Group Leadership Skills

Second Edition

Group Leadership Skills

Interpersonal Process in Group Counseling and Therapy

Second Edition

Mei-whei Chen
Northeastern Illinois University

Christopher Rybak
Bradley University

Los Angeles | London | New Delhi
Singapore | Washington DC | Melbourne

FOR INFORMATION:

SAGE Publications, Inc.
2455 Teller Road
Thousand Oaks, California 91320
E-mail: order@sagepub.com

SAGE Publications Ltd.
1 Oliver's Yard
55 City Road
London EC1Y 1SP
United Kingdom

SAGE Publications India Pvt. Ltd.
B 1/I 1 Mohan Cooperative Industrial Area
Mathura Road, New Delhi 110 044
India

SAGE Publications Asia-Pacific Pte. Ltd.
3 Church Street
#10-04 Samsung Hub
Singapore 049483

Printed in the United States of America

Library of Congress Control Number: 2017942488

ISBN (pbk): 978-1-5063-4930-5

This book is printed on acid-free paper.

Certified Chain of Custody
SUSTAINABLE FORESTRY INITIATIVE
Promoting Sustainable Forestry
www.sfiprogram.org
SFI-01268

SFI label applies to text stock

Acquisitions Editor: Abbie Rickard
Editorial Assistant: Alissa Nance
Production Editor: Kimaya Khashnobish
Copy Editor: Michelle Ponce
Typesetter: C&M Digitals (P) Ltd.
Proofreader: Lawrence W. Baker
Indexer: Marilyn Anderson
Cover Designer: Rose Storey
Marketing Manager: Katherine Hepburn

17 18 19 20 21 10 9 8 7 6 5 4 3 2 1

CONTENTS

PREFACE

The power of a group in action fascinates and humbles those who behold. No matter how many times you sit in a group, you cannot help but be captivated by the surprising richness and complexity of the forces at work within it. As members' interpersonal and intrapersonal processes wed, you are privileged to catch sight of an explosion of dynamics—each with a personality and a life of its own, commanding your unfaltering respect and appreciation.

Many therapists and counselors, however, shy away from leading groups because of this uncontainable richness and complexity, which, as we have seen, can dazzle even the most seasoned of therapists. Feeling ill-equipped to handle group dynamics, new group facilitators feel nauseous, and even break out in a cold sweat, at the mere thought of leading groups.

This sense of anxiety and inadequacy completely makes sense as many budding therapists feel like they lack the necessary skills and competencies to run a group—even with training. The fact is that with the one or two group training courses that they may have taken, their preparation has often been too general to provide an in-depth understanding of how to tackle the intricacies inherent in each group session, much less how to help group members transform. As such, numerous beginning group leaders thirst for practical and tangible instructions that provide not only conceptual discussion but also specific guidelines and illustrations to help them brave the many challenges of group counseling.

We believe that the first edition of this text met such needs through converting abstract concepts into concrete actions, by way of skill and technique illustration. From the feedback that we received from its active users, it was made clear to us that the practical, as well as tangible, skills and techniques within the text have made a significant contribution to the beginning group leader's foray into the unendingly fertile and intricate world of group work.

We have been told that they begin to triumph over their fear and anxiety of taking on this most complex modality of counseling and therapy by the help of this book's skills and techniques—much like a ship at sea, in dark and stormy waters, being shown safely to the shore by a lighthouse.

We hope to extend this vital impact with this second edition.

In this new edition, we continue to hone in on the power of the group. We continue to offer a wealth of case histories, creative ways of conducting groups, and examples for skills and techniques—all in an effort to get right to the heart and the action of the group practice, without lingering overly long in the realm of abstraction.

What, then, is new here? We add leadership skills from several theoretical foundations: solution-focused therapy, strength-based therapy, cognitive behavior therapy, and interpersonal neurobiology. We also add three new chapters to join the lineup:

Chapter 6: Leading Structured Group Sessions

Chapter 8: Unstructured Groups—Basic Level

Chapter 13: Using Psychodrama for Unresolved Pain

Taking the suggestions of our reviewers, we spread the here-and-now leadership skills over four different locations to suit varying stages of member readiness:

- Chapter 8 introduces *the first baby steps*, suitable for the early stages of a group.
- Chapter 10 ushers in the *intermediate steps*, fitting for the norming stage.
- Chapters 11 and 12 expound upon the *most advanced steps*, apt for the working stage.

Even at the advanced level featured in Chapters 11 and 12, the here-and-now techniques are further partitioned into several levels of intensity. The hope is that success with the less intense techniques will embolden new group leaders to apply those of higher intensity if it so suits the needs of their groups.

In addition, the entire manuscript went through a major makeover—a welcomed revision of the previous contents and a proud enhancement via the new research, new concepts, new cases, and new delivery style—giving the entire text a different feel.

Due to limited space, we let go of two old chapters (professional standards/best practices and further development of the group leader) so as to leave room for the added chapters.

The power of a group in action fascinates and humbles those who behold. No matter how many times you sit in a group, you cannot help but be captivated by the surprising richness and complexity of the forces at work within it. To work with this power, one must enter its sphere with utter openness, curiosity, willingness, humility, and a sense of awe—an attitude that can be best described as a Zen mind, or a beginner's mind. It is with this same attitude that we fashion this second edition.

ACKNOWLEDGMENTS

We feel privileged to be given the honor to create this book. The precise honor, however, must go to the numerous trainees and group participants who have given us insights into group dynamics and interpersonal processes that no amount of study in literature and theories can achieve. It is through seeing groups at work that the ideas and concepts in this text began to germinate.

It is with the deepest gratefulness that we thank our trainees and group participants, especially those who have given us permission to use their personal cases and journals, though anonymously, to demonstrate points in the text. We thank them for their generosity and the trust they have placed in us.

We want to thank Annie Huston and Wendy Haas. You hunt down and expunge flabby expressions, correct grammatical errors, tighten sentences, place words here and exchange words there—until the writing reveals its message in the clearest way possible. Your contributions quicken the pace of the book, making it easier and lighter to read.

Special thanks are to Ed Porter. This text has more to offer because of your linguistic acumen, scrupulous attention to detail, and insight into elusive group processes—a rare find of amalgamation of talents.

Thank you, Ana Ferraz-Castilho, for your assistance in updating the bibliography. What a patient researcher you are! Without your help, we would have been bogged down by the mammoth task of researching.

Thank you, Sarah Cozzi and Thomas Nedderman, for contributing your thoughtful ideas to several exercises in this text. And thank you, Kimberly Buikema, for so generously sharing with the readers the group proposal in Appendix A.

It is with utter gratitude that we thank the following reviewers—as "iron sharpens iron," the astute comments from you have sharpened our minds and visions as we go about completing this new edition:

Professor Jack Flight, Dominican University;

Professor Karin Lindstrom Bremer, Minnesota State University, Mankato;

Professor Kevin A. Curtin, Alfred University;

Professor Susan Claxton, Georgia Highlands College;

Professor Susan Glassburn Larimer, Indiana University;

Professor Tracey M. Duncan, New Jersey City University;

Professor Tracy A. Marschall, University of Indianapolis;

and Professor Charles Timothy Dickel, Creighton University.

Finally, thanks be given to Abbie Rickard, Kimaya Khashnobish, Nathan Davidson, Lara Parra, Kassie Graves, Alissa Nance, Jenna Retana, and our copyeditor, Michelle Ponce, at SAGE. Your professionalism and your passionate enthusiasm for this book make the undertaking of this project clear and focused; your supportive approach adds an extra measure of positive energy to the entire authoring process.

For our parents, family, partners, and friends, words are inadequate to express our gratitude for your unyielding support, understanding, and love.

The authors' ultimate gratitude must go to the larger community of group counseling and therapy through which the heritage of group work is maintained and through which precious knowledge is handed on to the generations of therapists to come.

About the Authors

Mei-whei Chen, PhD, Licensed Clinical Psychologist

Dr. Chen is a professor at Northeastern Illinois University. She teaches group counseling, individual counseling, theories in counseling and psychotherapy, mental health counseling, grief counseling, and stress management. In addition, she maintains her own private practice, on the side, in Illinois.

She has received three Faculty Excellence Awards from Northeastern Illinois University. As well, she received the Beverly Brown Award for Outstanding Contributions to the Field of Group Counseling from the Illinois Association for Specialists in Group Work (IASGW).

Besides the text of *Group Leadership Skills*, Dr. Chen also publishes *Individual Counseling and Therapy: Skills and Techniques* (3rd edition coming out in 2018) and has published many journal articles in related areas.

Christopher J. Rybak, PhD, Licensed Clinical Professional Counselor

Dr. Rybak was a professor and chair of the Department of Educational Leadership & Human Development at Bradley University and a specialist in group work. He taught group counseling, counseling diverse populations, practicum and internship in counseling, theories and techniques of counseling, and pre-practicum in counseling.

Dr. Rybak served as the director of the ELH Counseling Clinic and several times as president of the Illinois Association for Specialists in Group Work.

He received awards for innovative teaching and integrated learning, a research award, two Fulbright scholarship awards, and the Beverly Brown Award for Outstanding Contributions to the Field of Group Counseling from the Illinois Association for Specialists in Group Work (IASGW).

CHAPTER 1
THEORIES AND ASSUMPTIONS

Beneath any ordinary interaction among a group of people lies a fascinating world of interpersonal process—a world we often let pass as we go about our lives. However, upon a closer look, stretches of interpersonal terrain often lay themselves bare in front of our eyes—a member shutting down in communication; another using anger to keep others at arms' length; yet another constantly jumping in before others get an opportunity; and more.

We can neither confirm nor deny: festering within these exteriors might be certain perceived disapproval from others; flight from vulnerable feelings; evasion from anxiety; and what not.

The complex, fertile, and elusive nature of the interpersonal process in a group often baffles beginning group therapists, whilst keeping the most seasoned therapists on their toes, no less. Yet it is the very nature of its elusiveness that fascinates us, and it is the pursuit of the depth and richness of its underlying process that rejuvenates all involved.

From a pragmatic perspective, this pursuit also makes economic sense. Cost containment has become a major thrust in the healthcare industry. As a consequence, the length of group counseling and therapy is being cut shorter and shorter, and group therapists are increasingly called upon to search for therapeutic methods bringing forth client change in shorter and shorter timeframes. Placing interpersonal process at the heart of group counseling, we believe, is paramount to this end, as it maximizes group power within a brief time frame.

This text provides a comprehensive framework and a variety of methods through which you, as a group leader, can build your muscle in tackling the subtle and complex dynamics of a group. Through sharing our experiences, our treasure maps if you will, we hope you and your group can strike therapeutic gold.

This exciting journey will start with the base camp—the theoretical underpinnings—from which the interpersonal approach of this group work has drawn its origins. All leadership skills and intervention techniques in this text are solidly built upon the groundwork of the concepts and assumptions of the following theories. Granted, these theoretical approaches are immensely complex; an in-depth discussion will be far beyond the scope of this section. We, hence, highlight only those ideas connected with the theme of our text.

SULLIVAN'S INTERPERSONAL THEORY

Harry Stack Sullivan was the first to present a systemic theory of interpersonal relationships in psychotherapy (Sullivan, 2013; Sullivan & Perry, 1971). His work has since spawned a lineage of interpersonal theories and studies (Kiesler, 1982a; Strupp & Binder, 1984; Teyber, 2000). Steering clear of the prevailing trend at the time of focusing on intrapsychic processes, Sullivan, instead, put an emphasis on interpersonal processes. This focus, indeed, proved to break new ground.

Major Notions of Sullivan's Interpersonal Theory

To help you zoom in on Sullivan's interpersonal theory, we condense Sullivan's groundbreaking theory into the following major notions:

- Human behaviors are recurrent and recursive: Our idiosyncratic behaviors seem to be moded by "the relatively enduring pattern of recurrent interpersonal situations which characterize a human life" (Sullivan, 2013, pp. 110–111).
- We are driven by interpersonal needs: It is not the sexual drive but the need for control, affiliations, and inclusion (the three interpersonal forces) that influence human motivations and actions.
- Our anxiety is rooted in interpersonal disapproval: Anxiety in interpersonal relations is the central force that organizes human behavior. Most people have a pervasive anxiety rooted in the fear of being discounted, rejected, or disapproved of by others, especially significant others. Our behaviors are mostly motivated by our desire to reduce anxiety.
- Problems manifest themselves in interpersonal relations: Our problems are primarily embedded in disturbed interpersonal relations and often manifest themselves in handicapped interpersonal communication.
- We cocreate our interpersonal reality through a reciprocal feedback loop: Recurrent interpersonal patterns and communication styles create a reciprocal loop in our environment—a type of feedback loop wherein the effect and the cause become circular. Thus, we not only affect others but are simultaneously affected by our interpersonal cocreation.

From Sullivan to Yalom

Sullivan's interpersonally oriented theory and practice represent momentous insights into the nature of human suffering and healing—insights that continue to influence contemporary theorists, including Irvin D. Yalom, the most influential figure in group psychotherapy. Many of Yalom's concepts of group psychotherapy can be traced back in some form to Sullivan's original concepts (Yalom & Leszcz, 2005).

As for us, Sullivan's interpersonal theory deeply shapes the way we view group members' behaviors as well as the way we formulate leadership skills and interventions. Beginning with Chapter 7, we provide ways to explore the interpersonal patterns and coping strategies that play out in members' interactions with one another. Chapters 9–12 discuss how to directly address these often difficult dynamics, making them the grist for the mill of group work. All over these chapters, Sullivan's impact leaves its trace.

EXPERIENTIAL THEORY

Another theoretical model that greatly contributes to our interpersonal approach to group work is experiential therapy: a therapeutic approach that places emphasis on the *felt experience* (Elliot & Greenberg, 2007; Lietaer, Rombauts, & Balen, 1990).

Clients Need Direct Experiences, Not Cognitive Explanations

Experiential therapy springs from the humanistic school of therapy (Elliot & Greenberg, 2007; Pascual-Leone & Greenberg, 2007), which assumes that growth and change happen naturally when experiences are not impeded. Taking this assumption one step further, the experiential therapy approach emphasizes that for change to take place, clients need *direct experiences,* instead of cognitive explanations (Greenberg, Rice, & Elliott, 1998).

For example, the prominent existential psychotherapist Rollo May once said, "The patient needs an experience, not an explanation" (May, 1983, p. 158). This statement highlights the therapeutic tenet of experiential therapy.

From this precept, enters this notion: To truly know something, one must achieve that knowing through a personal, immediate experience, not just through discussion, listening, or abstract processing (Bohart, 1993; Elliot &

Greenberg 2007; Horvath, 1995). Only when the experience is felt directly are people then able to access a myriad of thoughts and feelings.

From Disowning, to Owning Up, to Reclaiming

An experience cannot be felt unless it is owned by the person having it. And to group therapy with an experiential slant, this ability to "own up" to one's experiences puts itself at the central point of the trajectory of its members' growth and change:

- Clients begin the group stuck in processing experiences or *disowning* their undesirable experiences.
- Clients, gradually, allow themselves to *own up* to their own experiences, becoming able to immerse themselves in their experiences.
- Clients reclaim their ability to process experiences, reconstruct the meaning of experiences, and respond to experiences in new ways.

This unfolding process, from disowning, to owning-up, to reclaiming one's self, is a process nothing short of splendid.

Learning Self-in-Relationship Skills Through Group Interactions

To apply experiential therapy in the group setting is to help members embrace what is happening; articulate what is unspoken or difficult to express; and reflect on the meaning of their here-and-now relationships in the group (Yalom & Leszcz, 2005). When emotionally engaged with their fellow members in this way, group members find themselves with a surge of energy and vivacity, inspired to reach deep within to uncover long-hidden issues, wounds, and emotions.

This experiential approach stands unsurpassed as a treatment choice through which members can learn *self-in-relationship skills* (Elliot & Greenberg, 2007; Furman, Bender & Rowan, 2014)—skills that are difficult to develop when one is alone, without others to practice with or to get feedback from. The experiential approach, with its built-in emphasis on here-and-now engagement, accelerates members' pace of delearning and relearning these self-in-relationship skills.

In Chapter 13, we provide a special kind of *experiential therapy* useful for group counseling, especially when it comes to healing unresolved pain, loss, and trauma—*psychodrama*. Packed with actions, basic techniques of *psychodrama* offer group therapists flexible and adjustable methods, applicable to various group settings, and at the same time, powerful in healing members' long suffered pain.

OBJECT RELATIONS THEORY

A client's issue is like an onion—multi-layered with each one closer to the core than the one before. Object relations theory helps therapists appreciate these many layers.

What Is This Obscure Term—Object Relations?

You may feel uncertain about the term *object relations*, but you need not. Simply put, *object* refers to people, including our internalized perceptions of people, while *relations* refers to relationships. Stripped down, object relations theory is precisely what we've been discussing thus far—interpersonal relationships.

Although object relations theory has been historically written about in obscure and impersonal terms, it is nevertheless a powerful theory. When fully understood, it can help therapists comprehend the core of their clients' predicaments.

The Quest for Connection Is What Motivates Our Behaviors

Although similar to interpersonal theory, object relations theory takes issue with Sullivan's postulation that human behaviors are motivated by our need to reduce anxiety. Instead, it believes that as humans, our ultimate motivation is to seek relatedness, attachment, and connection to others (Greenberg & Mitchell, 1983; Kohut, 2014; Sandler, 1981; Strupp & Binder, 1984; Teyber, 2000). Being crucial to our survival, attachment and connection play a central role in the ways we interact with our early caretakers, so much so that they tend to become internalized within us (Cashdan, 1989; Flanagan, 2016).

Our Internalized Others Are With Us Everywhere We Go

If our early caretakers are empathic and responsive to our needs, a sense of self-worth and trust will become the basic constituents of our psychic development.

On the other hand, when our caretakers and early home atmosphere deprive us of empathy and nurturance, this environmental deficiency can lead to a weakened, fragmented, or disordered self.

These childhood injurious and conflicted ways of interaction are deeply rooted within those who seek therapy. Impressed upon them and internalized within them is an enduring mode of perceiving—a cognitive schema—that shapes their relationships with others later in life.

Coping Strategies Are Just the Outer Layers of the Onion

Armed with object relations theory, therapists are equipped with a great tool to help their clients come to their recognition—their recurrent, problematic coping patterns are an upshot of their past unresolved issues, as well as a source of their current relationship difficulties (Greenberg & Mitchell, 1983; Kohut, 2014; Sandler, 1981; Strupp & Binder, 1984; Teyber, 2000). For example, people who come from a background lacking emotional nurturance, where their parents were emotionally unavailable, neglectful, or abusive, often felt immensely hurt and pained as children. The more their self and relations were injured, the more they felt disquieted and insecure, and thus, they chased affirmation and reassurance with a sense of urgency. When affirmation and reassurance are unavailable, the unbearable pain may drive them to apply more extreme coping strategies to up the ante.

If the process of therapy is like peeling the onion, then coping strategies are the outer layers, appearing in the form of intellectualization, rationalization, deflecting, caretaking, people-pleasing, dramatization, externalization, and impersonalization. Though initially useful, these coping patterns become problematic later in life.

In order to live productively, people need to develop new responses to manage the unique demands and tasks of each life transition effectively. The first step of developing new responses is to become aware that their entrenched coping patterns are getting them stuck in a rut.

Reaching the Reactive Inner Layers

Through the lens of object relations theory, group leaders have a deeper appreciation of our members' problems. As a result, we gain great respect and compassion for the pain our members endure on a daily basis. At the same time, we are inspired and encouraged to reach the heart of our members' issues—their recurrent relational patterns.

Peeling the onion by slowly leading the group to touch on members' more reactive inner layers represents a powerful way of working with counseling groups. Chapters 6 and 8 expound on processing method and leadership skills to reach to these reactive inner layers. This method fosters great insight, self-compassion, and motivation for a member to change.

FAMILY SYSTEMS THEORY

We will never appreciate enough the profound impact that a client's family of origin can have on his or her life. Family systems theory provides a rich understanding of how the roles and rules in family systems shape our clients and how this early learning is often at the center of our clients' present-day issues.

Unstated Family Rules About Roles Dictate Our Lives

Theorists in family systems, such as Gregory Bateson, Murray Bowen, Salvador Minuchin, Virginia Satir, and Carl Whitaker, have observed various overt and covert *communication and interaction patterns* in families, as well as various *fixed roles* that people play in their family of origin (Becvar & Becvar, 2013; Goldenberg & Goldenberg, 2013; Nichols, 2016). Though unstated, these patterns and roles—like unrelenting *family rules*—are, however, faithfully abided by all family members to maintain the family system's homeostasis. Unstated, these rules are thus outside of conscious awareness, making it difficult for people to change them.

Additionally, these roles and communication patterns are reciprocal and complementary. Roles reinforce each other, making all behaviors recursive. For example, a brother's domineering role reinforces his sister's submissive role, and the sister's submissive role reinforces her brother's domineering role. Similarly, a mother's critical role reinforces her son's passive role and *vice versa*. You can see that it takes multiple people to change such reciprocal, recursive relationship patterns. This adds to their resistance to change.

Our Family of Origin Remains Within Us

Family systems theory states that our family of origin remains within us throughout our life. Wherever we go, we carry the blueprint of its emotional and cognitive road maps with us. If the old blueprint schooled us to disguise our vulnerability by our reactivity, we will replicate this very behavior in new relationships. The closer the relationships become, the more they touch the deepest layers of our inner life and the more they have the potential to stir our primitive emotional responses.

From Reenactment Toward Awareness

The family systems perspective helps group therapists catch a glimpse of group members' recurring patterns of interaction in their lives when reenacted within the group. Unfailingly, the schematic perceptions and reactions—rivalry, separation anxiety, dependency, vulnerability, deficiency, or ambivalence—come to light in group interaction. Consistently, the group therapists can shift attention from the outward content of conversation toward the very family dynamics being reenacted in the group process, when it occurs.

Through the here-and-now—through the examination of the interpersonal process and communication patterns in the group interaction—members become aware of the roles they play. With that, they can start to challenge their unstated beliefs, needs, and feelings. Chapters 11 and 12 illustrate how to work with the roles that are reenacted within the group.

BRIEF THERAPY

At its core, brief therapy is about an attitude and mindset of doing therapy, not just the number of sessions.

Targeting Central Themes and Member Responsibility

From the perspective of brief therapy, the key to success is through focused intervention—treatment that targets central themes. To discover that central theme, the therapist may look into the past or the present for any indication of where the clients have gotten themselves "stuck." When the theme is found, it is easier to figure out how to get them "unstuck."

Another tenet to brief therapy is that clients hold the ultimate responsibility for their own well-being. For that reason, therapists strenuously avoid taking responsibility away from their clients (Hoyt, 1995; Kreilkamp, 2015; Levenson, 1995).

Those therapists who are used to conducting open-ended therapy may worry that the time limit inherent in brief therapy may shortchange their clients in terms of treatment quality. In actuality, the limited time can actually increase and intensify the work done in each session, compelling clients to become more active in the group throughout the course of therapy.

Thus, a time-limited framework often generates a sense of urgency, firing up group members to get quickly and deeply involved. This sense of urgency can serve as an antidote to passive attitudes toward change that many clients seem to harbor.

Informed by brief therapy, a group leader may choose to adopt a more focused leadership style that requires each group member to refine, reframe, and be held accountable for their goals—ones that are behaviorally concrete, specific, and achievable. The skills of goal setting (see Chapters 3 and 5), as part of the screening interview and the first session, clearly demonstrate this focusing element.

Embracing Here-and-Now and Small Changes

In brief therapy, our mindset must shift from idealism to pragmatism and optimism. Bound by a set time frame, therapists cannot afford to pursue an ideal or perfectionistic "cure" (Budman, 1994; Budman & Gurman, 2002; Hoyt, 1995) but must *focus on small changes*. These small changes have the power to snowball into significant changes later.

The concept of brief therapy reinforces a belief that group therapy should begin with members' current life situations. Then, the group can move on to the observations of their recurrent relationship patterns when appropriate. Less focus is spent on review of members' there-and-then history, and more focus is on the here-and-now. This here-and-now orientation is consistent with that of the experiential therapy approach. Chapters 11 and 12 specifically illustrate the pragmatic aspect of the here-and-now orientation.

Focusing on Trust and Group Cohesiveness

Within the brief therapy model, the leader also strives to quickly develop trust, empathy, and bonding within the group. In doing so, a safe group environment is built that allows for deeper self-exploration of the inner layers of client issues. As trust and empathy deepen within the group, group cohesiveness tends to strengthen. Group cohesiveness can be a powerful experience for many people who have difficulty in interpersonal relationships. Chapter 10 demonstrates leadership skills of how to facilitate greater risk-taking behaviors within a group as cohesiveness strengthens.

An Emphasis on Reflective Practice Between Sessions

Brief therapy also teaches us that most changes occur between sessions (Budman, 1994). This fact leads us to encourage reflective practice (Atieno Okech, 2008; Bolton, 2010) between sessions. We believe that intense interpersonal learning does not happen just within group sessions but also after the sessions have ended. Indeed, insight and self-awareness often begin just a few days after a particular session, when members have had some time to let the feedback sink in.

Throughout this text, we sprinkle journal entries of members and leaders here and there, illustrating their reflective practice between sessions. Chapter 15 specifically provides detailed rationales and methods for including reflective practice in group therapy.

Highly Direct Leadership Style

Under the influence of brief therapy, the process-minded leader will be active, clear, direct, and directive. To beginning group therapists used to the Rogerian style of individual counseling, this direct and directive style might feel unfamiliar and challenging. This highly direct style shall be intentional. Direct and directive leadership is requisite to hold members accountable for their own goals and tasks, as well as for the goal of the group as a whole.

The direct leadership style may trigger transference and authority issues for members having issues with boundary and power. Leaders need to be cognizant of this possibility. When these issues do arise, leaders can tackle them with sensitivity and nondefensiveness and treat them as grist for the mill, as illustrated in Chapters 9 and 10.

STRENGTH-BASED THERAPY

Strength-based therapy, an offshoot of the fast-growing movement of positive psychology (Lazarus, 2003), puts the energy of therapy on cultivating clients' resources, rather than on trying to fix their problems (Seligman & Csikszentmihalyi, 2000).

Tapping Into Clients' Reservoir

Strength-based therapy believes that the predisposition of all humans is such that it inclines toward adaptation and growth. However, though all people have a reservoir of strengths, they often leave many of their strengths unrecognized and unutilized (Epstein, 1998). Therapists, thus, aim to tap into clients' reservoir by coconstructing a realistic plan of action with the clients to bring these strengths out.

Without a doubt, strength-based therapy represents a striking *paradigm shift* from the traditional medical model of fixing what's wrong, toward one that builds upon what's right for clients (Seligman & Csikszentmihalyi, 2000; Walsh, 2004). It actually draws its concepts and techniques from several contemporary therapeutic approaches—including narrative therapy, solution-focused therapy, as well as a line of resilience literature and research.

Narrative Therapy: The Emphasis on "Change Talk"

The concept of *change talk* that strength-based therapy thrives on actually is borrowed from narrative therapy (White & Epston, 1990). In change talk, narrative therapists use the language of change to revamp the ways clients attribute meanings to the distress, trauma, or pain in their stories (Selekman, 1997; White & Epston, 1990).

As clients r-author the meanings of their experiences in the ways that serve them, they can revise their reactions and reclaim what strengths or resources they have, all to improve their lives. Meaning-reconstruction sits at the heart of this kind of change talk.

Solution-Focused Therapy

The *exception question* and the *miracle question* that strength-based therapy uses are drawn from solution-focused therapy (Jong & Berg, 2013). Armed with these two techniques, solution-focused therapists gain access to the problem-free areas of clients' life; thus, they get insight into what client resources to tap into.

Resilience—The Centerpiece of Strength-Based Therapy

Resilience literature and research are the cornerstones upon which strength-based therapy builds its foundation (Werner, 1995; Werner & Smith, 1992). Indeed, the notion of resilience is a centerpiece of strength-based therapy.

In life, success will always be accompanied with intermittent failures, setbacks, and disappointments. Even so, hardship will not dominate for long as small successes begin to accumulate and build our resilience. This resilience is the ultimate resource we all rely on to advance our lives.

Strength Born out of Overcoming Life's Hardship

The notion of resilience aligns well with the work of Riegel (1976), who believes that hardship gives birth to strength. From this position, a therapist can help clients go on with whatever lays ahead in life, without fear—because out of adversity, strength emerges (Desetta & Wolin, 2000).

The emphasis on client resilience not only allows clients to live without anxiety but also instills a sense of *hope*—a cornerstone of strength-based therapy (Davidson, 2014; Smith, 2006).

Help Members Find Their Areas of Resiliency

To apply strength-based therapy to group counseling and therapy, leaders first need to get members to get a firm grasp of the *paradox of adversity* so that they notice each other's resiliencies, and at the same time, appreciate the suffering that their problems inflict on them.

Get a firm grasp, they will. Search diligently enough, and members will always find many areas of resilience in each other's lives. The following areas, suggested by Wolin and Wolin (2013), are examples of what members can find as each others' resiliency: insight, independence, connection with people who matter, taking initiative, creativity, sense of humor, and the ability to abide by personal principles.

Once group members become aware of the strengths and resilience that they have forgotten or minimized, they may then begin to consider using their strengths to effect desired changes (Desetta & Wolin, 2000).

Don't Dismiss Members' Problems

One caution in applying this approach is that during the early stage of the group, the group members must take the time to come to a clear understanding of how members perceive their problems. Leaders must facilitate the group in listening to the problems members present and validate the feelings evoked.

If by mistake, the group dismisses the problems to focuses on the strengths too early, then any solutions that the group arrives at are likely to be rebuffed (Cowger, 1992; Selekman, 1997).

INTERPERSONAL NEUROBIOLOGY

In recent years, findings from neuroscience have helped us understand how our emotional brains function in our interpersonal relationships. This line of studies all gathers under a big umbrella—"interpersonal neurobiology" (Siegel, 2015). Interpersonal neurobiology has made enormous contributions to our understanding of memory, learning, and change and has validated most concepts in counseling/therapy (Fishbane, 2014). Still, much is to be learned about how our *mind* can work with our *brain* to deepen therapeutic change.

The constantly evolving field of interpersonal neurobiology can enhance our work as group therapists by expanding our understanding of the *deeply interpersonal nature of the human being* (Tootle, 2003). Major concepts of interpersonal neurobiology that integrate well into group therapy follow.

The Power of Emotional Brain Overrides the Cognitive Brain

Unlocking of the mystery of the emotional brain, particularly the amygdale, neuroscience contributes significantly to our therapeutic work (Damasio, 2006; LeDoux, 2015). The amygdale, the primary part of our brain, regulates our emotions (Tootle, 2003). Being more critical for survival, the emotional brain is given primacy, by natural selection forces, to the cognitive brain. For our survival instinct to immediately kick in when needed, emotions are given the power that overrides intellect. This is evidenced by the fact that there are twice the amounts of axons extending from the limbic area of the brain to the prefrontal cortex, as compared to the amount from other areas (Calvin, 1996; Damasio, 2006; LeDoux, 2015).

A Shift in Therapy Toward Honoring Bodily Rooted Emotions

As the primacy of emotions is revealed by the neuroscience revolution, the field of counseling and therapy also experiences a *paradigm shift*—a move away from treatment models that favor cognitive, top-down treatment, toward ones that place emphasis on the power of the bottom-up, bodily rooted emotions (Fosha, Siegel, & Solomon, 2011).

In the past, treatment focused on emotions and physical experiences could hardly get much recognition; now, however, emotion-based treatment and transformation are getting brand new respect (Fosha et al., 2011).

A New Understanding and Compassion for Resistance to Change

In counseling and therapy, we often have to deal with two conflicting forces within the client—to change or not to change—and the force to resist change can easily get an upper hand. With the help of neuroscience, now we come to appreciate the reasons why resistance is such an integral part of clients' experience.

The reasons have to do with Hebb's Law—"neurons that fire together wire together" (Siegel, 2015, p. 49). Over time, the connectivity between certain behaviors and certain messages, transmitted by neuron firing, becomes strengthened (Makinson & Young, 2012). In plain English, the more we do, think, or feel something, the more we are likely to do the same in the future. Hence, much of our functioning becomes automatic and ingrained; we become habitual. No wonder; those habits and personality characteristics formed early in life tend to be wired with such density in the brain that they gain a firm foothold, dead set against change.

We can say that when clients exhibit resistance, they are, in fact, stuck in their *neuronal ruts*. To change their maladaptive habits and behaviors is literally going against their neural wiring (Fishbane, 2014). This difficulty is universal; it does not reside within just certain clients.

Understanding Hebb's Law gives us a new level of compassion for people at the crossroads of change.

Group Therapy Brings About Neuroplasticity

Though not endowed with any knack in changing our habits, we are not condemned to perpetually replicate our past either. In the recent decade, neuroscience has demonstrated that the adult brain can and does change. Our brains' capacities to change and to create new neural networks are accounted for by a phenomenon called neuroplasticity—a phenomenon that happens essentially in an enriched environment (Makinson & Young, 2012).

Group therapy represents one form of such an enriched environment where clients learn to think differently, to feel what was previously blocked, and to make more conscious choices. Through such enriched interactions, new neural connections are made; defragmented networks are repaired; and the neuroplastic process is then activated (Cozolino, 2010; 2016). Of course, for new neuronal connections to take root via Hebb's Law, the new ways of thinking, feeling, and behaving need to be practiced over and over, until they feel like second nature. Only then will the new wiring be sufficiently strengthened.

These kinds of new learning brought about in group therapy can change the brain structurally and physiologically—literally *rewire* the way the mind works (Doidge 2014; Makinson & Young, 2012). Such a neural basis is the bread and butter of group counseling and therapy.

Process-Minded Leadership as a Necessity for Fostering Neuroplasticity

Cozolino (2010) proposes that neural plasticity is made possible in the following conditions:

- A safe and trusting relationship has been established.
- There are moderate levels of stress.
- Emotion and cognition are both activated.
- New meanings have been coconstructed for the clients' life stories.

We happily find that Cozolino's notions resonate with the principles of leadership skills and techniques proposed in this text, including the two tiers of here-and-now processing featured throughout this text. Learning to handle the group in the level of its interpersonal process, leadership has a surefire capacity to create the kind of environment to enhance members' neuroplasticity.

The First Step of Conflict Resolution Is to Calm the Amygdala

According to neuroscience, our emotional memories tend to be processed in the amygdala—a part of the limbic brain that mediates the fight-or-flight response. In other words, the amygdala scans the environment for danger, then quickly does what needs to be done without sounding the alarm to the prefrontal cortex (PFC), the thinking part of the brain (Fishbane, 2014; Makinson & Young, 2012). This highly reactive impulse of the amygdala serves to protect our survival.

In most people, the brain is in a delicate equilibrium between the cognitive (the PFC) and the emotional (the limbic system) (Makinson & Young, 2012). However, in a stressful situation, such as interpersonal conflict, the amygdala is likely to get an inkling of threat. This sends our bodies into the fight-or-flight mode, short-circuiting the thinking part of our brain. (Fishbane, 2014). This kind of emotional hijacking is typical in interpersonal conflicts, especially in open conflict within a group.

According to our clinical experiences, it is unrealistic to teach people in conflict to show empathy for one another. Others in front of us have to validate our experiences, thus calming the activated amygdala before we can call on the higher brain (the PFC) to reflect on the meanings of what has occurred intrapsychically and interpersonally.

In Chapter 9, you can find the steps for resolving open conflict in the group. Our principle of conflict resolution in the group is that the triggered amygdala must be calmed first, and then the PFC can be called on for a higher level of reflective processing.

UNDERLYING ASSUMPTIONS

With the previously discussed theories as the backdrop, the interpersonal approach to group work featured in this text assumes seven core premises about the nature of people's problems and about how problems can be resolved through the relationships within the group. This section discusses these seven core premises in detail.

Assumption 1: Most Problems Are Interpersonal in Nature

People come to counseling or therapy to solve the problems that plague them—they may feel isolated or depressed; have problems with their spouse, coworkers, or others; have a pressing issue that holds them back from building the lives they desire; or so on. The road toward the resolution, however, is not a direct line.

The first thing we as group leaders must realize is that we cannot directly solve our clients' problems. According to Yalom and Leszcz (2005), most clients in therapy share two common difficulties:

- Difficulties in establishing and maintaining meaningful relationships
- Difficulties in maintaining a sense of personal worth

These difficulties are interpersonal in nature, which can only be solved within the interpersonal context. The interpersonal process of the group provides the exact context wherein clients can learn a new way of healthy relating to replace the old, impaired one. This will likely rebuild their sense of self-worth and their interpersonal connection.

Assumption 2: Clients' Underlying Problems Will Be Played Out in the Group

A major difference between individual counseling and group counseling is that in individual counseling, clients tend to *talk about* relationship issues, whereas in group counseling, they *act upon* them, mostly without a trace of awareness. The group setting, therefore, allows therapists to do something that the individual counseling cannot afford—to witness what goes wrong interpersonally for clients.

For example, we get to see how members play out their distancing behaviors, build their walls, carry on impersonal communication styles, or get into off-putting behaviors, and then we realize how all of these play a part in their interpersonal problems.

Yalom and Leszcz (2005) point out that a group is indeed a "social microcosm" (p. 46)—a setting that affords us a glimpse into the bona fide interpersonal patterns in group members' outside lives. With that, the most important tool emerges right in front of us—the here-and-now interaction among members.

Assumption 3: Family Experiences: The Primary Source of Interpersonal Process

The question is, where do these interpersonal problems come from? Sullivan's interpersonal theory and object relations theory both inform us that people's interpersonal difficulties are often rooted in early childhood interactions, especially those within clients' families of origin. Family systems theory also informs us that many maladaptive interpersonal styles stem from hurtful interaction patterns in the family of origin (Goldenberg & Goldenberg, 2013; Nichols, 2016). These deeply ingrained interactions tend to manifest themselves in clients' current relationships.

For example, on the enmeshment-disengagement spectrum, clients from enmeshed families often find themselves still avoiding conflict and still suppressing their undesirable emotions, especially anger, in their current relationships. They often struggle with a sense of guilt whenever attempting to assert themselves or to set boundaries.

On the other hand, clients from disengaged families tend to lack a sense of introspection and are other-focused. They have difficulty containing their emotions, especially anxiety. Since people from a disengaged family often cut off their family members as a way to shut out rising anxiety in relationships, clients with this background generally lack experience in regulating, containing, or working through their anxiety in their current lives.

Group therapy represents an *interpersonal learning laboratory* where members get a chance to receive honest feedback from others about the patterns they inherited from their family experiences. Through awareness, new behaviors become possible (Drumm, 2006; Shaffer & Galinsky, 1989; Yalom & Leszcz, 2005).

Assumption 4: Group Galvanizes People's Interpersonal Patterns

Group interaction provides a platform where, sooner or later, members' interpersonal problems come out for all to see. Due to this natural tendency for people to *repeat* their past in their present, the group inevitably becomes a unique setting—*an emotionally charged setting*—where shame, guilt, abandonment, rejection, mistrust, and other dormant feelings all have a chance to come to the forefront through group interactions.

Although threatening, the experience of these charged interpersonal encounters is a blessing in disguise. The emergence of these feelings urges us to work through them as well as their attendant issues *within* the group. The evoked experiences become grist for the mill. They afford members an opportunity to examine how and why their interpersonal experiences get organized in a certain way. Subsequently, a sense of secure attachment, mastery, acceptance, and adaptive engagement with others—qualities that make up healthy living—can be experienced (Drumm, 2006; Furman et al., 2014; Riester, 1994).

Assumption 5: Here-and-Now Can Bring About Change and Healing

The here-and-now relationships within the group have the enormous creative potential for helping clients reconstruct the past and re-envision the future. For this to occur, the group therapist must strive to engage, intervene, participate, and transform maladaptive patterns of relationships (Blaney, 1986; Ferencik, 1991; Greenberg & Mitchell, 1983; Perls, 1992; Yalom & Leszcz, 2005).

The power of the here-and-now rests in its ability to provide a personal and direct experience of the interpersonal. When clients direct their attention to their *present* emotions as well as their *present* interpersonal relations, learning and healing will naturally come about. However, when the attention is directed to events back in time, the vitality of therapy is lost. The therapeutic focus, therefore, must be on the client's whole constellation of emotions, as they occur in real time in the group.

Assumption 6: To Last, Interpersonal Learning Must Be Experiential

As the saying goes, "I hear and I forget, I see and I remember, I do and I understand." In life, most of our significant learning comes from direct experience, not from speculation and intellectualization. In the group, learning about one's own interpersonal patterns takes place only when the group takes on an experiential method.

In their direct interactions with others in the group, members' "entire composite behavior is open to scrutiny within the group" (Leszcz, 1992, p. 50). In other words, the group gets to see everybody's patterns in the act. This direct experience of one another is an invaluable gift that only the group can bestow.

Assumption 7: Sustaining Change Can Happen Within a Short Time

In working with clients, try to assume that all group members, irrespective of their present issues, will respond to short-term group treatment unless they prove themselves too fractious for it. Try to believe that long-lasting change can happen within a short time (Hoyt, 1995; Levenson, 1995; Malan, 2012). This is the tenet of brief therapy.

The exact time limit does not define brief therapy, but the focused innovative interventions do. The awareness that there *is* a time limit can create the power of brief therapy. To invoke this awareness, we may start each session by asking group members to respond to this question: "What interpersonal skills are you willing to practice in today's session to bring about the change you desire?"

Within this question reside the key elements of brief therapy: *what skills, you, willing, change, today*. The emphasis on the here-and-now experience conveys a sense that therapy is present-centered and that change can happen in the experiences of pivotal moments of the present.

KEYS TO SUCCESS IN LEADING TODAY'S GROUPS

Successful individual counseling often points to a consistent trend in client change. Successful groups exhibit similar trends, particularly in interpersonal terms. To succeed in group leadership, leaders must be ready to take on certain tasks and directions. This section depicts what tasks and directions these might be.

The Growth in Self-Directedness, Present-Focus, and Connection

Although different in various ways, individual counseling and group counseling resonate with each other in the areas where clients' growth show.

Growth Shown in Successful Individual Therapy

In successful individual therapy, clients tend to change from being other-evaluated to self-directed (Dinerstein, 1990; Levant & Shlien, 1984; Rogers, 2003). Additionally, they tend to gradually face responsibility for present life, instead of blaming the past (Dinerstein, 1990; Levant & Shlien, 1984). The client often rediscovers his or her "me, here and now" (Rogers, 2003), meaning his or her attitudes, emotions, values, and goals as they currently affect one another.

As the self-work progresses and as clients sustain their own self with internal validation and approval, they tend to become more able to accept themselves the way they are. Their sense of self-worth increases, and they are more able to trust their own choices. As a result, they are baggage-free and have more capacity to connect with others and feel more fulfilled in their relationships.

Growth Shown in Successful Group Therapy

When a group is successful, members experience mental shifts quite similar to those in individual therapy, but the shifts are more in interpersonal terms. Research shows that in successful group counseling and therapy, members tend to grow toward *self-directedness, present-focus,* and *connection to others* (Salzberg & Kabat-Zinn, 2003; Yalom & Leszcz, 2005). Following are the details of successful group members' changes:

- Discovering and accepting previously unknown or unacceptable parts of their self
- Expressing to others what is happening inside rather than holding it in
- Seeing others taking risks to reveal embarrassing things or vulnerable parts of themselves and benefiting from it; therefore being inspired to do the same
- Accepting and appreciating honest feedback about how they come across to others in the here-and-now of the group
- Taking risks in expressing uncomfortable feelings (either negative or positive) toward another member in the group
- Taking ultimate responsibility for the way they live their present life no matter what kinds of past influences they received from others
- More willing to trust group members and other people in their present lives

Difficulties in Today's Groups: Unexamined Interpersonal Processes

This above-listed picture of successful group behaviors seems deceptively simple. The journey one has to take to arrive at these depicted outcomes, however, can surprise us with twists and turns.

As stated previously in this chapter, clients *talk about* their problems in individual therapy, but they *play their problems out* in group counseling. If only one member does this, there will be no sweat. Multiplied, however, it can make the group dynamics dazzling, if not confusing.

Indeed, most difficulties witnessed in today's groups arise from the subterranean interpersonal processes that remain unexamined, even by experienced therapists. Following is a list provided by S. D. Rose (1989) regarding the characteristic, subterranean, problems in today's groups:

- The group has low cohesion caused by a group-collusion among certain members, making others feel unsafe.
- Many members step back and allow one or two members to carry all the emotional work for the group.
- One or more members dominate the session, constantly speaking up to contribute, not giving quieter members their chance to contribute.
- Some members check out emotionally from the session.
- Some members don't self-disclose, making it difficult for other members to help them, support them, give them feedback, or challenge them.
- Some members are angry all the time, assigning blame or criticizing others in a negative way.
- Some members simply refuse to participate in the process at all and state their refusal early on.
- Some members establish subgroups, such as pairs, triads, or cliques, excluding others in communication.
- Some members resort to put-downs, defensiveness, or passive-aggressiveness as their mode of interactions with others without even recognizing it.
- The group as a whole becomes dependent on the leader; interaction occurs primarily between the leader and members.

Though most of these problematic interpersonal processes are miles away from the concerns that members bring to the group, these processes present that critical issues—*the elephants in the room*—that must be dealt with, if the group is to move forward.

Allow the Group Members Enough Time to Soak Up Their Interpersonal Dynamics

Some groups (such as psychoeducational groups, grief support groups, cognitive behavioral therapy groups, etc.) can afford to skirt around the interpersonal processes among their members—because they are so designed (Braaten, 1989; Furman et al., 2014; Shaffer & Galinsky, 1989). Most counseling and therapy groups, however, will eventually need to address these subterranean interpersonal processes.

Before tackling interpersonal process in the group, however, we need to slow down, giving the group enough time to get to a state where members are ready to tackle the interpersonal issues. Enough time should be spent to get the following foundations well in place:

- establishing a safe environment
- responding to members' emotions and inner needs
- observing how members' coping patterns sneak up in group interactions, how these patterns shed light on their presenting problems, and what the functions are of these coping patterns and how they have served the person

Before jumping into the here-and-now incidents to examine the dynamics, try to spend a couple of sessions mindfully observing how members' interpersonal patterns and central conflicts sneak up in the group interactions. Your observations will serve as your guidepost when the group is ready to grab the bull by the horns and deal with the subterranean interpersonal processes of the group.

Strive Toward a Process-Minded Leadership

To conceptualize members' problems from the perspective of interpersonal processes, a group therapist needs to develop his or her perceptivity to the process going on in the group. This is easier said than done. As Zaslav (1988) points out, most group leaders are not born with the innate capacity to see at the process level of group interaction. It is no wonder then that many therapists are repeatedly observed to have difficulty in directing the group to the process level of the here-and-now (Yalom & Leszcz, 2005).

To further magnify their difficulties, most new group leaders come from training programs that do not place significant focus on the process level of group work. They are adequate in leading structure-oriented or content-focused groups; however, when it comes to interpersonal process-oriented groups, they are left scrambling to keep up.

This text strives to fill this void in group leadership training. Becoming proficient in what is infused in this text, a new leader will feel confident and adequate in leading groups—not only in leading structure-oriented or content-focused groups but also process oriented-groups. To see the new generations of group leaders reaching this highest level of competency is our ultimate intent.

∞∞∞

In closing, beneath any ordinary interaction among a group of people lies a fascinating world of interpersonal process—a world we often let pass as we go about our lives. However, upon a closer look, stretches of interpersonal terrain often lay themselves bare in front of our eyes. A journey—to marvel this spectacular interpersonal terrain—has begun.

SELF-REFLECTION

Heightening one's self-awareness is a key aspect of development as a group leader. You are encouraged to reflect on the following questions.

1. Which of the theories addressed in this chapter do you think most fits with your view of group work? What is it about that theory that fits best with you?

2. Of the theories identified in this chapter, which least matches your present view of group work? What areas of this theory are in conflict with your outlook?

3. Is this your first introduction to any of the theories described in this chapter? If so, which ones? Are there aspects of these theories that you need to read more about?

4. What is your view of the role that experience should play in groups? Of what importance are the experiential aspects of a group as compared to other dimensions?

5. Of the assumptions about group work discussed in this chapter, which would you personally rank as the most important for a successful group?

6. Are there any additional assumptions about groups that you think should be added to the list?

CHAPTER 2

ON BECOMING
A GROUP LEADER

When done well, group therapy looks like a work of art—its process appears seamless and effortless, even though we know much work goes into the making. Arriving at this artful state of group leadership requires

- a wide range of knowledge about group dynamics,
- a set of skills and techniques to facilitate these dynamics, and
- a list of personal qualities conducive to bringing out the group power.

Among the above three rudiments, it is the personal part of leadership—the "self" of the group leaders—to which this chapter is devoted. The nuts and bolts of leadership skills and techniques will be covered throughout subsequent chapters.

THE DEVELOPMENT OF A LEADER

An effective group leader works neither as a technician nor a motivational helper—he or she functions so much more than that. The following portrays what an effective leader actually does and the process it takes to become one.

Effective Leadership Requires
the Ability to Facilitate, Not Persuade

Leadership calls, not as much for charisma or persuasion, as for the ability to listen at the process level; not as much for knowledge, as for the skills in facilitating interaction; not as much for being in charge, as for enabling the group to reach its goals.

Leading a group has nothing to do with curing members' symptoms either. No therapist can cure clients' symptoms, except to change the underlying processes that perpetuate their symptoms.

Essentially, a group leader inspires, mentors, challenges, instills confidence, and most importantly, helps members free themselves from whatever is blocking their personal growth.

These differentiations should be clear when you prepare yourself to lead.

Effective Leadership Can Be Taught

Through trial and error, most counselors can pick up some group leadership skills on their own but often at the client's expense. Proper training and development are imperative to effective leadership. Though a complicated art form, effective leadership can be taught. Of course, some therapists make better group leaders than others because of their innate gifts, yet the truth is, any counselor and therapist can be trained to become a skillful group leader. Even the most painfully shy person can develop the required leadership competence.

Ironically, those who believe they already have leadership skills down pat—and therefore don't need further training—are the ones who are apt to perform poorly as group leaders. They tend to close themselves out from the art of facilitation and intervention.

Practice Over Time, and You Will Appear Effortless

An indispensable first step in mastering any complex art is practice. Many piano players practice their techniques at any given opportunity, even when no piano is available. In the same vein, Ted Williams, one of the greatest baseball players, regularly swung a bat at imaginary pitches.

When practiced over time, the skills of the art become effortless, and the artist becomes self-confident. Likewise, the skills and techniques of group leadership will require practice over time. But once seeded in your consciousness, they will take root and grow throughout your professional life.

Self-Awareness Is the Key to Effective Leadership

Interpersonal processes and dynamics in the group are always in flux at any given moment. To handle something as fast moving as group dynamics requires that we have great awareness of our self and of others. Thus, developing the leader's self-awareness and self-knowledge is a focal point in group leadership training (Fehr, 2014; Zastrow, 1990). And that won't appear overnight.

The competency of a leader grows, bit by bit, through training and experience. You can accelerate your growth by developing self-awareness of both your interpersonal styles and your own unresolved issues. Later sections of this chapter discuss this part of personal development in greater detail.

IDEAL QUALITIES OF AN EFFECTIVE GROUP LEADER

It will take a long time to attain the "ideal" qualities of an effective group leader—if they are ever attainable. Still, we all can start to accumulate our leadership experiences before these qualities are perfected. The following qualities, therefore, shall be treated as aspirations, instead of expectations.

Calm Mind

A group leader needs to have a calm mind, or clear-headedness, to take the group in the desired direction (Corey & Corey, 2014; Kottler & Englar-Carlson, 2015; Yalom & Leszcz, 2005). A calm mind comes from having a wide range of conceptual and technical knowledge, including

- theoretical concepts of group work;
- knowledge of group dynamics;
- supervised group leadership experiences;
- knowledge of working with diversity and differences; and
- knowledge about effective communication, conflict resolution, reality testing, and constructive feedback, and so on.

Striking a Balance Between Supports and Challenges

When it comes to leading members to give support to one another, most beginning group leaders meet no problems; yet, when situations require them to guide the group to challenge or give corrective feedback to another, that is another story—that is where they bump into difficulties.

Looking closely at the way effective leaders work, we will find that they seem to achieve balance—between supports and challenges—in fairly consistent ways (Lieberman, Yalom, & Miles, 1974; Marmarosh, Holtz, & Schottenbauer, 2005; Thomas, Martin, & Riggio, 2013). Unwaveringly, they

- facilitate the needed amount of *emotional stimulation* within the group, such as *challenging* one another and promoting self-awareness;
- offer *support*, such as encouragement and protection, to members;
- use meaning-attribution skills, such as clarifying unspoken meanings and interpreting members' underlying patterns; and
- provide an executive function, such as setting rules, boundaries, limits, and norms.

How do they know when to direct and when to let be; when to stimulate and when to step back; when to interpret patterns and when to instill hope? It all takes self-knowledge and years of practice.

Cultural Sensitivity

Most group counseling concepts are developed for majority populations. Therefore, group leaders need to make certain modifications when applying these concepts and intervention techniques to minority group members so as to internalize a more self-affirming identity for them (Haley-Banez et al., 1999).

All culturally sensitive group leaders inevitably work from a *relational-cultural framework* (Han & Vasquez, 2000). This framework promotes healing through *validation*, *empowerment*, and *self-empathy* in group members. Validation helps counteract the disbelief and disregard that minority members frequently experience. Empowerment helps minority members overcome the internalized messages of inability and inferiority, while self-empathy allows them to reflect on the difficulties they have faced in dealing with oppression.

Trustworthiness and Compassion

"How much can I trust the leaders and other participants?" Members entering a new group often entertain this kind of doubt and question. Building trust usually begins with the group leader; one who offers honest feedback and genuine perspectives is more likely to earn trust from group members (Kottler & Englar-Carlson, 2015) than otherwise.

Furthermore, compassion for self and others—which starts with self-acceptance—can save the group a great deal of frustration. Without self-acceptance, group leaders may expect perfect group work, which is unrealistic.

Relaxed Attitude and Discovery-Oriented Practice

The complex nature of groups requires leaders to adopt a flexible and creative practice (Bohart, 1999) for each unfolding moment of the group—a practice only made possible with a discovery-oriented mindset. With this discovery-oriented mindset, a leader is more able to flow with the energy of the group, to be creative and spontaneous, even when the interactions and progress of the group become unpredictable (Kottler & Englar-Carlson, 2015). We encourage you to follow your intuition and let your creativity guide you where to go when applying group leadership skills. Experimentation is the key to discovery.

Total Concentration: The State of Flow

Leading at the interpersonal process level demands a total concentration of one's mind, similar to being in a state of "flow." One of the authors experienced this power of concentration firsthand. During Chris's training days as an intern, he led an experientially focused group that met each week for 90 minutes. One day, Chris developed a severe allergic reaction, and his eyes and nose would not stop running. That night he was unsure whether he would be able to lead the group since he was feeling so distressed and distracted by the severity of his allergic reaction.

The moment Chris walked into the group meeting, however, his nose and eyes completely cleared, as though someone had turned off a faucet. He proceeded to conduct the entire 90-minute group session without giving another thought to his allergies. Interestingly, the moment the last group member left the room, Chris's allergies returned and continued for several days afterward.

The mental demand of being totally present when leading an experientially oriented group had been so great that Chris's body had surrendered to his mind. He entered into the flow of the group dynamics, and his symptoms disappeared; in the absence of that demand, his symptoms quickly re-emerged.

THE FIVE PHASES OF GROUP LEADER DEVELOPMENT

Be patient and trust yourself on the journey of developing yourself as an effective group leader, because the skills and techniques of leading a group are complex and challenging. By and large, a new leader who embarks on the journey will go through *five developmental phases*, as indicated by the classical study by Zaslav (1988). Permeated within each phase are valuable lessons you will draw from.

1st: Group Shock Stage

Leading an experiential group for the first time can feel like a threat. Unlike individual counseling, each session in group therapy can inundate you with a vast amount of stimuli and at a fast pace. At any given moment, a minimum of four levels of dynamics await your mind to take in:

- The individual members' inner and outer reactions
- The intermember interactions and dynamics
- The dynamics of the group as a whole
- Your own inner and outer reactions

Facing this complex and multifaceted process, a new leader may feel overwhelmed, intimidated, or confused—an initial jolt called *group shock* (Zaslav, 1988). The following is a trainee's reflection on her first time leading a group and her experience of group shock.

> It's sort of like juggling nine balls at once. You have to keep your eye on every ball and keep your attention on the one that's about to fall.

Often the new leader attempts to cope with these overwhelming feelings with the following two coping strategies:

First, they *revert* to the comfortable *individual counseling techniques*, such as probing, reflecting members' feelings, or paraphrasing. This results in a series of *leader-member dyad interactions* that can frustrate group members. It prohibits the powerful interaction that the group needs.

Second, they focus on the *content level* and attempt *problem-solving* or *advice-giving*. This strategy creates a group atmosphere that is detached, lethargic, or intellectualized.

2nd: Reappraisal Stage

After the attempted coping strategies prove ineffective, a new leader may retreat into a more inhibited mode of functioning, feeling confused about how to get adjusted to the overwhelming complexity of the group. At this stage, inexperience with group dynamics can make way for self-doubt.

Eventually, though, efforts to *rethink* and *adjust* will produce results, and the leader will become more adept at recognizing the differences between individual and group counseling. As his or her reliance on individual counseling skills decreases, use of basic group facilitating skills will greatly increase.

3rd: One Step Behind

Once you begin to apply basic group facilitating skills, your ability to identify and track the various threads of group interactions grows. You may start to understand the interpersonal dynamics of an event happening right in front of you. You may be able to connect what happens within the group to the theory and intervention methods—all that you have learned from textbooks, lectures, and didactic materials.

However, it is not until after the session that a light bulb comes on in your mind, "Aha! I could have used this intervention to bring forth that new understanding for that member! Oh well, it's too late!"

As such, you are able to recognize the process level of group interaction, but you are not quite able to apply the process-focused interventions on the spot when crucial events occur—you feel as if you are always *one step behind*. Though you may lament about it, it is exactly where you should be at this point.

4th: Using the Here-and-Now

As your ability to recognize interpersonal process grows, there comes a point where you are able to actively apply interventions on the spot when interpersonal events happen right in front of you; you are able to go beyond the content level and zoom into the process level. At this point, you begin to *experiment* with here-and-now focused skills and techniques that allow for a greater intensity and greater illumination of the group.

Sometimes you make mistakes and your process-focused intervention is not effective because you did not deliver it precisely enough for the group to understand your intention. Other times your process interventions are spot on, and you shout "Zoop!" in your mind, viscerally feeling the power your here-and-now technique has on the group. This drives you to refine your skills and techniques, to dig in for more. A "group geek"—as some of the enthused new group leaders like to call themselves—is born.

As your experiences continue to grow, you observe that each process intervention has its own effects. You begin to develop a more intimate but realistic working relationship with the here-and-now applications. You begin to have a more comfortable, as well as a more theoretically consistent, personal style—you begin to attain a real sense of competence.

5th: Polishing Skills

In this phase, you continue to experiment with and polish various here-and-now activation and process-focused intervention techniques. You take risks in sharing more here-and-now impact disclosures of your own for the goal of transparency. You find creative ways to deal with difficult members. There is no end in this learning—the polishing of skills takes a lifelong journey.

When they finish their group leadership training, most new leaders land at the camp of "one step behind"—almost half way up to Mt. Everest. What an extraordinary expedition!

Application to Training and Supervision

Zaslav's classic model helps instructors and supervisors in training programs better assess and understand their supervisees' cognitive process. It is easy for us instructors and supervisors to forget the psychological and cognitive process that beginners must endure.

Zaslav's five-phase model indicates that instructors and supervisors need to spend sufficient time on *basic leadership skill*. This is in order to *scaffold* before more advanced abilities are developed. For example, when the supervisees are in the Group Shock and Reappraisal phases, the supervisor might need to calm their minds by asking them to focus on *fundamental leadership skills* and *techniques only*.

In addition, the supervisor may provide trainees with *strength-based feedback*. When their fears and anxiety are cushioned with a trusting and respectful supervisory relationship, trainees are more likely to venture further into the next stage (Ronnestad & Skovholt, 1993; Rubel & Atieno Okech, 2006).

At the One-Step-Behind and Using the Here-and-Now phases, supervisees may have increased confidence, yet they are still burdened with a sense of insecurity. They are not certain whether their impressions of the moment-to-moment dynamics are valid. Therefore, the supervisor might need to focus more on deepening trainees' understanding of elusive group dynamics and complex interpersonal processes.

Finally, if the supervisees are in the Polishing Skill phase, the supervisor is afforded the opportunity to draw attention to *the "self" of the trainee*. Such personal matters may include the following: personal strengths and limitations that impact their practice, transference and countertransference reactions, and the discovery of their own personal voice in their practice of group work.

THREE MODELS OF CO-LEADERSHIP PRACTICE

Co-leading a group provides a valuable experience in the beginning group leader's evolution. Given the economic pressures of managed care today, however, co-leadership practice is a modus operandi—more realistic in professional training programs but less possible in today's mental health agencies.

Overall, there are three models of co-leadership: the alternate leading model, the shared-leadership model, and the apprenticeship model (Jacobs, Masson, & Harvill, 2016).

1st: The Alternate Leading Model

In this model, co-leaders divide tasks. For example, one will do the opening, and the other will follow with an icebreaker. They *take turns* facilitating and intervening. A rhythm develops where each leader can predict what tasks he or she will take on.

Although dividing tasks may seem easier and more alluring, it does not provide the group with the model of mutual support and communication between co-leaders. In reality, this model tends to stifle the creative flow of the leaders.

2nd: The Shared Leadership Model

In the second model, there is no division of tasks or turn taking. Rather, co-leaders carry out every step of the group intervention and management together, flowing back and forth seamlessly.

Bouncing Off Each Other

In the shared-leadership model, both leaders are active and engaged in every step, every facilitation, and every intervention. If one leader initiates an intervention, the other leader helps to carry it through. If one leader's intervention is unclear, the other steps in to clarify the intention. The two leaders are there to *bounce off* one another.

For this to work, each leader should not say more than two or three sentences at a time. This allows for the other leader to pick up what needs to be said next. This requires each leader to listen attentively and be ready to pick up where the other leaves off.

Examples of How to Bounce Off Each Other

Here we use the following example to illustrate how two leaders can *bounce off* each other in the opening of a session:

Co-leader A:

Welcome back to the second session of the group. I hope everybody has had a good week.

Co-leader B:

We hope that after the first session, you are feeling more relaxed and ready to do some hard work together.

Co-leader A:

In this session, we will do a quick check-in and introduce two new members and their goals. The bulk of the session will then be spent in a structured activity to help everyone get to know one another.

Co-leader B:

Let's start with a quick check-in. For check-in, I would like everyone to share any realization or reflections that you have had since the first session, any lingering feelings, or any new events in your life.

Co-leader A:

We are not going to take turns or go around the circle, so whoever is ready, please feel free to jump in.

Co-leader B:

Yes, we like the check-in to be free flowing. You are welcome to show support and encouragement to one another during the check-in, but please keep it short as we only have 10 minutes or so for the whole group. If any major issues emerge during the check-in, we invite you to work on them during our processing portion of the group.

Co-leader A:

Thank you [to co-leader B] for the clarification. [To the group] Who would like to begin?

3rd: The Apprenticeship Model

In the apprenticeship model, one leader is typically more experienced, while the other is a relative novice. In the beginning, the experienced leader will take on the primary initiative and responsibility within the group. Later, when appropriate, the novice (the apprentice) begins to take on a more active role. In due course, the practice becomes a shared-leadership.

Advantages of Co-Leadership

Co-leadership provides a dual perspective and doubled energy for both leaders and members unavailable in solo leadership.

To Group Leaders

Group is inherently complex, so a beginning leader may feel overwhelmed at any given moment. Having a supportive partner can be an invaluable asset because attention and care to the group are doubled (Jacobs et al., 2016; Kottler & Englar-Carlson, 2015). In a situation where one leader is absent, the other leader ensures that group treatment remains uninterrupted. This continuity is important (Hoyt, 1995).

Another advantage observed through clinical experiences is that co-leaders complement each other; one plays the *bad cop,* while the other plays the *good cop.* When one co-leader challenges a member, the other may take on the supportive role. When one co-leader focuses on showing warmth, the other may press hard for self-examination. Each co-leader frequently shifts roles but is always there to take on a complementary function.

To Group Members

The presence of two leaders can provide a model of communication and cooperation for the group, especially when the group leaders are a male and female pair. Members also benefit from the experience and insight of two leaders. Different feedback and reactions from each may enhance member energy and interaction.

Disadvantages of Co-Leadership

Co-leadership is not without its *disadvantages*. Allow us to explain.

To Group Leaders

The planning process may actually take longer because there are two perspectives on every issue. If leaders' approaches and perspectives are not well coordinated, the session may not go as well. Personality differences may create tension in the pair; an extroverted leader might complain that the introverted partner does not carry an equal share of leadership responsibility. On the other hand, the introverted leader might feel deprived of leadership practice because the extroverted partner often jumps in first.

To Group Members

Group members may align themselves with one leader, in opposition to the other leader. This is especially common when they detect a discord between the leaders. On the other hand, two leaders may align themselves in influencing a group member to the extent that the recipient feels "ganged up on." This is especially true if both leaders unintentionally push too hard to break through a member's initial resistance, without balancing that challenge with adequate acceptance and support (Jacobs et al., 2016; Kottler & Engler-Carlson, 2015; Yalom & Leszcz, 2005).

SEVEN PRINCIPLES OF CO-LEADERSHIP PRACTICE

Abiding by certain principles can make a difference in therapists' co-leadership experience. These principles are detailed below.

1st: A Good Working Relationship

To be effective, you must have a good working relationship with your co-leader. This is of critical importance. We recommend the following to ensure this:

- Choose a co-leader whose theoretical orientation is compatible with yours.
- Adopt a shared-leadership model and avoid the alternate leading model.

- Avoid a power struggle; process thoroughly and regularly so that feelings and concerns are aired and not built up.
- Give refreshing feedback; help each other develop awareness of previously unknown blind spots.

2nd: Balance Each Other Out

The second principle of co-leadership practice is about balance. If one leader challenges a member, the other leader should offset this with some support.

The reason that co-leaders need balance is that there is an inner conflict involved whenever a member is stuck in a rut. A part of the member wants to get started on the hard work of therapy, but the other part is afraid, and so the member is stuck.

Given this, one leader can encourage the member's courageous side and press him or her to take on the hard work that is feared. The other leader can care for the member's anxious side, conveying acceptance when the member is not ready to take on such a task.

When co-leaders complement each other in this way, members are given the chance to see how their own dilemmas are played out between the two sides and can then choose more freely. Often the members choose to undertake the difficult tasks.

3rd: Support Your Co-Leader's Facilitation and Intervention

New leaders often feel alone and discouraged when members seem unresponsive to the facilitation or intervention they have initiated. This is where a co-leader can offer a big boost of morale by *stepping in to support* the other's initiatives.

A Member Sidetracking the Group From Maria's Facilitating Prompt. For example, Maria and Mike, two trainees, were co-leading a group. At one point, Maria initiated an intervention by saying to the group,

[To the group] Ted has told us the problems he is having with his boss. I wonder, would the group share with Ted what difficulties you sense in his experience that he might still be struggling with?

One member, Jean, acknowledged Ted's anger and hurt. Other group members were touched by Jean's validation of Ted's feelings but did not say much else. Another member spoke up, but about a totally unrelated subject.

The Co-Leader, Mike, Stepping In to Direct It Back. Seeing that the group would lose the moment of connection and intensity if he did not intervene, Mike stepped in. He redirected the group to loop back to Maria's original intervention. Mike said,

[To the group] "I sense that some people are still deeply touched by Ted's story. *Let's go back to Maria's question for a moment.* Do any of you want to share what unexpressed difficulties you sense Ted might have in this experience with his boss?"

Insights Deepened. With this redirection, the group was able to go back and explore the topic further. The group was able to reflect Ted's feelings of shame and humiliation that he had been unable to articulate. One member even pointed out that the way Ted reacted to his boss seemed similar to the way he responded to his alcoholic father. This observation provided great insight for Ted.

This critical moment of heightened understanding and awareness would have been lost if Mike had not stepped in to reinforce Maria's initial intervention.

4th: Pick Up the Slack When Your Co-Leader Is on the Hot Seat

Sometimes one of the co-leaders might be challenged by a group member and therefore stuck on the "hot seat." At this juncture, you as the co-leader should pick up the slack to facilitate or mediate toward a resolution. You can help by reframing the issues at hand, thus moving the group along. Vice versa, when you are on the hot seat, you can expect your co-leader to drive the group forward.

Enrique Got Confronted by a Member. For example, Enrique and Gilda, both group leaders in training, were co-leading a personal growth group. A group member, Sawetha, confronted Enrique, saying that he had allowed the group to overlook her when she related her story. The confrontation aimed at Enrique created instant tension in the group.

Gilda Stepping in to Help Process. At this point, Gilda stepped in to help Sawetha clarify her statement toward Enrique. Gilda facilitated while Enrique explained his decision to focus on other members' issues first and to return to Sawetha's story later.

As a result of Gilda's mediation, the group understood both leaders' high level of commitment to them, as well as reasons for specific decisions that had been made along the way.

5th: Active Communication Pre-/Post-Session

The fifth principle is for both leaders to engage in active communication pre- and post-session. Co-leaders need time to talk and to learn about each other's views and approaches to group leadership. The pre- and post-session communication can alert the co-leaders to critical incidents arising in the group and how best to address them. Without these meetings and discussions, erroneous assumptions may be made about the other leader's actions, creating unnecessary difficulties within the group.

This is not to say that group leaders cannot disagree. Actually, disagreement in front of the group can be good practice. However, serious disagreements between co-leaders are better resolved outside the group, so that the session does not revolve around the leaders' issues.

6th: In-Session Communication

The sixth principle of co-leadership is for co-leaders to have an open line of communication during the session. As stated by Kottler and Englar-Carlson (2015), co-leaders need to communicate frequently both *nonverbally and verbally during the group session*. The following illustrates verbal and nonverbal communication.

Verbal Communication. When issues arise in the group, co-leaders should acknowledge their need for communication with one another and proceed to talk openly about their reactions and intentions. For example, in one group session, co-leader Mike intended to let the group talk a bit longer about the issue presented by group member Eli. Mike was confused when Maria turned the group's attention to Tracy, a member who sat next to Mike and whose facial expression Mike could not see.

To clarify his confusion, Mike communicated with Maria during the session by saying,

Maria, I sense there are dimensions in Eli's presenting issue that remain unexplored. Are we going to come back to Eli later?

To this, Maria replied,

> Oh, thank you for checking that out with me, Mike. Yes, we will loop back to Eli later. I saw Tracy having some intense emotions just now and thought that we should help her explore what's behind those emotions. We can then return to Eli.

This kind of communication provides the group with a model of how to communicate honest reactions with each other. In addition, it demystifies any unrealistic status that group members might attribute to leaders. It helps increase leader transparency.

Nonverbal Communication. Co-leaders need to exchange eye contact or use agreed-upon nonverbal cues (such as hand gestures), in order to increase the understanding of their intentions. Although nonverbal communication is encouraged, whispering is not. Whispering tends to give an impression of secrecy, hampering the leader's intention of being transparent.

Sitting Across From Each Other. To enhance in-session communication, co-leaders need to avoid sitting next to each other. Sitting across from each other can help both verbal and nonverbal communication. It also helps each other compensate for any missed observation of dynamics of members sitting next to leaders.

In the earlier example, Mike was unable to see Tracy's eyes tearing up because he was sitting next to her. Fortunately, it was not missed by Maria, who was sitting across the room from Tracy and Mike.

7th: Resolve Disagreement in the Moment

As stated previously, serious disagreements between co-leaders are better resolved outside the session. Sometimes, though, spur-of-the-moment disagreement between co-leaders can happen in a session. When this does occur, it can actually become a learning experience for group members about how to handle disagreements in the moment (Lanza, 2007).

When co-leaders express their feelings openly in front of group members, it usually results in a positive experience for the entire group. Lanza (2007) recommends that co-leaders model what you want to teach members right in the session. If you want to teach the group conflict resolution, then nothing is better than to model conflict resolution right in front of the group.

Our clinical experiences resonate with the recommendations by Lanza (2007). We encourage new group leaders to seek out opportunities to co-lead and learn to be open about their feelings with their co-leaders in the session. Through co-leadership, we will learn more about our own selves than through any other avenue.

CULTIVATING YOUR INNER LEADER

The "self" of the group leader—the *inner leader*—is the most important instrument that decides the outcome of the group. This section focuses on the cultivation of the self of the leader.

The Use of Your "Self" in Group Work

Who we are as a person, our own experiences, thoughts, feelings, perceptions, intuitions, prejudices, and biases—all of these "inner workings"—pull together to shape the session we lead. What is alive inside us can be our best resource, or our foe, depending on our level of self-awareness.

When your "self" or your "inner working" is fine-tuned, you are able to be mentally and emotionally present, aware of your own feelings and of their impact on members, and able to use these data to funnel your actions as the session unfolds. In doing so, you are using your "self" as the instrument to bring about positive therapeutic outcomes (Baldwin, 2013; Moro, Scherer, Ng, & Berwick, 2016).

In the following, we suggest ways through which you can cultivate your inner leader.

Engage in Reflective Practice, Consistently

Reflective practice—the most important tool (Atieno Okech, 2008; Bolton, 2010) in the development of any professionals—is at the heart of cultivating our inner leader. Reflective practice asks that we critically examine our values, concepts, and assumptions. Doing so will widen our perspectives, develop the authority of our personal voice, and give clarity to our role, responsibility, and principles.

For details about how to go about engaging in reflective practice as a group leader, and how to use it to maximize member growth, please see Chapter 15.

Accept Our Own Anxiety

Another way to cultivate our inner leader is to *accept our anxiety,* instead of trying to escape from it.

When we accept our anxiety, we are more likely to differentiate our own "stuff" from what occurs in a group. For example, when experiencing emotional reactions, we are more likely to ask ourselves which parts strictly belong to me and which parts to members? When experiencing boredom, fear, anger, or disinterest during a session, we are likely to listen attentively to our inner self. We pay attention to particular sensations in our body (e.g., a queasy stomach, pain in the back, or a creepy, tingly sensation on the back of the neck).

One way to learn to accept our own anxiety is to practice open communication in our personal relationships, without slipping into withdrawal or defensiveness whenever anxiety arises. If we find ourselves unable to engage in this, seeking personal therapy might be helpful.

Push Beyond Current Capacity

There is no shortcut in developing our inner leader except for pushing beyond our current capacity in each step of professional development. To better understand this concept, let's visit the concept of "flow" experience.

According to Csikszentmihalyi (2008), when our skills are developed *enough* to meet a demanding challenge, we experience a sense of flow where we completely immerse ourselves in that task and forget about ourselves and time. We are *skillful enough but are still challenged,* therefore we are neither bored nor overwhelmed.

In this state of flow, all of our senses and thoughts are totally engaged in the activity, yet we have the confidence to meet the challenges being faced. We lose a sense of time and self-consciousness.

In a group session, being in a state of flow is likely to open ourselves to each unprecedented group situation and allow ourselves to be immersed in the present moment. We are likely to see group dynamics as they are and to respond to those demanding circumstances without fear.

Take Risks and Give Yourself to the Process

Many beginning group therapists fear to make mistakes in group interventions. Approaching group dynamics from a cautious, assiduous, perfectionistic distance will not get us far. We cannot possibly know what is best to do in every group dynamic, nor will we ever have it "all figured out."

We can learn to tap into the power of the group only when we give our self to it without reservation. We must take risks. Without this dedication, we are not therapists—but mere technicians.

When we take risks with new techniques, our first attempt may fail because of our lack of experience. After several attempts, however, our delivery of the interventions may become more sophisticated and effective. The new skill will eventually become second nature.

Allow yourself to experiment with different skills and techniques. Experimentation is the only way to further our own growth. Experimenting is not about using clients as guinea pigs, but rather *experimentation* means *constantly checking on feedback* and *adjusting therapeutic methods* until they work.

Develop Your Own Therapeutic Voice

To make group work personally gratifying, leaders must exercise their own therapeutic voice in it. To speak with our own therapeutic voice is to be ourselves and to be the best versions that we can be. The members will sense "the person" of the group therapist and feel that presence.

Developing our own personal voices is a lifelong process, an infinite journey that continues far beyond the professional training we receive. It requires continual direct personal experience, a personal evolution in every aspect of ourselves—there is neither shortcut nor cheating.

Reading and attending workshops will help only to a limited degree. We must do our personal work experientially to refine our own voice. Please see the next section for more details about how to do our personal work.

One-to-One Supervision

One-to-one supervision represents one of the precious components in preparing novice leaders to meet the challenges of leading a group (Li, Kivlighan, & Gold, 2015). Supervision can deepen, accelerate, and contribute to the overall quality of the learning.

The best way to use your time in one-to-one supervision is to discuss your emerging intrapersonal awareness: your thoughts, feelings, and impulses. For example, if you experienced feelings of uneasiness, fear, anger, or other sensations in any group session, you are encouraged to bring these reactions to the supervision session in order to identify their sources. Through exploration within supervision, the rich meanings behind these feelings may be appreciated, and your ability to lead more objectively will be enhanced.

Group Supervision

When one-to-one supervision proves unavailable, one may still benefit from group supervision. Group supervision has the following benefits (Christiansen & Kline, 2000; Rubel & Atieno Okech, 2006):

- Helps trainees make the most of the multimodal learning possibilities inherent in the group of people
- Illustrates an effective means of group interaction and leadership
- Helps trainees test out new skills in the supportive environment of the supervision group
- Enhances trainees' personal development, building up their self-confidence

Within the group supervision, the supervisees can explore just about every kind of feeling and concern about leading groups (Kees & Leech, 2002). Issues you can investigate in group supervision may include the following:

- Anxieties about dealing with conflicts, anger, or negative transference/countertransference in the group
- Personal pain or tragedy in your own life
- Personal barriers that inhibit you from leading your group effectively

Supervisees often go through a growth trajectory (Christiansen & Kline, 2001a). At first, they often *begin at a dependent level*, leaning heavily upon the supervisor to "show them the ropes." With time and experience, they gradually *move toward greater independence and initiative*. Later, when they are able to better trust themselves and their peers, they *move toward interdependence and intimacy*, which is the highest level of development.

STARTING A JOURNEY TO YOUR OWN INNER PEACE

Chris once heard an interesting story about someone who purchased a bicycle made in the Far East. Excited to get it assembled, he jumped into action only to find that the first line of the assembly instructions said, "First, have inner peace." The point here is that having "inner peace" is the exact condition where any complex activity should begin. It is the same for leading a counseling group. This section addresses areas for leaders to attend to so as to achieve that inner peace.

Resolve One's Own Unresolved Issues

We leaders are more vulnerable to the "interpersonal pull" or "button pushing" within the group if personal issues are left unresolved in our lives. See the following examples:

Mike and His Unresolved Issues. When a member, Alice, was describing a recent experience where she was violently attacked, the leader, Mike, found himself suddenly emotionally distanced and angry. He tried to divert attention away from Alice, but other members kept bringing the attention back to her. Mike finished the session feeling frustrated and confused.

As he was reviewing the circumstances in supervision, Mike recalled a childhood incident in which his brother was viciously mauled by a dog, and Mike was unable to stop the attack. This recollection helped Mike recognize his attempt to protect his old painful feelings by distancing himself, and his failure in helping Alice and other members.

With his supervisor's help, Mike worked out a plan to better deal with Alice's issues within the group. At the same time, he sought out counseling to work through his unresolved feelings about the attack.

Bridgett and Her Unresolved Issues. Bridgett was co-leading with Eckhart. In the sixth session of a group, a member, Suzy, disclosed that she had an abortion 2 decades earlier at the age of 14. In response to this disclosure, Eckhart noticed a look of contempt flash across Bridgett's face. Outwardly, Bridgett did not acknowledge Suzy's disclosure, nor did she respond to Suzy during the remainder of the group. This left Eckhart alone to acknowledge Suzy's disclosure and make connections to the work she was doing in the group.

Right after the session, Bridgett disclosed to Eckhart that she was a member of a fundamentalist religious group that taught its members to condemn and disassociate from those who did not follow the precepts of their sect. She said that she did not know how to respond therapeutically to Suzy because she had been taught that all abortions are wrong.

In supervision, a great deal of discussion was devoted to helping Bridgett find a way to work from a position of support, instead of exclusion and separation.

Bridgett was able to identify some immediate steps that she could take to help with this group and relate more effectively with Suzy. In addition, Bridgett identified a religious individual with whom she could consult, in order to resolve her inner conflicts between the doctrine of her religious sect and the ethical standards for a professional counselor.

Have a Visceral and Live Group Experience

Having live, personal group therapy counts as the most important part of group leadership training. Most group researchers (Pierce & Baldwin, 1990; Stockton & Toth, 1996; Yalom & Leszcz, 2005) agree that participating in an experiential group or therapy group is imperative in leadership training.

Learn Through the Visceral Experience of Being a Member. Through the personal experience of being a group member, we experience our own sense of vulnerability and become aware of our own dark sides, impulses, strengths, and weaknesses. Only by being a member of a live group will we come to truly appreciate the force of group pressure, the catharsis of telling our own story, the bliss of having our feelings validated, the influential status of the leader, and the painful but valuable process of receiving feedback about our interpersonal patterns and the kind of courage it takes to change (Yalom, 2009).

Plain Role-Playing and Cognitive Understanding Are Not Going to Cut It. Cognitive knowledge gained through reading, lecture, and discussion is not sufficient to help you become a group leader, nor is mere role-playing of the leadership skills. It is in a live group that we learn at an emotional level.

Group leader trainees consistently report being helped by personal group experience as they gain a better awareness, build a clearer understanding of their own behaviors within groups, and gain greater wisdom with the give-and-take of the feedback process (Comstock, Duffey, & St. George, 2002; Kline, Falbaum, Pope, Hargraves, & Hundley, 1997).

Participate Not Just to Improve Your Group Leadership. Mere participation in personal group therapy is not enough. To truly benefit, your goal should *not be confined to improving your own effectiveness as a therapist/counselor.* Rather, you need to allow yourself to explore your own personal issues. Without exploring your issues within the context of a live group, you are cheating yourself. This is what the "person-practice model" (Aponte, 1994) is about: to practice therapeutically, our personal issues related to interpersonal patterns must be identified and exposed in a therapeutic context.

Critical Reflection/Journaling as a Vehicle for Trainee Inner Peace

Many training programs offer an experiential group as part of the curriculum (Yalom, 2009). When a group is taking on the dual role of an experiential group and a training group, relationships become easily blurred. Steps must be taken to ensure that the setting is safe where trainees can feel free to deal with personal development issues.

Confine the Grading to Academic Assignments Only. To scale down the threat of dual relationships, *any activities related to personal disclosure during the experiential group must not be graded* (Sklare, Thomas, Williams, & Powers, 1996). Rather, only academic assignments, including *critical reflections on the group process*, are graded.

Limiting grading in this way will diminish trainees' fear of being evaluated by their instructors and make it possible for trainees to become more open to exploring the personal issues.

Critical Reflection as Assigned Homework. It would be wise for instructors to *assign critical reflection as a homework assignment* for trainees participating in the live experiential group. Cummings (2001) reported on *a journaling approach* where trainees were asked to write a reflection after each session about their personal experience of the group. After the experience was completed, almost all trainees reported that the journaling helped them understand their change throughout the various stages of the group, their own interpersonal process, and theories in action.

The writing of critical reflection should be part of the reflective practice that we have covered in the previous section. For more details, please read Chapter 15.

∞∞∞

In closing: When done well, group therapy looks like a work of art—its process appears seamless and effortless, even though we know much work goes into the making. To arrive at this artful state of group leadership, the leader first has to develop his or her personal part of leadership—the inner leader.

SELF-REFLECTION

1. In past groups in which you have participated, what group leader behaviors contributed most to the quality of the experience? How did the leader(s) balance safety and challenge within the group? What is the optimum mix of safety and challenge that you prefer for yourself?

2. What past experiences have you had serving in a leadership capacity? Did you find yourself focusing strictly on the task(s) at hand, or did you also attend to the emotional needs and experiences of others?

3. How confident do you feel at this point in your training to use your "self" as a tool for your work with groups?

4. Think back to a time when you had a fair to high level of confidence. How do you think this happened? What experiences did you have that contributed to building your confidence in this way?

5. If you have a low level of confidence, what kinds of experiences do you think might be beneficial in helping you develop it?

6. What are some options for you to increase your level of group leadership experience? What kinds of groups would these experiences include? What supervised opportunities exist for you within these groups?

7. How comfortable are you with using humor in your work with groups? What guidelines might assist you in deciding what is an appropriate use of humor as compared to what would likely detract from a group?

8. What are some ways in which you might bring some of your creativity into your group leadership? Can you identify some direct and indirect ways of incorporating it?

9. For you, what would be an ideal co-leadership arrangement? What are some key features that you would want in your co-leadership relationship? How will you try to ensure that these factors will be part of any arrangement in which you participate?

10. What factors described in this chapter will be most helpful in developing your group leadership skills? Are there factors not addressed in this chapter that you expect will also contribute? If so, what are they?

11. In terms of your current developmental level and your experience in leading groups, at which stage would you put yourself based on the developmental stages described in this chapter?

CHAPTER 3

TYPES OF GROUPS AND HOW TO START ONE FROM SCRATCH

Much work remains to be done before a group can launch into its therapeutic work. This includes the following:

- Attention to ethical and professional guidelines
- Program planning
- Member preparation and screening

The only way to bypass this altogether is when you adopt a group that has already been formed. In this case, you will have to bend over backward to fit yourself into a group that has already had its own history, dynamics, and unspoken rules. Given a choice, most leaders will opt to start their own group from scratch in an effort to ensure a solid foundation and optimal success for the group.

ETHICAL AND PROFESSIONAL GUIDELINES

Before serving our members, we must fully grasp the highest principles—the ethical codes and professional guidelines—that govern our behaviors and activities of *group* practice (Association for Specialists in Group Work, 2000; Thomas & Pender, 2008). This section stipulates just these.

Informed Consent

Prospective members have the right to know exactly what the group will be about. Therefore, before starting a group, the therapist must disclose relevant information to prospective group members. This information allows for prospective members to make an *informed decision* about whether the group will be appropriate for their needs. Informed consent is a fundamental ethical condition.

The most efficient way to fulfill this requirement is through a face-to-face *pregroup orientation* (detailed in a later section of this chapter). If face-to-face is not possible, the alternative is to give prospective members the necessary information via phone calls or letters.

Disclosure on Risks and Limitations of Group Counseling

Potential members also have the right to know the limitations and the potential risks of group counseling.

- *Limitations of group counseling.* Not all clients are appropriate for treatment through group counseling; individual counseling may be more suitable for them. For people who have difficulty opening up in front of a group of strangers, they will be best served to first receive individual counseling where they can benefit from in-depth self-examination and self-discovery in privacy. People with special needs, such as those suffering from personality disorders or major depression, would also need to be informed of the limitation of group counseling and be referred to proper individual therapy.
- *Potential risks with respect to the particular group.* Potential risks of participating in a group include periodically experiencing some level of *stress, dissonance,* and *anxiety.* Groups are designed to help people discover who and how they are in their relationships. *Increased awareness,* however, *is not always pleasant.* This awareness can lead individuals to reassess themselves and the quality of their relationships. *They may experience some degree of dissonance* if they begin to let go of overly narrow restrictions from the past, opening themselves to new choices and new ways of being.

Whether these advances are small or sweeping, *significant others in their lives may resent these changes and react in ways to try to "bring back the person they knew."* This may be the catalyst for either conflict or deeper levels of interpersonal understanding and intimacy, different case by case. Members need to be informed of this risk before joining the group.

Professional Disclosure

The professional disclosure should include information about the following:

- The leader's approach to group work. When providing information about your approach to group work, use clear and understandable language for the population coming to the group. *Avoid technical lingo or psychological jargon.*
- The leaders' professional backgrounds and experiences relevant to group work. In a regular group session, the leader would not normally disclose a lot about themselves. In professional disclosure for informed consent, however, you will need to share a bit more about your relevant professional background and experiences. Any applicable credentials should also be included.

Voluntary Participation

By ethical codes (Thomas & Pender, 2008), group members only proceed to their *personal disclosure* based on *voluntary* choice. Prospective members have the right to know that such standards exist—that they can reveal their personal information at the level and pace comfortable and appropriate for them. When not ready, they have the right to observe and wait until it seems fit for them to do so.

Of course, not all groups are voluntary. Sometimes therapists work with *mandated groups* wherein they serve court-ordered or school-ordered members in groups. Though mandated to be present physically, these members *have the right to determine the level and pace of their personal participation, mentally.*

Knowing how to work with *resistance* and knowing how to start from a place of encouragement and respect will go a long way when leading such a group. Allowing the reluctant members to watch one or two sessions, without personal participation, may help soften the aversion. After they have developed a sense of trust with the therapist, mandated members can actually benefit greatly from meaningful group work.

Chapter 6 provides more details of how to lead mandated groups with hope and encouragement and *how to use structured communication activities to help distrusting members open up gradually.*

Freedom to Withdraw

Group members have the freedom to withdraw from the group at any time if they find the experience unsuitable. However, it would prove therapeutic for everyone involved if they return to the group to share their reasons for withdrawal. This appearance helps the withdrawing member handle the departure in a responsible way and obtain appropriate closure. This also provides a sense of closure for the remaining members, rather than suddenly having a member disappear from the group with no explanation. Ways of handling premature termination will be detailed in Chapter 14 in the section on dealing with *uncommon termination.*

To prevent withdrawal from the group, leaders should inform prospective members early on that some anxiety is normal when joining a new group. When trust begins to build within the group after several sessions, this anxiety will dissipate.

For this reason, group leaders can *invite members to commit to a minimum number of sessions (e.g., four sessions)* in order to give the group a chance to prove itself. This is not meant to be a hard-and-fast rule but a way in which to remind members that it does take a bit of time to *build group cohesion and a sense of comfort* within a group.

Screening Interview and Member Protection

Ethically, group leaders must screen prospective members so that only those whose needs and goals are compatible with other members of the group are admitted. Those who may impede the group's work or whose needs cannot be served by the group should not be admitted to the group.

The purpose of the screening interview is to *protect group members*—to shield them from potential physical and psychological harm by other ill-suited members. More details on *the procedure of screening interviews* will be provided later in this chapter.

Confidentiality Within Groups

Prospective group members should be informed of their right to confidentiality, as well as the limitations on that confidentiality. Specifically, the issue of its limitation and its threats loom large in a group setting because fellow members are not bound professionally.

The antidote to this threat is having members commit to maintaining confidentiality between fellow group members. This commitment to confidentiality should be renewed several times throughout the existence of the group. If the group does not commit to confidentiality, the trust will be hampered, cohesion will be weakened, and members will not be confident in any significant level of self-disclosure.

Nondiscrimination

Ethically, group counselors and therapists must practice nondiscrimination. Respect is paid to all members, regardless of ages, cultures, disabilities, ethnicities, genders, races, religions, sexual orientations, marital statuses, or socioeconomic status. Differences are valued and appreciated. A mere tolerance of differences does not stand a chance in the group.

Even in a group where members have much in common, substantial differences may still exist. Some differences are quite visible; others are not as obvious. *Before they can trust the group, certain members might choose not to reveal their invisible differences due to fear of being ostracized.*

When obvious characteristics cause a member to appear alone, you, as the leader, should extend yourself to this individual in order to help him or her feel welcomed and supported. For example, if you have a Muslim member in a predominantly Christian group, you must make an extra effort to connect with this member of the group. This connection must be done with sincerity, sensitivity, and subtlety, lest the person feels embarrassed.

Practicing Within Competence

Group leadership is a highly complex discipline. Group counselors and therapists should only practice in this discipline when competent in group facilitation and intervention. If still training, they can only practice under close supervision.

Achieving competence in group leadership calls for a great deal of effort in acquiring applied knowledge, training, and practical experiences. One key element of clinical competence is the "self" of the group leader. To develop the self as the vital instrument for group work, you need to have sustained growth through reflective practice. For more details on reflective practice, please read Chapter 15 and review the section on "Self as the Instrument" in Chapter 2.

TYPES OF GROUPS NOT FACILITATED BY CREDENTIALED PROFESSIONALS

The variety of groups existing today never ceases to amaze us. The list that follows ever dazzles our eyes: counseling or therapy groups, growth groups, ongoing groups, time-limited groups, groups for specific interests (such as men, women, LGBT, social anxiety, eating disorders, medical illness, addictions), cognitive behavior therapy (CBT) groups, dialectical behavior therapy (DBT) groups, guidance and life skills groups (also called psychoeducational groups), task groups, support groups, consultation groups, self-help groups, cyber-groups, and so forth.

It takes credentialed therapists to facilitate groups. Exceptions, however, exist for support groups and self-help groups. This section focuses on just these types of groups.

Self-Help Groups

By their nature, self-help groups do not require therapists to facilitate the group process. Rather, they rely on "fellow sufferers" or *peers*, who have "been there, done that," to mutually help each other (Munn-Giddings & McVicar, 2007; Pistrang, Barker, & Humphreys, 2008). Not involving professional therapists, these peer-led groups are *free of charge*, affording those financially challenged to still receive the help they need. Examples of such groups may include the following:

- Alcoholic Anonymous (AA)
- Other anonymous groups (narcotics, gamblers, overeaters, codependency, etc.)
- Groups for those with physical illness (cancer, HIV positive/AIDS, etc.)
- Groups to help with loss issues (divorce, death, etc.)

Support Groups

A support group differs from a self-help group in that *a leader*, rather than a peer, provides the facilitation. However, *the leader of a support group is often not a credentialed therapist.*

Furthermore, a support group merely focuses on offering support, encouragement, empathy, and validation for group members. It *does not offer interpersonally oriented feedback, immediacy, challenges, or confrontation,* even if members' maladaptive interpersonal patterns show up in group interaction (Gitterman, 2005).

While support and self-help groups prove valuable and healing for many people, long-term change is not to be expected due to the lack of interpersonal feedback.

Growth Groups

Growth groups started decades ago to help well-adjusted people become more sensitive, aware, and self-actualized through the use of group process (Trotzer, 2006). The most common among them are sensitivity training groups (T-group) and encounter groups.

Encounter groups use more confrontations (Dierick & Lietaer, 2008; Young, Reysen, Eskridge, & Ohrt, 2013) and are therefore more oriented toward solving problems. On the other hand, T-groups highlight personal awareness and sensitivity toward self and others, thus are more process oriented. Encounter groups are much more intense than sensitivity groups (Trotzer, 2006).

Regardless of their differences, these types of growth groups share the following characteristics:

- Spontaneity
- Freedom of expression of feelings and perceptions
- Honest feedback
- Here-and-now

Unfortunately, a great deal of controversy exists concerning growth groups, primarily surrounding *the lack of credentials of their group leaders* (Trotzer, 2006). The lack of credentials lessens the credibility of their leaders, despite their charismatic leadership style. This is one of the reasons that growth groups are not included in the four group specializations (Thomas & Pender, 2008).

TYPES OF GROUPS LED BY CREDENTIALED PROFESSIONALS

Groups led by credentialed therapists can be divided into four categories: psychotherapy groups, counseling groups, guidance and life skills groups, and task/consultation groups (Association for Specialists in Group Work, 2000).

If you want to specialize in guidance and life skills groups or task/consultation groups, you will need to obtain the complex knowledge of *normal human development*.

If you desire to work with *counseling groups* or *psychotherapy groups*, then you need knowledge and awareness of *both normal and abnormal* human development, plus *an ability to work with clients with intense emotional arousal*.

In this section, we discuss the details of the four group specializations.

Task/Work/Consultation Groups

A group consultant can apply group leadership skills and strategies to help achieve the tasks and goals of a work or consultation group. This type of group may be in a school setting, a business/industry setting, or others.

- In the school setting: A school may hire a group specialist to facilitate task groups made up of parents, teachers, and administrators. These task groups are often charged with certain responsibilities such as developing curricula, individual educational plans, or social learning plans. Group specialists help these task groups improve their functioning so that what is charged to them may be accomplished. By assisting the task groups, group specialists indirectly promote the well-being of the students that these groups exist to serve.
- In the business and industry setting: These private settings also contract with group specialists to act as "process consultants." In this role, the group specialist usually employs various strategies to assist the project teams to streamline the system, improve interpersonal communication, and develop respect among various team members. This facilitation results in team members working more effectively together in achieving the goals charged to them and ultimately advancing the bottom line of the company (Conyne, Rapin, & Rand, 2008; Kormanski, 1999). These results make contracting a group specialist appealing to the business.

See the following examples of task groups:

Table 3.1 Examples of Task Groups

School parent/teacher consultation groups	A Native American powwow committee
Project development work groups	Product evaluation work groups
Case-centered consultation groups	

Psychoeducational Groups

Generally speaking, psychoeducational groups are *guidance and life skills groups* (Brown & Brown, 2011) serving two types of clientele:

- Clients with special *developmental* needs and issues
- Clients with limited ability to communicate

These two types of clients benefit greatly from psychoeducational groups due to a *sense of universality* (Yalom & Leszcz, 2005) that reduces the stigmatizing effects that they often suffer from. On a different note, such groups ease the burden of clinicians' tedious and repetitive maintenance work with individual clients. Though they involve credentialed professionals, by and large, psychoeducational groups resemble *support* groups. Its supportive nature is perhaps the reason why *disturbed clients tend to respond better to* psychoeducational group than counseling and psychotherapy groups (Remocker & Storch, 1999).

Psychoeducational groups can use *structured activities* to address clients' needs, identifying and building on their skills (see details in Chapter 6). For example, they may use a cognitive-behavioral approach to teaching coping skills and strategies to deal with various life stressors.

Psychoeducational groups are *developmental* and *preventive* in nature. This is due to their focus on building life skills to prevent future problems for clients or to keep current difficulties from getting worse.

See the following examples of psychoeducational groups:

Table 3.2 Examples of Psychoeducational Groups

Stress reduction groups	Grief support groups
Anger management groups	Assertiveness training groups
Phobia and panic management groups	Chronic pain management groups
Couples communication enhancement groups	Social skills groups
Caregiver training groups for adults with aging parents	Groups for new parents
Groups for chemical dependency early recovery	Chemical dependency graduate groups
Groups for persons coping with physical illness	Groups for chronically mentally ill patients
Large guidance group in a school setting	Small guidance group for human relations

Counseling Groups

Counseling groups serve two types of clients:

- Clients who are at risk for developing personal or interpersonal difficulties
- Clients who seek improvement in interpersonal functioning

An *unstructured, experiential* manner is the crux of counseling groups (Bemak, 2005; Bemak, Chung, & Siroskey-Sabdo, 2005). Research has found that *empowerment groups for minorities* typically work best in this manner. Compared to psychotherapy groups, counseling groups tend to be shorter—about medium-term.

Counseling and therapy groups work best with client issues that are *interpersonal in nature* (Berg, Landreth, & Fall, 2013). Budman and Gurman (2016) make clear this orientation:

> [Counseling and therapy groups are] interpersonally oriented rather than symptom oriented. This means that rather than emphasizing, for example, the depression or anxiety experienced by those dealing with strained relationships, *it is the nature of those relationships themselves that is examined.* The interpersonal environment of the group is uniquely suited to the examination of such issues. (p. 252)

Given this, leaders of counseling groups use a variety of intervention strategies to address interpersonal patterns, concerning maladaptive cognition, emotions, actions, and relational systems. Such interventions help people become more aware of themselves, their interpersonal behaviors, and their interpersonal interactions with others.

Counseling groups are considered *treatment* groups because they are not only *preventive* and *developmental* but also *remedial*.

Please note: For the profession of group work to thrive, asserts Vriend (1985), *the training of prospective group leaders must be based on the mode of counseling and therapy group*, rather than on that of the growth group. To the world at large, and the managed care industry in particular, we must demonstrate that group counseling/therapy does not exist just for skill building or just for growth enhancing, but it serves a *remedial* function for members who suffer from maladaptive behaviors, emotion disregulations, as well as intrapersonal and interpersonal malfunctioning.

Following are some examples:

Table 3.3 Examples of Counseling Groups

Interpersonal problem-solving groups	Cancer groups
Men's groups	Women's groups
LGBTQ groups	Minority women's groups
Groups for socially awkward men	Groups for at-risk students
Groups for couples with relationship problems	Divorce groups
Groups for adult children of alcoholics	Groups for codependents
Groups for adults molested as children	Empowerment groups for minorities
Groups for clients having recently left inpatient settings	Training groups for prospective group leaders

Psychotherapy Groups

Most people in our society and even some professionals in our field consider psychotherapy groups and counseling groups the same thing, but by design, they are different. Psychotherapy groups are more *in-depth* and tend to be *longer-term* than counseling groups (Trotzer, 2013).

Psychotherapy groups are *remedial* by nature and often *nonstructured*. This type of long-term group has the greatest degree of therapeutic leverage in reconstructing members' deeply ingrained personalities (Trotzer, 2013). Participants in psychotherapy groups may include the following:

- Clients who function at a level just to get by due to grave *interpersonal* and *emotional barriers* that limit their well-being in life
- Clients with a high level of maladjustment or a mental health condition that is *severe* and/or *chronic*

Psychotherapy group therapists use *interpretation* as a tool to address the clients'

- maladaptive patterns,
- psychological blocks (e.g., resistance, distorted perceptions, and defenses), and
- unconscious materials (e.g., transferences and dreams).

See the following examples of psychotherapy groups:

Table 3.4 Examples of Psychotherapy Groups

Long-term therapy groups	Groups for physically or sexually abusive individuals
Groups for the substance addicted	Groups for people suffering from schizophrenia

STARTING A GROUP FROM SCRATCH (I): PROGRAM PLANNING

This section focuses on program planning for *counseling and therapy groups.* Due to space limitation, planning for other types of group is not covered.

Good Intentions With Poor Planning: A Disaster

The importance of program planning can be illustrated with a story told by Conyne (1999):

Two therapists working at a human services center decided to offer a counseling group at the center because they noticed that individual therapists were becoming burdened with the demands of managed care. The two collaborated in private with such confidence that it didn't occur to them to first propose it to their director. When they brought it up to their colleagues at a clinical staff meeting, the result was a disaster. Due to the lack of program planning, the idea was not well received by the director or colleagues. Several colleagues were actually frustrated.

The two therapists ended up feeling embarrassed and discouraged. If the two therapists had done their homework and developed a good program plan, the result might have been different.

Program planning is the groundwork that group therapists cannot avoid. It involves *managerial tasks* including *needs assessment, proposal writing,* and *member recruitment.* Such managerial tasks may seem mundane, but they stand necessary. Do not attempt to leave them in the hands of an administrative assistant who has little understanding of group work.

Needs Assessment

Program planning, as a rule, starts with a careful assessment of the needs, demands, and interests of the population that the counseling group intends to serve. Needs assessment can help identify types of problems and unmet needs that exist as well as resources already available

Results of the assessment can help therapists determine what kind of group should be offered to *fill the gaps* in the service delivery system. What tools can be used to identify unmet needs?

Formal assessment. Formal methods usually involve the use of various types of surveys including mailed *questionnaires, telephone contacts,* and *personal interviews* (Lewis, Lewis, Daniels, & D'Andrea, 2011).

Informal assessment. Therapists may check with colleagues in local agencies to determine what services they currently provide and what needs are unmet.

How to Write a Group Proposal

After needs are identified, the next step of program planning is to develop a clear proposal. The functions of a proposal are twofold: It helps the leader achieve greater clarity for practical matters at hand, and it increases the likelihood of the plan being accepted. An example of the group proposal (for working with trans individuals) can be found in Appendix A.

When writing a group proposal, you should clearly indicate the features of your group in the following 12 areas:

Type and Purpose of the Group. Will the group be a psychoeducational or a counseling or therapy group? Will the group be a support or a process group? Will it serve clients with similar problems or clients with diverse issues? When it comes to the purpose of the group, you can use the findings of your needs assessment to help you formulate it.

Voluntary or Mandated Membership. Planning for school-mandated or court-mandated groups is different from voluntary groups. For mandated groups, you will need to spend more time planning how to use structured activities to handle negative attitudes that members may have about being in the group (Jacobs, Masson, & Harvill, 2016; Yalom & Leszcz, 2005). If resistance and resentment are well managed, even mandated groups can prove to be beneficial to clients who struggled to be there in the first place. See Chapter 6 for the section on *using structured activities for mandated groups.*

Is It a Closed Group? *Next is to indicate whether your group is going to be closed or open.* A *closed group* is one where no new members are admitted once the group begins. A *counseling group tends to be closed* because members are working to develop trust and intimacy with each other and hold one another accountable for working on their goals within the limited life of the group. Members in a closed group also greatly *benefit* from going through the various stages of group life together. The progression of group development often leads to deep personal exploration and working through difficult issues.

Is It an Open Group? An open group is one where members come and go at various points throughout the life of the group. This format is best suited *for a hospital or residential treatment* environment. In these settings, group services must remain open to the changing membership (new arrivals or members graduating) on a weekly basis.

Open groups certainly present *challenges* for leaders and group members. For members, the challenge rests in the fact that they do not have the benefit of progressing through various group stages before departing. For leaders, the challenge is the need to constantly orient newcomers to the group and to say goodbye to those who leave. *Cohesiveness* is difficult to establish in an open group. However, it is possible to increase cohesiveness by having the remaining members "carry the torch" for new participants. That is, current members can mentor new members as to how the group functions. This mentorship can cultivate a sense of continuity within the group.

Group Size. Group size greatly influences dynamics, and it should be indicated in the proposal. When a group is too big, full participation from each member becomes unattainable. A large group often leaves some members' needs neglected. When a group is too small, you will face greater challenges: First, the dynamics become strained because more pressure is placed on each member to talk, with less time to ponder and reflect. Second, it may lack adequate perspective and stimulation for members.

The proper size of the group will depend on its purpose and the population of the members. An ideal size for a counseling/therapy group with an adult population is approximately eight. A psychoeducational or support group can be slightly larger in size: approximately 12 members. For younger populations, the group size should be smaller with around three or four members for children or six to eight for adolescents (Corey & Corey, 2014).

The Length of Session and Frequency of Meeting. How many minutes will your group session last? For young children, sessions should only be 30 to 45 minutes due to limited attention spans. In a school setting, the session usually corresponds with the class period, ranging from 40 to 50 minutes (Jacobs et al., 2016). These groups can *meet twice weekly* to compensate for the shortness of the sessions.

Groups for adolescents outside of the school setting can have a slightly longer session length and meet just *once weekly*.

Adult counseling or therapy groups are usually conducted for 90 minutes to 2 hours per session and meet *weekly*. Such length is necessary for members to get emotionally engaged with one another. If sessions are too short, members will have difficulty getting into issues of any depth and therefore will not accomplish very much.

Adequacy of the Location. Is privacy adequate where the group meets? To make group members feel comfortable enough to open up, the meeting room should ideally be closed and free from intrusion or distraction. There should be flexibility in seating so chairs can be moved to form a circle. *In counseling and therapy groups, no tables should be placed in the center* of the circle. Tables create distance and erect barricades between members. In task and psychoeducational groups, tables present less of a problem.

Leaders' Qualifications. In the proposal, indicate your qualifications to be a group leader. Basic competencies of a group leader include experience in working with individuals, adequate training in group theories and dynamics, personal experience in group, knowledge of the topic specific to the group under consideration, and awareness of the best practices in group counseling and therapy (Thomas & Pender, 2008).

Screening Procedure. To protect group members from unnecessary emotional harm, leaders have an ethical responsibility to screen unsuitable members from the group. In the proposal, it is advisable to state the criteria that will be used for screening. Methods of screening will be covered in later sections.

Ground Rules. Including ground rules in your proposal will ensure the reviewer that the group will be carried out within agreeable boundaries and will be in good order. Although they vary from group to group, typical ground rules may include, but are not limited to, the following:

- No fraternization is allowed outside of the group among members.
- Maintain confidentiality for fellow members.
- Bring any outside conversation that relates to the group, to the group.
- Call to notify the leader of any absence.
- Be punctual.
- No food, chewing gum, or beverages are permitted during the session.
- No alcohol or substances may be used before or during the session.

Structures and Techniques. Whether the groups are structured, semistructured, or unstructured, the format must be clearly stated in the proposal. Please see Chapter 6 for a structured format, Chapter 7 for semistructured, and Chapter 8 for unstructured.

When deciding the format of the group, consideration should rest primarily on the cognitive and emotional developmental levels of the group members. In general, a structured group may benefit less-developed individuals while it may stifle those highly developed.

Possible Issues or Topics. In the proposal, you may want to list possible issues and topics that group members would work on. The findings in the needs assessment that you conducted previously will help cultivate the concerns, issues, and areas of life that should be explored to best address the members' needs.

Recruiting Members

Once your proposal is approved by the reviewer, it's time to look for ways to recruit potential members. Three strategies can be used for recruitment:

1st: Peer and agency referrals—Your peers and other therapists at other agencies know you and tend to have a high level of confidence in the group that you provide. Many times, your targeted population is already receiving some type of counseling or other services. You might want to contact the agencies and therapists who work with the population appropriate for the group you are planning to lead. Flyers and other written descriptions can be made available for them to give to their clients.

2nd: Informing key individuals in the community—With some populations, especially those that are traditionally underserved by counseling and therapy services (e.g., minority and immigrant populations), you will find it helpful to talk to key individuals within those communities and to provide them with written information about the group.

These key individuals include religious, educational, or business leaders who are highly respected within the community. They often have influence over whether someone outside of the community might be given an opportunity to work with community members. These key individuals might also have in-depth knowledge about the special needs and issues of that population.

3rd: Advertising extensively—All things considered, it is worthwhile to advertise extensively through nontraditional or traditional methods of advertising: social media, listservs, flyers, newspaper articles, and posters placed in key locations frequented by members of the population being considered.

STARTING A GROUP FROM SCRATCH (II): PREGROUP ORIENTATION

Once you have begun to advertise, interested individuals may start to call in with various questions. Asking the secretary of your agency to answer such questions is not appropriate, but answering them on an individual basis by yourself will consume too much of your time. Therein lies pregroup orientation.

Pregroup orientation is not a luxury but an ethical obligation. It fulfills the therapist's ethical duty to provide *professional disclosure*, obtain *informed consent*, and maximize *member preparation*. It may be said that orientation is a pretreatment training.

Orientation as Pretreatment Training

Pregroup orientation is a type of pretreatment training; it gives you an opportunity to lessen potential members' fears and eliminate misconceptions about the group. The time and energy spent in member preparation will be well worth it as this preliminary training often greatly reduces subsequent dropouts.

When deciding whether to join a new group, potential members often experience a high level of anxiety. Lack of familiarity with a group experience magnifies this anxiety. Apprehension can be reduced by educating the potential members through a pregroup orientation (Sklare, Keener, & Mas, 1990).

In group therapy, premature termination has been found to depend most on members' expectations (Hannah, 2000). When expectations are not met, members tend to drop out quickly. Given this, it is wise to use pregroup orientation to educate potential group members. This may prevent unrealistic expectations during the initial stage of the group before therapeutic factors have kicked in.

In preparing people for group experiences, we must inform the prospective members of three things: *group rules, the necessity of self-disclosure,* and *the need to be patient.* In our experience, it is especially important to educate potential members about the need to attend at least *four sessions* before judging its effectiveness. When properly educated, interested individuals will be prepared to have an optimal response to the challenges inherent in a new experience.

Orientation also clears up any misconceptions that potential members might have about groups. Even if members are joining the group on a voluntary basis, they often come to the group with certain fears and *myths about groups*. Myths that potential members might harbor include the following:

- Group counseling is only for people with major issues.
- Group counseling waters down real counseling because there are more clients than counselors/therapists.
- Group counseling is less effective than other types of counseling.
- Group counseling would be entirely unnecessary if only there were more counselors/therapists available (Carter, Mitchell, & Krautheim, 2001).

Make the First Contact Engaging and Validating

Pregroup orientation is perhaps your first contact with interested individuals. In this initial contact, potential members will form impressions about your interpersonal skills and communication skills, your likeability, and your level of competence. In a sense, they are sizing you up.

If you are a new leader, you will need to prepare the orientation well so that you can be as professional, knowledgeable, empathic, and enthusiastic as possible. The pregroup orientation should truly reflect who you are as a professional and your beliefs in the group process.

There are many tasks to complete during this first contact. Tasks include providing professional disclosure about the following: the purpose of the group, the expectations of member participation, requirements for joining and leaving the group, guidelines about the handling of and limits to confidentiality, necessary information about the time frame and cost for the group, and potential results of participation.

As you can see, there is much to cover. If you address all of them in a lecture or speech, the orientation may appear dry and boring and consequently discourage the audience.

One way to make the pregroup orientation more engaging is to provide a handout that covers basic information. A handout can serve as a written professional disclosure. Handouts allow you to use the precious face-to-face time in a more personal and dynamic interaction. Please see Appendix B for the following handouts for pregroup orientation:

- Rights and Responsibilities of Group Members
- Orientation to Being in Group

- How to Get the Most from Group
- Informed Consent Form

If your potential group members are young, you may need to tailor the handout, using age-appropriate language.

The time saved via using handouts can be spent in *allowing potential members to ask questions.* A question-and-answer session can make your orientation *interactive and engaging.* You are also afforded the opportunity to connect with potential members with your empathic and supportive responses.

Clarify Mutual Expectations

One of the major tasks in pregroup orientation is to define mutual expectations between member and leader. Hannah (2000) emphasized that leaders must inform potential members what is expected of them prior to the beginning of the group. These expectations include the following:

- Member commitment to working on personal goals in the group
- Nonhierarchical group interaction
- Honest sharing of feelings and perceptions based on the here-and-now experiences of the group
- Member-to-member empathic support
- Members taking appropriate risks and testing out new behaviors in group

By clarifying expectations, you help potential members gain a realistic picture of appropriate group behavior, which may prevent premature dropout.

Since time is short while the list of expectations is long, we encourage you to overcome this challenge by use handouts as exemplified in Appendix B, which help clarify client rights, responsibilities, and what they can expect from group counseling.

Make Connections, Provide Hope

With some of the important information covered in a handout, you can spend the majority of the time answering audience members' questions and making connections with them.

To make connections, allow yourself to convey the feeling and core message behind each question. To do this, you need to

- listen deeply to the questions asked,
- reflect the audience's *implicit feelings* behind the questions, and
- provide hopes by *reframing* the audience's concerns *into positive group outlooks.*

For example, Ginnie, an audience participant, asks in the pregroup orientation, "If someone in the group dominates by talking all of the time, how will the group handle that?" Rather than just responding to the content of this question, you should try to sense what is behind it. *What is the feeling underlying this question?*

If you sense apprehension, you can convey your understanding of this fear by saying,

> [To the audience] Yes, I can see how anyone would *feel frustrated and discouraged* when someone dominates and no one does anything about it. [reflection of feelings] In group counseling, domination by a few members may happen because a group is just like any other interpersonal setting. What is different in the group though is that we, the leaders, are here to make sure that the group interaction moves in a way that *those difficult things can be talked about and resolved in a safe way. This way, each member gains a greater awareness and grows from it.* [positive reframing]

Eddy, another audience members, asks, "Aren't people going to think that I am weak or that I have psychological problems if I decide to join the group?" Again, you can answer with empathy and positive reframing. Consider the following answer:

> [To the audience] It's understandable that we might *worry about being seen as weak* when thinking of joining a counseling group. Judgment from others is a very powerful force in our lives. [empathic response] If we look deeply, we will find that *seeking change is not a sign of psychological problems but rather a sign of courage.* Most of us in society have some *internal blocks* that need to be worked on so that we can expand our capacity *to live a more ful-filling life* and form closer ties with people we care about. Therefore, joining a group is actually *a wise investment for all.* [positive reframing]

The Challenge of Confidentiality

Another topic frequently asked about during orientation is confidentiality. As a group leader, you are ethically and legally obligated to maintain confidentiality.

Group members, however, are not legally bound in a similar way. This presents a challenge for the group. You must stress how important it is to maintain confidentiality if people are to build a sense of trust for the group. You are encouraged to discuss ethical issues of privacy in the pregroup orientation and in the screening interview.

Additionally, the issue is likely to arise during group sessions, both directly and indirectly. During pregroup training, acknowledging the impact that confidentiality can have on a group will help establish a foundation for later work.

Frequently Asked Questions During Orientation

The following represents the common questions asked by prospective members in pregroup orientations. Before gaining personal experience and acquiring knowledge of group process, you may not be able to answer these questions thoroughly. We include these questions here because questions have a way of provoking and accelerating our learning. After finishing group counseling training, you can come back and visit these questions. At that point, you will find that you are able to provide answers with confidence and competence.

Questions frequently asked in pregroup orientation include the following:

- What kinds of problems are suitable to work on in the group?
- If the problem that I want to work on is different from those of others in the group, how will the group be able to help me?
- How can the group help people with so many different concerns and problems at the same time?
- Are all people suitable for group counseling? What kinds of people are appropriate for the group? What kinds are not?
- If my husband wants to know what's going on in the group, can I tell him what happens in the sessions?
- After the group starts, if a friend of mine wants to join the group, would she be admitted?
- What's the next step? Are we admitted to the group now since we have come to the orientation?
- What can I expect during the screening interview?
- How am I going to know whether I am making progress in the group?
- If I figure out after a few sessions that I really don't like the group, can I drop out?
- If I miss a few group sessions, will it matter?

- Will there be a lot of homework assignments for members to do between sessions?
- If someone in the group dominates the group by talking all the time, how will the group handle that?
- If I have a pressing issue to talk about in a session but someone is more aggressive and thus prevents me from having time to discuss my situation, how will this be handled?
- I am a very quiet person; will I really get a chance to talk about my issues among other more vocal people?
- If I don't get along with someone in the group, what will happen?
- If I have a problem with someone in the group, can I consult with the leader in an individual meeting?
- I am very afraid of confrontation. I am afraid of being attacked by others. What would you say about that?
- If I find myself attracted to someone in the group, may I date that person outside the group?
- Is there anything I should be cautious about before deciding to join the group?
- How long does a session usually last? How many sessions will the group run?
- I am in individual counseling now. Is it possible to participate in group counseling concurrently?

STARTING A GROUP FROM SCRATCH (III): CRITERIA FOR MEMBER SELECTION

Before conducting member screening interviews, try to determine the criteria that you will use to best select your members. Poor selection can significantly impede the work of the group. A group composed of problematic members can instigate mistrust, anger, guilt, or impatience. This section covers potential areas for you to consider before selecting your group members.

Membership Match

The functioning level is the most important group composition factor. Ideally, for a group to work well together, members should be homogeneous in terms of their functioning level. You may be able to gauge an individual's stage by determining his or her willingness to change, excitement about joining the group, awareness of reality and self, openness to feelings, willingness to tolerate anxiety, willingness to disclose, sensitivity to others, risk-taking ability, creativity, and nonaggressiveness (Riva, Lippert, & Tackett, 2000). When showing *a goodness of fit* in these characteristics, the group of individuals will likely be a good match.

Gender is an important factor in groups for *children*. Mixing boys and girls can have a negative impact, especially when dealing with developmental issues or issues specific to gender. For adults, however, a group of mixed gender can provide greater interpersonal learning for each gender.

Diversity Factors

The more homogeneous the group, the more rapidly trust can be built and greater cohesion can result (Han & Vasquez, 2000). However, members of homogeneous groups may be hesitant to challenge one another, even when it would be in their best interest to do so.

The more heterogeneous a group, the more its members have the opportunity to be stimulated by their differences. However, if not properly facilitated and processed, power dynamics may become difficult (Han & Vasquez, 2000). Leaders must be sensitive to marginalized members, such as an elderly woman, a gay man, or an individual with a disability. You must make sure that the group norms validate the experiences of these people.

One specific diversity factor worth noting is rates of verbalization (Han & Vasquez, 2000). The *rate of verbalization* involves how assertively a person takes his or her space to verbalize his or her views. Certain cultures, such as Mexican Americans, American Indians, and Asians, encourage *noninterference* as a way of showing respect when other people are talking. People of these cultures will *seldom interrupt each other. When these people are in the group, they often find it difficult to chime in or take the floor.* Leaders must make sure that the participation needs of these nondominant group members are met.

Best Candidates

People who can best benefit from group counseling are those who

- are motivated to change,
- understand the benefits of group work,
- feel isolated or lonely at times, and/or
- struggle with self-esteem and social skills.

Those who are not likely to benefit from groups are people who are not motivated to change; people who do not believe in group therapy; sociopathic individuals; or people with brain damage, extreme narcissism, paranoia, acute psychosis, or extreme depression (Yalom & Leszcz, 2005).

Other poor candidates include people with high levels of resistance to participation; individuals who are hostile, passive-aggressive, or actively abusing drugs or alcohol; and those with cognitive retardation, poor skills in managing anxiety, or excessive neediness (Riva et al., 2000).

The individuals mentioned in this section are likely to present serious *management problems* in groups. They need special attention and are usually *best referred to specialized programs*. At a minimum, *they need to be stabilized* before entering group counseling and therapy.

Concurrent Therapies

Concurrent therapy happens when a member receives individual counseling and group counseling at the same time.

Benefits: The benefit of concurrent therapy is that issues identified in group counseling can be explored further in individual therapy (Taylor & Gazda, 1991). For example, concurrent therapy is *good for people with borderline and narcissistic personality disorders* because these clients need both extensive intrapersonal exploration in the individual setting and external support in the group setting.

Problems: For most people, however, concurrent therapy creates a problem: These clients may *save their self-disclosure for individual therapy* and *talk less in the group.* The opportunity to work on interpersonal issues within the group is thus lost. Furthermore, *other group members might feel shortchanged* by this member's lack of engagement.

Solutions: If a member needs to be placed in a group and individual counseling concurrently, it is best if the individual counselor and the group counselor can support each other's therapeutic efforts through *mutual consultation.* However, do remember to *seek client consent* (American Counseling Association, 2014) before consulting with the other therapist.

STARTING A GROUP FROM SCRATCH (IV): SCREENING INTERVIEW

In an ideal world, members should be screened before entering a group. Equivalent to an intake for individual counseling, a screening interview for a group is simply more *time consuming*. To the already tight schedule of a therapist, the screening interview adds more demand. Ethically, the therapist needs to go through this process despite its laborious nature.

The Ideal of a Pregroup Screening Interview

A pregroup screening interview serves three functions:

1st: Protecting prospective members—The *Best Practices Guidelines* by the Association for Specialists in Group Work (Thomas & Pender, 2008) state that group practitioners need to properly screen members to protect future members. An unscreened group may be an unsuitable collection of individuals, which can result in causing psychological harm to its participants.

2nd: Building groundwork of rapport—In the screening interview, the leader gains an opportunity to build rapport with the prospective members and thus reducing their anxiety of joining a group.

3rd: Helping potential members define goals—A clearly defined goal leads to a definitive vision and focused task. Goals motivate us and dictate how our energy will be invested. The screening interview can help members hone in on a workable goal in the group.

Realities and Limitations

A couple of difficulties stand in the way toward carrying out pregroup screening. The first centers on the issue of time. A screening interview may take anywhere from 30 minutes to an hour, depending on the depth you go into. Additionally, if you meet the interviewee together with your co-leader, it will double the expenditure of time.

The second has to do with the mandated group. When working with a mandated group, therapists often do not have the control over group parameters that they would like. The idea of screening out unsuitable members is simply *not possible for addiction or court-ordered groups*.

As you go through your training, this is the best time to follow this ethical requirement and muster up your skills of proper screening. In your future practice, you will need to be flexible and realistic in your considerations.

Help Interviewees "Flesh Out" Their Goals

Most people need help to "flesh out" their goals in order for them to become practical and achievable (Barker, 2013). The major task of the screening interview is to help the interviewee frame a goal in a *specific* and *workable way* for the group context.

If a potential member becomes unresponsive or defensive toward your efforts in shaping an achievable goal, this likely indicates how he or she functions interpersonally. You will need to be judicious when making your decision concerning this person's suitability for your group.

The following suggests several steps for conducting the screening interview. You may tailor them to suit your specific circumstances.

Greeting

This step provides continuity from pregroup orientation to pregroup screening. It also gives the interviewee a general picture of what the procedure will involve. The therapist may say something like,

Hi, Tom. It's nice to see you again. It was a pleasure to have you in last week's pregroup orientation. I'm glad that you are interested in joining. Today we have about 30 minutes together. To decide whether the group is suitable for serving your needs, I need to gather some information from you. If any of the questions I ask are too personal, you can decide to what extent you would like to answer. Toward the end, I would also like to know whether you have questions to ask me.

Ask Clients About the Issues They Want to Work on

With the brevity of time, it is wise to right away get to the heart of business—what the client wants to achieve in the group. If a client is uncertain of where to start, it may be helpful to ask about his or her issues of concern. *These issues can be later translated into a personal goal.*

Following are some possible questions to initiate this discussion of goals. *Avoid asking one question after another* like an interrogation. *Remember to reflect back or summarize client responses* in an effort *to establish rapport* with the prospective members.

Example 1:

Question:

Have you ever been in a group before, Tom? If so, what was the experience like?

Later reflection:

I am sorry to hear that your previous group experience was not productive for you. Despite that, it seems that you remain open to pursuing another group. I have great respect for your determination to try this.

Example 2:

Question:

Group works best when members can identify certain concerns or areas in their lives to improve on. If you were to identify an area that you would like to work on, what would it be?

Active listening followed by reflection:

So you tend to either flare up into anger or shut down into depression when things are not going as you expected. You would like to find ways to manage this problem, which has been a struggle for you for quite a while now.

Example 3:

Question:

Could you give me an example of how your anger flares up?

Active listening followed by reflection:

I can see that it is a big concern when you are not able to channel your anger properly. You have a tendency to blow up, sometimes even break things or throw things across the room.

Example 4:

Question:

Tom, what made you decide to make a change at this specific stage of your life?

Active listening followed by reflection:

So, you went through a divorce a few years ago, and it was very painful for you. Now you are in a new relationship that is very important to you, and you want to make sure that things go smoothly in your new relationship.

Example 5:

Question:

If these problem areas are not taken care of, what might be the possible negative outcomes?

Active listening followed by reflection:

Tom, I can see that you care about your relationship with your fiancée and her daughter very much. You are afraid that if your anger and depression do not improve, you might end up ruining the new relationships as well. I can see that this is a serious concern, and I am glad that you are pursuing group counseling to seek change with this issue.

Translate Problems Into Personal Goals

There are two keys to successful goal setting: (1) Translating the presenting problems into a personalized goal and (2) Making the goal concrete and achievable. Following are prompts that you can use to translate the presenting problem into a personal goal:

Example 1:

Question:

By the end of the group, what change would you like to see happen in terms of your anger and depression issues?

Active listening followed by reflection:

> I see. So you would like to feel more at peace with yourself and with others, rather than flare up or shut down. [Client's goal is broad and nonspecific.]

Example 2:

Question:

> So, when you feel more at peace with yourself and with others, what will you be doing that is different from what you are doing now? How would it appear to an outsider? [Probing for concreteness and specificity.]

Active listening followed by reflection:

> Tom, you are saying that you would be able to communicate your frustration with words rather than with your hands and that you would be more able to express your emotions rather than act them out. Am I hearing this right?

Another active listening followed by another reflection:

> I see. So it is not only negative emotions that you have trouble expressing but also positive emotions. You feel as if you are disconnected from your feelings. So to be able to *connect to your feelings* will be your primary goal. To be able to effectively *express your emotions, positive or negative,* will be your secondary goal. Does that sound right, Tom?

Interview Clients About Their Interpersonal Backgrounds

Our *family of origin* represents our *first group experience,* literally. Gathering specific information about clients' interpersonal background, especially the family of origin, offers the group leader an opportunity to get a sense of where clients come from. Influenced by object relations theory and family systems theories, we often look into clients' earlier life and family experiences by asking questions such as these:

Example 1:

Question:

> Our family is like our first group experience. I would like to get a picture of what your first group looked like. Specifically, how did your family of origin interact? How did your family of origin handle anger, intimate feelings, and other intense emotions? How did your family respond to differences within and outside the family? I am asking a lot of questions here. Please respond in a way that you feel most comfortable.

Active listening followed by reflection:

> So there were a lot of fights in the family. Your father walked out when you were six, and your mom was depressed for as long as you can remember.

Example 2:

Question:

> While all these things were going on in your family, what did you do? How did you cope? In other words, what was the role you played in your family of origin?

Active listening followed by reflection:

> So not only could you not get much attention from your mom because of her depression, but you also had to take care of your younger siblings. Two things cross my mind right now. I may be wrong, but first, it sounds like the model of emotional expression that you got in your early life was one of the outbursts and angry confrontations. Second, the heavy responsibility of taking care of your younger siblings at such a tender age, in addition to the lack of emotional support from your mom, seem to have driven you to suppress your feelings in an effort to survive each day.

Example 3:

Question:

> How do the coping strategies you learned as a child affect your life as an adult? Do you handle emotions the same or differently?

Active listening followed by reflection:

> There are two things that I heard you saying, Tom. First, as an adult you find yourself continuing to suppress your emotions and your needs. It is becoming difficult for you to get in touch with your emotions, even the positive ones. You use work as a distraction from your emotions. You are a high achiever at work but often feel anxious in your personal life. It is as though you are a ticking time bomb. Second, you continue to play the caretaker role in your personal relationships, in a similarly lopsided way. You often feel unheard, and your needs are unmet, leading to your frustration. When bottled up for too long, your frustration turns to angry outbursts or depression. Am I correct?

Summarize Clients' Goals in Behavioral Terms

Near the end, try to summarize the large amount of information obtained from the client, especially that which relates to his personal goal. Summarizing the goal in behavioral terms makes it clear and succinct.

Example:

> Tom, our time is running out pretty soon. Before we end, let me summarize what you have said so I know I heard you correctly. Your goal for joining the group is to learn to express yourself in a way that is not defensive when your needs are unmet, when you feel unheard, and when you feel frustrated. You want to learn to express yourself in a way that is respectful of others' views. At the same time, you want to be truthful to your needs and feelings, rather than bottle up your emotions as you have done in the past. Am I hearing you correctly?

Prepare Interviewees for Group Interactions Yet to Come

If you still have a few minutes left, prepare the interviewee for subsequent group interactions:

Example:

> In a group, people work together to help each other toward change. However, there might be a time when interaction gets a bit intense and disagreements occur. How do you see yourself in this type of situation?

Active listening followed by reflection:

> I am glad to hear that you have realistic expectations about group inter-action. You appear to welcome these potentially heated situations where you will need to use new coping skills of expressing your emotions in a way that matches the goal you want to achieve. I am very touched by how determined you are to learn new coping skills.

Give Clients a Chance to Ask Questions

Before ending the screening interview, allow the interviewee a chance to address any questions he might have.

Example:

> Tom, we have about 2 minutes left. I would like to see if there are any questions about the group or about me that you would like to ask.

Close the Interview

Close the interview by thanking the interviewee for his sharing. You should also identify future steps, so the interviewee knows what to expect.

Example:

> Thank you, Tom, for sharing this very meaningful information with me. I feel very touched by your openness and your motivation to change. You should expect to hear from me within a week.

After the Interview

The interview is not complete until the screening decision is made, and the notification contact is accomplished. Two steps are involved after the screening interviews:

1st: Making decisions on membership—During the screening interview, the group therapist uses all his or her senses to absorb any information that might provide insights about the interviewee. Afterward, the therapist must put all the pieces together and decide whether the interviewee is a good match for the group. The decision will be based on clinical judgment around the following aspects:

- Is this person motivated to change?
- Will this person benefit from the learning environment of a group?
- Can this person contribute to the group?
- Is this person likely to bring serious management problems to the group?
- Is there a good fit between this person and other candidates in terms of functioning level?

If a serious concern surfaces in the process of clinical assessment, the group therapist will need to make the difficult decision to not accept the client. A *tactical explanation* must be provided for the rejection.

2nd: Making after-interview contact—After the screening decisions are made, the therapist contacts the interviewees about the results. The method of the contact (e.g., by phone, e-mail, or by snail mail) should be defined by the interviewees. If they are accepted, you may want to remind them to bring the signed consent form to the first group session. If a client is not accepted, the language of the notification should be *phrased in a way to reduce the person's sense of rejection*. The language should sound as though the group and the therapist are to blame for not having the capacity to serve the client, regarding his or her needs. If possible, the person should be referred to a resource better equipped to provide for the person's care.

∞∞

In closing: Much work has to be done before a group can launch into its therapeutic work. With your attention to ethical and professional guidelines, your thorough program planning, and your labor on member preparation and screening, you are all geared up to launch your group out into the deep.

CASES IN POINT: SCREENING INTERVIEW NOTES

After the screening interview, a therapist should compile the *interview summary notes*. The summary notes serve not just as a part of the routine of record keeping but also as an important narration for you to review during the course of the group. Reviewing these screening interview notes refreshes your memory of critical information about members' starting points, their original problems, and struggles. The notes can be short and succinct unless you choose to provide further details.

The following are two examples of screening interview notes that are more detailed.

Interview Summary of Anne

The group's work with Anne can be found in the 1st case example in Chapter 7. Following are the summary notes that the leader compiled after the screening interview.

Issues of Concern. Anne is a 31-year-old single woman who works in the city as a first-grade teacher. Anne's issues surround the fact that she has difficulty in forming a long-term relationship. The longest relationship she ever had was shy of 6 months, and that was back in high school. Anne says she generally dates two types of men: the noncommittal and the "nice guys."

She finds the noncommittal type exciting and intriguing at first, not knowing when he will call or what he's thinking. However, she soon finds that this type has little interest in going deeper emotionally or investing in the relationship, and it eventually ends.

The second type is the nice guys. Anne interprets these types as being needy, so she soon grows tired of their requests to see her on a regular basis. She gets downright annoyed, and her pattern is usually to shut herself off quickly to avoid further involvement. Anne states that a nurturing and kind man turns her off, but that the nurturing relationship type is what she ultimately wants.

Anne said that people perceive her as always happy and at ease in any situation. She has a confident manner and is always smiling. She admits, however, to feeling insecure inside. She covers it by being a good listener. Anne does not divulge a lot of information about herself. When this was pointed out in the intake, she was able to get to the real issue.

Anne's Real Issue. Anne's real issue is that she doesn't want people to reject her, and therefore, she doesn't open up. She is able to keep her emotions in check because she never really invests much of herself in a dating relationship. This lack of emotional investment makes it easy on her when the relationship ends. Anne justifies her actions by stating that she doesn't want to hurt anyone by prolonging a relationship that isn't going to last.

Family Dynamics. When we look at her family history, some of Anne's behaviors become understandable. Her parents have always had a troubled marriage. Her mother and father argued constantly while she was growing up. She has two brothers; both are much older than she is, and both are married with children. She feels close to one brother and talks with him often.

Becoming Her Mom's Confidant. Anne remembers a defining moment with her mother during her teen years. Because her parents were constantly arguing, her mother needed someone to confide in. Anne became her mother's confidant. As a result, Anne learned to be a listener instead of a person who shared her inner self. She listened to all of her mother's complaints and provided the support that her mother needed. However, in the process of helping, Anne did not develop the ability to communicate her own needs and wants or share her inner thoughts and feelings.

Difficulty in Intimacy. As I (the interviewer) sat and listened to Anne, her issue became more apparent. Because she developed such a good capacity for listening, people turn to her with their problems. She is a good sounding board and listens intently and patiently to what they have to say. With this role so ingrained in her, Anne doesn't get the opportunity to practice revealing and opening up to others. It's very difficult to develop intimacy with others when one doesn't share one's inner self through warm and open conversation.

As Anne is not used to disclosing personal and meaningful parts of herself, intimacy becomes difficult to develop. Thus, her romantic relationships do not endure. In addition, she feels insecure that what she has to say might not be substantial or interesting and might be rejected.

Anne's Goal in the Group. As Anne's issue became clearer, she narrowed her goal to one that she felt would be very worthwhile for her. Anne stated that her goal is to practice opening up to members of the group in a personal and intimate way. This goal will allow her to experience firsthand how people respond to her when she is doing the revealing, as opposed to the listening. She hopes that when she changes her behavioral pattern and the role it has in her life, she might be able to carry her new self into her romantic relationships.

Interview Summary of Brooke

Difficulty Talking About Herself. Brooke is a female in her late twenties, working as an assistant at a law office. She explained that she found it hard to talk about herself with others. She felt that talking about herself would feel selfish or self-absorbed. During conversations, she asks other people many questions about themselves to keep the attention away from her.

Current Issues With Anxiety and Depression. Brooke then stated that her current issues revolve around problems with anxiety and self-esteem. When looking at her family history, it is clearly identifiable where her anxiety and self-esteem problems began.

Tumultuous Family Dynamics. Both of her current issues seem to stem from the "tumultuous" relationship that her parents had while she was growing up. Brooke explained that the communication style in her household was either yelling or silence, and this often caused her to feel defeated. She was often caught between her parents' bickering, serving as the middleman. It was not until 2 years ago that her parents got a divorce and peace finally settled on her household.

Self-Esteem Taking a Toll. A lot of Brooke's self-esteem issues have developed from the constant yelling from both of her parents and, in particular, her mother. She always felt that she could never do anything right. Brooke described her mother as a self-absorbed perfectionist. If Brooke would go to her mom to talk through a problem that she was having, her mother would turn the problem around to make it seem like it was Brooke's fault. The resulting low self-esteem has led to feelings of anxiety for Brooke.

Anxiety in Relationships. Along with self-esteem issues, Brooke experiences anxiety in relationships. She explained that when she is single, she is very confident about herself and what she is doing. However, when in a relationship, she feels that she is very self-sabotaging. If she senses any threat in the relationship or feels that an individual may have a slightly undesirable trait, she ends the relationship. She does this to prevent a negative relationship from forming, much like the one between her parents.

An Adult Child of an Alcoholic. After learning more about her family, her presenting problem becomes clearer. Her father is a recovering alcoholic, and her mother is a perfectionist. She has an older brother, 15 years her senior, and he is a drug addict.

Being surrounded by this mix of individuals has led Brooke to become very cautious about whom she lets into her life. If she meets someone with similar traits to her father or brother, she immediately puts her defenses up.

Part Daughter, Part Middleman. Growing up in a family where she was part daughter, part confidant to her parents, Brooke had to mature quickly. She never had the chance to focus on herself or her own feelings. As her issues became clearer and more defined, Brooke was able to narrow down her goal to dealing with relationship anxiety and learning how to be true to herself while surrounded by others. With this goal in place and her mind set on growth and potential change, Brooke seems ready for the challenges of group counseling and reaching her goals.

EXERCISES

Scenarios for Your Practice

1. As you are interviewing potential group members for a general counseling group, one person blurts out that he is open to being in the same group with anyone except homosexuals. As a group leader who abides by the American Counseling Association's *Code of Ethics and Standards of Practice,* what are some possible ways you could handle this situation? Suppose that this person claims his religion tells him to condemn and avoid homosexuals. What are some appropriate possible responses?

2. Suppose a respected colleague refers to you a potential member for a general counseling group, but that person is struggling with alcoholism. What are your thoughts about including this type of member in a general therapy group that will likely focus on such things as personal growth, unresolved grief, lingering depression, loneliness, and social anxiety?

3. As you move into the third session of a group, a member states that she overheard another member at a local restaurant recounting to friends various personal issues shared by group members. As the group leader, how would you address this issue? Would you consider it as mere "tattling" and quickly move to the agenda the members have set for the day? Would you immediately toss out the offending member? Or would you discuss the issue with the group members and then vote on whether to remove the offending member? Might you ask the accused member to explain and then review the issue with the group for possible responses?

4. Having just graduated with your master's degree in counseling, you are looking for ways to earn extra income. An acquaintance offers you a chance to work with a sexual predator group for an attractive level of remuneration. However, you are informed that there are no supervisors to guide you in your work, and you have no experience in working with this type of group. What issues should you consider in deciding whether to accept this offer?

SELF-REFLECTION

1. Visualize a prospective group member who is considering entering a new group. Imagine the different feelings he or she might have. Can you imagine any fears he or she may have? Would he or she have any general anxiety? Might he or she experience doubt about how he or she will fit in with the other group members? What actions on the part of the group and the group leader will be most helpful?

2. What types of questions do you think people have when joining a new group? Are there specific kinds of information that might help to address those questions?

3. When a member enters a new group, what might be some of his or her concerns about the group leader? About the other members?

4. What kinds of feelings will be most difficult for a member to share in a new group? Are these the kinds of feelings that you as a leader would want to encourage members to share with one another?

5. How does a person decide what level of commitment to make to a particular group? Have you ever stayed in a group that you were unsure about at first? If so, what happened to you as a result?

6. As a group leader, what are your primary concerns about maintaining an ethical group practice in a world where profit and loss sometimes take center stage for administrators?

7. As a developing specialist in group leadership, what qualities might assist you in promoting the ethical practice, even in a subordinate position in relation to individuals who have no knowledge or understanding of group leader ethical principles?

8. In which group specialization do you have the most interest? Least interest? Why?

9. What are some ways that you might be able to increase your familiarity with each of the four group specializations?

10. At this point, what are your deepest concerns about screening and selecting members most appropriate for a potential group?

CHAPTER 4

FUNDAMENTAL SKILLS FOR GROUP FACILIATION AND INTERVENTION

"**A** journey of a thousand miles begins with a single step" says Lao-tzu (604 BC–531 BC), a Chinese philosopher. Your trek toward mastering the group leadership skills also starts with a humble step—learning the fundamentals. This chapter focuses on the crux of the matter of group facilitation and intervention.

GROUP FACILITATION AND INTERVENTION

The term *facilitation* has been so overly used that it has come to mean almost anything. Before getting into the skill set, we opt to clarify what facilitation actually is in the discipline of group counseling.

What Is NOT Group Facilitation?

Perhaps it helps to start with what group facilitation isn't. Frequently, neophyte leaders assume group facilitation is the action of helping members to open up. With this assumption in mind, they use probing, reflection of feelings, paraphrasing, and interpreting to engage members, helping them talk, all the while not knowing that these skills are actually "*individual counseling*" *skills*.

Misused in the group, these skills inevitably result in a series of leader-to-member, as well as member-to-leader, dialogues, rendering the group into a setting of a *multiple-individual-based counseling*. This kind of faulty facilitation cannot help but rob the group of the *member-to-member interaction*, giving rise to a detached, lethargic, or intellectualized group atmosphere.

What Is Group Facilitation?

Facilitation, simply put, is the art of helping members communicate more easily *with one another*. Without proper facilitation, a group often slips into turn-taking, advice-giving, unproductive silence, one-to-one conversation, boredom, frustration, dominance by a few outspoken members, and so on.

A group leader's ultimate goal is to facilitate an atmosphere of acceptance and understanding, of safety and trust, within which therapeutic work can happen. Seems simple enough, yet it will take a wide range of facilitation skills to arrive at this goal. Entering a group without a comprehensive skill set, you might find yourself overwhelmed by the group's complex and ever-changing characteristics—yourself in a state of an extreme sense of inadequacy called "group shock" (Zaslav, 1988), as we have discussed in Chapter 2. Therefore, your first charge is to equip yourself with as many *fundamental facilitating skills* as possible before you embark on this journey.

What Is Group Intervention?

Differing from facilitation, group intervention refers to the action of *stopping, redirecting,* and *correcting* maladaptive member behaviors when they impede group function. Group intervention techniques are less talked about in most textbooks. As a result, new leaders often feel like stepping outside their comfort zone when intervention techniques are called for. In addition, many leaders don't feel as comfortable in applying intervention techniques as facilitating skills. Thus, this is an area requiring extra effort to master.

LEADER AS OBSERVER-PARTICIPANT

A basic concept that a leader must have a firm grasp on is that he or she is both a group participant and a group process observer/facilitator—for short, an "observer-participant" (Yalom & Leszcz, 2005, p. 153). This section focuses on how to make this dual role work.

1st Component: Leader as Process Observer and Facilitator

To facilitate the group interaction, you must finely hone your ability to *observe what's going on* in the group, often by stepping back to attend to the group dynamics and interpersonal process. As you do so, you are more likely to notice how one member is having difficulty in owning up to his or her feelings by talking abstractly, how another feels compelled to rescue any member who is just getting in touch with deep pain, how yet another member becomes defensive when challenged by the group, and so on.

With the data of all the relational dynamics going on in the group gained through your keen observation, you will know what to facilitate or intervene to bring the group interaction into a productive flow.

Of course, we can never be a completely impartial observer. At times, we may find ourselves "hooked" or "sucked in" by members' interpersonal pulls. Later chapters in this text will provide you with advanced leadership skills and techniques regarding how you can "squirm loose" from the hook so that you can help the group get to the heart of the issues at hand.

2nd Component: Leader as a Participant

In the midst of observing group process and facilitating interactions, you also need to participate in whatever activities you direct the group to do. For example, if you are inviting the group to reflect on the feelings that a member, Tracy, is experiencing, then you also need to participate in getting into Tracy's inner world, sensing what she might be feeling, and then verbally conveying that understanding to Tracy.

And if you are inviting members to disclose their gut reactions toward the behaviors of yet another member, Santiago, then you need to disclose your inner feelings toward him as well.

In sum, this dual role of being an observer-participant allows you to be the best of who you are in the group. By being both a participant and an observer/facilitator, your presence is felt, and you are fully engaged, instead of being only a clinician.

Mistakes of Underparticipating or Overparticipating

The multifaceted leadership responsibilities often overwhelm new group leaders, leading to either of the following mistakes:

Underparticipation. Many beginning leaders are simply so nervous that they focus entirely on facilitating, completely forgetting about being a part of the group, overlooking the opportunity to offer members their validation and feedback. This underparticipation makes the leader appear remote and separate from the rest of the group.

Overparticipation. Some new leaders, on the other hand, participate too much. They rush in to give empathy, insights, feedback, or to share personal feelings even before group members get a chance to do so. The session, unfortunately, turns into a leader-dominated extravaganza. Members are left feeling unfulfilled, muffled, and frustrated.

How Much to Facilitate and How Much to Participate—A Rule of Thumb

We are often asked by new group leaders, "How much of my leadership time should I spend on facilitation/intervention and how much on participation?" Striking an appropriate balance is itself an art, and it takes a lot of clinical intuition and interpersonal awareness to arrive at that delicate point. Risking oversimplification, we propose a modus operandi called "the 70:30 rule."

If there are 10 people in the group and 90 minutes for a session, a *group-centered* leader might talk for 15 of them, leaving each member a mere 7 minutes to talk about their concerns. Talking any longer, the leader will run the risk of dominating the group.

So out of that 15 minutes of your time, how much should be used in facilitation/intervention and how much in participation? It depends on the developmental stage of the group. In the early stage, new leaders are usually more occupied with getting the group rolling, and thus they tend to do more facilitating and intervening and less participating. We estimate the ratio could be about 80:20.

As the group progresses, it has less need for structure; the ratio may drop to 70:30. Later on, when the group moves to the more advanced stage, the ratio might drop further to 60:40 or even lower.

Let's say that Alex adopts the 70:30 ratio. A translation of the ratio to time will yield 10.5 minutes for facilitation and 4.5 minutes for participation. Not to be a cut-and-dry rule, but to be kept in mind, this sense of time frame can help leaders avoid overparticipation, preventing them from overshadowing the group, especially when it is young.

The Best Time to Facilitate/Intervene

The above ratio is an oversimplification of how much a leader talks in a group but does not give us any guidelines. Alternatively, we suggest that you use the following situations as indicators, pointing the best time for you to facilitate or intervene:

- When a silence is overly long and unproductive
- When the group discussion gets sidetracked
- When some cross currents of feelings go unrecognized by the group
- When a connection appears between members' concerns
- When emotions in the group get intense and members don't know what to say
- When some members make it difficult for others to express themselves freely

However, the following situations shall indicate that you avoid doing any facilitation:

- When a member detects certain feelings in another and responds in a manner that deepens that member's self-exploration
- When the group interactions are productive

On these two occasions, the leader is wise to remain quiet and let the group carry on by itself (Rogers, 2003). If it would benefit the group, you could participate by sharing your empathy, feedback, personal feelings, or here-and-now reactions, but don't do so just to meet your own emotional needs.

Members Participate First, and the Leader Pitches in Later

When it comes to participation, you would want to let members participate first, delaying your own input just a little. The reasons are threefold:

- The leader will not end up dominating the group interaction.
- Members will take an active role of being helpers to one another.
- Members will experience the power of altruism by giving empathy, understanding, reactions, insights, and acceptance to one another, leading to increased sense of self-worth and feeling more at home in the group.

Once the members have shared, you then can pitch in, giving whatever might be missing from the group contribution. In so doing, you fulfill the role of being a process observer/facilitator and a participant at the same time.

A Good Prompt Is at Times
More Effective Than Modeling

Some group leaders may ask, "Don't we need to go first to provide modeling?" This is a great question because sometimes members won't know how to respond to each other, especially after someone reveals something painful or intense. But if you give members a good prompt, they will surprise you with compassionate and wise responses beyond your expectation, even without your modeling.

This is evidenced in the following case. In a structured activity called "inside and outside," a member, Yasmine, revealed that none of her family had been in the inside circle. After some probing from group members, it became clear that Yasmine was a parentified kid. Since she was little, she had to take care of her younger brother and her mother who suffered from depression, while watching her father slowly die from alcoholism. Yasmine often displayed an unfeeling front, but as she peeled back the layers, some emotion showed through her eyes.

The group was silent, not knowing what to say to show understanding, acceptance, and validation to Yasmine, without minimizing her pain. Rather than rush in to reflect Yasmine's sadness as a way to provide modeling, the leader gave the group a facilitating prompt instead:

[To the group] I can sense that everybody is deeply touched by Yasmine's sharing. I would like the group to tell Yasmine, *what you imagine it was like to be Yasmine* in the way she grew up?

Responding to this facilitation, the group pored out their nurturing, validation, and understanding, without the leader having to first "model" how to say things.

BASIC PRINCIPLES OF
FACILITATION AND INTERVENTION

Before venturing into the wide variety of facilitation skills and intervention techniques, you will want to familiarize yourself with their basic principles.

Intentionality: Heed What You
Are Doing and Why You Are Doing It

The first principle—With every facilitation or intervention, you need to beware of what you are doing and why. Not all techniques fit all members at all stages. You pick your facilitation and intervention intentionally, that is, with a clear purpose.

Above all, seek to figure out where your members are regarding the following measures (Juhnke & Hagedorn, 2013) before you venture forth into what you try to do:

- The trust level of group members
- Your members' worldviews and cultures
- Your members' past experiences
- The interpersonal processes manifested in members' issues
- The specific timing in the session

Speak to the Group Members Using "I-You" Language

When talking to members, address them using "I-you" dialogue, rather than "I-they" descriptive style. For some reason, new leaders seem to fall to the "I-they" descriptive language a lot, unknowingly creating distance in between. Since the members are right in front of you, therefore, you should address them in the language of "*you*," as if saying "*you guys*" or "*you all*." See the following illustrations:

Don't say:

Many members look thoughtful. *I* wonder what *they* think George was trying to say?

Some members are nodding *their* heads. *I* wonder whether any member would like to share *their* experiences with George.

Do say:

Many of *you* look thoughtful. *I* wonder what *you* think George was trying to say.

Some of *you* are nodding *your* heads. *I* wonder whether any of *you* would like to share *your* experiences with George.

Create a Safe Climate for Members to Open Up

Across cultures, fear stands strong as an emotion, blocking people from letting others in. For some members, it is the fear of drawing attention to themselves; for others, the fear of letting the gate open and their emotions surging out of control. In opening themselves up in front of the group, most members fear the following:

- Rejection
- Judgment
- Pressure to perform
- Looking stupid
- Burdening others
- Discovering abnormal patterns
- Attack
- Not being able to cope once opening up

For members to open up without fear, leaders need to create a safe environment free of judgment.

For example, Tricia did not say a word for the first 45 minutes in a structured session. She stared at the floor, making it difficult for people to see her facial expression. The leader looked in her direction several times but resisted calling attention to her, trying to respect her tempo of participation. When Tricia finally shared her story, it was short and impersonal.

The leader could see that other members were becoming concerned about Tricia's lack of participation. At this point, he tried to make the group a safe environment for Tricia by inviting the group to acknowledge Tricia's experience in the group:

[To the group] I wonder whether anyone could imagine what worries, feelings, or thoughts Tricia might be struggling with right now that make it difficult for her to share in the group?

As the group compassionately reflected on Tricia's inner struggles, Tricia was surprised that she actually felt more relaxed and free.

She went deeper to say that during her college years, her friends often ridiculed her when she opened up about personal stuff. She felt a lot of rejection in her circle of friends and started to shut down. In this session, it was the first time that she didn't feel judged. When Tricia shared this, everybody sensed *the trust in the group increasing,* shown by *their forward-leaning body posture.*

Don't Stimulate Clients Into Immediacy Issues Too Soon

In the early stages of the group, members often focus more on relaying stories, seeking venting and relief, staying within their comfort zone, and avoiding vulnerable emotions (Shapiro, 1978). This is healthy and normal and something that we must respect. As Leszcz (1992) states: "Frequently this resistance centers around the issue of subjective feelings of safety and vulnerability (p. 56)."

We need to allow new members certain time to dwell on the telling of their stories. We need to constrain ourselves from pursuing immediacy issues lest they over-stimulate members' affects beyond the capacity of the group as a whole (Leszcz, 1992).

Knowing when to and when not to stimulate the group is something beyond what a few tips can cover. As Friedman (1989) states, "knowing when to focus on here and now and when to focus on there and then is something of an art born of experience, sensitivity, and good instincts" (p. 115).

Consider the following example. During the screening interview, the leader learned that there were a lot of abuses in Ediltrudis's early life. In the first session, Ediltrudis strived to talk intelligently in the group, but something about her intellectualized way of expression did not engage members. Since it was early in the group, it was much too soon to dig into Ediltrudis's intellectualizing and members' tuning out on her. It would have overstimulated the intense and chaotic emotions that Ediltrudis so carefully orchestrated to shield herself from.

Instead, the leader tucked the immediacy issues away, noting it in her mental file and chose to facilitate *a less stimulating but equally meaningful exchange* between Ediltrudis and the group. The leader said,

[To the group] After you listened to Ediltrudis's story, what inner strengths and resources can you see in Ediltrudis that she might not have seen in herself?

Honoring her inner qualities, then, the group earned the privilege to address Ediltrudis's interpersonal pattern later, when it resurfaced in a future session.

Avoid Problem-Solving and Feedback-Giving Too Soon

When listening to another member sharing his or her concerns, most members feel responsible for taking the struggles away from the person presenting. They rush in to provide advice or a solution, only to find their enthusiasm be met with resistance. Their frustration can be avoided in the first place if a leader takes a preventive measure by engaging the group to give something much more needed by the person presenting.

For example, Michael, a member with difficulty using "I" language to express himself, shared that everyone in his life comes to him for help, no one ever asks him how he feels, and he is constantly feeling stressed out. A couple of years ago, his stress had become so unbearable that he even thought of taking his life. He did not succeed. But after that everything just went back to "normal": no one shows interests in his feelings.

As the leader looked around the room, she noticed that the rest of the group was struggling with how to make Michael feel better. Knowing that the group can easily slip into advice-giving and problem-solving unless she gives specific prompts, she takes precaution to avoid asking two kinds of questions as below:

"What do you think Michael can do to eliminate his stress?"
"Michael, how do you think the group can help you reduce your stress?"

Instead, she decided to get Michael in contact with his disowned experience. So she said,

Michael, I noticed that you used the general "you" language to describe your personal agonies. It has a distancing effect on me. Would you please change it to "I" statements?

Michael did not even notice that he used the distancing "You" language to describe his life stories. As he started to use "I" statements, he became much more clear about his sense of bitterness and actually felt liberated. Finally, he had a sense of ownership of his resentment. Finally, he gave it a voice.

To the group's surprise, Michael came to his own senses that perhaps he, to a great extent, contributed to people not asking how he feels. The sessions that followed, Michael worked diligently to explore ways of expressing himself to allow others in and know his needs and feelings.

Listen From the Heart, Not From the Head

When listening to fellow members presenting their concerns, most members tend to listen from the head and operate in an analytical mode. In such mode, they

- ask question after question so as to collect more information,
- interrupt so as to clarify, and
- evaluate, so as to "fix" the problem.

This analytical mode of listening will not impart warmth and understanding to each other. A group must shift its listening from the head to the heart level. To this end, you will need to help members learn to slow down by engaging their imagination and intuition. A facilitating prompt like the following tends to do the trick:

[To the group] After you listened to Fujita's story, what do you imagine to be his core message? What do you imagine to be his deepest hopes and desires?

Tune In to an Angry Member's Unmet Needs

If a member is angry, he might be distressed about some unfulfilled needs of his own in the group. After you tune into his unmet needs, you may say something like the following:

Dale, I get a sense that you are upset with me because you need someone to show that you matter, especially when you are under stress, but I have failed to lead the group to fulfill your needs.

You might then get the group involved in helping the member by the following facilitation prompt:

[To the group] Dale has been feeling as if his stress is put on the back burner by the group. I wonder how we as a group can *modify our interaction* to make sure that Dale feels that his concerns matter?

Facilitate Mutual Empathy: The Key to Group Emotion Co-Regulation

In individual counseling, a therapist's empathy has the power to *co-regulate* clients' effects (Edwards & Davis, 2013)—the same *co-regulation effect* happens in the group, only the empathy comes from even more persons.

Since empathy is the key of group co-regulation, the leader has got to be skilled at using prompts to facilitate mutual empathy in the group:

[To the group] Let's pause for a moment. Imagine that you were Julie and you had been struggling to find a mate for quite a while now. Please *guess* what Julie might be feeling *but has not yet been able to articulate*. When you are ready, please speak directly to Julie.

Can any of you help Mary identify the *core emotions* beneath *the obvious frustration* that she has with her husband?

Beyond the sense of loss and abandonment that Bruce has shared, do any of you sense any other emotions that he may be struggling with *but is not aware of at this time?*

The power of empathy as a co-regulation agent is reflected in the following journal entry by a member:

When Brooke shared about her alcoholic father and their relationship, I was brought back to *my own alcoholic father* and *my feelings about him.* I felt so compelled to share that but continuously stopped myself. Finally, I jumped in and it was such a breakthrough for me. As I looked around the room, I was able to see that *my fellow group members did not recoil in disgust from my story, but they responded with empathy.* For so long I'd held back from telling this truth about my father; it now feels so good to let it out. I was proud of myself for taking such a big leap of faith. It warms my heart to hear *the compassion in my fellow group members' voices.*

Allow Members to Experience the Power of Giving

The power of the group reaches its maximum when members are granted the chance to give to one another. Their giving shows in

- tuning in to the other's spoken and unspoken emotions,
- communicating their understanding, and
- connecting to the others in meaningful ways.

The givers benefit just as much as the receivers. Being the givers, members feel that they have offered something precious. They feel a sense of *altruism.*

Altruism is one of the key therapeutic factors for a group (Yalom & Leszcz, 2005). This sense of "having something to offer" bumps up group members' self-esteem and gives them a sense of meaningfulness and mutual connection that overcomes the feelings of isolation and emptiness bringing them to group originally.

Bring Out the "Inner Strength Detectives" in Members

The more we focus on the inner strengths of a member, the more his or her inner resources are activated. A sense of hope is thus installed, empowering the member to become the person he or she wants to be. This is the tenet of strength-based therapy (Seligman & Csikszentmihalyi, 2000; Wolin & Wolin, 2010).

To apply strength-based therapy in the group, we need to engage the *inner strength detectives* in all members. All we have to do is simply give some prompts like the following:

[To the group] As you listen to the story shared by Bala, what inner strengths do you catch a glimpse of? What are things that you find remarkable in her that she might not know of herself?

[To the group] Despite having experienced so many heartbreaks in her life, what do you experience as the special qualities in Mary that keep her love robust in her relationships?

[To the group] *What aspects of Bruce* do you think *his late father would feel proud of?*

[To the group] Through Linda's responses to other members' concerns in our group, *what clues* do you get *about Linda's skills* in dealing with difficulties in her life?

Applaud Members' Progress and Effective Behaviors

Having their progress acknowledged by the group, members tend to thrive even more to bring about desired changes (Desetta & Wolin, 2000; Wolin & Wolin, 2010). Given this, whenever any sign of a member's improvement, wisdom, sense of humor, or creative talents comes to our attention, we shall call on it, affirm it, amplify it, and celebrate it. For example,

[To the group] Something very important just happened here. Lee just said something that he never told the group before. That is a very big step for him. Do other people in the group also notice Lee's new progress?

In order to acknowledge members' growth, we need to be a group historian, able to describe how each member is pressing forward from his or her original issues toward his or her desirable outcomes. For example,

> Masumi, I remember that your goal in the group is to work on being more willing to share your vulnerability with others. In the past, you had difficulty with this issue. Yet, today you took risks to reveal something so personal and so delicate about yourself. I am impressed by the risk you took today. It is a step toward reaching your goal.

> Phyllis, you really took some risks today by expressing your desire to have the group attend to your issues a bit longer. This seems to relate to your goal of becoming more assertive. How does it feel for you to express yourself in this way today?

BASIC FACILITATION SKILLS (I): HOW TO OPEN A GROUP SESSION

The way you open a session sets the tone for the rest of the meeting. An effective check-in goes a long way in launching the group into the session. This proposes several options of how to do just that.

Simple Greeting

This is the best time to ask members to turn off their cell phones.

> Glad to see you guys again. We had a productive session last week, and I hope we will have a fruitful one today as well. To that end, let's make sure that all of our *cell phones or other electronic devices* are turned off so that we have a relaxed and calm environment for our sharing. Thank you!

Brief Relaxation Exercise (Optional)

After greeting, you may take an optional step to conduct a brief relaxation exercise. Members often arrive after a hectic day, exhausted by their daily hassles. A brief relaxation exercise can do wonders to set the mood for the session. A 2- to-3-minute relaxation exercise can help members feel more centered and focused.

Appendix D provides three examples of such relaxation exercises. You can choose one of these to open the session or tailor them to suit your own group's needs.

Simple Check-In

The major step in opening a group session is the check-in. The simplest way to do a check-in is to have a quick go-around (without any particular order) where members share any lingering feelings or unfinished business from the previous session.

Remember to mention the *time frame* (such as 10 minutes) lest members start to get into their concerns or to ramble away the check-in time:

[To the group] Let's start today's session with a quick check-in. *We have about 10 minutes for this.* If you have any lingering reactions or unfinished business from the last session, please use a few sentences to share what it is. [pause] Whoever is ready, please jump in, without in any particular order. Let me add that while you are listening to the other members checking in, please feel free to respond to one another with a few words, if you feel a need to make a comment.

Make the Check-In Solution-Focused or Strength-Based

To apply solution-focused or strength-based therapy (Jong & Berg, 2013) into the check-in, you may gear it toward any positive features suitable for the group. For example,

Let's start our session with a quick check-in. Perhaps we can briefly state how we can *make this group session as useful as possible?*

Let's start our session with a quick check-in. Perhaps you could specify *what you want to get out of this session* today?

Identify an Interpersonal Skill to Practice (Optional)

An optional addition to check-in is to ask members to identify an interpersonal skill that each will practice during the given session. This gives members something personal to work on even when not talking about their own issues, putting the ball in members' courts, so to speak. This is especially important for time-limited or brief group.

It does take a while for members to get a clear sense of what areas of interpersonal functioning they may need to work on, especially within the session. Appendix C provides numerous examples of interpersonal skills often observed within groups.

> [To the group] Let's start today's session with our traditional check-in and an extra piece. *First*, if you have any *lingering reactions or unfinished business* from the last session, please use a few sentences to share what it is. [pause] If you don't have unfinished business, please share what new behaviors you have been practicing outside the group. [pause] *Second*, for the extra piece, please use just one sentence to state what *interpersonal skill* you would like to practice during this particular session. An example could be "I would like to practice speaking up more today even if I worry that others might disagree." Get the idea? Okay, whoever is ready, please jump in.

The following is a personal reflection by a member, Natsuko, on how setting interpersonal skills to practice during the group session really benefits her:

> Each time I take risks to practice a new interpersonal skill in the group, it is a springboard for me to take more risks, which continues to bring me to a deeper, more honest level of interaction with my fellow members. Tonight is an example. I asked Matt to clarify the meaning of his laughter that seemed to target me.

> Afterward, I felt ready to cry. In asking Matt, I was letting the rest of the group see the neurotic, self-conscious side of me—the side of me that I go to great lengths to hide. This exposure was a huge risk for me. However, it was a great relief to hear from Matt what his laughter was about, rather than letting my imagination go out of control.

> I have always feared being laughed at. I tend to read into other's behaviors and then withdraw from them. Perhaps if I start to take the risk of asking people the meaning of their behaviors, it will help reach a higher level of honesty and closeness in my relationships. When I first began the group, I admit feeling skeptical about ever changing myself. Now each time I practice the interpersonal skills of clearly stating my feelings or asking

someone for clarification, I am beginning to feel better. I have seen small, continuous improvements in the past three sessions. Especially tonight! I left the session feeling charged, ready to go out in the world and practice these new skills.

Check In About Progress and New Realization (for Later Stages)

If the group is in a later stage of development, the leader may want to encourage members to report on their progress or new realizations to further instill the sense of hope in the group:

> Let's start our session with a quick check-in. Last week, several of you shared difficulties that you've experienced in your lives, and you were able to gain insights into these difficulties in the group session. I've noticed that some of you have tried out some *new approaches here in handling difficult issues*. I'm wondering whether anyone here has been able to *test out new behaviors in your life*. If so, I hope you will share them with the group.

The following is a personal reflection by a member on how reporting on his practice of new behaviors outside the group really benefits him:

> I'm glad the leader asked the group to talk about the new behaviors that we have been practicing outside of the group. Since joining the group, I am becoming more conscious of my interactions with others. I am also making progress toward strengthening my interpersonal relationships with significant others in my life. Since I notice a difference in myself, I am curious to know whether other members are making progress toward their goals in their lives outside the group as well.

Check In and Restate Goals (for Later Stages)

Another option during the check-in is to invite members to restate their goals. Members frequently change their goals after being in the group for a few sessions. Perhaps other members' soul-searching disclosures, or perhaps their own personal reflections, lead members to a new understanding of what they really need to work on. Inviting members to restate their goals during the check-in gives members a chance to inform others of this new change and to hold one another accountable.

> Before we start, let's do our traditional check-in, but please add one more piece—remind the group what your original goal was and whether you have changed it to a new one. I have a sense that some of you have narrowed down your goals to something more specific and that others have completely changed them. So it would be helpful for the group to know where you are and where you are heading. Who would like to begin?

Handle Issues That Emerge During Check-In

Some intense emotions involving other members, due to unfinished business, may emerge occasionally; open conflicts may even surface during check-in. A rule of thumb is to handle these hot emotions with care, stopping the check-in right away, and *acknowledging* the issue at hand.

> [To the group] As we are checking in, I sense some tense emotions among Tammy, Tom, and Tengfei, due to the unfinished business from the last session. I just want to acknowledge these emotions for now. When the discussion floor is opened, I would like to invite the group to give our priority to resolving this issue.

> Susan, this seems to be an important yet complicated issue for you. If you would like to get a clear perspective on it, you could present your issue when the discussion floor is opened. Would you like to do that?

If a member is absent from any given session, ask the group members whether they have any reaction to the absence of the member during check-in:

> I just want to acknowledge that Patty is not with us today. If you have any reaction to Patty's absence, please feel free to share it with the group once we open the session.

BASIC FACILITATION SKILLS (II): HOW TO INCREASE GROUP MUTUAL ENGAGEMENT

For the bulk of the session, leaders need to find creative ways to get members fully engaged in meaningful interactions. The leader is there to "host" the member-to-member conversations and to nurture their dialogues. This section presents a series of fundamental skills needed to maximize group interactions.

Simple Acknowledgment

Simple acknowledgment serves as a lubricant, helping things to move along. When a member finishes speaking, you can nod with acknowledgment without saying a word. But when you wish to stop a member's long-winded talk, you can simply say something neutral without being abrupt:

Thank you!

All right!

Shift Focus Between the Speaking Individual and the Group

As an observer-participant, a group leader must observe the reactions of the entire group, rather than fixate his or her eye contact on the member speaking. Unfortunately, unprepared leaders tend to obsess about what to do or say next (Li, Kivlighan, & Gold, 2015), forgetting to scan the room to take in nonverbal communication and various group responses.

To scan the room correctly, spend a couple of minutes establishing adequate eye contact and rapport with the member speaking and in getting the sense of what he or she is talking about, then slowly and subtly shift away your contact to observe the nonverbal signs in the room. After the brief moment of observation, come back to make eye contact with the member speaking. In other words, you shift your focus between the individual and the group, back and forth, subtly and continually.

Invite Participation When You Notice Nonverbal Cues

Poring over the broad view of group interaction, you will notice a lot of nonverbal signs that cue you about what the group needs next.

The Forward Lean

Leaning forward indicates that the individuals are listening, thinking, and perhaps have something ready to say (Borg, 2009; 2012; Pease & Pease, 2006). Seeing this, you shall feel confident to invite the members to speak:

[To the group] As Kwanza talked about his family problems, I see that many of you are leaning forward, absorbed in what he was sharing. Would any of you like to speak to Kwanza about what his sharing evoked in you?

Tracy, I noticed that you were leaning forward while Jean was talking about her efforts to reconnect with her family. I wonder, what would you like to say to Jean regarding the topic of family issues and reconnection?

Slow Head Nods

Head nods may indicate one's understanding or *relating* to the speaker's experiences (Borg, 2009). *Slow head nods* particularly indicate that the listener is interested in what is being said (Pease & Pease, 2006). You may go ahead to invite a contribution if these members have not volunteered themselves:

[To the group] I see several members nodding; would any of you like to share your thoughts right now?

Matt, you were nodding when Sue was mentioning her anger. Would you like to share what's on your mind?

Facial Expressions

Our facial expression is the barometer for our emotions (Borg, 2009) associated with disapproval, confusion, joy, surprise, sympathy, admiration, suspicion, contempt, and so on. Seeing facial expressions, you can go ahead and invite members to express their inner reactions:

[To the group] By many of your facial expressions, I can sense that there are a lot of reactions to what Dale just said to Steve. Would any of you like to share your reactions?

Lily, by your expression, I guess that you have some reaction to what Matt and the others are saying. Would you like to share your thoughts?

Leg Movements or Body Shifts

The further away the body parts are from our head, the less they are subjected to our conscious control (Pease & Pease, 2006). Especially "the feet and the legs are the most honest parts of the body" (Borg, 2009, p. 153); their movements often betray the anxiety or a sense of *unease* that a person is feeling.

The same can be said about the body shift. Posture shifts during the session often indicate *confusion, tension, boredom,* or *irritation.* Observations like these shall cue you to invite members to talk about how they're feeling:

[To the group] I may be wrong, but I sense that the group seems uneasy at this juncture. Would any of you like to share how you are feeling right now?

Direct Members to Talk to One Another, Not Just to You

In individual counseling, you want the client to talk to you, while in group counseling, to the group, instead. This new orientation spells difficulty for many new leaders. Added to the difficulty is that members in a new group tend to speak to the leader primarily. A leader-centered group cannot help but result in the following negative results:

- The rest of the group members feel excluded and lose interest.
- The leader is too preoccupied with individual members to pay attention to the way that the group is reacting.
- The leader nonverbally encourages the speaking member to go on and on, leaving other members to fall on the sidelines.

To avoid these problems, you need to *direct members to talk to one another by using hand gestures or using facilitating prompts.* For new leaders, it does take practice to break free from the habits of individual counseling. Once you crack it, however, hosting member-to-member conversation will become a treasured experience for you.

Avoid This Cookie-Cutter Prompt: "Can Anyone Relate?"

Some new leaders have the habit of repetitively asking "cookie-cutter" prompts, such as "Can anyone relate?" Overused, the "relating" prompt can turn the session into runaway storytelling.

For example, Pauline shared that she grew up in a huge family, and she had to fight and use a loud voice to be heard in the family. Now, in her marriage, she also has to fight to be heard by her husband. In addition, she tends to read negatively into the messages in others' communication, convinced that others are not interested in what she has to say.

Given her history, Pauline really needed the group to hear her and show interest in her. Unfortunately, in an effort to help Pauline not feel alone, the innocent leader used the very cookie-cutter prompt that should have been avoided, "Can anyone relate to Pauline?"

Lo and behold, other members started to share their stories, one after another, compelling as ever. Meanwhile, Pauline, falling on the sidelines, feeling just as unheard and alone in the session as in her life, became irritated and shut herself down.

A prompt with the intentionality to support Pauline would have been a better choice:

[To the group] Can anyone imagine what it's like for Pauline to have to fight and be loud to be heard? [Intentionality: Facilitating member-to-member empathic responses.]

Or

[To the group] In addition to feeling unheard, what other feelings might Pauline be struggling with in her situation?

Or

[To the group] After listening to Pauline's difficulty, what do you think are Pauline's unmet needs, and what can our group do to meet her needs?

Allow Adequate Time for the Group to Respond to Prompts

Seeing that members are not responding to the offered facilitating prompts immediately, many new leaders become so anxiety ridden that they jump in with another prompt, thinking that it will move the group along. Failing to allow members sufficient time to pause and ponder, the leader's quick pace actually stops members' internal processing in full flow.

When it comes to the question of how much time to give members before you barge in, three principles are worth considering:

First, after you give a facilitative prompt, allow about *7–14 seconds* for members to ponder how they will respond. Treat this pause as a super-mini meditation.

Second, honor members' pace of processing. If only one or two members respond to your prompt, it does not mean that the rest of the group has nothing to say. Most likely, they are just taking their time to put their thoughts and feelings together and into words. You can actually show appreciation to their pace of processing by saying,

> [To the group] I have heard from one member responding to my question. It seems like many of you are still taking your time to think. When you are ready, please feel free to share with the group what comes to your mind.

Third, sometimes members wanted to respond to your prompt, but the discussion got sidetracked, and they lost their opportunities. In this situation, you can simply restate your prior facilitating question:

> [To the group] I was asking whether any of you have observed any recurring themes in what has been shared. Then we got sidetracked a little bit. Let's come back to the original question for a moment. Anyone want to share any other recurring theme that you observed?

Provide Modeling of Desired Responses When Necessary

On those occasions when members are unable to put their reactions into words, the leader can go ahead to provide modeling of desired responses. For example, a leader wants to guide group members to show empathy to another member, Gina, so she invites the group by the following prompt:

> [To the group] It seems that Gina not only lost her father in the car accident but she also lost her relatives because of the cut-and-dried way they treated her loss. I wonder if anyone in the group can imagine what feelings Gina might have struggled with under those circumstances?

The group members feel strongly for Gina's pain, but for some reason, they struggled to put their empathy into words. After waiting for a while, the leader went ahead to provide modeling by expressing her own empathy to Gina:

> Gina, I sense that you feel re-injured each time when you run into those relatives who stir this pain in you. Their aloof treatment makes you feel invisible. You feel hurt and lonely.

Learning from this response modeled by the leader, the group pored its empathy and understanding out to Gina. It moved Gina to tears as it was the first time since her father's death that she felt understood and validated.

Invite Quieter Members to Have Their Voices Heard

Not outwardly quick and expressive, quieter members actually often have rich thoughts and feelings whirling in their minds. Unfortunately, the wheel of conversation in the group turns so fast that these members seldom get their turn to share.

The stress of not being able to speak up quickly enough is well demonstrated in the following journal entry of a member:

> When Ann began sharing her issues with weight, I could really identify. I have serious struggles with my weight also. I have every intention to exercise daily, but it just does not seem to happen. I wanted to express this, but it was so hard to get a chance to chime in. I am now nervous about the next session because I am afraid that I will still be unable to speak up because I am just not as vocal or quick as others.

If you want to give a quieter member a chance to join in, invite him or her together with other quieter members *collectively* so that you don't need to single out a person who is already self-conscious. Consider the following examples:

> Before we move on, I would like to *set aside a few minutes* for people who have not had a chance to express themselves yet. Do those of you who have not yet responded want to go ahead?

> I have not heard from some of the members *on this side of the group*, I wonder whether *some of you* would like to take the opportunity to contribute?

> I see that *some of you* have not had a chance to share but have been nodding. Would any of you like to share your two cents?

Sometimes, it's necessary to *individually* invite quiet members to speak. You may use any of the following simple encouragement, coupled with a genuine smile, to invite quieter members. For example,

> Jeff, it looks like you are in deep thoughts. Would you like to share what's in your mind?

John, I notice that you have been quiet in this session. I'd like to hear from you, but only if you feel comfortable.

Helen, I can see that you have been wanting to talk about that issue for a long time, and until today, you have not been able to. Somehow Nelson helped you to open up. What did he do?

In inviting participation from quieter members, you might want to consider the principles below:

- Do not draw people out unless it is needed. Members may develop a dependency on the leader if the leader extends an invitation too frequently.
- Do not try to draw out uncommitted or resistant members. Give them time to watch and observe the group until they feel comfortable enough to get their feet wet.
- Be sensitive to multicultural dimensions regarding participation patterns. Members from some cultures may need more time to observe before jumping in. If your invitation is met with hesitation, do not try to crack them open. Support their pace, and allow them time to watch and learn.

Be Sensitive to Difficulties Experienced by Members of Diversity

Many things shared in the group can be difficult for a member to talk about. Due to the limitation of space, we will illustrate with just one example: the pain of subjugation experienced by members of transgender and LGBTQ is often difficult to share (Comacho, 2001; McGoldrick & Giordano, 2005). When they build up their courage to share, these members need to be heard and acknowledged, especially.

To help members of diversity feel heard, the leader can give prompts to the group guiding them to communicate how they understand *the pain* expressed:

[To the group] Marcus has just shared with us some very painful experiences of rejection and isolation in staying true to his sexual orientation. If you could walk a mile in Marcus's shoes, so to speak, what would it be like for you? Please speak to Marcus directly when you are ready.

Your prompt will likely draw out more sensitive and compassionate comments than letting people respond on their own.

If someone responds with judgment to transgender and LGBTQ members, you definitely need to intervene:

> Penn, thank you for your comments. I did notice that you seem very certain about what Marcus should do to get rid of his confusion. You are so convinced in your own view that you have not been able to take in what was expressed here by Marcus. I wonder if you would be willing to slow down a bit and consider if what Marcus gets right now in the group is similar to what he gets when he tries to share this part of his identity with his family and friends?

Invite More Members to Disclose Around a Similar Core Issue

When a member presents his or her issue, all eyes tend to be on him or her. This can overwhelm the member presenting. To temper, ask yourself, "What is the core issue of this member's presentation?"

After you get a sense of it, for example, "not living up to family's expectations," you can *spin it off*, inviting more members to get involved along this line. This will help all members feel included, and at the same time, the person presenting will not feel overwhelmed by the exclusive attention. To do so, you may say,

> Matt, thank you, for your sharing! The group has given you some food for thought. I would like to invite you to reflect on what has transpired in the past 10 minutes, and then we can come back to hear your reflection. [Turn to the group] *Right now I would like to hear from the rest of the group.* I wonder, *what kind of memories or reactions has this issue of "not living up to family's expectations" brought up for you?* Would anyone like to jump in first?

Acknowledge Members' Tears—When Trust Is Not Yet Established

When your members cry, don't try to be "socially correct" by getting them to feel better. Stopping a member from crying actually takes away something that has the power to eliminate his or her stress, something that he or she needs precisely to feel better ultimately.

The way that leaders deal with crying really depends on the group stages. When the group is still young and trust has not been firmly established yet, members may not be ready yet to dive in to express deep-rooted feelings associated with the tears. In this case, just gently acknowledge the tears or simply reassure members to allow their pain to come alive through tears:

> Dale, I can sense how much it hurts to lose your brother when you were so young! I can sense that the group is as touched by your tears as I am.

> Mike, please take your time to stay with your pain. We are in no hurry. Please know that we are here to support you.

Honor Crying as an Open Space of Healing—When Trust Is High

When the trust level is high as is usually the case in later group stages, you can encourage members to plunge deeper into emotions. Crying often indicates that the topic is touching a deep reservoir of feelings. If processed properly, these emotions open a space for healing to happen. This kind of processing will take a few steps.

First, you can give support to the member's emotions by saying something like:

> You are doing good work, Kyung. Stay with that feeling for as long as you can. Don't feel guilty about taking the group time. Your feelings are very important to the group.

After the member has gone through the waves of emotion, you may encourage her to talk about it:

> Kyung, if you are comfortable, would you like to share what your tears are trying to say? See whether you can put your tears into words.

If the group is ripe for the *here-and-now encounter*, you can go further to explore this member's feelings about crying and being vulnerable in front of the group:

> Kyung! Thank you for sharing! I really appreciate your trust in sharing these intimate stories with the group! *How does it feel to cry and be vulnerable in the group's presence?*

Before moving on, ask the group members to express their *here-and-now feedback* to the member who cried:

[To the group] We had a few intimate moments of staying with Kyung while she gets in touch with a very moving memory of her past. I wonder, *how each of you experiences Kyung today? I am not asking how you imagine Kyung is feeling but how you are experiencing her today.*

Don't Rush in With "Kleenex"

To offer the box of Kleenex or not, when a member is crying? This is a question long debated in our field. There is no definite answer. Some members might feel comforted by the tissues, others might interpret this as an *indication to stop crying*, while still others might feel distracted by the passing of the box.

Following is one member's reflection about how the offering of Kleenex dampens her emotions:

When I began to speak in the group, something unexpected happened inside of me, and I just began to cry. *I became a little upset when people quickly moved to offer the box of Kleenex* because it distracted me from what I was trying to say, and I also saw it as an effort to stop my tears.

As a leader, you cannot predict how a specific client might respond. Overall, we (the authors) prefer to wait for a while so that a member crying has a chance to *fully experience his or her own pain,* and the group members have a chance to stay with the member with full emotional presence. After the crying has subsided, the group then can go ahead to pass the box of Kleenex.

Alternately, you may put a box of Kleenex on the floor in the center of the room. This will allow a member who is crying to reach for the tissue in his or her own time frame.

Help Members Better Receive Others' Input

Members receiving group input often want to explain away their situations or add more and more information for clarification. If allowed, the back and forth of inputs and explanation may cycle continuously, leading to details not conducive to focused group processing. To nip this tendency in the bud, the leader may need to instruct the member specifically about how to receive inputs from the group.

First step:

> Kyung, when the group gives you their input, please just listen without trying to explain or judge immediately. Later, you will have a chance to share your reactions.

> Gina, as the group shares their perspective with you, please just listen in. We will come back to you to hear your reactions.

Later step:

> Kyung, after listening to the input from the group, what do you realize about yourself that you did not before today?

> Gina, after listening to the group's validation regarding your double loss, what do you take away? What are your new beliefs about yourself?

Summarize the Common Threads of Group Discussion

It is wise to periodically summarize common experiences before moving on to the next activity. Summarization helps members internalize their learning from the shared discussion and helps the group make connections. You may synopsize the common experiences by saying something like:

> [To the group] Many members have shared the experiences of growing up in an alcoholic family. It seems that the anxiety of not living up to expectations, the angst that things are ready to fall apart at any point, the need to be overly responsible or to be perfect, and the tendency to be mistrustful are common threads that *run through our discussion today*.

You may also have group members sum up for themselves:

> [To the group] We have had a great deal of personal sharing for a while now. I wonder, would anyone like to summarize the common threads that have run through our discussion so far?

BASIC INTERVENTION TECHNIQUES (I): BLOCKING AND REDIRECTING

Group interactions can go off the track at any point, and it is entirely the leader's responsibility to intervene, steering the group back toward productive inter action. New group leaders often feel *more at ease with facilitating skills* such as inviting, drawing out, or initiating activities while *less confident with intervention techniques*. The actions of blocking, redirecting, refocusing, or correcting do, in fact, unnerve many. Still, these intervention techniques warrant a special space in your toolkit.

This section covers the first two intervention techniques: blocking and redirecting.

Dare to Stimulate Members With Blocking and Redirecting

Some counterproductive member behaviors often organically show up during group interaction (Jacobs, Masson, & Harvill, 2016), such as the following:

- Repeatedly jumping in first
- Becoming negative
- Giving a long-winded explanation
- Rambling
- Arguing
- Rescuing
- Intellectualizing

Without leaders' intervention, these behaviors will chip away at group dynamics. The ways of tackling these behaviors do vary depending on the group stage: In the early stages, it is more appropriate to just redirect them (as shown in this section). In later stages, however, it is more productive to employ here-and-now processing (see Chapters 11 and 12).

To redirect, we first need to *stop* the behavior and then *guide* it into a different direction. New leaders tend to feel ill at ease with these actions due to fear of hurting members' feelings. This fear is valid, but blocking does not necessarily hurt the receivers. It actually stimulates them to think about the unproductive nature of their old behaviors and about the alternatives.

The Rules of Blocking

Keep in mind the rules of blocking:

- Don't let members ramble on for too long, argue for an extended amount of time, or jump in to rescue others from intense or painful emotions before blocking them.
- Don't lecture on the unproductive behaviors. Your goal is to stop, not to judge.
- Follow the intervention with a facilitation prompt to steer the group to a more productive group interaction.

If subtle signs do not do the trick, progress to more direct interventions.

Start With Subtle Ways of Blocking

To ease yourself into the techniques of blocking, start with the subtle ways. You may use *avoidance of eye contact* to give a *hint* to a specific member for him or her to wind down.

Or you may use a *hand gesture* to give the person a "hold on" or "stop" signal. Many times, a slight gesture is all that is needed to stop an unproductive behavior.

Block a Rambling Behavior and Turn to Other Members

If avoidance of eye contact does not get your hint across, then sum up the rambling member's core message in one simple sentence (this way it won't appear abrupt), and then turn to the rest of the group to invite them onto a more productive topic:

Thank you, Dale! It seems you are saying that all of us fear being taken advantage of by others [summing up a rambling member's core message in one simple sentence]. [turning to the group] I would like to hear from *other* group members about the *trust issue that we were just starting to get into*. Does anyone want to start? [Finish the invitation by smiling toward the *quieter* members.]

Shift the Focus to Strong Emotions Pulsating at the Moment

Listening to other members' stories, a member might react emotionally, such as tearing up, to the topic being discussed. Don't let this moment slip by; stop the discussion, and shift the focus to that member:

Urszula, would you please excuse me for stopping you for a moment! I notice that *Marcelina is in tears* as the group is on the theme of the abandonment issue. [turning to Marcelina] Marcelina, if you could, would you please share with the group what your tears are trying to say?

Lily, would you please let me stop you before getting into another detail? It seems that Jane is reacting to what you just said, and I want to give her a chance to comment. [turning to Jane] Jane, would you like to share what's going on?

Block Members' Arguments and Conflicts

Argument and conflicts will definitely happen sooner or later in the group. In Chapter 9, we will cover detailed methods of working with conflicts within groups. For basic intervention, you just need to *block the negative exchange* and replace it with a facilitated dialogue. There are many different ways of managing it.

- If the argument is mild, you could ask,

  John and Jeff, I'd like you both to pause for a moment, and then do your best to summarize what the other has shared up to this point. [pause] John, would you like to go first and summarize what Jeff said? And later, Jeff, I would like to hear your summarization of what John said.

- If the argument is intense and emotional, both parties in the argument will probably be in a *short circuit* (see Chapter 9) and unable to hear what the other has been saying. You will need to get the group involved to calm down the emotional reactivity of the conflicting parties. For example,

  John and Jeff, please allow me to stop you for a moment. You two are trying so hard to make the other see things from your point of view. But I don't think either of you is hearing the other. So please stop for a moment, and we will get some help from the group. [turning to the group]

I would like the rest of the group to share what you observe is going on between John and Jeff? *What* do you think *makes sense* in both John's and Jeff's reactions? Does anyone want to start? [Getting the group to give empathy to calm down the conflicting parties.]

Redirect When Members Are Rescuing

Rescuing is not the same as helping. To rescue is to make the other feel better by "taking away" the painful or negative emotions someone is experiencing. In contrast, to help is to aid someone to resolve these feelings via fully experiencing and working through them. Most new members, however, won't be able to differentiate between them and will be inclined to rescue. The leader will need to block or redirect. For example,

Sue, may I stop you for a moment? I see that you are very eager to cheer Jane up so that she won't feel so much pain. I appreciate your good intention [start with a positive]. I believe that what is helpful for people doesn't always involve making them feel better immediately but rather allowing them to experience the pain more fully, no matter how uncomfortable it is for us to witness. [providing an educational moment] [turning to the whole group with psychodrama redirecting] As you all can see, Jane felt ashamed and isolated due to her painful childhood experiences. I would like each of you to take on a role of Jane's family member and say from your heart what Jane needed to hear from her family member but never did. [For more psychodrama methods, see Chapter 13.]

Block a Complicated Issue
Near the End of the Session

Sometimes members may start digging into a complicated issue near the end of the session. Leave such a complicated issue to unfold, and you will find the group unable to close on time. A can of worms will be opened, and the group has no sufficient time to explore it. A better alternative is to block the action.

Barry, this seems like a complicated issue that deserves the group's full attention to helping explore it. Since we are near the end of the session, may I ask you to hold this until we meet next week? How about we put your issues as the first priority in the next session? Is that okay with you? [turning to the group] Now with 5 minutes left, let's wrap it up by each of you using just one sentence to share what you take away from today's session.

BASIC INTERVENTION TECHNIQUES (II): REFOCUSING AND CORRECTING

Just as important as blocking and redirecting are the intervention techniques of refocusing and correcting. There are several ways to do this, and most take courage from the leaders to implement.

Loop Back and Refocus

When a group wanders into something irrelevant, the leader has to act quickly to put it back on track. This action is called *refocusing*. Don't wait too long because the more the group goes astray, the harder it will be to bring it back to focus. Consider the following example:

[To the whole group] We were just starting to get deep into the topic of 'wearing masks and how this coping strategy creates disconnection. Somehow we got away from it. Can we go back to where we were 5 minutes ago when Judy was talking about it? [turn to Judy] Judy, when you were talking to George, you seemed to be near tears. What was happening inside of you?

[To the whole group] Please pardon me. We seemed to be getting off track right now. Let's go back to talk about our reactions triggered by Mia's sharing of her needs for self-cutting. Anyone want to share how Mia's experience affected you?

[To the whole group] Let's stop a moment and stay with Mark for a few more minutes. [turn to Mark] Mark, would you say again when and how you started to feel regretful about your decision to cut yourself off from your family?

Change the General "You" or "We" Into "I" Statements

Using *the general* "you" "we" "people" statements in describing a personal experience, members can successfully *distance themselves* from their own feelings, protecting them from feeling exposed or vulnerable (Bernstein, 2010). Habitual use of this kind of impersonal language, however, prohibits others from understanding them or feeling close to them.

For example, a member, Malachy, said, "When people only come to you when they have problems, and when you have problems, no one is there for you; you feel that nobody cares. It can make you so mad, like wanting to smash things. It's not worth it to live like this."

Upon hearing Malachy's sharing, everybody knew that he was actually talking about his own experience, but everybody felt detached from his experiences due to his use of the general "you" language. People nodded their heads but did not have much to say.

To nip this problem, the leader simply asked Malachy to repeat what he just said but in "I" language:

> Malachy, what you just shared is very weighty. But when you use the general "you" statements to describe your personal experiences, *it feels detached and impersonal, making it difficult for people to connect to you.* Would you please restate what you just said, but this time, change it to an "I" statement, as in "When *I* feel _____ (fill in the blank) that nobody _____ (fill in the blank)." Would you please try that?

Have a Member Talk Directly "to" Instead of "About" Another Member

As a member hearing other members *comment about* him (as if he were not here), instead of talking directly *to* him, the member often feels gossiped about or excluded. For example, after Malachy changed to "I" statements, the leader invited the group to respond to Malachy in a way that showed understanding and acknowledged his unspoken feelings. Shizuko responded to the invitation, saying, "I think *he* probably feels alone and invisible."

Aloneness and a sense of invisibility actually spoke to Malachy's underlying struggle, but this comment did not help him feel understood. Malachy kept his head down, his feet fidgeting. Sensing Malachy probably felt left out by being commented on, the leader took action to amend the situation:

> Shizuko, your perceptions are really on target. Since Malachy is here with us, would you please say what you just said, but this time talk directly *to* him, instead of making comments *about* him?

Allow Productive Silence

A leader will run into two types of silence in group interaction: productive and unproductive (Jacobs et al., 2016). Productive silence happens when members are quietly taking in what has been said in the group. You can actually feel *a sense of energy* and *a depth of connection* in productive silence.

The following reflection by a member, Susan, illustrates what might go on inside members during a moment of *productive silence*:

> During check-in, Carol broke down in tears over her mother's illness. As she sat there with her face covered, I could feel the silence in the room. I was struck by *how comfortable I felt in the silence that lingered*. It was obvious to me that Carol was struggling with her intense emotions and *the group was giving her the gift of their presence in silence, without rushing in to take her pain away*, so she could begin to process these feelings.

When encountering a productive silence during group processing, let it linger for a while; members need the silence to process their thoughts, feelings, or memories. If a member starts to speak when everyone else is still absorbed in quiet processing, you may use a hand gesture to add to your intervention:

> [To the group] Let's wait for just a couple more minutes. It looks like people are still processing.

After enough time passed, you may break the silence:

> [To the group] We have just had a moment of silence here. I would like the members to share what was going on inside of you during the time of silence.

Deal With Unproductive Silence

Unproductive silence haunts a group when its members are bored stiff or tuned out by certain dynamics that cannot be named. A sense of *tension* seems to fill the room.

If the nonproductive silence happens during the *early stages*, you may promptly shift to a topic more conducive for group discussion. For example,

[To the group] It seems like we are ready to move on. Let's shift gears a bit. A moment ago, Jeff mentioned something about the *trust issue,* but we did not have a chance to talk about it. What personal experiences or concerns do you have surrounding the issue of trust?

Or

[To the group] We just had a moment of silence. I'd love to hear from you guys what went through your mind in that quiet time.

If an unproductive silence happens in *later stages* of the group, address the tension, boredom, fear, or so on. Invite members to share their observations. Examine together as a group what caused the silence. This is called "process examination" and is detailed in Chapter 12.

Address Members' "Advice-Soliciting" Behaviors

Almost every group has some members who habitually *solicit advice from others.* They may say something like, "I have this problem, and I just want to hear what advice you all have to give so I can make a decision about what I should do."

Though appearing open to others' input, these members are not up to implementing whatever advice was given to them. What they might really be on to is using *advice-solicitation to disguise their anxiety* of not knowing how to connect to others.

As a leader, you need to differentiate the genuine request from a disguised anxiety. When a group is faced with pressure to give advice, you may say,

[To the group] Although Denise seems to be asking for advice, and we all want to help her solve this problem right away, we do need to acknowledge that we know very little about her issue so far. So let's slow down a bit and try to understand more. [turning to the soliciting member] Denise, the group will be willing to give you some fresh perspectives if you allow them to gain some more insight into the nature of your problem. This will take a bit of exploration. So when you are ready, please let the group know. Is that OK with you?

BASIC FACILITATION SKILLS (III): CLOSING A GROUP SESSION

After a productive and engaging session, it is time to close the session. This section spells out principles and methods of closing so that you can put the icing on the cake.

Get the Group to Close on Time

More often than not, the group has more to process than what the time permits. Tempted to squeeze more discussion into the last few minutes, the group can easily end up closing 20 minutes beyond the hour. Even if members are so generous as to stay for a longer session, the boundary within the group might be crossed unintentionally.

One way to close on time is to make it one of the group's ground rules. Make sure that your members understand the rationale of this rule and have a consensus on it. Another way is to gently announce that time is running short and to sum up the common thread before proceeding to the check-out:

[To the group] We are approaching the end of the session. I feel encouraged by the work that was done here today. When I look back, I see that *a sense of loss—be it the loss of job security, attachment to loved ones, or untapped potential—has been a connecting theme in today's session.*

Sometimes we run into some members who habitualize on *waiting until the last minute to pore out a significant disclosure—*a phenomenon called *the doorknob disclosure*. Don't let it petrify you, just acknowledge the issue, and table it until the next session:

Steve, thank you. That seems like an important issue for you, yet we are running out of time today. If you would bring that up at the beginning of our next session, we will certainly spend some time on that.

Check-Out

Check-out gives group members a chance to reflect on the session or to air any unspoken reactions. You may use a quick go-around, in no particular order, to accomplish this. Be creative to customize any of the following options to suit the needs of your group:

- Option 1: What they learned about themselves.

  We have 7 minutes to wrap up the session. Before we do, I would like to hear from all of you *what you have learned about yourself* from today's session. Who would like to start?

- Option 2: What they like or dislike about the session.

  This is our first unstructured session and a very emotional one. We have 7 minutes left to wrap up for today. Before we leave, let's have a quick go-around, without any particular order; each of you can share *what you like or dislike about how we worked together* today.

- Option 3: What progress they made in the session.

  Before we wrap up, I would like each of you to share *the progress that you made today*. Please tell the group what steps, however small, you have taken in this session toward reaching your goal.

Or

I was aware that a number of group members took some important risks here in the group today relative to their goals. Can we do a quick go-around and each give a short description of how you've *made progress on* your new skills today?

- Option 4: What self-designated effort they can implement during the week.

  We have 7 minutes to wrap up the session. Let's have everyone share how they feel about the session today. Also, please identify *what personal work or goal you would like to focus on in your personal life during the week*. Who would like to start?

The Reminder

The last step of the closing is a reminder. This helps members to be mindful about confidentiality and of continuing their personal internal processing during the week. You may say,

Thank you all for sharing and contributing to the group process today. Just two reminders before we leave: (1) Please remember that in order for the group to be in a safe place, we all must adhere to the rule of *confidentiality*. (2) Please spend some reflective time to write in your personal *journals* so that you have a space to reflect on your intense emotions that often come up *after* the group. Of course, you are welcome to share those emotions with the group next session. Thanks again, and have a wonderful week!

∞∞∞

In closing: "A journey of a thousand miles begins with a single step" says Lao-tzu. Your trek toward mastering the group leadership skills also starts with a humble step—learning the fundamentals. These fundamental skills turn out to be not so humble after all. We hope you give yourself time to muscle up these skills.

EXERCISES

Scenarios for Your Practice

1. About halfway through the second session of a personal exploration group for laid-off white-collar workers, Bob states, "I don't know why we must listen to all these tales of woe from everyone here. What we need to know is how to find a new job."

   What are some possible group leader responses at this stage?

2. About 30 minutes into an experiential group session, Joan directs the following question to you. "I don't think that what Melanie has been talking about is relevant to what our group is doing. Don't you agree?"

   What would be an appropriate response from a group leader?

3. At the start of the fourth session of a grief group, there is a great deal of silence and lack of responsiveness to your general invitation for someone to begin. As you scan the group members, you notice that most of them are avoiding eye contact and gazing into the distance. You also notice that Molly is red-eyed and she is twisting a handkerchief in her hand. You recall that in the last session, she had been the focus for most of the group for what you perceived to be an especially productive session with much input from others.

As the group leader, what would be a helpful response that you could make at this stage?

4. Ten minutes before the end of a group session of ten individuals, Alice makes the following statement: "Well, I've been thinking that half of us are much better at this than the others." You notice that all of the members sit upright at this statement. Wayne expresses his agreement with Alice that he also has been better at group than others but asks in a very demanding tone, "What do you quieter members have to say about <u>that</u>?"

Given the short amount of time left in the session, what would be a helpful response that you as group leader could make at this stage?

5. In an experiential group, Jeff describes a painful experience with his supervisor at work. At the same time, you notice that Walt gets an angry look on his face but doesn't say anything.

What are some of your options to deal with this? Why might you make these choices?

6. As you are concluding a session for an experiential group, you ask for a quick go-around for each member to briefly comment on what he or she learned or experienced during the session. Most comments are fairly positive, but Wally blurts out, "You know, I wasn't given a chance today to tell you of the traumatic experience I had this afternoon."

What are some options for responses as group facilitator?

Self-Reflection

1. What personal concerns might you have about stepping forward as a group leader to block rambling, counterproductive, or argumentative behaviors by group members?

2. What difficulties do you anticipate having with scanning the room and being aware of what is happening with all the members of a group of 12?

3. As a group facilitator *and* participant, it is likely that you will at some point find your own issues bubbling up. How can you use this to further the group process and still find the balance between facilitating and participating?

4. Since the ultimate goal of group facilitation is to help people communicate more easily with one another, how can you model such communication as the facilitator and/or participant?

5. As a group leader, what does *intentionality* mean to you when it comes to group intervention?

CHAPTER 5

THE FIRST SESSION
AND THE FORMING STAGE

Half the success of a group relies on a good start. The first session, just like the first stage of a group, sets the tone for the remainder of the group life. Foster a sense of connection, trust, and hope right off the bat, and the group will launch itself onto a positive trajectory. This chapter provides concepts and skills for such a successful group launch.

LEADERSHIP AND THE FORMING STAGE

Filled with apprehension and uncertainty about the unknown, members in the initial stage of a group need structure and orientation. This section depicts features of this tender stage of the group and leadership principles.

The Five Stages of Group Development

Groups tend to move through stages during their life spans. Some group models identify four stages (Corey & Corey, 2014; Gladding, 2015), whereas others identify five (Lacoursiere, 1980; Tuckman, 1965; Tuckman & Jensen, 1977). In this text, we adopt the five-stage model, as it corresponds more precisely with the framework and the skills that we employ.

Following, we outline the five stages of group development, and Table 5.1 provides a quick view. When you read the group stages, please remember the following: In theory, group stages seem clear-cut; in reality, they are often fluid and seldom linear.

- The 1st stage—the *forming/acquaintance* stage
  - o This stage focuses on goal setting and boundaries, getting to know one another, and nourishing a sense of safety. The group relies heavily on the leader for structure and active facilitation.

- The 2nd stage—the *storming/transition* stage
  - o This will be a stage inundated with covert and overt tension as well as competition. Conflicts may become the undercurrents that the group must wade through.
- The 3rd stage—the *norming* stage
  - o This stage strives to develop a solid sense of cohesion that enables members to gain confidence in risk taking and delving deeper into group work.
- The 4th stage—the *working/performing* stage
  - o A heightened level of productivity tends to occur at this mature stage. The group harvests deepened self-disclosure, honest feedback, caring confrontation, a sense of humor, reality testing, and intense here-and-now work.
- The 5th stage—the *termination* stage
  - o As the group completes its task, its members say good-bye to each other while preparing to move onward in their lives with a renewed sense of competence.

This chapter will focus on the 1st stage of group development.

Table 5.1   A Quick View of the Five Stages of Group Development

Stages of Group Development	Tasks	Possible Format
1. The *forming/acquaintance* stage	• setting goals and boundaries • getting to know one another • nourishing sense of safety	structured
2. The *storming/transition* stage	• processing covert and overt tension and competition • honoring differences	unstructured with themes focus
3. The *norming* stage	• achieving a solid sense of cohesion • gaining confidence • learning to take risks • preparing toward here-and-now focus	unstructured with themes focus
4. The *working/performing* stage	• here-and-now intense work • deepened self-disclosure • honest feedback • caring confrontation • laughter and humor • reality testing	unstructured with a here-and-now focus
5. The *termination* stage	• saying good-bye • preparing to move onward	unstructured or soft structured

The Forming/Acquaintance Stage

The forming/acquaintance stage of a group parallels *childhood* of a human life. This is a stage marked by looking forward, setting goals, a need for structure, and a dependency on the leader for active facilitation.

Members often feel anxious and apprehensive when attending a new group. They worry about safety and familiarity issues. A myriad of questions run through their minds: What will the group be like? What will discussions entail? What does the group expect of its members? Is it safe to be myself in the group? What types of members will be in the group? How will I feel amongst a group of strangers?

With a sense of anxiety and unfamiliarity, new members often fancy the leader to be *an expert* on building and maintaining the success of the group.

Work Both on the Task and on the Relationship

From the onset, the leader must focus on *two keys* for a successful group: *task and relationship* (Bales, 1953; Kivlighan III & Kivlighan Jr., 2016).

The Task. Every group has a predetermined task. For example, members follow the group's *ground rules* and *reach their goals.*

The Relationships. The group must provide a safe environment for members to explore their issues without fear of judgment or rejection. A safe environment nurtures a sense of connection, trust, acceptance, and hope for all. Therefore, an equal amount of leadership effort should go to *forging relationships* among members that are therapeutic for them.

"The Need of Inclusion" in the Forming Stage

At the heart of all group members lay three universal needs: *inclusion, control,* and *affection,* as indicated in the classic study by Schutz (1958). Each of these needs becomes most critical at a particular stage:

- The need for *inclusion* seeks to have its thirst quenched in the *forming stage.*
- The need for *control* screams for satisfaction in the *transition stage.*
- The need for *affection* smiles to allure close connections in the *working stage.*

Since a group in the *forming stage* must meet its members' *need for inclusion,* the group's leader needs to use facilitating prompts to invite members to respond to one another and show mutual interest (Hetzel, Barton, & Davenport, 1994; Shechtman & Toren, 2009).

Provide Structures in the 1st Stage of the Group

To soothe anxieties and meet expectations of the members, a group leader needs to provide enough structure in the first session. Ways of providing structure may include the following:

- Having the group identify basic ground rules
- Having members *set clear goals*
- Using a "go-around" format to ensure inclusion for every member

Simple structures such as these listed above can foster *a sense of orientation* and *reduce anxiety* about the unknown (Lacoursiere, 1980; Pan & Lin, 2004).

LEADERSHIP SKILLS FOR THE FIRST SESSION

To guide a group to work simultaneously on its tasks and relationships (Kivlighan III & Kivlighan Jr., 2016), a leader's best bet is to have members *share their problems and goals* in the first session. An extraordinary thing occurs when people share their difficulties, issues, struggles, and areas in which they desire changes. *A sense of universality* (Yalom & Leszcz, 2005) sets in while isolation melts away, and the bond amongst members begins to forge.

If you are a first-time group leader, your leadership of the first session may be stunted by the phenomenon of "group shock" (as described in Chapter 2). Prepare to make adjustments, including changing from individual counseling mode to that of group counseling.

To help you lay the groundwork for success, the following section presents pragmatic ways to provide structure for the first session and to deal with potential stumbling blocks.

Greeting

A greeting provides a warm and soothing way to open a session, much like a welcoming. Greetings should be short and succinct. No need trying to be chatty or sassy.

Hi, everybody! Welcome to our first group session! I'm glad that everyone made it here tonight. We have about 90 minutes together. During this time, we'll start to learn a little bit about one another.

Conduct an Ice-Breaking Exercise

Mixed feelings often come with people when they enter a new group. If not properly expressed, these feelings may hinder their mental presence in the group. As a principle, expressing feelings regarding the present moment may help clear the way and forge group bonding.

On this, one leader reflected, "I found that through the initial disclosure of feelings by everyone, we had begun a bonding process." To initiate this ice-breaker, you may say,

[To the whole group] Before we start our first session, I'd like everyone *to tell us your name* and *one sentence about your current feelings.* It's common to come to the first session with mixed feelings. These feelings are important to the group, and our sharing them will lead to a more relaxed environment. We have about 7 to 10 minutes for this, so let's have a quick go-around. Whoever is ready, please start.

Handle Concerns as They Come Up in the Ice-Breaking

Don't be surprised if some immediate concerns, such as the issue of confidentiality, arise during the ice-breaking exercise. Any concerns and their accompanying feeling ought to be acknowledged, and the leader should facilitate the group to discuss the issues:

Judy, it sounds as though you're worried that what you say in the group may reach others outside the group. This certainly would make you feel unsafe. [turning to the group] At this moment, I would like the group to talk a bit about where each of you stands on the issue of confidentiality and what each of you is willing to commit to in order to protect your fellow members' right of confidentiality.

Once everyone agrees on ground rules regarding issues brought up, you should return to the ice-breaking exercise:

[To the whole group] Now that we all seem to be on the same page regarding confidentiality, I would like to go back to sharing your names and feelings about the first session. Who wants to go next?

Transition to the Next Activity by Summarizing the Common Feelings

A transition moment creates a breathing space between two distinct activities. After an icebreaker, the best transition summarizes *common feelings* shared amongst members. This serves to forge a sense of *universality*:

[To the whole group] Thank you for sharing how you feel at this moment. It sounds like most of you feel excited about the group and yet ambivalent about what challenges might be ahead of you.

Kick Start the Introduction of Members' Goals

Now enters the most important task of the first session: members introducing their personal goals. This will occupy the bulk of the first session.

It is very common for members to be curious about what brings others to the group. Once they hear what their fellow members want to work on, then they can begin to *help one another* and *hold one another accountable for working on their goals.*

If you are leading a group composed of people with higher levels of anxiety, such as adolescents, it can be beneficial to *put members into pairs first.* This gives the young members the opportunity to feel more at ease talking about their issues. Later, you can open the floor for individuals to present their goals to the entire group. This allows members to feel more in control.

When initiating this major activity, remember to explain its purpose and time frame:

[To the whole group] For the bulk of the session, I would like for each of you to introduce your personal goal to the group. [pause] As we only have 12 sessions for our group, *it is important that we know one another's goals so that you can hold each other accountable to these goals.* [pause] With 8 members here, we will have around 7 minutes for each person. That is, each of you will have about *3 minutes to share the issue that you want to work on and the goals that you want to achieve. Then, the group will spend about 4 minutes responding to what you have shared.*

You can also clarify your expectation of spontaneous group interaction during the process:

[To the group] After one member introduces his or her goal, I would like the rest of you to feel free to jump in to show your understanding, make a comment, or to ask a clarifying question. Please interact spontaneously. There is no need to raise your hand or seek my permission.

Since *the first person will set the tone for the rest of the group,* it is advisable to invite someone more emotionally open to begin goal introduction. Again, the first person tends to set the tone for the rest of the group. To facilitate this, you may say,

[To the group] Are there any questions? If not, then let's start off with Jeff and then go this direction [hand gesture indicating the direction; choose Jeff knowing he is likely to set the tone for emotional openness].

Help Members Give Their Personal Goals a Context

When introducing their goals, some members may feel overwhelmed by a roomful of strangers. As a result, they leave out the context (the issues and problems) where the goals are embedded. Others, from backgrounds that discourage personal disclosure outside of their own family, may hold back. As a result, they skip over the context, making their goals less personal or meaningful.

For example, a member, Gabi, gave minimum context in her goal introduction. She simply stated, "I want to learn to be more open with others" and then abruptly stopped. The group was unable to understand the full context of her goal. At this juncture, the leader stepped in,

Gabi, would you tell us what makes this goal so important at this stage of your life? Was there something in your life that occurred that inspired you to want to be more open? Would you share a bit with the group the background of this goal?

The Virtue of Having Clearly Defined Goals

After a member opens up, the next step is to help him or her flesh out a clear goal. During the intake, you have helped members flesh out their goals, but in the group session, you may need to do it again with the help of the group. Starting with a well-defined goal is the best way for the group work to succeed (Drumm, 2006; Haley, 1991).

As stated in the previous chapter, goals serve as an engine that drives human motivation and directs our behavior. An optimal goal is one that paints a clear mental image of the desired outcome. With that image, a momentum is set for it to become a reality (Needham-Didsbury, 2012).

Further, when a member's goal possesses a definite visual, other members are able to see whether the goal has been achieved at the end of the group (Barker, 2013).

A member, Abram, originally had difficulty in setting a personal goal. Looking back on his group experience, he realized the virtue of goal setting. Abram wrote,

> I found the first session to be compassionate and fun, rather than confrontational or intrusive, as I had previously feared. Certainly, this is due to the emphasis on empathy and respect, as well as my fellow members being so sincere, forthcoming, committed, and generous. Yet, most important is the whole idea of "having a purpose, having a stated goal." I think this concept accounts for the success of the group. I think *there is a lesson in goal-setting* in the group—even in life. If you have a purpose—a stated goal—your personal experience is transformed.

Define Goals in the Positive Direction

Another way to create attainable goals is for members to define the goals in positive descriptors, rather than negative.

A goal with positive descriptors points out what we *do* want, instead of what we *do not* want. A negative goal will not lead to the desired outcome. As Barker (2013) states,

> Many people come to therapy with *negative goals*. They want to feel less depressed, or to stop eating so much, or to stop smoking. Or they want their children to stop fighting, or their teenage daughter to stop refusing to eat the food they provide. These are all good reasons for seeking professional help, but they are not adequate as outcome frames. (p. 67)

It takes a certain leadership skill to guide members to define their goals in the positive direction:

Gaston, I understand that you *don't want* to feel depressed. So, when you don't feel depressed, what is your life like, and what will you be doing?

Zemin, I hear that you want to *stop* smoking. When you do stop smoking, what *positive activity* will you be doing to release your emotional stress?

Yang, you said that you want to *stop* binge eating. What will you be doing to nurture yourself when you don't binge eat anymore?

Fine-Tune to a More Tangible Goal

Even when members' intentions are stated in positive terms, they may still be too vague to be useful. For example, members may say that they want to "feel happier," "have more energy," or "be able to decide what I want to do with my life." As Barker (2013) pointed out:

Such statements are all right as the starting points for the discussion of treatment goals, but they are not in themselves adequate outcome frames. What does "feel happier" mean? Happier than what or who? Under what circumstances does the person want to feel happier? How will the client and the therapist know that the desired degree of happiness has been achieved? (p. 68)

Leaders need to guide members in fine-tuning a more tangible goal. For example,

Pedro, you said that you want to have more energy at the end of the group. When you do have more energy, how will you act differently from how you act now?

Catharina, it seems like you want to feel more content in your life. How will we, as a group, be able to see that you are reaching your goal?

Get the Group to Respond With Support and Empathy

When listening to each other's issues and goals, members often have difficulty responding to one another in a therapeutic way. To amend this, the leader needs to design certain facilitating prompts to draw out the group's empathy, support, and empowerment for one another. Please review Chapter 4 for details. Following are three different ways of drawing out support and empathy in the group.

- To draw out empathy

  [To the group] What do you understand to be Joe's struggles and his desires to change?

  [To the group] Do any of you understand the point Mary is trying to make? Would you tell Mary *what you understand*?

  [To the group] Can any of you imagine what it is like for Luka to live in constant fear of being reported to the authorities?

  [To the group] Can any of you imagine what unspoken messages Rukmini receives from her family?

- To draw out similar feelings

  [To the group] Some of you might feel similarly to Eunice, *feeling disconnected even though you are staying connected digitally* through texting and Facebook. Who would like to share their feelings with Eunice?

  [To the group] I can see that *being betrayed* by someone she loves so much has created a lot of pain in Tracy. Have any of you experienced *the pain of being betrayed* or some similar feelings?

  [To the group] I believe that just like Delmira, some of us have similar difficulties in *letting others know how we really feel and even putting on a brave face when we feel like crying inside*. Would anyone like to share their feelings with Delmira?

- To draw out empowering comments

  [To the group] From the goal that Hanako just shared with us, what do you imagine to be the priority in her life? What does this priority tell you about Hanako?

  [To the group] After you listened to Hazim's presenting issues, what inner strength stood out for you, even though he did not speak about it himself?

  [To the group] As Yanni was speaking, what did you find significant in his ability to rise above the hardship that has occurred in his life?

Stay Away From Problem-Solving and Rescuing

When listening to fellow members' presenting issues and goals, new members often feel tempted to offer reassurance, advice, or problem-solving. These incidences often require leader intervention.

For example, Katie expressed concern that her brother might be drafted. Dreadfully worried about his safety, Katie became visibly upset as she continued sharing her presenting issues. Upon hearing this, Julie said to Katie,

> I don't think the war will happen. The threat is not that great, so you don't need to be worried.

Even though Julie's reassurance was given with the best intentions, it had the effect of dismissing or discounting Katie's fears. Unbeknownst to Julie, Katie had been getting the exact same reassurance from her father and friends. They all negated her feelings as illogical, and now Julie had done the same.

Seeing this, the leader intervened to prevent the rescuing behaviors from continuing:

> [To the group] I wonder, do any of you understand Katie's deep fears about the draft?

The group responded with plenty of empathy and compassion, allowing Katie to feel heard and validated. The leader followed this up with a facilitation question for Katie.

> Katie, it seems that when the group really hears your concerns and your worries and doesn't just give you reassurance, you immediately appear more relaxed. Does this shed any light on what is important for you?

Responding to this question, Katie expressed a need to be able to fully experience her own feelings. For too long, she had learned to suppress them due to her belief that no one would ever understand. This became her goal within the group.

Transition to the Next Member

With proper facilitation, the group has succeeded in providing support and understanding for Katie. This allowed her to shape a more relevant and realistic goal. It is then time to transition to the next member. It takes a simple acknowledgment to transition:

> Katie, thank you for sharing your issue and personal goal! Due to the time factor, may I have your permission to move on to the next member? [Katie responds positively] OK, who would like to go next?

Summarize Members' Commonalities at the End

After all group members have taken a turn introducing their personal goals, it is time to wrap up. Prior to wrapping up, summarize common themes that emerged from members' issues and goals. Doing so fosters a sense of bonding. For example,

> [To the group] Thank you, everyone, for sharing your personal issues and goals with one another. From what you have said, I noticed two common threads. First, it takes a lot of strength to open up. Second, many of you share a common desire to work on being truer to your feelings, taking responsibility to express your own needs, and clearing out some unresolved issues from the past so that you can live more fully in your present relationships. Are there any other common threads that you have noticed as well?

Discuss Ground Rules

In the first session, the group often does not have sufficient time to discuss group rules thoroughly. It's normal to take a couple of sessions to complete the group's ground rules. If any issues related to group ownership do emerge, you may want to provide the group some time to come to an agreement about any of the following issues:

- Confidentiality
- Attendance
- Tardiness
- Smoking and eating in the session
- Recording
- Getting involved socially or intimately with other members
- Members' rights and responsibilities

After the group discussion, try to summarize:

[To the group] These issues we've just discussed are very important for all of us. Since the group is of our creation, I would like for us to continue to address these issues as they emerge.

It may take a few weeks for the group to complete the list of rules. Encourage members to freely add to the list any rules they consider important. This should be done until they feel like their needs for boundaries and safety have been taken care of.

Check-Out

A quick go-around provides an opportunity for each member to express their experience of the first group session. You may combine the announcement of the closing and the check-out.

[To the group] We have 5 minutes left for today. Before we leave, I would like to have a quick go-around where each of you shares how you are feeling at the end of today's session. How about starting with Katie, and then going around this way?

You may also include your own response in this final go-around:

I feel very good about our first meeting. My respect goes out to all of you who took a big risk in revealing your issues and your goals. I am also impressed by the vastly different experiences that each member brings to the group.

Give Reminders

A reminder can serve as a guidepost, giving members a sense of how to prepare themselves for the following sessions.

[To the group] Just a few reminders before we leave: Please remember that in order for this to stay a safe place, we all must adhere to the rule of confidentiality. I would also like to encourage you to take some time *during the week* to reflect on the goal that you set for yourself. If any thoughts come up, please write them down and share them with the group next time. Have a great week!

SPECIAL CONSIDERATIONS FOR THE FIRST SESSION

To ensure the success of the first session, you may want to take note of the following considerations.

Avoid In-Depth Therapy in the First Session

The first session is not the time to jump into "in-depth" therapy. This is not to say that the first session should remain superficial. Just the opposite in fact: the first session should be as engaging and meaningful as possible.

The concept of not going in too deep means that the leader should avoid spending an extended length of time, such as spending more than 15 minutes, focusing on one single member, digging into his or her deeply rooted issues.

It will be tempting to explore what hides behind the tears a member has as he or she shares his or her issues and goals, but it is wise to hold back. Most members are not ready for this type of in-depth work during the first session.

Exposing members to deeper therapy too early can actually frighten them away. This fear of exposure can be illustrated by Vasilissa's reflection:

> Although I'd heard about how powerful group sessions can be, I was not expecting to have such a strong reaction myself. I was the last one to introduce my goal. I surprised myself by starting to cry almost immediately after I started talking. I was, of course, aware that this was a painful issue for me to talk about, but honestly, I didn't think that I'd break down this way and during the first session, no less!
>
> I have to admit I felt pretty *embarrassed* by my outpouring of emotion. I felt extremely *vulnerable* in front of a roomful of group members. Although I trust some of them, I still felt really *exposed* and kind of silly and overly dramatic.

Deal With Members' Emotional Distress

What to do when members show powerful emotions in the first session? We suggest the following:

If a member is visibly distressed when introducing her issues and goal, simply acknowledge the feelings and provide a sense of direction:

Amelia, I can sense how hurt you feel to be so rejected by your own parents. The group is an excellent place to explore such issues. Perhaps you can spend some time working on this issue *in future sessions when you feel comfortable.*

If a member is already in tears, respect her pain while also reducing her sense of embarrassment:

Tracy, it is totally okay to cry. Your emotions are very important to us. Please take your time and stay with your feelings for a moment. We are in no rush.

After the tears have stopped, acknowledge the member's feelings and provide a sense of direction, just like the previous example:

Tracy, thank you for sharing your tears with the group. I can sense that there has been a lot of pain in these past few years since you discovered your husband's affair. The group is an excellent place to explore such emotions and issues. Maybe you can spend some time working on these issues *in future sessions when you are ready.*

Take Opportunities to Address Ground Rules as Situations Arise

Never begin the first session talking about ground rules as it may set a tone of constraint and control. Do not wait until the end of the session, either. Rather, *the rules should be addressed as situations arise.*

When a situation arises, have the group discuss what ground rules they need to prevent it from happening again. Undesirable behaviors, when allowed to become entrenched in a group, become difficult to change.

Ground rules should be established in due time, *with the consent of all members.* This way, they are more likely to have a sense of ownership and the motivation to follow through. Some examples include the following:

If during the first session, a member reveals a *fear of confrontation*, it signals a good opportunity to set *the ground rule about confrontation*:

[To the group] The issue about the confrontation that Jamie just addressed is an important concern. I would like our group to establish a ground rule where no one is allowed to attack another member. We are here to learn from one another, not to attack those who have different opinions or life choices from us. How do all of you feel about having that as a group rule?

If a member brings up a concern regarding trust, you may take this opportunity to establish a ground rule about trust:

Ken, thank you for mentioning the issue of trust; it is a legitimate concern in a group setting. [turning to the group] Before anyone begins sharing something personal, I want to emphasize the rule of confidentiality that we briefly discussed earlier. If we want to build a group where we can trust one another and feel safe, it is imperative that we keep others' personal sharing within our group. Can everyone commit to this rule?

If members ask about whether or not they can share certain details of the group with a significant other, this is a good opportunity to educate them on this matter:

[To the group] I see a difference between sharing with your significant other what you yourself are working on in the group versus talking about what your fellow members are working on in the group. Keeping confidentiality means that you don't share any other group member's information with anyone outside the group. Regarding discussing what you learn about yourself, you may freely do so as long as you don't mention how your fellow group members contribute to your learning. How do you guys feel about this rule?

Time Management

Time management issues in the first session tend to be caused by the following mistakes:

- Ice-breaking activity goes too long, leaving inadequate time for goal introduction
- Group discussion lingers on a member for too long without a leader's proper facilitation

Without a doubt, effective time management requires the leader to be active and directive. Review the facilitating skills and intervention techniques of Chapter 4 to increase your confidence in taking on this role.

For example, you see that a member is rambling on while sharing his story. To prevent loss of group time, you simply acknowledge his issue and redirect the group interaction:

John, it seems like a complicated situation; I hope you bring it up again in a future session so the group can help you. [turning to the group] Before we move on to the next member, I want to make sure that everyone understands what John's goal is. Could anyone use one sentence to summarize what John hopes to achieve in the group?

Avoid Turn-Taking

A major disruptor to group interaction is turn-taking. Do not let the group slip into the habit of taking turns to talk. Encourage the group to interact spontaneously.

The only time it is appropriate for the group to takes turns is when the leader uses a *go-around* as an exercise. This type of go-around is especially useful in *the check-in or the check-out,* where everyone is included. Even so, the go-around does not need to follow a particular order.

∞ ∞

In closing: Half the success of a group relies on a good start. The first session sets the tone for the remainder of the group life. With your skillful facilitation, intervention, and special considerations, the group starts to form a sense of connection, trust, and hope right off the bat—the group has launched itself onto a positive trajectory.

REFLECTIONS ON THE FIRST SESSION

The following reflections, as experienced by both members and the leader, give you a glimpse into the ambiance of a first session. All names are fictitious.

Louise's Reflection on Her First Session

I went into the first session thinking this process would be easy, especially after having worked on my issues in individual counseling. I now know that the hurt surrounding my trouble with my family is far from over; it continues to live just below the surface. I surprised myself when some of my emotions started creeping in as I described the issues surrounding my goal. What surprised me most was that I could identify with a lot of issues presented by each member; I could connect to some aspect of each and every person's dilemma. . . .

After this first session, I feel positive and optimistic. I really trust everyone in our group and feel a sense of security. I left the session feeling that each member has the best interests of the group at heart. But I am also realistic, knowing that it is inevitable that, sooner or later, the conflict will arise. But I am very interested and curious to see what will develop as we begin to challenge one another to delve deeper into and work on our core issues.

Leader Session Narrative Notes— Regarding Louise's Work in the Group

Louise's goal is to gain the means to not rely on approval from others. I was touched by her openness about her struggles concerning her father not showing the slightest trace of approval for her accomplishments in life.

The group seemed to understand what she was dealing with. After some group interaction and clarification, Louise's goal seemed to change to achieving inner approval instead of from others. Emotion swelled in her as this notion of inner approval struck a chord in her and she seemed to make a valuable connection.

As I looked around the room, I noticed that many members had a contemplative look on their faces, nodding their heads in agreement to Louise's restated goal.

Karen's Reflection on Her First Session

The first session for me was very intense and scary. I started out feeling that no one would be able to relate to anything I was going through. This was the first time that I'd ever had a chance to sit down and talk about things happening in my life. I was very nervous and a little apprehensive about talking. My mind was racing with thoughts of how the group would react to the things I would say and how they would view me.

But when Louise began speaking, I found myself really in tune to what she was saying. My thoughts went, "finally, someone is having similar issues and goals as me."

When it was my turn to speak, I became very nervous. But as I started talking, I tried to observe everyone's reactions and expressions. The group's responses really make it easy for me to express myself. My goal is to have the ability to find someone in my life to whom I can talk and feel comfortable with. I want to be able to trust that individual.

After I finished introducing my goal, I thought this was the first step toward developing trust in myself and in others. . . . Even though this is my first group session, I felt a sort of peace, sitting there listening, learning, and observing the group of relative strangers who I will be interacting with for the next 11 weeks. I have to thank the leader for setting the tone and keeping the interaction flowing.

Leader Session Narrative Notes— Regarding Karen's Work in the Group

Karen spoke cautiously as she revealed to the group that her goal was to learn to trust others. I sensed that she had been hurt many times by people whom she placed her trust in. Knowing this made me feel even more privileged that she was able to open up and trust the group. This step demonstrated her strength of character, despite the wounds and hardships that she had gone through.

She admits that she began building walls around herself to protect her feelings ever since she was a child—a period of time when her mother had never supported her emotionally. The group listened quietly, and I wondered if they ever had to deal with this type of pain before.

"Testing the waters" in this first session, where members shared a glimpse of their lives with one another, was the first baby step for Karen. I believe the small increment of trust gained from this session will continue to strengthen and grow throughout further sessions.

AN OVERVIEW OF THE FLOW AND TIME FRAME OF THE FIRST SESSION

Before going over the details of leadership skills, it is helpful to provide an overview of the flow of the first session, as presented in the following table. Each step is to be detailed subsequently.

Table 5.2 An Overview of the Flow and Time Frame of the
First Session

A. Opening the first session

-Greeting (1 minute)
-Introducing names and breaking the ice (7 minutes)
-Transition by summarizing common feelings (2 minutes)

B. Members introducing personal goals (65 minutes)

-Initiating the introduction of personal goals (2 minutes)
-First member (about 7 minutes)
-Member sharing issues and setting the goal
-Group interacting with the member in empathic ways
-Staying away from problem-solving and rescuing
-Transitioning to the next

(All along, the leader facilitates, intervenes, and participates to maximize member-to-member interaction, while balancing the focus on both task and relationships.)

-Second member (same as above)
-Next member, and so on
-Last member
-Summarizing members' common themes (2 minutes)

C. Discussing group ground rules (time varies)

D. Closing the first session (10 minutes)

-Announcing the closing
-Checking-out
-Giving reminder

EXERCISES

Scenarios for Your Practice

1. It is the first session of a counseling group. As the group leader, you have invited all members to share their identified goal with the group. Lou, Sally, and Bill offer fairly focused behavioral changes that they want to work on.

When it comes time for Sue to speak, she begins very slowly, "Well, when I was six, I had to go live with my grandmother for 2 years while my parents divorced, and my mom found a good job. . . ." For another 10 minutes, Sue continues to describe her painful feelings about this experience.

What would be a helpful response that you could make at this point in her story?

2. After you have explained the group ground rules to everyone, and each person has identified a goal for the newly started group, Jared comments to Alphie, "I think that everyone has identified a solid goal except you. Your goal is silly."

How might you respond as a leader who wants to set useful and effective norms for the group?

3. In the first session of a new group, after each of the members has identified a goal, Curtis asks you directly, "I hope that you will be instructing us on exactly what to do. I can't see much benefit in following a policy of letting the blind lead the blind."

What are some possible responses for you as a group leader?

4. Mary states that she felt reluctant to come to the group, but that her husband Phil encouraged her because "he feels that I will learn to better fulfill my duty. In fact, Phil said that he would call the leader from time to time to make sure that these matters receive enough attention."

What aspects of this statement would you want to address? Why? What would you say?

5. Sylvia says she learned of this group through her individual counselor who encouraged her to come. She says that she doesn't understand how a group is going to help her because she is a shy person.

How might you speak to Sylvia to help her find a way to work within the group?

Self-Reflection

1. What are your personal experiences concerning the issue of inclusion?

   What would you do to make every member feel included?

   What would you do with members who appear shy?

2. As a group leader, you are responsible for screening potential members to determine which ones would be appropriate for a particular group. As an interviewer, you might not have the same level or type of anxiety as the prospective members who are interviewed.

   How might you stay in touch with and be sensitive to their anxiety and need for inclusion within the group?

3. There are times when you may enter an already established group as the "outsider" to lead or consult. How do you envision working through your own need for inclusion and other expectations with a group that could be mistrustful or even hostile, depending on the circumstances? Perhaps you joining the group may even represent some threat to the established roles and feelings of inclusion for current group members.

   How might you sensitize yourself to the underlying concerns that members may have about your presence in the group?

4. Think back to some recent time when you've set goals for yourself.

   What was helpful for you in clarifying those goals? How did you find resources that assisted you in clarifying your goals?

5. For goals that you've been able to attain in recent years, what factors do you think contributed most to your success in reaching them? Support from others? Sheer perseverance? Wise plan of action?

6. What principal emotions tend to be stirred in you upon entering a new group? What thoughts are likely to accompany these emotions? How do you react to these thoughts and emotions? Do you act or react in certain ways in order to deal with any discomfort?

CHAPTER 6

LEADING STRUCTURED GROUP SESSIONS

Just like a well-built vehicle, a properly designed structured exercise can take the group anywhere you want—except that you need the key to turn its engine on. This chapter hands you that key—a method of conducting and processing structured exercise—that starts the ignition, sending the group off down the road.

MANDATED GROUPS: HOW TO MAKE THEM WORK

Most group therapists, green or seasoned, dread the thought of leading groups made up of mandated members. Yet, as Jacob and Schimmel (2013) state, "people don't mind being led if they are led well" (p. 8). Mandated members can be led well, if we have a firm grasp of the realities of mandated groups and, at the same time, a suitable method of working into the needs and hopes that they hold dear.

A Number of Challenging Populations, to Begin With

Mandated groups typically consist of the following populations:

- Students with behavioral or academic problems
- Employees with certain issues, such as anger management issues
- Partners facing an imminent end to a relationship: break-up or divorce
- Child abuse or domestic violence offenders
- People in substance abuse/addiction treatment programs with possible criminal offenses, such as DUIs or drug possession

Challenging, to begin with, the aforementioned often raise their resistance just as expected when forced to attend a group setting (Snyder & Anderson, 2009).

On top of this, several factors, as depicted in the following sections, also play a part on their resistance.

Still in the Precontemplation Stage—Unaware and Unwilling

The first roadblock is that many group members deny having a problem or a need to change. Fitting them into the Transtheoretical Model of Change (Prochaska, DiClemente, & Norcross, 1992), these members are squarely in the precontemplation stage. Even those aware of the need for change are seldom willing to make any significant sacrifices for the change (Hagedorn, 2011; Hagedorn & Hirshhorn, 2009).

Distrust of the System—Reluctance to Open Up

To the clients, a mandated group often represents the very institution—"the system"—that ordered them to attend. For example, mandated students may perceive the group as the school's "punishment" for whatever wrong they may have committed. Group leaders are pitted in conflicting roles (Kupers, 2005)—as therapists who champion confidentiality and trust, and conversely, as reporters of client "progress" to the school administration (Miller & Rollnick, 2012).

As a result, confidentiality—the bedrock of a trusting client-therapist relationship—is compromised (Meyer, Tangney, Stuewig, & Moore, 2014). It is no wonder that mandated clients generally feel suspicious, anxious, and defensive (Osborn, 1999). This inherent distrust leads to reluctance to open up.

In one study, a woman stated that opening up in her mandated group was uncommon (Cantora, Mellow, & Schlager, 2016). Another client in the same study stated, "I couldn't care less, to be honest. I'm just doing it because I have to. I'm not looking for help. And none of us really want to hear it neither. Like everybody in there really just wants to get it over with" (Cantora et al., 2016, p. 1025).

The Group Process Being Questioned

With this atmosphere of mistrust, the group process will undoubtedly be questioned (Osborn, 1999). The questioning may appear indirectly, in the form of *not* being present *mentally and emotionally* or directly, in the form of sulking, silence, complaining, or defensiveness.

Some will challenge your leadership by defying you, transferring their anger toward you or accusing you of conspiring with the authorities; others will view the group as a complete waste of time, a total interference to their daily life.

No wonder so many group leaders panic at the mere thought of leading mandated groups!

The Failure of the Confrontational Approach

One approach that has been previously used, but proved ineffective, is a confrontation. Confrontation is typically used to tear down a mandated client's resistance or denial, especially when blaming, minimization, or rationalization is involved (Taft & Murphy, 2007). For example, the widely adopted multidisciplinary Duluth Model, designed to address domestic violence, staunchly uses confrontation in the face of resistance in order to increase client accountability (Levesque, Velicer, Castle, & Greene, 2008; Pender, 2012).

This type of confrontation can come across to mandated clients as an attack, leading to even greater defensiveness and a damaged therapeutic alliance. Indeed, the Substance Abuse and Mental Health Services Administration (SAMHSA) argues that a confrontational approach cannot help but fail in treating substance abusers (Center for Substance Abuse Treatment, 2005). Velasquez, Stephens, and Ingersoll (2006) agree that confrontation only serves to promote increased resistance of mandated clients.

Rays of Hope

Given the reputation of mandated groups, a majority of leaders have been advised to develop a thick skin and not take it personally when mandated members downpour them with negativity (Schimmel & Jacobs, 2014). This, of course, is not a realistic expectation.

Kelly's field report providing a ray of hope—Interestingly enough, an interview by Enos (2006) with John F. Kelly, associate director of addiction research at Massachusetts General Hospital, shows that even for mandated clients, change is possible and may actually come sooner than expected. In the interview (Enos, 2006), Kelly surprises us with many of his field observations:

- Mandated clients can actually benefit from treatment *from the start.*
- Treatment doesn't have to be voluntary to be effective.

- Interaction among members in group treatment led to decreased *arrest rates* for mandated clients.
- The arrest rates remained at a low-level post treatment whereas *employment rates* increased.

Another positive field report—With the help of several grants, a group therapist in Chicago and his colleagues have been able to provide group services for court-mandated clients. These clients have either been convicted of domestic abuse or a DUI and other substance abuse problems. The group therapist indicates that when skillfully led, *these groups are actually quite productive* because *members eagerly bond*, *openly* discuss their experiences, and whole-heartedly support and encourage one another. Indeed, most members are far from hostile or uncooperative (Petras, personal communication, 2016).

These field reports further prove the idea that "people don't mind being led if they are led well" (Jacob & Schimmel, 2013, p. 8). The key to success with these particular populations is to engage, establish rapport, and earn their trust (Cantora et al., 2016).

Member Preparation Through Motivational Interviewing

In order to lead well with mandated members, it is necessary to kick start the therapeutic relationship through a special kind of member preparation. Preparing members prior to beginning the group gives mandated clients the readiness they need for therapeutic work (Behroozi, 1992).

Enter motivational interviewing!

Motivational Interviewing (MI) was created by Miller and Rollnick (2012) as a client-centered approach to helping people with addiction problems who are *ambivalent about change*. The critical element of MI is to highlight what the client values in his or her life and contrast it with the client's behaviors.

Motivational interviewing can be used *during intake* (Horvath & Symonds, 1991; Pinsoff, 1994) to boost client readiness. After MI, leaders can apply structured communication activities to increase group interaction.

Though effective during intake, MI is *not suitable for group interaction* since it relies on *individual-focused techniques* to address a client's sense of ambivalence. If used in a group session, MI techniques can reduce group therapy into individual counseling, albeit with multiple clients together (Lundahl & Burke, 2009). Research finds that groups using motivational interviewing as the primary approach are less effective in achieving treatment goals (Lundahl & Burke, 2009).

Allow Venting, Avoid Lecturing

During the first quarter of the first session, providing mandated members an opportunity to vent their frustration and anger is often an effective way to take care of their negative feelings (Schimmel & Jacobs, 2014). However, be prepared to practice detached engagement during venting, lest you react to the negativity. This initial stage often tests our patience but is a necessary step in allowing for more productive sessions.

In the first session, avoid going over the ground rules or lecturing on the dangers of whatever destructive behaviors that have been brought to the group. Lecturing may deter and bore group members already frustrated and angry about being mandated to attend group (Schimmel & Jacobs, 2014).

Be Active and Use Well-Designed Structured Activities

Prepare to use an active leadership style when leading mandated groups. If you are under the impression that the group will carry itself, you are in for a rude awakening: the session will fall apart, and you will end up frustrated and miserable. Echoing this sentiment, Schimmel and Jacobs (2014) warn that those who wishfully think that they can put the responsibility of the group session on mandated group members will be in dire straits.

To be an active leader for a mandated group is to carefully design certain *structured activities*—communication activities that provide you with a sense of control, that engage the members, and that draw something out of even the most resistant members. This highly structured environment can also prevent mandated clients from *playing out disruptive behaviors* in the group (Thylstrup & Hess, 2011).

Keep an Eye on the Phases

Not all structured exercises are made equal for all phases of the group. Using structured sessions with each group phase in mind allows the power of the group to do what individual counseling can only dream of achieving.

For the early phase, choose positive and meaningful topics. In the early phase of the group, it is wise to choose structured communication activities consisting of *positive and meaningful* topics. Positive-focused topics tend to relax members and decrease their defensiveness—the exact effect desired when needing *sufficient time to earn their trust*. When the first two sessions go well, the group atmosphere will lighten up, and members may even look forward to attending group (Enos, 2006).

As a reminder, positivity does not equate with superficiality. Don't let precious group time wear away on members' personal interests, hobbies, sports, movies, TV programs, and other recreations. Chatter amongst members, no matter how positive, contributes little to a productive atmosphere.

In the later phase, mix in more personal topics. When members are even more relaxed in the later stages of the group, it is an opportune time to slowly *mix more personal topics into the positive ones.*

At long last, focus on sensitive issues. When members are trusting enough, you then move on to *the most sensitive issues of all*—the issues that brought them to the mandated group. For example, at this phase, the communication topic for domestic abusers may be "I tend to hit those I love when _____ (fill in the blank)" while for mandated substance abusers, "If I give up drugs, it would mean _____ (fill in the blank)" (Schimmel & Jacobs, 2014).

In closing: Mandated members can be led well, if we have a firm grasp of the realities of mandated groups and, at the same time, a rich knowledge of how to use *structured activities*—communication activities—to provide you with a sense of control, to engage the members, and to meet their needs and hopes.

The following sections demonstrate how structured exercises can maximize the effectiveness of three different group settings:

- Mandated groups
- Psychoeducational groups
- Counseling and therapy group

I. STRUCTURED EXERCISES FOR MANDATED GROUPS

Without a focus, conversations in mandated groups easily derail into storytelling and drunkalogues. With a well-design communication topic, the session becomes engaging and meaningful, providing members with the tools to learn about one another and alleviate boredom. Above all, a group with a communication focus will *meet the requirements of a functional group* expected by agencies or by the legal systems (Schimmel & Jacobs, 2014).

The human brain yearns for novelty, and as leaders of the mandated group, there is no limit to the multitude of structured activities that can be created.

Structured Written Communication Exercises

When using structured communication exercises, the initial exercise can be written. Writing provides an alternative outlet for someone who doesn't want to talk. Further, while listening to what other members wrote, reluctant members may become interested in what others have to say. They may compare their own reactions to those of others and may even read aloud their own, all without the pressure of thinking about what to say (Schimmel & Jacobs, 2014).

Though many thought-provoking communication exercises should be in our toolbox, ready to put to use for any occasion, only one exercise should be used per session (Schimmel & Jacobs, 2014). Avoid using multiple exercises just to fill up a session.

As previously discussed, structured exercises that evoke positive emotions are especially helpful in the initial sessions. An example of one is called the *List*. You can create many varieties with it:

List things that you feel most proud of about yourself.

List persons who are most supportive in your life.

List some of your accomplishments.

List things that you like about yourself.

List three persons who have had the most positive influence on you.

List some unforgettable moments in your life that you wish to go back to.

Tailored Fishbowl Activity

The fishbowl (detailed later in this chapter), also called the inner-outer circle (Schimmel & Jacobs, 2014), is a structured activity that can be tailored for mandated groups. In this structured activity, members slightly more willing to talk sit in the inside circle, while those reluctant to talk sit outside the circle.

As members in the inner circle talk, those outside the circle observe. This partition eliminates the chance that negative energy from reluctant members may spoil the work of those inside the circle. When they are ready to open up, members outside the circle are encouraged to join those inside.

Experiential Exercises

When it comes time for mandated groups to discuss more sensitive issues, leaders can move it one notch up to include *experiential group activities* (Hagedorn, 2011)—activities that have the capacity to normalize the difficulties of change and, at the same time, continue to sidestep client resistance and ambivalence (Miller & Rollnick, 2012).

One such experiential activity is "Writing a Letter to My Substance/Behavior" by Hagedorn (2011). In this exercise, Hagedorn gives members several prompts to which to respond. We have rephrased the prompts as follows:

- My relationship with my drug of choice
- How I feel about saying goodbye
- My reasons for saying goodbye
- The possible negative and positive things about saying goodbye
- The changes that need to occur after I say goodbye
- My level of confidence in making these changes

Members are given 15 minutes to write these letters and then 45 minutes for the group to share their letters aloud as well as to process their reactions and realizations.

Experiential exercises, such as letter writing, allow mandated members to share positive and negative aspects of their behaviors. When faced with their contrasting behaviors, members tend to feel motivated to change. In addition, being a right-brained activity, letter writing can evoke clients' deeply held emotions. In the private space of a letter, clients can express these deep emotions, without feeling pressured to answer questions posed by the group (Hagedorn, 2011).

II. STRUCTURED EXERCISES FOR PSYCHOEDUCATIONAL GROUPS

Psychoeducational groups are frequently the treatment of choice in substance abuse programs, schools, and community mental health agencies. This section discusses psychoeducational groups and how to use well-designed structured activities to increase your success with them.

The Characteristics of Psychoeducational Groups

The general purpose of psychoeducational groups is to

- enhance member knowledge about psychological issues,
- teach skills on how to deal with challenging situations or emotions, and
- provide extra community resources.

Groups in school settings often contain all of these components.

A drastic difference from counseling groups, psychoeducational groups focus neither on the underlying dynamics of members' behaviors (Champe & Rubel, 2012) nor on members' long-term transformations. Clients seeking to restore their interpersonal effectiveness in order to achieve long-term transformations shall be referred to a counseling /therapy group.

Structured Activities and Adolescent Psychoeducational Groups

When it comes to working with groups of adolescents, psychoeducational groups are the foremost treatment of choice (Rose, 2016; Shechtman, 2014). Using structured activities for group discussion, psychoeducational groups assist students in building the basics of specific skills and indirectly repairing certain deficiencies (Johannessen, 2003).

For example, a structured anger management group (Potter-Efron, 2005; Reilly & Shopshire, 2014) uses specially designed structured written exercises to help members build the skills necessary to identify what triggers their anger and how to deal with their anger without acting out.

In the same vein, groups for assertiveness training (Brown, 2011; Miltenberger 2012) use structured exercises to help members look into their faulty assumptions and replace them with correct methods and skills for assertiveness (Corey, 2017).

Due to the educational component, some psychoeducational groups use videotapes, audiocassettes, or lectures as a part of the session. It is acceptable if these educational activities are followed by *facilitated discussion* and *role-playing*—two keys to increasing member interaction and helping members internalize what they have just learned.

Role-Playing in Psychoeducational Group

Role-playing is an integral part of a psychoeducational group. One of the most effective ways for clients to develop skills is by trying out their learned skills in action (Brown, 2011; Hammond & Wyatt, 2005; Miltenberger, 2012). This can involve as few as two people or as many as the situation requires.

Role-playing involves two parts: first, leaders spell out the underlying mechanism of how a skill works (Rose, 2016; Zipora, 2014); second, members choose a specific problematic situation and put their learned skills into action. Combining these two parts ensures that members have the skills down pat.

After role-playing, leaders can request that the group members give each other *feedback* regarding the strengths and weaknesses of their skill execution. Knowing their own strengths and weaknesses in skill execution is imperative for adolescents because they gain understanding best through *practice* and *feedback*.

When guided well, most members should not have difficulty role-playing. Some members, however, might need extra help. For example, members who have *performance anxiety* or *attention deficit issues* may struggle to put skills into action on the spot. It is recommended that you ask these members to write down key phrases on *index cards* as personal reminders—a simple action that helps many members with special needs feel more relaxed about role-playing.

A Structured Exercise Carried Through in a Series of Sessions

Who says that a psychological group cannot go deep? One example that contests this typecast is a model called "Achieving Success Everyday" (Rose & Steen, 2014). Consisting of several components, this structured activity carries a psychoeducational group to a profound place.

In a beginning session, students develop a timeline of powerful experiences from their lives. (This structured activity is also called "Life Line" and can be found in examples near the end of this chapter.) In sharing their timeline, the group members recognize a great deal of *universality* in their *shared struggles* and are able to demonstrate *increased empathy toward one another* as the group moves forward.

In a later session, members identify current stressors and the ways in which they are coping well and are resilient. In yet another session, the members project their timelines into the future, incorporating identified goals and newly developed life skills.

As a result of their interaction through the *series of structured activities*, members' self-reflection greatly increases and their resilience is fostered.

Brazilian Mask-Making Structured Activity

A fun and engaging activity for psychoeducational groups is *Brazilian Mask-Making* (Molina, Monteiro-Leitner, Garrett, & Gladding, 2005). Here members are instructed to *design a mask* from any available materials, such as clay, paper, or even an existing mask.

Once made, members *personify the masks* by telling their own stories *from the perspective of the mask*.

Mask-making is fun and engaging *for young populations*. The mask gives them the opportunity to speak about things they might typically not be forthcoming about.

Colored Candy Go-Around

Another fun and meaningful structured activity for psychoeducational groups is "Colored Candy Go-Around" (Lowenstein, 2011). It is perfectly suited for *young kids*.

In the activity, the leader distributes 10 to 15 candies to all members, instructing them to sort their candy by color. The leader makes sure that *each member receives at least one candy for every color*. Each color requires a specific description of the owner. For example, green calls for a few words describing yourself, purple for ways you have fun, orange for things you'd like to change about yourself, red for things you worry about, and yellow for good things about yourself.

The leader asks one member to pick a color (say, red) and has the rest of the members say how many red candies they have. Let's say that Maria has two red candies; she would then give two responses to the following question from the leader:

What words would you use to describe the things you worry about? [red color represents worry]

Other members then take turns responding to the same question. When finished, another color may be picked out, and the activity continues.

At the end, the group members process what they take home from the activity: what they learned, what surprised them, and how they would work toward making changes or improvements (Lowenstein, 2011). Through processing, these young kids are able to identify areas of improvement that they want to address.

Seeing young kids at such a deep level of open communication and self-learning is something that truly moves us. If kids can do it, adults can, too. It's simply a matter of being well facilitated.

Common Mistakes to Avoid in Leading Psychoeducational Groups

Sad to say, psychoeducational groups in many mental health agencies and school settings often fail to tap into the groups' potential. This failure is caused by misusing psychoeducational groups as *classes* or *lectures*, devoid of member-to-member discussion (Brown, 2011; Corey, 2017; Lothstein, 2014).

Just like anyone else, members of psychoeducational groups have an innate desire for self-expression and engagement, as well as the need to feel heard, affirmed, included, and understood (Chen & Giblin, 2018; Graybar & Leonard, 2005; Maslow, 1943). These needs are even more pronounced when it comes to kids and youth.

When groups are misused as classes or lectures, these universal needs are negated. It is no wonder that kids and youth feel *checked-out* and *unable to sit through* these sessions.

III. STRUCTURED EXERCISES FOR COUNSELING GROUPS

Structured exercises benefit counseling groups as well. Bolstered by a few sessions of such devices in the beginning stage, a counseling group can speed up the pace of trust and connection. This gets the group ready for the upcoming *storming stage* and for its transition into the unstructured format (Berg, Landreth & Fall, 2013). Beyond this, many other benefits await our recognition.

Reducing Member Anxiety

In the beginning, the group experience can seem scary, unpredictable, and ambiguous. It's no surprise that new members of counseling groups are often plagued with anxiety (Fall, 2013; Page & Berkow, 2005; Rutan, Sonte, & Shay, 2014).

A couple of sessions with structured activities can settle nerves, decrease the anxiety of the unknown, and get members at ease with group interaction.

Fulfilling the Needs of Inclusion, Especially for the Introverts

Members' emotional connection to one another is what determines whether a group will gel or not. Members only connect when their need for inclusion is met. A key to fulfilling members' need for inclusion is to make sure that every member has an equal share of floor time, no one monopolizes, and no one gets left out (Mason, 2016).

An easy way to achieve this is by conducting structured communication exercises for a couple of sessions. In particular, these exercises are a big help for *introverts*, easing them into interacting *with those more extroverted and vocal.*

Improving Member Engagement

Increasing member engagement is the key to group success, and structured activities give you an excellent way to engage the entire group. As each person begins to talk, members are given the opportunity to feel more comfortable around each other and learn to trust each other. Trust is critical prior to the more intense encounters of later stages of a counseling group.

In addition, structured activities also lead to cognitive and reflective exploration (Leichtentritt & Shechtman, 2010). This paves the way for insight and cognitive examination that will come in later stages.

Preventing Second-Session Letdown

Beyond the first session, the excitement of sharing may wane. Some members may become reticent about disclosing on a more personal level; while others may expect that the group can quickly bring resolution to their problems. Needless to say, the group cannot live up to these high expectations. This is why during the initial stage of a counseling group, members may experience a *second-session letdown* (Jacobs, Masson, & Harvill, 2002).

Neophyte leaders often find themselves stressed from this letdown because they mistakenly believe that the energy of the first session will carry on through the life of the group. Unprepared, they feel distressed by this change of atmosphere.

Fortunately, using certain structured communication activities will guide the group toward more engaging and personal sharing through the early sessions. In so doing, you will lessen the impact of the letdown and allow the group members to immerse themselves into a deeper level of group work.

MISUSE OF STRUCTURED EXERCISES

The key to the success of a structured session is not the exercise itself but the processing that follows the exercise. Unfortunately, structured exercises are often misused in the field of group work. This section addresses pitfalls to steer clear of.

Mistake 1: Doing One Exercise Right After Another

Due to their anxiety or lack of training in group processing, new leaders tend to err by doing one exercise after another. This misuse will deter members or give them the wrong impression that group work is nothing more than gimmicks.

Communication exercises are best used to initiate communication and focus members on certain meaningful topics; they should not be used just to fill time. A false concept in our society is that group is a manufactured, thus phony, environment (Carter, Mitchell, & Krautheim, 2001). This notion is mostly caused and reinforced by those group leaders who overuse structured exercises, taking away members' sense of ownership, authenticity, and autonomy.

Mistake 2: Using Published Structured Activities Without Customization

Some group leaders rely heavily on published structured activities. They accept them wholeheartedly, thinking that if they are in print, they must be effective (Vannicelli, 2014). Those who created the materials could not have possibly considered the special needs and challenges of your particular group members. For example, materials prepared for team-building groups usually don't measure up when applied to members of a highly resistant, mandated group.

Careful examination of published materials is critical in order to determine their usefulness for your members. If these materials are given to you by your agency, it is advisable to select certain ideas from them and then customize them to fit the specific needs of your members.

The Limitation of Structured Exercises

Before deciding to use structured activities, beware of potential setbacks.

No long-term change. Yalom has done extensive research on the effect of structured exercises on group outcomes. Results show that leaders who use multiple exercises are *popular* with their groups. Exercises create *immediate results*, leading members to perceive the leaders as more *competent*, more effective, and more perceptive than those without using many exercises (Yalom & Leszcz, 2005).

However, the long-term outcome shows quite the opposite. Groups that use the most exercises actually have much less positive outcomes and fewer behavior changes. Even when there are changes, they are less likely to be maintained over time.

Crippled group autonomy. Relying heavily on structured exercises inevitably stifles group dynamics, making a group less effective long term. Yalom's research shows that structured exercises quickly open the door on members' expressivity but bypass the anxiety and the difficult stages. This *immediate result* seems fantastic at the time, but it comes with a price. Like a child being rushed into adulthood, the group's autonomy and self-assertion can be crippled.

Stifled interpersonal styles. Structured exercises make it difficult for members' interpersonal styles to emerge and therefore delay the transition to the here-and-now of interpersonal learning. It is no surprise that in their study, Hetzel, Barton, and Davenport (1994) conclude that unstructured sessions are significantly more helpful than structured ones. A reflection by one of the members in their study best illustrates this point, "I feel like the group really took off once we stopped doing exercises" (p. 59).

Less intrinsic rewards for leaders. Many untrained paraprofessionals have a fondness for structured exercises and predesigned communication topics because these exercises spare them of challenge and anxiety. For a trained group leader, however, leading a structured group consistently provides *less intrinsic reward* because of a lack of depth in interpersonal learning.

The following table provides a visual display of the pros and cons of using structured activities in group sessions.

Table 6.1 The Pros and Cons of Using Structured Communication Exercises

	Pros	Cons
For Leaders	More control over group engagement	Illusion of control
	Greater ability to predict session outcome	Leader stagnation
	Perceived as more competent, more effective, and more perceptive	Seen as using gimmicks
	Less stressful, less challenging, less anxiety-provoking	Loss of leader personal growth; *less gratifying*
For Members	Bypassing the anxiety; no ambiguity in group interaction	Loss of spontaneity
	Having something to say. No struggles with initiating self-disclosure	Loss of autonomy
	Equal time to share. Less need to deal with someone who dominates	Boredom
For Group Dynamics	No complicated group dynamics to deal with	Interpersonal dynamics or patterns having no chance to emerge
	Group feedback tends to be more supportive	Group feedback tends to be more superficial, less insightful
For Group Outcomes	Group engagement immediately improved	Less depth of interpersonal learning
	Atmosphere change could be immediate	Changes tend to be short-lived

HOW TO CONDUCT STRUCTURED EXERCISES

The general consensus among group specialists is to use structured exercises as little as possible. However, as Hetzel et al. (1994) state, a *few* structured exercises, especially during the initial sessions, can provide the catalyst for group cohesion. If you decide to include a structured exercise in your early group sessions, consider the procedures detailed below.

Introduce the Exercises

The first step is to introduce the exercise and explain its purpose:

In a minute, I am going to ask the group to do an exercise. This exercise will help all of us get in touch with our thoughts and feelings about people that have greatly impacted us.

This exercise will help us gain some insight about our selves and about each other. We will take about 8 minutes to complete the writing portion of the exercise, and then we will spend the rest of the session sharing what we learned.

Are there any questions before we begin?

Conduct the Exercise One Step at a Time Without Preview

The second step is to guide the group in carrying out the activity. Don't go over every procedure at once, lest members become worried about missing out. On the contrary, when you guide them one step at a time, you *pique their curiosity* about what is to come.

To begin this activity, I am going to pass out paper and pencils to everybody. [wait] Ok, now please draw a circle, not too big and not too small, on your paper. [wait]

Now, on the inside of the circle, please write or draw the people in your life whom you get most emotional support from. You have about 3 minutes to do this. [wait until members are finished]

Ok, it has been about 3 minutes. If you need more time, please let me know.

Now on the outside of the circle, please write or draw the people in your life from whom you wish to get emotional support from but have had difficulty getting it. You also have about 3 minutes to do this. [wait until members are finished]

By and large, *leaders do not participate in an exercise* because it might ignite feelings, thoughts, or unfinished business that will inhibit the leader from giving their full attention to the group members.

HOW TO PROCESS AFTER STRUCTURED EXERCISES

The processing of the exercise can make or break your group session (Delucia-Waack, 2009; Jones & Robinson III, 2000; Skudrzyk et al., 2009). With this in mind, a leader should not leave it to chance but thoroughly work on processing what comes out in the structured exercise. How will the leader go about doing the process? To answer this question, the following section proposes a working model and its principles.

Avoid Dry Reports on the Content Level

The first principle of processing is to avoid dry reports on the content level. To process something means *to attend to* or *sort out* what has been brought forth by an experience. In a group, processing can extract insights, new perspectives, and meanings from an activity.

This action sounds abstract and may be subject to misunderstanding. For example, some group leaders mistake *content reporting* for *processing*. This misperception is exemplified by the reflection of a new group leader:

> I was pleased with the way I smoothly conducted the structured exercise. However, in terms of the processing portion, the group fell flat. I thought I was helping the group process, but perhaps I was mistaken. By having the group report their written content, they went into a story-telling mode, and I could not make a crack on it.

Here is a tip to avoid dry reports: Ask your members to *put their paper aside* or *under their seat* after they are done writing. This way, members will have neither the convenience nor the temptation to look down and read their writing.

Good Materials for Processing

The second principle of processing is to give members hints on materials for a productive processing portion. For example, the following are good materials for processing:

- Sensations stirred *inside of them* during the exercise
- *Feelings and thoughts triggered by the exercise*

- *Realizations or discovery about themselves* through the exercise
- What about others' sharing that struck a chord with them

The Working Model: Playing With Common Themes

An effective working model of processing is to play with common themes. An effective group leader needs to take on the following responsibilities, much like a shepherd to his sheep:

- To tend, feed, and herd the group in the processing portion
- To allow the highest degree of autonomy for the group to discover meanings from their own experiences

Playing with common themes allows the leader to achieve the previous and following tasks:

- To provide enough structure for a new group to get orientated
- To afford opportunities for members to build a sense of connection
- To allow members maximum freedom for self-expression and self-discovery

This way of processing quite resembles the basic-level unstructured group (see Chapter 8), with one major difference: In the structured group, the leader uses a structured exercise to set up the stage for members to jump into processing immediately, while in the unstructured group, the leader uses none.

Initiate the Processing

The first step of the processing portion is simply to initiate it. If the group is new, a bit of instruction will go a long way:

Now we are going to move on to the bulk of the session, which is the processing part. I would like each of you to please put your paper under your seat; let your hands go free. Now close your eyes for 2 minutes and think about what you realized, learned, or discovered about yourself, your belief system, your world view, your self-talk, your coping style, and your relationships, as a result of this exercise.

Next,

> OK, if you are ready, please open your eyes and feel free to share. We are *neither taking turns nor focusing on one member at a time*. We are going to process whatever topics emerge along the way. Who would like to start?

Pick up the First Member's Core Message and Spin It Off

A member may take your offer and go first. The disclosure may turn out too abstract or too brief. Try to draw out some rudiments of the story. Warmly affirm members' every effort of self-disclosure. Listen deeply to the core message of each story. When you get a grasp of the message, offer the core concern to the group:

> [To the whole group] From what Dan shared, it seems that this exercise brings up feelings that he has struggled with for quite some time. Deep down, he feels like he is never good enough for anyone. I wonder how the feeling of "I am never good enough" strikes a chord with you?

Spin a Common Theme off to the Group and See How It Gains Traction

As the group chimes in to relate to the issue you just offered, they will discuss it back and forth, zigzagging here and there. From their collective sharing, you may pick up a common theme, such as "self-doubt," "disconnection," or something else. You will then spin it off to the group again.

> [To the group] From what a few members have just shared, it seems like *feeling disconnected* [key phrase] is *a common experience* among them. I wonder if this *feeling of disconnect* [key phrase] has come up in your life, too?

This common thread may or may not gain traction. Play around with it, and don't become attached to the outcome. Continue to listen, and you will find another common theme—for example "feeling flawed." You spin it off to the group, just the same.

[To the group] From some of your stories, it appears that many of us see ourselves as *flawed*; leading us to *hide our true self or compromise our standards*. I wonder, *what memories come up for you* surrounding the theme of *being flawed*?

Some members may respond to this new common theme; others may connect it to the previous two themes; still, others may go astray to a completely different topic. Don't attempt to control this.

From there, you might pick up yet another common theme. Again, spin it off to the group:

[To the group] A theme I am hearing from several members just now sounds like this, "Damn it. I have worked on this for 25 years, and I cannot believe I am still so easily triggered by it." I am wondering how this theme is striking a chord with you.

Surprisingly, this common theme gained traction big time. The whole group perked up and became completely immersed in a deep and intimate discussion.

Allow Improvised Responses to Play at "the Edge of Chaos"

The processing part of a structured group is playful in a sense. Just like *an unrehearsed jazz ensemble*, as one tune emerges, other musicians join in on the beat. Another tune emerges, inviting another synchronization. Just when harmony dominates the melody, out of the blue comes something contradictory, causing a bit of disarray. Yet, born out of the disarray, something emerges that takes our breath away.

As such, group processing is never neat or linear but rather "ever messy and muddy" as so lamented by a new group leader. Underneath the muddiness may hibernate a creative force that can burst through the hard topsoil in due time, giving birth to a new plant. Long fascinated by chaos theory, I (Mei) am exhilarated to see its working principles take effect in group processing. According to chaos theory, "the edge of chaos" (Waldrop, 1992, p. 12) pulsates the most adaptive and creative force in a living system. This very working principle is alive and kicking in the group processing.

Common Themes Associated With Reactive Emotions

A saying (originated from Shakespeare) goes like this, "There is a method to the madness." Upon careful examination, there is an amazing order to the seemingly disordered array of issues that members presented. Under this system, we can simplify members' presenting issues into two genres of common themes.

One type of common theme deals with certain universal emotions, reactive in nature. These *reactive emotions* are called *secondary emotions* (Greenburg, 2008; Greenburg & Pascual-Leone, 2006; Johnson, 2004). Among them, we often hear frustration, guilt, anger, discouragement, worry, anxiety, and so on.

Reactive emotions are typically elicited by certain *recurrent life struggles or themes* and are significant enough to warrant group processing. These themes may include the following:

- Isolation, disconnection
- Being unheard
- Being unappreciated
- Not fitting in, misplacement
- Not getting needs met in relationships
- Discrimination, oppression

When spun off to group discussion, these common themes can easily propel group discussion. Most members have much to talk about and feel a sense of relief when others can relate.

Common Themes Associated With Primary Emotions

Another type of common theme deals with certain life experiences that are less reflected upon because they often illicit universal, vulnerable, deep-seated emotions. Referred to as *primary emotions* (Greenburg, 2008; Greenburg & Pascual-Leone, 2006; Johnson, 2004), they may include shame, unworthiness, loneliness, and so on.

Themes associated with these primary emotions can often be sourced back to a life experience associated with *deep-rooted and attachment-related deprivations or wounds*. They may include the following:

- Abandonment/rejection
- Being unwanted

- A sense of being flawed
- Broken trust
- Loss of self, emptiness
- Betrayal

The discussion among members may bounce back and forth between these two types of common themes, and this is precisely the way it works. There is no set way to have group members follow a neat sequence. From outside looking in, the processing seems to flow effortlessly. From inside looking out, only the therapist knows how much intuition and deep listening it takes to pick up the themes and how much concentration it takes to corral the group discussion around the themes.

Spin a Coping Strategy off and See Whether It Gains Traction

As members continue their discussion surrounding common themes in an intimate way, coping methods naturally emerge. Some are healthy, while others are quite maladaptive. The maladaptive style of coping eventually causes more suffering:

- Wearing a mask; hiding the true self
- Building walls
- Denying
- Escaping into social media, food, shopping, substances, sex, work, or so on
- Blaming
- Complaining
- Passive aggressiveness
- Being confrontational
- Overaccommodating
- Placating

If you want to steer the group toward reflecting on a coping style that you detect, you may say:

[To the whole group] From the sharing of several members, I hear that many of us "build walls" as a way of coping with the pain of not being appreciated for who we are. Who else would like to share a similar coping style?

Or

[To the whole group] From some of your stories, it seems that some of us cope with a sense of *shame* or a sense of being *flawed*, by *hiding our true self* [the coping strategy]. I wonder, what other ways you cope with feelings of *shame* or *being flawed*?

Collectively reflecting on one coping style has the power of *uniting the group in a profoundly honest place, which group members would not have done alone.*

Extract Meaning From Difficult Life Experiences

Upon discussing their coping styles, some members will start to talk about an alternative path they are taking. This presents an opportunity for the group to head in a new direction. If the group has not yet picked it up, you, as the leader, can bring it up to see what may happen:

[To the whole group] When Amelia talked about her life-long pattern of being a caretaker and her way of overcoming it, she mentioned that she shifted her focus from the end product to the process—every minute of it. When she said that, I saw sparks glisten in the eyes of many members. Something new and meaningful seemed to awaken in you guys. Who would like to share what this new thing is?

Or

[To the whole group] Jessa seemed to say that even though her parents' rejection still causes her pain and internal turmoil, it does not define her or dictate her destiny. She is exactly where she needs to be on her journey. When she said that, I saw many of your faces light up. Would you care to share what awakened within you just now?

As members take part in the discussion, and as they extricate meanings from their difficult life experiences, a sense of spirituality or transcendence often fills the room.

It may take one session of muddled processing to get members to arrive at the other side of the shore, or it may take multiple sessions. But when they do, you will know that your group has struck their therapeutic gold.

OTHER CONSIDERATIONS DURING PROCESSING

Disclosing personal, emotional, or intimate aspects of themselves in a group can leave members feeling vulnerable and exposed. A safe environment must be secured in order for members to feel supported and validated when they disclose. When ineffective communication styles emerge during processing, the leader will need to intervene.

Know When to Give Space and When to Invite

If a member is slow to participate, give him or her space and time to observe. On the other hand, if a member is emotional or crying, attention should be given to him or her immediately. You may ask the group members if they will stop and stay with the person's emotions for a moment. If the member is willing, you may briefly process the emotions:

> Thank you for sharing your experiences with the group, Katie. I see that you are fighting back some emotions right now. From what you just shared, I am not sure what is triggering them for you. I wonder if we could stay with these emotions a bit and you can help us understand them if you are ready.

Deal With a Member's Excessive Questioning

A member, Jenny, is asking a series of questions centered on a third party, which leads to excessive storytelling. This is a good time to intervene:

> Jenny, thank you for asking questions about James's experience of being betrayed by his friend. I think it would be helpful for James if you shared your own personal experience surrounding this topic.

Handle a Member's Invalidating Comments

Another member, Apple, is trying to provide supportive comments. Yet, her comments have a problem-solving or rescuing tone to them and end up invalidating or discounting the other member's feelings or needs. You may intervene as follows:

As Apple was making comments to Katie about how to communicate with her parents, I notice several facial expressions and body movements occurring within the group. I wonder what it was about Apple's comment that was causing this stir? Would anyone like to share your reactions or observations?

When a Member Is Talking "About" Another Member

Tony responded to your invitation by talking "about" Apple indirectly, as if she was not in the room. To this, you may intervene as follows:

Tony, since Apple is in this room, it would be more personable if you could address her directly, rather than talking about her. Would you mind repeating what you just said but this time say it directly to Apple, using an "I-you" statement?

When a Member Is Self-Referencing

Andre tries to validate James's experience by relating a story of his own, but he rambles on without relating to James's underlying needs, struggles, or feelings. To this, you may intervene:

Andre, I appreciate your kindness in trying to help James feel less alone with your own story. Would you please narrow it down a bit by naming one or two feelings, needs, or thoughts through which James might be able to feel a connection with you?

VARIOUS EXAMPLES OF STRUCTURED COMMUNICATION EXERCISES

This section presents structured communication exercises we have used in group settings over the years. These exercises work effectively in promoting group interaction. However, the level of depth that the group will reach is dependent on your methods of processing.

How to Choose Structured Exercises

When choosing a structured exercise, please make sure to match the intensity level of the exercise with that of your group. The emotional intensity of the group's interactions tends to directly increase with group development. Exercises that lack intensity may frustrate members who are ready for high-intensity interactions (Corey, Corey, Callahan, & Russell, 1992; Jones & Robinson III, 2000).

Also, please consider choosing structured activities that help the group *see the inner world of a member*. This is particularly important for introverts in the group.

Among all the structured communication exercises, written ones tend to be the most versatile, engaging, and useful. They are especially handy in the beginning stages of a group for members who feel nervous having to perform on the spot. They include sentence completions, lists, two-paper exercises (e.g., one-and-another, inside-and-outside), and expressiveness.

Team-Building Exercises Not Included Here

Some team-building exercises can be effective in increasing group bonding. For example, *icebreakers* help members get to know one another in a non-threatening way. This is especially true in the first session as it can be quite intimidating for a lot of people.

Others, like *physically engaging exercises, team-oriented exercises,* and games, are useful for groups with *teens* because these exercises can nurture collaboration, trust, and respect. Others, like wilderness activities and trust-building games, may help members develop confidence in their peers and in themselves.

Due to space limitation, we are unable to present examples of team-building exercises.

26 Examples of Structured Communication Exercises

1. Sentence Completion

In this exercise, you make up a sentence stem and leave the rest of the sentence blank for group members to complete. Examples of sentence stems are as follows:

When I enter a new group, I feel _____.

In a group, I am most afraid of _____.

When people first meet me, they _____.

I trust those who _____.

I regret _____.

If I had to do it all over again, I would _____.

2. Mannequin Exercise

I would like to have everybody think of an important person in your life who you *look up to* or *feel close to*. We will pass around a small wooden figure called a mannequin. When you hold the mannequin in your hand, please use it to connect to this particular person in your life. Then, have the mannequin face the group, and speak for the mannequin as to what this person would say <u>to the group</u> about you. Next, turn the mannequin toward you, and speak for the mannequin on what this person would say <u>to you</u> about you.

3. Letter of Gratitude

Please answer the following question on a piece of paper: If you could write a letter of gratitude to someone in your life, to whom would that be, and what would you write about?

4. Lists

In this exercise, you ask the group members to make a list. Examples of lists that focus on positive attributes may look like the following:

List what you feel most proud of about yourself.

List the most supportive people in your life.

List three people who have influenced you greatly in your life.

List some of your accomplishments.

List three decisions that you have made that have changed your life.

List things that you like about yourself.

List some unforgettable moments in your life that you wish you could relive.

Examples of lists that describe life stressors may look like the following:

List things that are stressful for you.

List feelings that you have felt most often recently.

List recent problems that concern you the most.

5. One-and-Another

Variation 1:

On the first piece of paper, draw a picture of your face that reflects how you think <u>it appears to other people</u>. Please remember how you feel on the inside as you are drawing this picture. [wait until members complete] Now, on a separate piece of paper, please draw another picture of your face that reflects <u>how you actually feel</u> [give enough time for members to complete].

Variation 2:

On one piece of paper, draw a picture or write down key words to illustrate where you <u>actually are now</u>, that is, how you are feeling and what your current life situation is. Don't be concerned about being artistic. Just let your pen lead you! [wait until members finish] Now, on another piece of paper, draw or write how you <u>wish</u> to be in the future [give enough time for members to complete].

Variation 3:

On the front side of the paper, please write a sentence or draw a picture to describe <u>where you are</u> in your life. On the back side of the paper, please describe <u>where you want to be</u>. <u>Then describe what small changes you need to act upon</u> to help yourself arrive at that desired version of yourself. (This is a good exercise for the beginning sessions of an adolescent group.)

6. Inside-and-Outside

Inside-and-outside can help members discover who they are and what their lives are about.

Variation 1: Attachment figures

> Please draw a circle, not too big, nor too small on your sheet of paper. Inside the circle, please write or draw significant people in your life with whom you feel comfortable being your authentic self and with whom you feel comfortable turning to when you want to talk about things that are on your mind. You have about 3 minutes to do so.
>
> Now, on the outside of the circle, please write or draw significant people in your life with whom you wish you could be your authentic self but have difficulty doing so and people with whom you tend to hold back from when you really need to talk about the things on your mind. You have about 3 minutes.

(*Notes*: This exercise has been able to generate intense discussions filled with tears and laughter for three consecutive sessions, for a group of 10 adult members. One 90-minute session of processing does not typically complete the processing. Subsequent sessions are needed to finish processing. It can start with a one-by-one processing and organically shift to unstructured, spontaneous processing. From what I (Mei) have witnessed, *attachment-based* topics bring up some of the most powerful and charged emotions in our lives.

Variation 2: Pride/inadequacy

> On your sheet of paper, draw a big circle. Think of things in your life that you are proud of, and then write or draw these things inside the circle. [wait for members to complete] Now, think of things in your life that bring you a feeling of uneasiness and inadequacy, and then write or draw those things outside the circle.

Variation 3: Control

> On your sheet of paper, draw a circle, not too big, not too small. Within the circle, please draw or write things in your life that you feel are within your control. Now, on the outside of the circle, please draw or write things in your life that you do not appreciate and feel are out of your control.

During processing, it is important to ask members to define what control means to them and what events in their life have impacted their definition of control.

Variation 4: Safety/fear

Within the circle, please draw or write things in your life that you feel safe and secure about. On the outside of the circle, please draw or write the biggest fears you currently have in your life.

7. Three-Columns Exercise

"Think of a specific memory from your childhood that you experienced that involved your family of origin. This moment should be one that you feel was not resolved.

Reflect on the items in the three columns (see Table 6.2), and write down your reflection.

If you have time, write on the back of the paper about what you have learned from this activity."

Table 6.2 Three-Columns Exercise

Feelings I Could Express	Feelings I Couldn't Express	How These Relate to the Goal That I Am Working on in This Group

8. Expressiveness

On the sheet of paper, write down some of your hopes and fears surrounding being a part of this group.

Maybe each of you can take a few minutes to think of an animal with which you identify. Then write a few sentences to describe how this animal deals with change and uncertainty.

Other expressive exercises involve storytelling, poetry, drawing, and music. They all have the capacity to act as catalysts for members to open up and express their inner experiences that might otherwise be kept hidden.

9. Fishbowls

In Fish Bowl exercises (Hensley, 2002; Kane, 1995), the group forms two circles in the room: one is a tight <u>inner circle</u> in the middle of the room, and the other a loose <u>outer circle</u> that wraps around the inner circle.

First round

Doing the Exercise: You ask a few volunteers to sit in the inner circle and openly discuss an issue that either you or the group chooses. Members of the outer circle will quietly observe what is happening in the inner circle.
There can be many different ways to form the circles in the fishbowl exercise. You can design the inner and outer circles based on gender, race, presenting issues, or position on certain issues.

Processing: Once completed, ask the members of the inner circle to reflect on what they have learned about themselves through the open discussion. Most importantly, how they experienced being watched like a fish in a fishbowl.

Engaging the outer circle: Then ask members in the outer circle to provide feedback to the inner circle about what they have observed. Most importantly, ask the outside people to reflect on what they have learned about themselves as observers. Simply hearing what others have to say often helps increase the observers' awareness about their own perspectives.

Second round

Changing roles: If suitable, you can have the circles switch. Those in the inner circle will now sit on the outside as observers and vice versa. This new inner circle will discuss the same topics as did the first inner circle.

Processing: Reflection and feedback portions follow the completion of changing roles.

To conclude: Fishbowl exercises are particularly useful for groups where members are still *hesitant* to openly discuss sensitive issues. Sitting in the outer circle, members have the freedom to observe others in action while silently looking inward and contemplating their own issues. For example, in a mandated group, you could place the most resistant members in the outer circle first, so that they can slowly warm up to the idea of sharing with the group.

10. My Family

Topics centering around family are usually sensitive for many people, so it's best to use this exercise when the group has already been with each other for at least two sessions. The introduction of this exercise is as follows:

Please look at the sheet of paper that we have handed out. Printed on the paper are three questions we would like you to answer.

1. The family member I am most similar to is _____.

   And this is why _____.

2. The family member I am least like is _____.

   And this is why _____.

3. If I could openly and honestly speak with any family member without ANY chance of hurting his or her feelings, I would choose _____.

   And this is what I'd tell him or her _____.

We have 8 minutes to complete this exercise. After everyone has completed the activity, each group member will have the option to share with the group. Are there any questions before we begin?

11. Four Relationships

Here are 4 small pieces of paper with different colors. Each of you will take all four pieces of paper. First, think of four relationships in which you would like <u>to be supported differently</u>. For example, it could be a relationship you have with a family member, friend, significant other, co-worker, supervisor, or so on. On the top of each piece of paper, write down one of your names, and underline it.

Second, under each name, please write down the kind of support that you would like to get from that specific relationship. For example, "I would like to him or her to listen and understand me better."

12. Life Events and Confidence

First, on a scale of 1 to 10, please rate how confident you feel about yourself. Then, please write down events in your life that have impacted your confidence level.

Variation: Self-esteem

On a scale of 1 to 10, please indicate how you feel about yourself. Then, please write down the factors in your life that have shaped your self-esteem.

13. Life Line With Peaks and Valleys (Also Called Timeline)

In this exercise, you will have an opportunity to chart the peaks and valleys in your life in terms of your confidence and sense of well-being.

I am giving everyone a piece of paper. Please position the paper horizontally. Draw a straight line down the middle of your paper to represent your life line.

Now, recall life events that made you feel happy, full of pride, or proud of yourself. These will be the peaks dotted <u>above</u> the line.

Then, recall any events that made you feel sad, depressed, or unhappy. These will be the valleys dotted <u>below</u> the line.

Remember, this is a time line of your peaks and valleys in your life up until this point, so try to go as far back as you can.

If you can, write down your age next to the dots on the peaks and valleys.

Finally, please connect the dots of the peaks and valleys.

14. Life Episodes Rating

Recall four critical episodes that have occurred in your life. Rate these critical life episodes on a scale of 1 to 10, with 1 being helpless and 10 being in control.

15. Expectations

On the top half of the paper, please describe your self-expectations. As you write, indicate which ones are realistic and which ones are not. On the bottom half, please write down others' expectations of you and whether they are explicitly or implicitly conveyed to you.

16. Caught by Surprise

On a sheet of paper, please describe a life event that most caught you by surprise, either in a positive or negative way.

17. "Who Am I?"

On a sheet of paper, please answer this question: 'Who am I?'

18. Fear in the Hat

This exercise touches on sensitive topics and is, therefore, better used when members have established trust with one another.

I am going to give everyone a paper and pencil. Please don't write your name on the paper. Now, if you don't mind, please write down your answer to the following question:

"What do you fear the most in life?"

Remember that no one will know your answer. OK. I am going to pass around a hat, and you will fold your paper into a unique shape and throw it into the hat.

Now, I will pass the hat around again. Please draw a paper that is *not* yours.

Good, now each of you has another person's paper without knowing who this person is. I would like to have each of you read the fear written on that paper <u>and reflect on how this person might be feeling inside</u>.

Variation: Secrets in the Hat

What's a secret that you have that you feel you cannot go to anyone with?

Benefits of this exercise:

Putting one's problem in a hat and having someone else read it out loud and reflect on it could potentially afford the person the opportunity to detach from the problem and hear it afresh in someone else's voice. This gives the person a chance to look at himself or herself from the outside and possibly receive some new and helpful insights.

19. Inside and Outside Discrepancy Exercise

This exercise motivates members to reflect on a past experience in which they created a *false sense of self* by not expressing their true emotions. It also asks members to reflect on *how others responded to the false self*. This exercise has the power to inspire people to be more real and to focus on the heart of their issues.

Table 6.3   Inside and Outside Discrepancy Exercise

(1) Situation	(2) Inside feeling
(3) Outside appearance to others	(4) Discrepancy between Box 2 and Box 3, and the impact of this discrepancy on your life

Write down a situation in which you experience stress and grief.

Now, name some inner feelings you have when you experience this situation. "Inside I feel _____."

Now, write how you appear to others during this situation. "On the outside, I appear as if _____." Please use feeling words as well as observable behaviors.

Now, think about the impact that the discrepancy between Box 2 and Box 3 has had on your physical self, your behavior, and your emotional self.

20. Four-Box Exercise

Variation 1: Hurtful and Grateful Events

Table 6.4   Hurtful and Grateful Events Exercise

(1) Hurtful event	(2) Your wish in this event
(3) Grateful event	(4) Why this event touched your heart

To begin this activity, please use the paper and pencils we just passed out, and fold your paper once horizontally and once vertically to create 4 boxes (demonstrate the folding).

Now, please think of a time when someone in your life hurt you in some way. Think of a specific event and when and where it happened. In the top left box, please briefly write down what the other person said or did that was so hurtful.

Now, underneath your description, in the bottom left box, write down what that person could or should have said to make this memory less painful for you.

Next, think of a time when someone in your life did something that made you feel grateful, special, or appreciated. In the top right box, please briefly write down what the other person said or did that was so meaningful.

Next, in the bottom right box, write down what made this memory so meaningful to you at this point in your life and why this event touched your heart.

Remember that there are no events that are too big or too small to have an impact. Trust your instincts and go with the first memory that comes to mind.

Variation 2: Hurt and Moving On

Table 6.5 Hurt and Moving on Exercise

(1) The event that hurt me	(2) How has it impacted the way I am today?
(3) What would need to change inside of me to be able to move on?	(4) How does this relate to my group therapy goal?

In Box 1, please write an event that hurt you.

In Box 2, please write how it impacted the way you are today.

We have about 3 minutes to work on these two boxes.

Now in Box 3, please write what would need to change inside of you to be able to move on.

In Box 4, please write how this relates to your group therapy goal.

We have about 3 minutes to work on these two boxes.

21. Letter Writing to a Person With Unfinished Business

On the sheet of paper attached to the clipboard, please use the next 10 minutes to write a letter to someone in your past or present, to whom you have some unexpressed feelings and realizations toward.

These unexpressed feelings and realizations are usually related to some unfinished business that you have with that person. When there is only 1 minute left, I will give you a signal to wrap up. Any questions?

22. Intimacy

On the sheet of paper, please define intimacy in your own way. Then please answer the following questions:

"What intimacy issues are you currently struggling with?"

"What blocks your intimacy with others in your life?"

23. Internalized Oppression

This exercise may suit LGBQT members who have had difficulties in their coming-out process.

First, on the top half of the paper please write down a list of negative things that you have heard *from others* regarding a member of the LGBQT community.

Now, on the bottom half of the paper write down what negative messages on the above list that *you have said about yourself*.

Finally, on the back of the paper write down how this internalized oppression has impacted and reinforced your sense of self-worth.

24. Ranked Position by Perceived Life Experience

Before we do this, I ask that from this point forward, you are not to speak until I say otherwise. There should be no talking.

Now, I would like Tom and Tracy (the chosen two members) to <u>sit down</u> right where you are and close your eyes.

For the rest of the group, please stay in a standing position and form a single line over on the other side of the room.

I would like to ask Cassie, Lindsay, and Jack (another chosen three) to take the task of reorganizing the group into perceived age order. Please start with those who you perceive to be the youngest or with the least life experiences at this end of the line and those with the most life experience at that end of the line.

Now, please bring the two members (Tom and Tracy) who are sitting with their eyes closed, into the age order line. Cassie, Lindsay, and Jack, please position yourself in the line as well.

Again, please remember not to make any communication during the whole process.

When the exercise is complete, lead the group in processing their experience using the following question:

How does your participation in this exercise run parallel to that in the relationships of your day-to-day lives, outside of our group?

25. Where I Am in the Group

Please take a minute to review the words and statements in the box located at the bottom of the paper. Then, as honestly as you can, place the words or statements from the box into the appropriate column. Please feel free to include words or statements that do not appear in the box. Try to avoid spending too much time on the task because no one will be passing judgment.

Table 6.6 Where I Am in the Group Exercise

I feel like I have done the following:	I feel like the group has done the following:
I feel like I have not done the following:	I feel like the group has not done the following:

Table 6.7 Where I Am in the Group Exercise

Taking risks	Violating trust
Self-disclosure	Confronting others
Showing empathy	Being confronted
Respecting others	Disclosing thoughts/feelings
Disrespecting others	Feeling connected
Being honest in giving feedback	Feeling disconnected
Listening to the heart of the issue	Being sensitive to my feelings
Tuning into others' feelings and needs	Being open-minded
Being supportive	Taking responsibility and self-initiative
Allowing me time to share	

26. Eye-Gazing Exercise

I would like everybody to stand up and walk around the room in silence for a few seconds. Now, stop. Please turn to the person nearest you. Now, the two of you will look into each other's eyes in silence for 2 minutes. Be present for this experience. [2 minutes pass.]

OK, stop. Step away from each other, and walk around the room again in silence for a few seconds. OK, find the person nearest you, and form a dyad again. Look into each other's eyes in silence for 2 minutes. Again, be present for this experience. [2 minutes pass.]

OK, return to your seat. Let's process how you experience this eye-gazing exercise and what it has stirred inside of you. We are going to process this structured exercise in an unstructured fashion. Who wants to start?

∞∞

In closing: Just like a well-built vehicle, a properly designed structured exercise can take the group anywhere you want—if you have the key to turn its engine on.

Knowing how to play with common themes and knowing how to sort out the reactions and self-realization coming out from the structured exercise, you now have the key—the key that starts the ignition, sending the group off down the road.

With the numerous examples of structured communication exercises as your fuel, with the model of processing as your road map, you can take the group anywhere you want— regardless of whether you are leading a mandated group, a psychoeducational group, or a counseling/therapy group.

CASES IN POINT: PARTICIPANT REFLECTIONS ON STRUCTURED EXERCISES

Case 1: Inside-and-Outside Exercise (Second Session)

Reflection by Tim

The Inside-and-Outside Exercise. Session 2 was a profound session for me. We did a structured activity where I was instructed to draw a circle on a sheet of paper. On the inside of the circle, I was *to write down the names of the people in my life with whom I could be the most authentic and vulnerable. For those who I felt challenged to be authentic with, I was instructed to write their names on the outside of the circle.*

Fear of Vulnerability With Loved Ones. I was both surprised and horrified to see that I placed all of the people to whom I feel the closest on *the outside* of my circle. Someone in the group nailed down my experience saying that it is as if the people on the outside were the "high stakes" people—they are the ones with whom I have the most to lose and with whom I feel the most vulnerable. Consequently, they are the ones I am the most afraid to expose myself to.

Strangers Are Safer. Throughout the years I have bared my soul to people I don't know as well. They are safe; they can't really hurt me or reject me. But the opposite is true about those who I love and care about the most.

Not Feeling Alone in the Group. As the group continued processing, others disclosed that they too struggled with intimacy with those who they love. It seems, and not surprisingly so, that many of my fellow group members struggle with the same fears of being vulnerable and feeling safe with those who they love . . . those with which the stakes are high.

I must say that there is a great deal of comfort in knowing that I am not alone. I knew cognitively that I wasn't alone in such feelings, but it is powerful to physically feel relieved and validated through experiencing the commonality firsthand. Suffice it to say, challenges with intimacy are a theme that is pretty universal.

I also felt a real sense of relief that others, such as Sabrina, were as emotionally expressive as I was. It made me feel not so "out on a limb by myself" when my emotions come out so strongly. Miquel also passionately expressed his frustration with not being heard by his family. I definitely was not the only one with strong feelings and visible emotions.

The Boundary Between Me and My Mother. I am glad that my open and honest sharing helps pave the way for others to do so as well, but I sometimes feel a little overexposed. I am feeling a real need for some self-preservation in order to lessen my feelings of overexposure. Perhaps what I'm really speaking of is finding my boundaries. I'm not really speaking about boundaries in the group, but the boundary between me and my mother.

A Heartfelt Conversation With My Mother After the Session. I want to be able to move some of those on the outside circle into my inner circle. And, I can proudly say that my desire to get authentic with my loved one is outweighing my fears of intimacy now. As a result of the impact from Session 2, I had a very honest, heartfelt conversation with my mother a few days ago. It's been a long time coming, but I know it was necessary.

Two Adults Having an Honest Discussion. Perhaps there was even some Divine timing. This occurred after my group experience as opposed to my trying to force a conversation prematurely. In any case, I felt heard, validated, and understood by my mother. More importantly, I didn't feel like I had to take care of her or manage her feelings like in the past. We were simply two adults having an honest and poignant discussion. That hadn't happened in a long, long, time.

An Honest Conversation With My Partner After the Session. I also had a similarly open, honest, and vulnerable conversation with my partner. While that conversation felt a little more challenging, the end result is that we both felt closer to each other. It's definitely a nice starting place to explore where we want our relationship to go in light of the recent events that I've disclosed to the group.

Buttons Pushed by a Member. I have to say that my buttons are pushed when I hear Miquel giving anyone feedback. His feedback is always precipitated by his own stories. I sometimes feel lost and even impatient with what he is trying to say. I wonder what button is being pushed inside of me? It definitely gives me pause.

Perhaps my feeling of being lost by Miquel's stories is similar to how I have often felt lost in my mother's story. Back when I was a child and adolescent, the focus was always on my mother and what she needed rather than on me. In fact, my mother would report quite willingly and even proudly that "my son raised me." That idea almost elicits a sick feeling inside me.

The Theme of the Parentified Child. Another theme came into our group—children being the caretaker of their parents or being the parent for their siblings. For example, Sabrina caring for her family and not wanting to be another burden after her brother's suicide; Eleshia being the caretaker of her disabled brother as well as her depressed mother; Sala listening to her father's problems for hours on end.

The Theme of the Absent Father. I also never heard Eleshia mention or say much about her father. I wonder where the father is, in all the heaviness within Eleshia's home life. This is another theme that I suspect we will dig deeper into as the weeks go on. I've heard many people struggling with relationships with their fathers. This is a theme that I know is universal . . . the absent father.

I know I definitely have issues with this, and it indeed is the reason that I so readily recognize it in others. Perhaps a better way to name this theme is abandonment.

My Father's Abandonment of Me. My father's abandonment of me has had one of the greatest effects on my self-worth. It leaves me with a feeling and an internal message that says "I don't matter." That feeling of low self-worth molds everything. It affects every area of my life.

I found this group thing fascinating, and I am so glad that I am a part of it.

Case 2: Eye-Gazing Exercise (Fourth Session)

Reflection by Mateo

The Eye-Gazing Exercise. We did an "eye gazing" structured activity in Session 4. I was really surprised by my reaction to the activity; I found that sustained eye contact is deeply unsettling for me. It made me feel extremely vulnerable.

Obsession With Others' Perception of Me. My internal dialogue during the activity centered on my own concerns over how I was being perceived. For example, I kept telling myself to "use open posture" and "stand still." My anxiety during this activity was heightened. If this were a social setting, I would have looked for the first available opportunity to escape.

Trapped in My Own Head and Insecurities. The processing following the structured activity provided me with some interesting insight. For instance, Kate spoke passionately about truly seeing the other person and enjoying the shared connectedness. Hearing her response that was other-centered really opened my eyes to a way of being I had not even considered. This led me to become conscious about how often I miss out on being truly present with another person because I'm so often trapped in my own head and insecurities.

Observation of Others' Coping Patterns. I sense that Toby seems especially vulnerable when sharing personal feelings evoked by the structured activity. Other group members, such as Diego and Brooke, have accurately pointed out that Toby tends to joke when experiencing uncomfortable emotions. Toby acknowledges this pattern and that it extends back to childhood. It gives him a place to hide and feel safe, especially within group settings. I do want to acknowledge that he has greatly decreased the joking behaviors.

A Family That Rarely Showed Emotions. My goal is to remain emotionally open and present, especially in situations where I feel stressed or vulnerable. I think I have made several positive strides in the last few sessions. Earlier, I would become highly uncomfortable in situations where others were experiencing strong negative emotions. I realize that this reaction goes back to my childhood and was reinforced within my family where we rarely showed strong emotions, even within the home.

Open to a New Sense of Connection. This past week, when Brooke was sharing her experiences with her father, I was able to feel not only her emotions but my own emotional reaction as well. Historically, this would have been a very unsettling experience for me. However, in staying present in the moment I felt a sense of connectedness with Brooke that was extremely powerful.

My hope is that I become more aware of my own barriers to interpersonal intimacy. This means that I need to worry less about the ways in which I am perceived and instead focus on truly understanding (and honoring) the person who is in front of me. This also means a willingness to open not just my mind but heart and soul, too. I am actually very excited for this.

Case 3: Outward Persona and Inner Reactions (Fourth Session)—Leader Reflection

The Persona and the Inner Reaction Exercise. In group Session 4, I asked members to draw a picture or write words, on one side of the paper, about how they think their face appeared to other people during a recent stressful event—in other words, what are the personas that they project to the outside world? Then on another sheet of paper, group members were asked to draw or write key words about how they were really feeling and reacting during that event—what was really happening in their internal worlds.

A Processing Revealing Much. I was excited to see that this exercise became the impetus for a rich discussion and processing amongst the members.

Although it started with a structured exercise, the processing revealed many issues and themes amongst the group members.

Very quickly after the processing started, issues of identity, acceptance, wanting validation, and creating intimacy within relationships all rose to the surface.

Lost and Got Back on Track With the Help of My Co-Leader. The pace of the processing was fast! Very quickly, things were happening, and I was lost. Fortunately, my co-facilitator was able to get us back on track when she brought forward the theme of "self-worth." This is exactly the moment when the dynamics of the group shifted into poignant and even riveting dialogue amongst members.

Validation and Acceptance Especially Craved by Minority Members. The shift really deepened when Sabrina and Miquel entered into what proved to be an enthralling dialogue about their need for validation and acceptance because they are both *culturally a minority*. I could palpably feel how others in the group were relating to what was being said, even without a word being spoken. This really showed the power of the group and how when one examines his or her thoughts, feelings, and emotions . . . other members witness the courage taken to do so.

AN OVERVIEW OF THE FLOW AND TIME FRAME OF A STRUCTURED SESSION

This section provides you with an overview of a productive structured session. Please remember, a table will not provide you with the richness of the flow of a live group session where multiple actions and circular interactions often occur simultaneously. Details of each step will subsequently be covered.

EXERCISES

Scenarios for Your Practice

1. In the first session of a substance-abuse mandated group, Richard expresses his extreme distrust for the leaders of the group. He advises the other members of the group to be distrustful, as well. As the group leader, how will you respond?

2. During a divorce group, Bobbie states that he feels like a failure; Tony says he feels like a weight has been lifted from his shoulders; Jack says he doesn't know how to feel about his impending divorce. As a leader, how might you link these statements?

Table 6.8 An Overview of the Flow and Time Frame of a Structured Session

A. Opening the session (10 minutes)

-Relaxation exercise (optional)

-Check-in: Members sharing lingering feelings and interpersonal skills

B. Conducting the structured activity (10 minutes)

-Distributing materials

-Guiding the activities one step at a time

C. Processing (60 minutes)

-Members share what they have learned about themselves through the exercise

-Extracting common themes from group sharing

-Working on the common theme, guiding members to provide validation and feedback to one another

-Going deeper by extracting meanings from the sharing experiences

(All along, the leader facilitates, intervenes, and participates, to maximize member engagement)

D. Closing the session (10 minutes)

-Announcing the closing

-Checking-out

-Reminder

3. During Tricia's intake, her motivational interview revealed a desire to change from being self-critical to being self-accepting. Now in the third session of the group, Tricia states that she does not believe she needs to change in any way. She states, "Being self-critical keeps me out of trouble with other people." How will you respond?

4. It is the fourth session of a personal growth group, and Jason, a very outspoken and influential member of the group, is responding to everyone by critiquing their feelings and doling out advice. The group momentum is lost, and everyone becomes silent when this happens. As a leader, how will you address this situation?

5. During a mandated substance abuse group, Jamal is deflecting with humor. In response to the following "fill in the blank" statement he answered: "If I give up drugs it would mean <u>I am such a good boy and</u>

<u>deserve a cookie.</u>" The group laughs at Jamal's joke. How do you respond?

6. In the third session during a structured activity, Greta becomes very upset and is inconsolable. She keeps apologizing for her tears and beats herself up saying, "I feel like I'm just doing this for attention. I don't deserve the time I take from this group." Many of the members reply with statements expressing the opposite, but Greta cannot accept their statements. As a leader, how do you respond?

7. In the second session of a school behavioral intervention group, Terrence refuses to participate saying, "Anthony is here, and he has bullied me since the second grade. Why would I give him more reasons to bully me?" He is speaking directly to you, the leader. How will you respond?

8. In a mandated group for DUI offenders, Maria refuses to accept others' feedback since her blood alcohol level was just barely over the legal limit. As the leader, how do you respond?

9. In the session, Darrell rationalizes his battering behavior. Angela, another member, responds by further rationalizing his behavior with this statement, "Your wife should know what happens when she pushes your buttons; it is her own fault." How do you respond?

10. In a group, Jim has a lot of experience as he is much older than the rest of the members. As a result, Jim is taking every opportunity to police and govern the group with statements such as, "It feels like we are just trying to get someone to break down and cry by probing them about their childhood." Some members of the group are offended by that statement and cross their arms. How do you respond?

11. In the fifth session of the group, Sun-Kim has still not spoken other than answering direct questions with single-word responses. In the previous session, other group members expressed interest in her and frustration with her lack of participation. Sun-Kim responded by saying she'd try in Session 5. How do you respond?

12. In a group, Tanya's goal was to speak up for herself more often with others in the group. It is the sixth session, and Tanya is interrupting others and steering the group back to her. You see other group members shifting and rolling their eyes when this happens. How will you respond?

Self-Reflection

1. What have been your personal experiences with structured exercises?

2. Under what circumstances did you find them to be especially useful? Under what circumstances might such activities actually take something away from the group experience?

3. Think back to some of your most challenging encounters with others. What frame of mind helped or hindered you the most in the situation? What are some of the ways in which you are able to cultivate a resilience or a *thick skin* in these sort of encounters?

4. Imagine yourself as your opposite. What traits would be different? How would you behave differently? What would your opposite look like in a group therapy setting?

5. Examine your thoughts and feelings about the different types of mandated groups. What are your negative beliefs about each population? Positive? How might these beliefs help or hinder your abilities as a group leader?

6. Imagine yourself as a group leader. In the group, you see someone who strongly reminds you of yourself or of someone you know. How will you effectively work with this person? Do you foresee any certain reactions such as rejection or empathy?

7. Reflect on your levels of intimacy with the people in your life. Do you readily trust someone with your feelings and thoughts? How long does it take you to open up to someone? What factors influence your decision-making?

8. Think back to your experiences in groups (e.g., school, sports, hobbies). What reactions did you have to other members of the group, and why? Did you notice any patterns or certain personality traits that drew you in or pushed you away? Were you caught off guard by any aspect of group work? How did you function in a group, and what influence will that have on you as a group leader?

CHAPTER 7

LEADING SEMISTRUCTURED GROUPS

Working on Agenda Items

S tanding between the colossal structured group (Chapter 6) and the tall-order unstructured group (Chapter 8), a humble format of group therapy—the semistructured group—finds a sliver of blue sky for itself. Humble it may be, lowly it is not. For this format offers members the autonomy lacking in structured groups and, at the same time, disbands the anxiety teeming in unstructured groups. What's more, this format affords budding group leaders their much needed scaffolding before they press forward into the advanced leadership they may practice later.

As semi as it is, this format is not *a hybrid*. Rather, the semistructured group is *an idiosyncratic method* of its own genre, distinct with its own features and leadership methods. This chapter puts forward the nitty gritty of how to launch a semistructured group successfully in the early stage of a group.

FEATURES OF SEMISTRUCTURED GROUPS

A semistructured group prides itself as a *member-centered* group. Here, members, rather than the leader, own the "say-so" of deciding *agenda items* for group discussion. Why do we call it "semistructured"? It is because the processing style of this format begins *sequentially*, but then the interaction often becomes more spontaneous as the group discussion progresses.

What Are Agenda Items?

Agenda items are topics of discussion for a meeting. In a group, members often discuss topics associated with *distressing issues* happening in their lives outside the group—there-and-then life experiences (Kivlighan, Jauquet, Hardie, Francis, & Hershberger, 1993).

Almost all topics can be welcomed as agenda items, especially depression, interpersonal conflict, addiction problems, relationship problems, anxiety, low self-esteem, weight problems, decision-making difficulties, academic struggling, employment difficulties, and so on. Though mostly related to specific situations (Ferencik, 1991), these topics, upon exploration, tend to reveal fascinating roots in long-established behaviors.

Meeting the Needs of Inclusion, Control, Order, and Meaningfulness

During the check-in, it is apt for members to determine if they have an agenda item to explore later. Putting forth agenda items on the table, everyone in the room now gets a sense of what work is in store for the session.

Though differing from each other, each agenda item, through group exploration, might find common elements among them. This commonality helps members feel a sense of being "in it together," thus meeting members' *needs of inclusion*—one the most vital universal needs (Seppala, Rossomando & Doty, 2013; Schutz, 1958) in humans.

Having the power to decide when to begin substantive work via presenting his agenda item, the member gets another universal need met—the need of control (Schutz, 1958).

Working on the agenda items also affords members a sense of *order and predictability*, and at the same time, a sense of *meaningfulness* when group exploration touches on *their long established behavioral patterns*.

As such, working on the agenda items is a leadership format that suits *beginning group leaders* trying to get a hang of leading counseling groups. Success on this basic level leadership practice will certainly *scaffold beginning group counselors into more advanced leadership* typically required for unstructured groups later.

Agenda Items Acting as a Springboard for Group Interaction

When working on members' agenda items, try not to single-mindedly aim at solving member's presenting problems. But rather, allow agenda items to serve as a *springboard* for creating a forward momentum of the group discussion.

As members become actively involved with one another, *their interpersonal styles will emerge*. These interpersonal events will become the grist for the mill for the group to explore and to come to a better grasp.

As you can see, the member presenting the agenda item is *not the only one* who benefits from the discussion, *but all* involved will surprise themselves at how much they get to know their own interpersonal patterns.

Balancing Supports With Challenges

Working on agenda items can give the group opportunities to provide support and challenges to one another.

The group treats each agenda item with sensitivity and explores it with care. While one member is working on his or her agenda, the whole group is on board to provide empathic, supportive, and honest responses. As such, the member presenting the agenda item gains validation and understanding typically scarce in his or her daily life.

The agenda items presented are *there-and-then oriented* and rightly so. But sooner or later, the group interaction will start to provoke members' behavioral patterns, affording the group the opportunity to engage in corrective feedback and challenges—the forces that bring about insight and change.

Although some members need more support, while others, more challenges, the leader is wise to strike a balance between the two. When challenges are balanced with support, a group member's experience reaches its optimum.

GETTING AGENDA CONTRACTS

To maximize its effectiveness, the group must garner *an agreement* from a member before diving in to explore his or her problems. You may see this agreement as an "agenda contract" (Yalom, 1983). This section discusses ways of securing members' agreement to having their issues explored in the group.

Never Work on a Member's Issues Without His or Her Agreement

A member has to *consent* to put himself or herself in the center of attention before the group can dig deeply into his or her issue for any length of time. Many new leaders make the mistake of diving in to examine a member's issues when a member is simply describing a problem or concern, albeit with dramatic expressions. Such dramatic presentation is misconstrued as the sign that the member is in great distress, in dire need of the group's help. The leader and the group then dive right in to address the member's problems, only to be met with "Yes, but" responses or resentment from the member. The group members end up feeling frustrated.

These hesitant responses make complete sense if we appreciate where they come from. Some members have a history of externalizing their problems or blaming others, with no desire to take charge of their own lives. Others are frightened of committing themselves to a plan of action in front of others. Others again have worked through their concerns and are simply sharing a past experience for whatever it is worth. Still others just want to vent the feelings associated with a situation and are not really prepared for any type of personal transformation.

Get Agenda Contracts Through Check-In

To avoid spending time on members not ready for change, leaders will need to get an agenda contract before moving forward with them. You can get the contracts through check-in.

During the check-in, if a member reveals any crisis or stressful event that seems to need the group's attention, you might invite him to put it on the table as an agenda item:

> Jeff, this event seems to bother you very much. Would you like to put this concern on the table as an agenda item so that the group can later help you explore a little bit more?

Or

> Jeff, this seems to be a complicated issue. Before getting into more details, would you be willing to wait until we finish our check-in, and then the group can work together to help you make some sense out of it? Would you agree?

If Jeff does want the group's help, then you have a deal of an agenda contract with him. If he does not, then his wish should be respected. Don't try to sell the idea to him too hard.

Obtain Agenda Contracts Through Agenda Request

Another way of getting agenda items is through an "agenda go-around" devised by Yalom (Clemans, 2011; Yalom, 1983). Yalom uses this ritual at the beginning of each session where group members are asked to formulate their agenda items. We believe that this go-around really *puts the ball in members' court*, where they have to take responsibility for pronouncing what they wish to get from the session. To initiate this process, a leader may say something like,

> If you are interested in having the group help you sort out a certain issue on a deeper level, please use one sentence to briefly indicate that you would like to put an agenda item of yours on the table, without going into too many details. We aim to work on at least three agenda items for today's session.

Identify Interpersonal Skills for Practice

For those members who do not have any agenda item at hand, you may ask them to name an interpersonal skill for practice while interacting with others in the session. By doing so, you engage them in self-reflection even when they are not working on their own issues. Thus, everyone is taking responsibility for determining the kinds of group experiences they want to create for themselves.

Please review Chapter 4 (on basic facilitation skills of how to open a group session) for what you might say to ask members to identify an interpersonal skill to practice in the session. Appendix C also provides a list of interpersonal skills for your members' consideration.

Deal With the Challenge of Having Too Many Agenda Items

If too many agenda items are offered, then inform the group that it might not be possible to work on all of them in the given session. This forewarning can prevent members from feeling neglected if their items have to be tabled until the following week. You might say,

> Okay, we have a number of agenda items on the table today. We will work as hard as we can to cover all of them, but please remember that

realistically we may not be able to bring all of them to closure in one session. If that is the case, we will continue working on the items in the following weeks. Are we all on the same page?

Decide Which Agenda Item to Go First

If several agenda items are on the table, you may decide who goes first by judging the sense of urgency of the issues. The basic principle is to let the member flooded with emotions go first. You might say,

Jane, you seem to be already in the depth of your emotions. Why don't you start first?

If no particular issue is pressing, you may ask those with agenda items to decide among them who should start:

Since no agenda item on the table is especially pressing, we will let those of you whose agenda items are on the table to decide who will go first. So, who among the four of you would like to start?

Handle Some Delays

If by the end of the session some of the agenda items have not been addressed, you need to carefully handle the feelings of those members whose items will be delayed:

We are running out of time today, and we haven't had a chance to work on Tom's agenda item yet. [turning to Tom] Tom, would you allow the group to put your agenda item as the first priority in the next session?

In the following session, when it is time to work on agendas, remember to remind the group:

Last week we did not have a chance to work on Tom's agenda item, so today we will put that first. [turning to Tom] Tom, would you still like to pursue your issue today?

In the following session, if someone is experiencing a crisis and needs the group's immediate attention, you will need to consult with Tom to see whether the member in crisis may go first:

> Tom, I know that your agenda item was tabled in the previous session, and we should give yours the first priority. But Betty is having a crisis today and is feeling quite shaky right now. She seems to need the group's immediate support. Would you be willing to allow Betty's issue to be addressed first, followed by yours?

The Challenge of No Agenda Items— Address Safety and Vulnerability Concerns

Nothing is more dreadful for a leader than getting no agenda items at all after going around the circle. Oftentimes, members are just struggling with anxiety and self-consciousness—the typical fear and anxiety preceding any major learning. The absence of agenda items tells us that members are not ready to put themselves on the line, exposing themselves in front of others.

Don't take members' reluctance personally as if it were your personal failure or their rejection. Rather, *take the opportunity to have members discuss the safety issue and the sense of vulnerability that they are feeling.* When members know they are not alone in their fears and anxiety, they will be more willing to come out of their shells. To this end, you may say,

> No one appears eager to put forth an agenda item at this moment. It seems like many of you still feel apprehensive about divulging your struggles in front of other people. I wonder whether we can spend some time *talking about these feelings.* In addition, can we talk about *how to make this group a safe and nonjudgmental place* for all of you to share your private struggles and feelings? Would anyone want to say a few words about this?

Later,

> I am glad that feeling safe is a priority for all of the people here. I'd like our group to make a commitment to an atmosphere where everyone feels safe, accepted, and supported.

Usually, after feeling safe and not alone, members will start to feel more at ease in putting their agenda items on the table.

Deal With Lack of Worthiness

Through the discussion above, the group may find that sometimes members don't put forth their agenda items because of not feeling worthy enough to have the group attention. They struggle with a deeply entrenched sense of *low self-worth* that discounts the importance of their issues. If this is the case, you may say,

> Harvey, I just heard you say two things. The first was that it bothers you that sometimes you don't choose to express yourself in your personal life and at work. The second was that you think your issues are not as important as those of others, therefore, not worthy of a place on the agenda. I would like to invite you to take a look at this belief. I don't believe that the group is reserved only for extreme problems. All kinds of personal concerns are appropriate for this group and are worthy of the group's attention.

TOWARD A MORE PERSONAL LEVEL OF SELF-DISCLOSURE

After members put forth their agenda items, the group will start to work on them. The first step involves getting members to disclose the issues they face in life. *Self-disclosure in the group setting is actually not as simple as what one imagines*. This section presents several techniques needed to facilitate self-disclosure toward a more personal level.

Peel the Onion—Start to Disclose at the Content Level

No member will benefit from the group experience without honest self-disclosure (Yalom, 2009). But the process of self-disclosure is like that of *peeling an onion*—starting with *the outer, less sensitive layers*, while the vulnerable core remains hidden. We can anticipate that most members will start talking about their issues at the *content level*: what it is, how it got started, and how it has had an impact on their lives.

This kind of self-disclosure, also called *there-and-then disclosure*, is absolutely essential in group counseling and therapy. Actually, if a member has not been in counseling and therapy before, he or she is highly likely to recoil from any type of self-disclosure in front of a roomful of strangers.

Steer Clear of Pseudo-Self-Disclosure or Storytelling

Starting with the *content level* of self-disclosure is all right as long as members eventually open up to a more reflective level of their inner experiences. But some members never get there. Their disclosures are so content-focused (or others-oriented) that they fall into a *superficial storytelling*, giving dry, factual, or nonreflective details about what's going on in their daily lives—a disclosure called *pseudo-self-disclosure* (Rains, Brunner, & Oman, 2016).

Pseudo-self-disclosure or storytelling keeps people at arms' length, damping down group intimacy. You will need to steer such members to a more personal level of disclosure by saying something like,

> Matt, I am aware that you are giving a lot of details about several people in your life. They are not here, so we are not able to work with them. But we can definitely work with your feelings and reactions toward them as well as how these reactions affect your life and relationships. Would you like to tell the group a bit about how you personally react to these events?

Engage the Group to Help Members Open Up a Bit More

Some members choose the safer way by expressing themselves vaguely, such as "I'd like to stop the way my life is right now." "I want to feel less distant from my sister." "I want my wife to be more understanding."

Presentations like these do not give anything tangible for the group to latch on to; too many major pieces of the puzzle are missing. In this situation, you may *engage the group* to help the member open up a bit more:

> [To the group] Some of you look puzzled. Would you like to ask Matt some clarifying questions so that you can get a clearer picture of what his underlying concern is?

You may also participate in clarifying the issue by making a comment like one of the following:

Matt, you said that you are hurting. I have been listening attentively to that feeling, yet I am not sure I get it.

Or

Matt, has your sense of feeling like an outsider ever happened *in other situations*?

Listen to Core Issues

While a member is presenting his or her issues, you, as a leader, need to listen conscientiously to identify what the core issues might be. How to do it? You listen for *keywords* or *key phrases* that seem to carry more energy, that seem to lie beneath the stories, and that seem to indicate some hidden dynamics of relationships and their implications. Chapters 6 and 8 list some of these key phrases that may help you have an easier time for identifying them.

Once you get a sense of a member's stories and the key phrases, you will be ready to go to the next step, which is to facilitate a supportive group interaction with the presenting member.

FACILITATING A SAFE AND SUPPORTIVE GROUP INTERACTION

The second element of working on agendas is *creating a safe and supportive environment during group interaction*. This section focuses on various facilitation skills that build safety and trust in the group. All of them center on one key: validation.

The Importance of Validation

Members often feel vulnerable and alone after sharing the issues they struggle with. Fear of judgment kicks in the moment there is a silence. This is the moment when they most need to feel safe and supported. And it takes a certain kind of group interaction to achieve that.

Many things can go wrong once members start to respond to others' self-disclosure. For examples, members typically jump in and

- give advice,
- problem solve,
- take sides with the member, criticizing the third parties in the stories,
- self-reference—refer back to their own long-winded stories,
- ask too many content-oriented questions, and
- change topics, shifting to the irrelevant elements of the stories.

These kinds of responses are unhelpful and invalidating, to say the least. No wonder many people have a hard time opening up to others.

Most people have been hurt in relationships and have had to lick their wounds alone; they do not have the luxury of receiving validation. Indeed, underlying many people's developmental problems and their insecurities lies *a sense of invisibility* in their home lives as children. The above invalidating responses tend to add salt to the wounds.

The antidote to that sense of invisibility comes from the experience of being seen and heard by other human beings, of being validated and acknowledged on the reasons behind one's particular emotions. The group is the exact place where this kind of validation can be afforded.

Helping people feel psychologically visible fuels the therapeutic power of the group; this power of healing is foremost for minorities and for those who have had many experiences of being rejected or excluded.

Receiving acceptance and validation from the group constitutes an essential part of the corrective emotional experience (Yalom & Leszcz, 2005). In order to give validation to one another, members have to attune to the inner experiences of the other. Mutual attunement will bring compassion and warmth to the group, enhancing group cohesiveness. It is at this level that another universal need, the need for affection (Gitterman, 2005; Schutz, 1958; Seppala et al., 2013), can be fulfilled.

Following we propose three options for helping group members validate one another.

Option 1: Validate via Naming the Feelings

The first easy way of validation is through *naming a person's feelings*. Without being named, feelings, particularly pain and self-doubt, remain buried; their validity and vivacity are depleted. But when named, feelings come to see the light of day; their vivacity brings the person alive, allowing the person to reclaim his or her lost self.

When steering the group to name the feelings, don't just ask, "Can any of you relate to what Matt was saying?" The word *relate* may inadvertently prompt the group members to reference back to their own stories. Relating may reduce aloneness, but it may also steal the thunder, taking the intensity away from the member's crucial moment.

Another thing that you don't want to say is, "Would any of you like to say *anything* to Matt?" The word *anything* probably means to be inclusive, but being so vague, it may inadvertently prompt members to ask too many questions or give advice, derailing from the original intent of giving validation.

To effectively facilitate validation and empathy in the group, you need to be specific in your prompts. There are two ways to do that: (1) naming feelings by using a sentence-completion exercise and (2) naming feelings by guessing.

Name the Feelings by Sentence-Completion Exercise

A sentence-completion exercise can vastly help a new group. To prompt the group to name a member's feelings, you may say,

> [To the whole group] Matt has been talking primarily about his wife's feelings as she goes through the cancer treatment. But it seems that he has difficulty taking the time to feel his own feelings. So, I would like the group to try to complete this following sentence. The sentence is, "I am Matt, and I feel _____ because _____." When you complete the sentence, please address it directly to Matt. Okay, whoever is ready, please jump in at any time.

Name the Feelings by Guessing

Having members simply imagine or guess at the member's feelings can achieve the same:

> [To the group] Rick has opened up to us about his abandonment issue and how it ties to his constant struggles in his current life. At this moment, I would like the group to *imagine* what it must have been like to grow up as Rick did. When you are ready, please feel free to jump in and speak directly to Rick. If you prefer to pass, that will be respected.

> [To the group] Imagine yourself to be Bill; how do you feel after you have experienced this loss of marriage and two near-death events?

Upon feeling heard and validated, the presenting member usually *feels safe* enough to plunge into the deeper levels of his or her experiences. This is the reward granted to an empathic group.

Option 2: Create Safety via Sharing Similar Experiences

A less powerful, yet still meaningful, way to create a safe environment in the group is by linking together similar experiences or reactions. As humans, most of us experience a certain sense of *interpersonal isolation*, thinking that we are alone in our problems and distress.

But this aloneness dissipates as soon as we hear others disclose similar reactions, dilemmas, and life experiences that reflect the human condition. Knowing that others have to deal with equivalent difficulties can comfort our tired souls, tendering *a sense of universality* (Yalom, 2009; Yalom & Leszcz, 2005)—a sense of "we are in the same boat!" and "welcome aboard!"

Watch out for some members' habit of slipping into a long, winding road of self-reference as they divulge their experiences. If someone does just that, loop the attention back to the person who should be receiving the validation.

An effective way to prevent irrelevant story sharing is to incorporate key phrases, reflecting a member's core issues, in your prompt:

[To the group] I can see that Jackie has a sense of *being out of control* [stating the member's core message by using his or her *key phrases*]. I wonder whether anyone can recall an instance in your lives when you felt a sense of *being out of control* [repeat the key phrase]. When you are ready, please talk to Jackie directly, showing her that you understand her struggle.

[To the group] From many members' facial expressions, it seems that Maria's sharing about her *fear of being judged* [stating the member's core message by using his or her *key phrases*] has struck a chord with many of you. Would any of you like to share *the fear of being judged* [repeat the key phrase] that you have experienced? Please speak directly to Maria.

Matt's reflection below demonstrates the powerful effect of hearing others sharing similar experiences when he thought he was alone:

I felt especially warm and grateful toward Dory as she described a similar experience to my own. Hearing that someone else felt some of the same things had a powerful effect on me. I felt some of my own self-judgment melt away in being reminded that I was not so terrible to the extent that no one else could possibly relate to my experience.

Option 3: Create a Safe Environment via Recognizing Strengths

In Chapter 4, we stressed the importance of bringing out the "inner strength detective" in members so that they may validate and empower one another. Here in the semistructured session, the leader will continue to have members verbalize the strengths that they see beneath one another's presenting issues. Consider the following,

[To the group] As you listen to Maria's response to Jackie, what strikes you as remarkable? What are the strengths that you see in her that she might not know of herself?

[To the group] What inspired you about what Bill just shared when he opened up to Rick?

[To the group] Through his responses to other members' concerns in our group, *what clues did you get about* some of *Jesse's skills* that he might not know of himself?

Work on Multiple Issues by Inviting Members to Share Triggered Memories

After members have responded to your prompt, you can use the member's agenda item as a springboard to getting *multiple agenda items involved. This will lead to* a rich and touching group interaction.

[To the group] Thank you all for participating in validating Matt's experiences. I would like to take another step and ask you guys to share *what you were going through internally when you said what you just said to Matt. What memories or reactions were triggered inside of you?* Would anyone like to start? [Launching the group into a widespread engagement.]

Work on Multiple Issues by Connecting Members' Reactions Together

Another way to get multiple agenda items involved is to connect members' reactions together. Oftentimes, a member's presenting issue reminds another of his or her previously neglected issues:

[To the group] Many of you seemed to get deeply in touch with something painful when you responded to Matt's sharing. Would any of you like to share what it is that connects you to Matt's experience?

Once multiple members open up, many use the method of working on *common themes* to help members find meanings from their experiences. For details, please refer to Chapter 8.

Loop Back to the Original Presenter

When you launch the group into multiple-member processing, sometimes you have to loop back to the person who originally presented the agenda item, if his issue has not been thoroughly processed.

[To the group] We have had quite an intense exchange about the issue of loss [stating the theme]. Many of you have shared how this issue has triggered deep feelings inside of you. Your comments have been very helpful for all the group members. Right now, though, I am aware that Matt's agenda item hasn't reached closure, so let's go back to Matt for awhile.

Leader Participation in Giving Validations

Most new group leaders tend to err on being too preoccupied in facilitating the group to participate in the group themselves. Remember that in the initial stage of the group, you might want to use about 30% of your air time for participation (see Chapter 4). Especially after giving group members their prime opportunities to validate one another's feelings, you should take liberty to contribute the empathy and feedback that you have for the member.

And if the group seems lost, not knowing how to convey their understanding to one another, then this is the juncture where you need to take the lead in validating members' experiences so as to provide modeling for appropriate behaviors.

You may give validations on two levels: the individual level and the group level.

A Leader Validating Individual Members' Experiences. Individual members need to feel that their leaders understand and hear them. Here is an example of how you could validate your individual members' experiences:

> [To an individual member] Matt, you *feel sad* to see your daughter so stressed out by your wife's illness. You wish she could just talk about her feelings instead of yelling at her brother, yet you don't know how to talk to her about this. If I were in this situation, I would feel powerless just the way you do.

A Leader Validating the Group's Collective Experiences. The group members' collective experiences are often not explicitly articulated. The leader can help put these unspoken reactions into words. Openly acknowledging these reactions, positive or negative, helps the group develop cohesiveness more quickly. For example,

> [To the group] It seems like *the group is deeply touched* by Matt's struggle. I can feel a sense of connection in this room right now as if all of us are in touch with similar *longings and pain* buried somewhere inside of us.

> [To the group] I sense that the group is *very tentative* right now and does not want to address Tracy's deeper feelings for the moment. I can see that you guys all *care* about Tracy and don't want to make Tracy feel even more vulnerable than she already does.

Intervene When Unhelpful Group Interaction Happens

To make the group a safe environment, the leader needs to intervene when inappropriate actions or unhelpful comments take place during group interaction. Your job as a leader is to keep half of your attention on the presenting member's issues while another half on the rest of the group's interactional dynamics. This is called the *"half-and-half" principle.*

To put this principle in a nutshell, don't focus so exclusively on the presenting member that you overlook some ineffective interpersonal communication patterns hindering the group's chance of developing a sense of safety, trust, and intimacy. This principle will be further expounded in a later section on intervention techniques.

If a member was giving premature advice to a presenting member, you will need to intervene:

Jeff, I appreciate your good intentions in trying to solve Matt's problem, but at this moment I don't think we know enough to do that. So let's try to understand a bit more of what's underlying Matt's struggles. How does that sound?

If a member rushes in to stop another member from fully experiencing painful or undesirable emotions, you may intervene by saying,

Ahmet, let's allow Matt a moment to be with his pain. I think he knows that we care. [turning to Matt] Matt, please realize that we care, and we are supportive of the emotions you are feeling right now.

Should a member talk *about* Matt rather than *to* him, you may intervene and say,

Isolde, since Matt is here, would you please *talk to* him directly, instead of *talking about* him?

More intervention techniques will be presented in a later section.

FACILITATING GIVING THERE-AND-THEN FEEDBACK

The third element in working on an agenda is facilitating feedback giving. Used precisely, feedback can bring about much self-awareness and self-knowledge to members. Feedback reveals the receiver's reality that he or she may not be aware. As a result, members come to see clearly their relationship patterns as well as their personal strengths and gifts.

Only after the group has spent sufficient time in giving validation can the rest of its time be spent on giving feedback. There are two types of feedback: here-and-now feedback and there-and-now feedback. For the early stages of a group, the there-and-then feedback—a less intense feedback not involving the immediacy issues among members—will meet the group's needs. As the trust level increases, the group may proceed to give the more intense here-and-now feedback as detailed in Chapter 10. This section specifies the many facets of how to facilitate the group to give there-and-then feedback.

Self-Esteem Boosting: The Power of "Giving" Feedback

Some members of the group, suffering from low self-esteem, feel as if they have nothing valuable to offer. Others, wreaked by self-absorption, feel as if they cannot step outside themselves to see the greater needs of others. The more members are self-absorbed, the less they give, and the lower their self-esteem will be. In the end, both types of people arrive at the same place—unhappiness.

The act of giving cures unhappiness. Members feel better about themselves immediately with absolutely no side effect. As a principle, the group leader shall create as many chances as possible for members to give to one another. Among all things, feedback is the gift to give without a penny spent.

The weight of giving feedback shall not be entirely on shoulders of the leader. Indeed, most members prefer to receive feedback *from their fellow members* (Corey & Corey, 2014; Toth & Erwin, 1998; Yalom & Leszcz, 2005), rather than from the leader.

Be Aware of Poor Forms of Feedback

As powerful as it is, feedback, when offered at the wrong time and in the wrong form (such as *advice, reassurance, problem-solving,* or *personal opinions*) is unhelpful at best. Although given with good intention—to *take the pain or intense emotions away from* those who are experiencing it—these poor forms of feedback can actually derail the recipients from staying with their experiences long enough to allow for therapeutic work.

Avoid the General Terms of "Feedback" in Your Prompt

To prevent the poor forms of feedback in the first place, you might want to avoid general prompts such as, "Would any of you like to give Matt any <u>feedback</u>?"

As a psychological term, the word *feedback* carries a definite connotation in therapy. But regrettably, in our society, laypeople often use it in such a loose way that it means almost anything, including advice, opinions, solutions, suggestions, impressions, lecturing, and so on.

A leader is better off to assume that members, by and large, do not know what feedback actually implies or what kinds are helpful. This assumption should help you avoid the word altogether. As a result, you would use more *specific prompts*, like the following, when facilitating feedback-giving.

Option 1: Give Feedback That Identifies the Functions of the Behaviors

A useful there-and-then feedback usually *identifies patterns* that run through various areas of a member's life. When given gently and with care, this kind of feedback can soften the grip that the coping pattern has on the member.

It is advisable to look at *both the positive side and the unfavorable side* of *the function* that the behavior has served in the member's past. This way of giving feedback is an act of challenge, and at the same time, support.

> [To the group] It seems that Matt feels well heard and supported by the group. Now I would like to take things a step further. I wonder, after listening to Matt's stories, *what pattern runs through Matt's various areas of life?* What *function has this pattern served him in his life?* And how might this old pattern *hinder* Matt in his current life? [Identifying there-and-then pattern; exploring both sides of the functions; the word *feedback* is intentionally avoided.]

Or

> [To the group] Thank you all for your empathic support for Matt. When you look back at Matt's multilayered story, what patterns of behavior in his personal relationships become clear to you? How have these patterns *helped Matt in the past*? And how are these patterns *hindering relationships in his current life*? [Identifying there-and-then pattern, exploring both sides of the functions.]

Another example,

> [To the group] After listening to Julie's and Mary's stories of growing up in alcoholic families and using rationalization to cope with the pain, how would you *appreciate the different functions* that this coping pattern has served them at home in their past? And how is this coping skill *not working* for them in their current lives? Your perceptions will add some new self-awareness for Julie and Mary. Is anyone ready to start? [Exploring both sides of the functions of members' coping pattern.]

Option 2: Give Feedback That Connects the Dots

A useful there-and-then oriented feedback may also connect two seemingly unrelated issues (two distant dots) with a *theme*. When dissimilar issues are pulled together, and when an *underlying theme* emerges, surprising insights can result.

> [To the group] Let's shift our focus a bit at this moment. Tracy seems to feel distressed and ashamed by the fact that she could not help but slip into affairs with other men whenever she was bickering with her boyfriend whom she loves very much. [the first dot] We also heard Tracy say that she has cut off contact with her father for many years. [the second dot] Do any of the group members see any connection between Tracy's cutting off from her father and her difficulty in handling tension in her intimate relationship? [connecting the dots; pause] If you do, please talk to Tracy directly about what you see to be *the theme* connecting the two events in her life. [pause] Who would like to start?

Leader Participation in Giving There-and-Then Feedback

The leader's participation in giving feedback constitutes an important part of leadership. There are two types of leader feedback: there-and-then oriented leader feedback and here-and-now oriented leader feedback. During the early stages of the group, the leader can safely give there-and-then oriented feedback that is moderate but with adequate value. Consider the following there-and-then oriented leader feedback:

> Tracy, I noticed that you stiffen up whenever you talk about how you cut off contact with your dad, who you called a loser. There seems to be a lot

of unresolved emotions related to your dad. [the first dot] Minutes ago, you also said that whenever you had a fight with your boyfriend, you would pick up the phone and set up an intimate meeting with another man. [the second dot] In these two situations, *the common thread seems to be a need to run away from the anxiety stirred up by any conflict.* [connecting the dots and identifying the pattern] *I appreciate how running away has been helping you deal with disappointments and pain in your life.* [the positive *function* of the behavior pattern] Yet, I also see that *the more you try to run away from it, the more the anxiety seems to sneak up on you.* [the unfavorable function of the behavior pattern] It's as if the anxiety is trying to convey that something needs to be resolved. [interpreting the meaning of the symptom, anxiety] Does that make sense?

Redirect Unhelpful Feedback

If some members slip into their old habits of giving advice or asking impersonal questions during feedback, you will need to intervene.

Jeff, you asked Matt a question just now. Would you please *make it into a statement* of what you really tried to say to Matt behind your question?

Nita, when you give feedback to Matt, please tell him how you personally perceive his life rather than telling him what he should do.

Coach Members to Listen to Feedback Without Immediate Response

Listening to feedback given by the group, the recipients often feel compelled to respond immediately. Their minds busy rehearsing what to say in return, they hardly can hear the messages being given. If allowed to go ahead to respond to each feedback, they will start to have an extended dialogue, aggravating the group.

To avoid this, you will have to coach the recipients on how to quiet their minds and just listen. The more silent one's inner dialogue becomes, the more one is able to become aware of how the body and emotions are affected by the messages in the feedback. In so doing, the recipient may allow a wealth of information to flow to him.

Matt, the group seems to have several areas of feedback for you. While they are giving you the feedback, *you may just remain centered and simply listen for awhile without thinking about what to say back.* [Part 1 coaching] Also, you don't need to accept all the feedback wholesale. You don't need to reject some of it immediately, either. Just allow some time for the feedback to sink in, and notice how it affects you later. [Part 2 coaching] If you want to respond to anything today, there will be time for you to do that when the feedback has been completed. [Part 3 coaching] Do these suggestions make sense to you?

Help the Recipient to Respond to Others' Feedback

After the member has listened fully to the feedback from the group, you can invite the recipient to share how it affects him or her. This last step completes *the feedback component* of working on agendas.

OK, Matt, now that the group members have given you their input, what do you realize about yourself that you did not know before the feedback given today?

Or

Matt, the members have shared with you some of their observations and comments. I wonder, among all this feedback, what strikes you the most?

Or

Matt, it sounds like there is a lot for you to take in right now. Since our time is running short, I invite you to reflect on this feedback during the week. When you come back next time, would you share with the group what feedback fits you the best and what insights have come out of it?

Deal With Dismissal to Consistent Feedback

If a member dismisses a consistent feedback from many members, the leader needs to intervene:

Jane, four members have made similar comments to you. It seems that you have difficulty listening to this feedback. I would like to encourage you to pay attention to any consistent feedback because when it comes from so many people, it is likely to have a certain degree of validity.

Seek Consensual Validation of a Feedback From the Group

If a particular valuable feedback is resisted by a recipient, the leader can seek *consensual validation* from the group (Dewane, 2006; Marmarosh & Tasca, 2013) about that feedback.

First, you restate that feedback concisely and then ask the rest of the group if they also observe the same patterns. Faced with the consensus of his fellow group members, the recipient tends to be more willing to reconsider the feedback.

[To the group] The group has provided Matt with a lot of interesting feedback. Among them, *Tom's feedback seems difficult for Matt to hear*. Tom was saying that Matt has a tendency to push people in his life away by his people-pleasing behaviors. [restating the very feedback in point] *I wonder, do other members also notice this pattern in Matt's presented issues?* [seeking consensus of the feedback from the group]

Make the Transition to the Next Agenda Item

Ideally, the group should work on multiple agenda items simultaneously, but new groups may not have the capacity to handle multiple presenting problems concurrently. For such groups, working on agendas items one at a time may decrease the mental load of group members. Later, as the group matures, it will increase its capacity for working with multiple presenting issues simultaneously. Chapter 8 provides methods of how to do just that.

For now, working on agenda items one at a time requires that the group transitions from one item to the next. However, *members in new groups often do feel uncomfortable with discontinuing the issue on the floor and moving on*. You, as a leader, can simply give them a clear direction to achieve the transition.

[To the group] Matt, thank you for your hard work and your trust in the group. I hope you have something to take home and reflect on during the week. Is it okay that we move on to the next agenda item now?

INTERVENTION TECHNIQUES

Working on agenda items requires that we follow the *"half-and-half" principle*—about half of the group's energy should be spent working on the task (the agenda items) and the other half spent on raising members' awareness about their ineffective interaction styles. To the aim of raising member awareness, leaders have to step in to intervene when situations call for such firm action. This section presents just the kinds of intervention techniques that the leader needs to practice.

A Scenario Requiring the Leader to Intervene

The following example represents a situation where a leader needs to step in to intervene. When working on Susan's agenda item, several events happen during the course of the group interaction:

- Mike cannot speak directly to Susan.
- Brenda jumps in to rescue Susan from her pain but shuts down when Tracy confronts her rescuing behavior.

These interpersonal events represent just the kinds of behaviors that slip away from members' awareness but nevertheless have the power to impede group progress—the kinds of behaviors calling for the leader's intervention. Still in its early age, the group may not have geared up for the here-and-now methods of intervention (as presented in Chapters 11 and 12), yet may be well primed for the basic level of intervention techniques, such as *blocking, redirecting, refocusing, and correcting*, as have been presented in Chapter 4.

Due to space limitation, we will provide just a few intervention examples here. Please review Chapter 4 if you need more of them about how to tackle ineffective member behaviors when working on agenda items.

Prevent and Block Rescuing Behaviors

When a member, such as Susan, sheds tears or begins to sob while talking about her issues, some members might rush to her side, trying to comfort her; others (like Brenda) immediately say something to reassure her, with the good intent of taking her pain away.

Certainly, group members are free to show support, care, and concern, but rescuing a member from experiencing pain is not helpful. Therapeutically, the member needs to fully experience her own pain, rather than be rescued from the pain.

Before any rescuing behaviors happen, you can prevent it by saying:

[To the group] Let's allow Susan to be with her pain for a bit longer! I think it is important for her to experience this part of herself. [turning to Susan] Susan, please know that we care, and we support your emotions and the work you are doing right now.

If Brenda still jumps in to rescue Susan from her tears, you will need to explain why rescuing is not helpful:

[To the group] Let's stop for a moment. As Susan is struggling with some issues that are painful, she doesn't need our sympathy, reassurance, or advice. The best way to show our care is to let her feel that her emotions are important in their own right, and that we are willing to listen to her and support her in whatever she is going through. Are you willing to try that?

To deal with the above scenario, you might also need to use redirecting to help Mike speak directly to Susan, and to help Brenda understand Tracy's good intention despite her lack of tact in her delivery.

Redirect Domineering Behaviors

When a member dominates the group, he or she often does not do it purposefully; indeed, the member thinks he or she is doing something good for the group. To redirect, you will need to use gentle, nonconfrontational language since the member being redirected may feel a bit sensitive about it. For example, when Senna was dominating the group interaction, the leader gently intervened by saying,

Senna, let's hold on for a moment! I notice that many members in the group have been waiting for an opening to say something. Let's give everyone an equal chance. [avoid confrontational language, then turning to the quieter members] Who would like to make some comments to Matt?

Another example:

> Let's stop for a moment. [using hand gestures] I have heard a lot from this side of the group [avoid singling out Senna], but I haven't heard much from this side. Let's shift gears a bit. I would really like to hear from the members who haven't had much chance to talk yet.

Correct Labeling Behaviors

When members unknowingly practice labeling, such as calling themselves "loser," "victim," or "wimp," you need to bring this behavior pattern to their attention so that they don't continue to cement self-defeating labels to their personalities:

> Luc, I notice that you have used the word *wimp* to describe yourself two times thus far. I hate to see you categorize yourself with such a label. I want to invite you to confront the behavior pattern itself rather than assign a label to your own personality.

Invite Those Unable to Get Words In

Just the way they are outside the group, quiet members often find themselves unable to chime into the group discussion. Similarly, those who feel isolated in their lives find themselves unable to break free from the shells that keep them separated from others. Be gentle with these members at this stage of the group. Just help them a bit to break through their habits of self-censorship or isolation without pointing out their patterns yet:

> Pat, you seemed to listen quite attentively to what Jen was saying. Is there something you would like to say to her?

> George, I noticed your eyes tearing up as Carissa described her mother's death. Would you be willing to share with Carissa what you are experiencing right now?

∞∞

In closing: Standing between the colossal structured group and the tall-order unstructured group, a humble format of group therapy—the semistructured group—finds a sliver of blue sky for itself. Humble it may be, lowly it is not. The semistructured group prides itself as a member-centered group where members, rather than the leader, own the "say-so" of deciding their *agenda items,* which then serve as a *springboard* for creating a forward momentum of the group discussion.

In this special format, the budding group therapist gets to learn how to facilitate a safe and supportive environment where members go deep in their self-disclosure and receive insightful feedback that brings about much self-awareness and self-knowledge.

CASES IN POINT

Case 1: Anne

Anne's original presenting problem was discussed in an example of intake summary in Chapter 3.

The Habit of Hiding Her Pain. During the check-in of the third session, Anne reported a weekend visit with her family. There seemed to be some turmoil during the visit, and the leader could see that Anne was struggling to keep a smile on her face when speaking to the group. Anne agreed that she might be up for presenting her issues with the group in the session. When Anne finally unfolded her story, she got tearful and really struggled with her emotions. It was obvious that she felt very vulnerable in her pain. She seemed to want to hide, as she brought her hands up to her face and nervously chewed on her fingers and looked down.

"Something Was Wrong With Me." The group became very still and quiet. At this moment, the leader broke the stillness by saying,

It's perfectly okay to cry, Anne. We are all supportive of what you are struggling with right now.

Anne felt somewhat relieved and gathered her courage to reveal to the group that she felt like something was wrong with her and that she thought others looked upon her as so because she seemed to be unable to have a long-term relationship.

Growing Up as Her Mother's Confidant. In response to Anne's revelations, the leader tried to make Anne feel safe by drawing out empathic responses from the group. Feeling understood and validated, Anne went on to tell the group how she grew up as her mother's confidant, to whom her mother unloaded her feelings about her troublesome marriage. As Anne peeled back layer after layer of her story, she continued to be tearful. She constantly apologized for her tears, and at times, tried to make a joke about her tearfulness.

A Pattern of Distraction. It was obvious that when confronted with uncomfortable feelings, Anne had a pattern of joking to distract herself or others from her feelings.

Sentence-Completion Exercise. At this moment, the leader asked the group to do a sentence-completion exercise that successfully initiated an animated exchange between the group and Anne. The leader said,

> I would like the group to complete this sentence: *When I see you crying, Anne, I feel _____ toward you.* Please jump in when you are ready, and please speak to Anne directly.

The Members Speak. The members' consistent remarks were that they felt drawn to and closer to Anne and had a desire to nurture and reach out to Anne when they saw her showing her vulnerable side. But they felt hesitant to do so when she displayed her all-smiling side.

Anne was surprised to hear these positive responses. It was then that the group felt a sense of cohesiveness. There was a bond of trust and a sense of safety in the group that allowed Anne to continue disclosing more about her issue with intimacy.

Ran's Feedback About the Wall Hit a Sore Spot. Ran said that he felt drawn to Anne because of his own feelings and experiences. He revealed his past experience as a member of the clergy and discussed how he learned to *build walls* that did not allow others to see who he really was. Ran actually moved his chair closer to the circle and leaned forward when he spoke. He expressed fear, loneliness, and resentment at having to hide. His tone of voice had much emotion and kindness in it when he spoke to Anne.

Ran, who made several insightful observations during the session, suggested that Anne had also built a wall around herself and was not allowing people to get to know the real her and that perhaps she used her listening skills to focus on others because she did not feel worthy of being the topic of discussion. Ran then asked Anne why she felt so undeserving.

This insight obviously hit another sore spot in Anne, as she nodded in reflective agreement and shed more tears.

Hypothetical Enactment. As the group strived to give Anne feedback about the pattern they saw in Anne's life, the leader created a hypothetical enactment (see Chapter 11 for this here-and-now technique) for the members to respond to. The leader said,

> I would like the group to respond to this hypothetical situation. If you were an invisible light, and you were allowed to follow Anne to a date that she has with a man, what would you be likely to see happening during the date? You can be spontaneous, but please speak directly to Anne.

Insights Given Through the Enactment. One member said that Anne probably would use her listening skills as a wall to keep the man at a distance so he would not get to know the real Anne and reject her. Another member stated that she saw Anne using humor as a way to deflect the focus off herself.

Another member suggested that if Anne turned the focus of conversation back onto the man when things got too revealing, the man would wonder what he did wrong and beat himself up over it. The response was spoken humorously, and the group laughed.

Still another member shared with Anne that she thought Anne would get resentful after a while because she would do so much listening and feel that nobody listened to her; her needs would not be met, and so she would become frustrated and end the relationship.

The Impact on Anne. At this point, Anne's face resonated with insight. Anne agreed that what was said in this exercise was true. She admitted that often she really just wanted to tell people to shut up and listen to her for awhile, but she never did.

As the group wrapped things up, Anne was grateful for the words of insight and felt she needed some time to absorb everything. The leader encouraged Anne to write down her thoughts and spend some time during the week reflecting on what had been exchanged in the group.

Snippets of Members' Reflective Journaling

Anne's Reflection

I came into the third session not sure whether I was ready to open up or not. It has always been easier for me to focus on others' problems than to talk about my own. I knew what I needed to get off my chest was a very emotional issue for me. But the thought of getting upset in front of a roomful of members of the group made me very uneasy. I surprised myself when I put my agenda item out on the table when the group was opened. And I panicked inside when I went first for the night. Even more, I was surprised by my tears. They seemed to come almost instantly as I began to talk.

I am the type of person who tries to keep a smile on my face even if I am upset. I cover a lot of emotions with humor, most of it self-deprecating. I was instantly worried about how everyone in the room was seeing me. I did not want them to pity me or think that I was a total nut case. It seems weird to me since I would never think that about anyone else if they shared a problem or cried, but I could not help thinking that about myself.

Once I began crying and struggling with talking to the group, the leader told me that the group was with me in my pain. Seeing and hearing the sincerity in her voice made me feel a little bit more comfortable. As comfortable as I was, I still could not stop fidgeting, biting my nails, and avoiding looking the rest of the group members in the eyes.

When I let the group know how unnerving it was to get so much focus on me, Ran made a comment that shook me up. He asked me why I felt so undeserving. I had never thought of it in that way.

When I went home I could not stop thinking about it. I realized that there have been many times in my life where I have wanted something but have made excuses why I shouldn't have it. Or if I did get it, I would give a million reasons as to why I did not deserve it. For instance, when I won a teacher-of-the-year award at my school, I felt guilty and could not enjoy it because I thought others were thinking the same thing—my undeservingness. I wondered what made me act this way.

In this group, I felt a real connection with Ran. I remember hearing him say that one reason he had joined the clergy was to avoid relationships. When I heard this, I felt that he could understand where I was coming from.

When the group gave me feedback, I found it a little odd that the group felt drawn to me when I was being so vulnerable. I had never had anyone relate to my emotions in that way or with those words. I really felt like the group heard me and understood. It was a nice feeling—one that I do not get to experience often, especially lately.

Everyone in the group was so encouraging to me. I was especially touched by Joe, who gave me a hug before I left. This was an exceptionally helpful session. I know that my journey has just begun.

Ran's Reflection

Today I decided that the interpersonal skill I wanted to practice in the group was to really try to listen, not only to the words, but also to the feelings, and to let myself feel without going to my head and being clogged by my thoughts.

As Anne shared how she would not let people see her real self, I could relate to that behavior very much. I could also understand her fears. Instead of jumping in to tell her pieces of my story, as I used to be inclined to do, I remained reflective and tried to become even more intensely focused on what Anne was saying.

As she was talking, I responded and reflected back to her the loneliness that I also have felt, since I am used to keeping things on the surface and not letting others in to see the real me behind the facade. I had that same fear very often. But the result was a huge hole in my life that created a sadness along with the loneliness.

I was surprised at the interconnection of Anne's story about her family and the image of her family being "all together" that they always presented when going to church. I saw the connection right away and shared with the group and with Anne that it seemed like Anne lives her life as if she is "in church"—presenting herself in a certain way and not being able to just be herself and let others see the "not so together" side of herself. After all, it isn't appropriate to be naked (not literally) in the church.

Anne mentioned that she was surprised that others would be drawn to her when she felt open and vulnerable. I do hope that sharing in the group like this might be a big step in learning that she can be vulnerable and open and let others in to see her deeper self.

When I left the session, I sensed a feeling of "togetherness" that was exhibited by the whole group walking and talking together as we left the building. I am pleased with my practice in the group this session, and I think I made progress on my own awareness. Anne's sharing has served to open me up to look at myself more deeply and to recognize the patterns of my relationships and the fears that cause me to control so much. This recognition challenges me to let down the walls I build.

Case 2: Sara

Sara's original presenting problem was self-censorship in her communication with people in general and with her father in particular. Her goal was to become more self-assured and confident in her communication.

Sara's Complicated Relationship With Her Supervisor at Work. In the fourth session, Sara presented a problem that had been causing stress for her recently. She spent quite some time speaking about her complicated and stressful relationship with her supervisor at work. As she spoke, it was obvious that she wrestled hard to control her emotions.

The Group Was Stuck on the Details of the Stories. Since Sara's story was quite complicated, the group made several clarifying inquiries to get the full picture of the situation. Mindful of Sara's obvious struggle in letting her emotions be known, the group made an effort to give her empathy and genuine understanding about the difficult feelings that she was not yet able to articulate. As empathic as they were, however, the group members became stuck in the particular details of the struggle between Sara and her supervisor, and they were unable to move beyond them.

Feedback About the Parallel. Just as the group was about to slip into problem-solving mode, the leader navigated members to provide connection-focused feedback:

> I am very touched by the support the group gave to Sara. As I listened to the group, I started to remember that Sara's original goal was to develop a better relationship with her father without censoring her own voice. Although her difficulty with her supervisor seems to stand as a separate issue, I am wondering whether any of you see *any parallel between Sara's relationship with her father and that with her supervisor?*

Group Feedback Leading Sara to a Sudden Realization. Sara was already fully in tears, but this question opened the floodgates to some deeper level of emotions. The group was jolted awake by the leader's question and by Sara's immediate reaction to it. Several members commented on the similarities they saw between the two relationships. These comments oddly led Sara to a *sudden realization* in the following that took the group by surprise.

Sara shared previously that her father suffered from chronic depression. Under the spell of depression, he was usually harsh. This was very oppressive to Sara since she had to censor her own voice and walk on eggshells around him. The way Sara dealt with her father had become so entrenched in her that she often censored herself around others.

Shaken by Her New Realization. But during Sara's emerging difficulty with her supervisor, her father had conveyed to Sara in his own idiosyncratic manner that he felt for her. He noticed her pain. He was, to her surprise, sensitive to her sadness even when what Sara expressed was an irritation.

As Sara shared this realization about her father's new emotional availability to her with the group, her emotions escalated rapidly. She was very moved and shaken by how her father was able to step out of his own depression and show her the affection that she had been longing for all her life.

Looping Back to Sara's Habit of Silencing Herself. Watching Sara become engulfed in her deep emotions, the group felt unspeakable tenderness toward her. For the first time, they felt close to her. But they did not stop there. They went one step further to give Sara their perceptions about her behavior patterns.

For example, Alice hinted that frequently Sara did not get the kindness she needed from people around her perhaps because of her habit of silencing herself. Julie wondered whether Sara's voice of amicability kept her from expressing her true feelings, particularly in situations involving authority figures who were harsh and unfair like her father and supervisor.

Snippets of Members' Reflective Journaling

Sara's Reflection

This fourth session was unlike any event I have witnessed or experienced in my life. It's an amazing feeling to have each member's complete understanding and empathy. Most importantly, the directing of my thoughts toward my father's recent efforts to connect with me was extremely powerful.

Each member attempted to give me thought-provoking insight. It was enlightening. I had felt a slow tension building within me over the past few weeks since the start of my work situation. But as today's session progressed, a sense of calmness came over me. I was able to get a better perspective of the situation.

I'm hoping that as I have more time to contemplate the empathic remarks and patterns that my fellow members offered to me, I will be able to alter my coping pattern and be the person I have the potential to be.

Lastly, I was moved when some members of the group gave me hugs after the session. My only regret is that Kathy was not present to share in this event. I missed her contribution.

Lori's Reflection

This was, without a doubt, the session that made me feel that our group was building trust and cohesiveness. It was full of emotions. As Sara shared her agenda item, the group could sense her frustration and pain. She was, evidently, fighting hard with her tears when she spoke of her father's unexpected support during her time of struggle.

It was at this point that I became tearful because *I, too, have a similar relationship with my father*. Near the end of the session, I told Sara that this instills hope not only in her relationship but also in mine with my father. I felt very close to Sara at that moment. In the next session, I will continue to work on sharing less people-pleasing remarks with others. I am feeling more confident of myself so I am looking forward to the next session with anticipation.

Rose's Reflection

As I listened, I noticed how Sara kept her body in control. Usually, when Sara talks, she uses her hands. This time, her fingers and hands stayed interwoven in her lap. I don't remember seeing them move, even when she was in tears. With the leader's prompt for feedback, I began to see the connection between the current situation and Sara's goals of building a better relationship with her father and of being more assertive.

As Sara began to see how the relationship with her supervisor was so closely connected to that with her father, her eyes began to tear again. As Sara worked on her agenda item, *I found myself reflecting on the relationship with my dad*, and *I told her so*. At the end of the session, I noticed a smile appearing on Sara's face. It indicated new hope and new strength!

AN OVERVIEW OF THE SESSION FLOW AND TIME FRAME OF A SEMISTRUCTURED GROUP SESSION

Before getting into the details of each element, let's take a look at the following chart for the flow of the session and the time frame for each component of a semistructured session.

We understand that presenting this process in such a simple fashion may run the risk of oversimplifying group action and reducing complex leadership practice into a simple linear procedure. A table can never do justice in representing the richness of the flow of a session where multiple actions and circular interactions often occur simultaneously within a live group.

Table 7.1 An Overview of the Session Flow and Time Frame of a Session Working on Agendas

A. Opening the session (15 minutes)

-Relaxation exercise

-Check-in: Sharing lingering feelings, agenda items, and interpersonal skills

B. Working on agenda items (65 minutes)

Working on the 1st agenda (time varies)

-Member self-disclosure

-Group giving empathy (creating a safe group environment) and member deepening self-disclosure

-Group giving feedback and member responding to feedback

-Transitioning to the next agenda

(All along, the leader facilitates, intervenes, and participates, to maximize member-to-member interaction, while balancing the focus on both task and relationships.)

Working on the 2nd agenda item (time varies)

Working on the 3rd agenda item (time varies)

C. Closing the session (10 minutes)

-Announcing the closing

-Checking-out

-Reminders

EXERCISES

Scenarios for Your Practice

1. In a group session, after several members have put their agenda items on the table, Bo states, "I'm just here to learn what I can. My wife joined a group like this a couple of years ago, and she thought it was great—all the feeling of support that she got. She said that it would be

good for me and for our relationship. So here I am." As the group leader, how might you respond to Bo's comments?

2. In the third session of a group, Stephanie recounts at some length her difficulty in expressing herself and feeling heard by others.

   Stephanie reports, "It's as if others sort of hear me but then discount what I say by going on to some other topic that they prefer." She pauses, and then adds, "It makes me feel . . ." Her voice breaks, and her lower lip trembles. Without waiting for more than a few seconds, Wayne interjects, "Well, that must be pretty annoying, but, hey, I get annoyed at work all the time. Like today, a coworker jumped all over me just because my cell phone rang a couple of times during our department meeting. Well, duhhh, people want to talk to me." As the group leader, how might you respond?

3. In a subsequent session of the group, Stephanie makes the following statement, and you notice several others in the group nodding their heads in apparent agreement as she says it: "Wayne, I have something to say to you. You have yet to acknowledge any of the comments that several of us have made to you about how we experience what seems like your lack of listening." Wayne instantly responds, "I think that it is just the other way around in here. It's none of you who are bothering to listen to me. I think that I've had some pretty good insight into what's wrong with people here, and yet no one seems to notice." As a leader, how might you respond to further this feedback exchange?

4. During a session of a group for interpersonal skill development, Jamie says to Bhavani (who is from India), "Bhavani, I don't know if you are afraid of talking in this group because you haven't said very much. I just don't know what you're thinking over there half the time." Bhavani looks puzzled but does not immediately respond.

   As a facilitator, how might you work with this issue from a diversity perspective?

5. It is the third session of a personal growth group. While mostly looking at you, Bill describes in lengthy detail his troubles and fears at work, but he doesn't pause or ask the group for any specific input. What are some of your options for a response as the group leader?

6. During a session of a personal growth group, Sue describes her feelings of missing her father and home life after her parents divorced. Alphie expresses

her feelings concerning her husband's unexpected death. Bob mentions how he felt betrayed by his company when they gave him his layoff notice. What links could you, as the facilitator, make between these experiences?

7. In the third session of a group, Max asks Faroud, "Can I offer you some feedback?" Without pausing to wait for an okay, Max continues, "You seem like a very timid person because you don't say much in this group." As a facilitator, how would you respond to this kind of feedback statement?

8. It is the fifth session of a group for laid-off white-collar workers. Tina took the first job that became available to her but is having some second thoughts about whether it is a good fit for her and whether she can accept the questionable business practices of her new employer. Sheila asks Tina, "How can you look at yourself in the mirror while working for an outfit like this? I would never take a job with a company like that. What were you thinking?" As a leader, what issues would you identify in this exchange? How might you want to manage the discussion?

9. After Martha gives a very brief outline of a dilemma with which she is struggling at work, Jill stares right at Martha and says, "That is just immoral." As the group leader, what options do you have for handling this type of encounter?

10. It is the fourth session of a personal growth group. Marie has described some of her relationship struggles, including those with her spouse. You've heard Bonnie (who was only recently divorced) make a statement implying that if Marie had any courage, she, too, would seek a divorce. What are your options, as the leader, for directing feedback around these issues?

Self-Reflection

1. If you were to join a personal growth group now, what are some of the agenda issues that you might formulate for yourself? As you envision setting out these agenda issues in front of strangers, what feelings are evoked for you?

2. Imagine yourself as a group member. What kinds of feedback would you like? Would it all be positive and supportive? Would you prefer to receive challenges along with support from the group to help you develop new alternatives?

3. Think back to some of your own significant emotional experiences in your life. What factors were present that made those emotional experiences significant to you? What were you able to learn from them? How were you able to implement changes in your thoughts or behaviors as a result?

4. When family and friends are experiencing difficult times, how do you react? Do you tend to jump into problem-solving mode and tell them how to fix things, or do you tend to respond more by acknowledging their feelings and understanding their reactions?

5. Envision yourself as the leader of a group being faced with unhelpful group member actions. What frame of mind will help you to assist the members in redirecting their behaviors to more positive channels?

6. Imagine yourself as a group leader receiving various kinds of feedback from group members. How might you react to positive feedback? Negative? Mixed? How would you like to respond to each type of feedback?

7. Are there any unresolved strong emotional issues in your life? If so, how might you respond to clients with similar unresolved issues?

CHAPTER 8

UNSTRUCTURED GROUPS—BASIC LEVEL

At the core of all counseling and therapy groups lies an *unstructured* group interaction (Bemak, 2005; Bemak, Chung, & Siroskey-Sabdo, 2005)—a style of interaction that harnesses the group's therapeutic power. Be it the second session or the fifth session, the leader can quicken the pace of a group by switching to an unstructured format.

Since unstructured group leadership involves an incredibly intricate skill set, and since complex skills get internalized more easily when broken down into palatable bits, this text has split unstructured group leadership into two levels:

- Unstructured groups—Basic level: orienting the group and reducing anxiety (this chapter)
- Unstructured groups—Advanced level: focusing on intense here-and-now experiences (Chapters 11 and 12)

FEATURES OF UNSTRUCTURED GROUPS

The spirit of an unstructured session is its inherent *freedom*. With this freedom comes a sense of *ambiguity, choice, and responsibility*. All of these elements work to create a unique environment, unlike that of a structured or semistructured group.

No Set Topics or Agenda Items

In an unstructured group session, the leader uses neither structured exercises to arouse member reactions (Chapter 6), nor agenda items to secure discussion topics (Chapter 7). Instead, the leader *leaves the group free to discuss whatever issues*

239

organically emerge. Such choice promotes maximum member-to-member *interaction*—the heart of group therapy (Bernard et al., 2008; Carlson, Watts, & Maniacci, 2006; Choate, 2010; Overholser, 2005; Page, Weiss, & Lietaer, 2002; Shechtman & Pastor, 2005; Yalom, 2009; Yalom & Leszcz, 2005).

Be on the lookout for a typical error of mistaking an unfacilitated group for an unstructured group. They stand miles apart. Left unfacilitated, an unstructured session can easily slip into chit-chatting on safe or irrelevant topics. If facilitated at the optimal level, however, the group will head for the greener pastures of interpersonal learning.

Ambiguity and Uncertainty: Actually an Advantage

Having to face the ambiguity and uncertainty inherent in an unstructured format, members tend to fall back on their established patterns of interaction (Carlson et al., 2006; Levine, 2011; Nicholas, 2013; Schwartz, Nickow, Arseneau, & Glissow, 2015; Yalom, 2009; Yalom & Leszcz, 2005), for an example, putting up walls to fend off anxiety. From the group members' perspective, this represents an advantage.

As such established patterns of interaction come alive, members have something interpersonal in nature to latch on to when they give each other feedback. Such feedback has much power to motivate members to make conscious choices to change. In the above example, a member habitually putting up walls may slowly learn—through feedback on the impact of that specific interpersonal pattern—to let others in.

Not Suitable for Anxious Clients or Task-Oriented Groups

With its potential to provoke *anxiety* (see next section), unstructured groups may not work well with members suffering from intractable anxiety issues. One of the reasons addiction groups run mostly structured (Washton & Zweben, 2006) is that people with addiction issues tend to have grave anxiety problems.

In addition, unstructured groups do not work well either for clients with *cognitive challenges* or for those working on *behavioral goals of a more specific nature.* For example, cognitive behavior therapy (CBT) and dialectical behavior therapy (DBT) groups tend to have precisely defined behavioral goals, requiring a narrow focus on those goals (Barkowski et al., 2016; Petrocelli, 2002;

Roney & Cannon, 2014; Teachman, Goldfriend, & Clerkin, 2013; White & Freeman, 2000). These groups are best run with a structured format.

LEADERSHIP PRINCIPLES OF UNSTRUCTURED GROUPS

To lead well, a leader must understand the principles of leadership that make unstructured groups work. This section touches on these principles.

Share Authority/Control Without Foregoing Facilitation

An unstructured group is a *member-centered* group where the leader readily shares *authority and control* with members. This principle empowers group members to create a session of their own making.

Your job as a leader is to strike a balance between letting members have their own authority/control and steering the group toward productive dialogue. It requires you to use a leadership style that is neither overly directive nor overly passive but just active enough to get the group interaction flowing, intervening only when things go astray.

Allow the Sense of Ambiguity to Do Its Work

Being so loosely open, an unstructured group has a built-in sense of vagueness and uncertainty to it. *Sitting with this vagueness and uncertainty,* members will sooner or later display their *interpersonal characteristics*. At these junctures, a leader needs to stay away from habits of overexplaining, micromanaging, or problem solving.

Instead, we can choose to allow *silence* to linger, *tension* to be felt, and *group reactions* to build up. These are, indeed, the grist of the mill for group work.

Of course, if the group is still at too early of a stage to examine these interpersonal impacts, members may benefit from the leader's simple redirection or intervention as depicted later in this chapter. If, however, the group is in a more mature stage, it will benefit most from close examination of *the dynamics* between group members (Dayton, 2005; Kauff, 2009; Yalom, 1980; 2009).

Addressing the interpersonal process is something that often eludes members; indeed, it appears irrelevant to them (Yalom & Leszcz, 2005). This task, therefore, falls squarely upon the shoulders of the leaders. Dealing with interpersonal processes within the group requires quite a different set of leadership skills and techniques; therefore, parts of Chapters 9 and 10, as well as the entire Chapters of 11 and 12, are devoted to these.

Build a Safe Environment for Self-Disclosure and Uncontrived Intimacy

Freedom and authenticity in the unstructured group are the "recipes" for uncontrived intimacy. However, the more free and authentic the group interaction becomes, the more it needs a safe environment to nourish it. The more members disclose who they are and what personal issues concern them, the more they need to feel safe in doing so.

To build that safe environment wherein members can take risks in self-disclosure and enjoy uncontrived group *intimacy* (Lasky & Riva, 2006; Perrin-Boyle, 2012), a leader needs to find gentle ways to prompt the group members to validate each other, especially when members feel vulnerable. Please review Chapter 4 for related concepts and skills.

EASING MEMBERS INTO SELF-DISCLOSURE BY WORKING ON MULTIPLE MEMBER CONCERNS

With its freedom and ambiguity, an unstructured group can provoke anxiety in many members. But one method may ease that anxiety while boosting both the effectiveness and the depth of the group. This method is working on multiple member concerns simultaneously. This section spells out the major concepts of how this method works. Please note that a few of the concepts might ring a bell for you as they appeared briefly in the section on spontaneous processing in Chapter 6.

The Effects of Member Self-Disclosure

Members benefit from a group experience, in part, through self-disclosure. The act of self-disclosure actually signals positive mental health. Research has found that people who self-disclose are more content, adaptive, competent, perceptive, and trusting toward others, as compared to nondisclosing persons. Sharing one's emotional life not only improves one's health by helping prevent disease but also lessens one's interpersonal problems (Johnson, 2012). Further, self-disclosure increases our self-awareness (Bach & Deutsh, 1971) because, in the process of describing ourselves, we organically sort out our feelings, make clear our inner needs and fears, and take ownership of our choices.

The effect of self-disclosure is contagious. When a member discloses something personal, others in the group cannot help but feel inspired to reciprocate with their own personal disclosures. Such reciprocal disclosure decreases the sense of shame and loneliness, nurturing more trust in the group.

The Anxiety of Self-Disclosure in an Unstructured Setting

As beneficial as it is, self-disclosure in an unstructured group is not for the faint of heart. Not knowing whether others might judge or reject them for what they disclose, members often feel vulnerable and exposed. This sense of vulnerability mushrooms in an unstructured group setting.

In members' imagination, self-disclosure could lead to all kinds of devastating results (Yalom & Leszcz, 2005). Those with distorted beliefs about themselves particularly have the propensity to assume that they will be rejected if they tell others who they really are, what they really think or feel, and *how they feel toward others* in a relationship.

In reality, this distorted belief is completely unfounded. When opening up, most people receive great interest, acceptance, and understanding from their fellow group members. This disconfirmation of one's distortion lies at the core of a corrective emotional experience, as Yalom and Leszcsz (2005) state, "to have that calamitous fantasy disconfirmed is highly therapeutic" (p. 376). This is the key to long-term change.

Ease Anxiety by Working on Multiple Member Concerns Simultaneously

As mentioned, a method that may both ease that anxiety as well as boost the effectiveness and the depth of the group is to work on multiple member concerns simultaneously. The following list summarizes its benefits:

- No member will be singled out for group attention for an extended time.
- Members feel more at ease with self-disclosure.
- The discussion flows effortlessly.

- The topics speak to members' *universal* concerns (Schlapobersky, 2015).
- The discussion touches on members' deep emotions.
- The group reaches maximum mutual engagement.
- All members feel deeply connected.

Beginning with such a low-intensity self-disclosure can prime group members for taking more and more risks (see Chapter 10) in the personal work yet to come.

Mine a Theme From Members' Stories—The Search for Therapeutic Gold

This method does come with a potential pitfall. Without a focus, working on multiple member concerns can lead to chit-chatting and storytelling, preventing the group discussion from reaching any depth. To avoid this, the leader must skillfully navigate the group discussion toward a certain meaningful focus.

To find a meaningful focus, the leader will need to raise his or her "rabbit ears" (Yalom, 2009, p. 49), listening to the common elements, or common threads, among stories shared by members. And this is no small task.

At the very least, we must work against the group's propensity for taking a nose dive into the first issue that a member presents. Left to its own design, the group will lavish a great deal of its time on this member, leaving other members waiting on the sidelines unable to get their needs met. So, the leader must do something to steer the group away from this inclination.

This something is *finding a common thread* around which members can focus their self-disclosure.

A common thread, also called a theme, is the focal point for group discussion. Not every topic counts as a theme. It has to be something that *carries "psychological significance"* (Rogers, 1965) and touches on certain common human conditions or psychological experiences.

In individual counseling, most seasoned therapists know how to find a theme of a client's life and turn it into a focal point of therapeutic exploration (Chen & Giblin, 2018; Ottens & Klein, 2005; Söchting, O'Neal, Third, Rogers, & Ogrodniczuk, 2013). In group counseling and therapy, an experienced leader needs to know how to find a theme among different members' stories and turn it into a focal point of group exploration. We must "mine the gold" of members' stories.

Go Beyond Presenting Problems

New group leaders often confuse a *presenting problem* for a *theme*. What is the difference? A *presenting problem* is a member self-disclosure surrounding *stressful life events* that a member bemoans. A *theme*, however, is something that entwines across many areas of a person's life or something *common* that interweaves across many members' self-disclosure.

For example, Eltha presents a problem about her distress around *seeing her mother struggling with recurring cancer treatment*. Although Eltha's distress surrounds her anticipated grief, it is something she has already learned to adapt to and is therefore *not* the essence of her issue (although a new leader may mistakenly want to focus on it).

Further exploration uncovers, however, that during the 6-year period of focusing on her mother's recurring life-threatening disease, Eltha has put her own needs aside, so much so that she is feeling increasingly burnt-out and empty. Her sense of who she was is lost. And this loss spills over to many areas of her life.

This kind of insidious loss is difficult for Eltha herself to recognize. Sensing this, the leader acknowledges it as the "loss of self" and invites the group members to let Eltha in on their own experiences around this theme.

As other members start to disclose their experience around "loss of self," the group energy immediately picks up. Due to its psychological significance, this theme speaks directly to the hearts of many members who have faced a similar predicament. As a result, Eltha feels supported, understood, and connected while the group members feel closer with one another, gaining heightened self-awareness around this central issue.

Reactive Emotions and Life Experiences Associated With Them

Leaders must learn to differentiate between presenting problems and central themes worthy of group exploration. To increase your ability to separate the wheat from the chaff, so to speak, you will need to learn to zero in on two types of emotions: reactive emotions and primary emotions. You will find your gold mines here.

Reactive Emotions. Listening carefully to member stories, we will soon find this: even though the stories told might differ, they seem to hit a chord of similar emotions. They carry *charged energy* and resonate with group members.

These are *reactive emotions* (Greenburg, 2008; Greenburg & Pascual-Leone, 2006; Johnson, 2004)

The process of working with clients is just like peeling an onion (Chen & Giblin, 2018), and at the upper layer of the onion are these reactive emotions. They many include but are not limited to the following: frustrations, guilt, anger, discouragement, worries, and anxieties over major life events.

Life Experiences Associated With Them. These reactive emotions are often connected to certain *recurring life experiences* that *carry some "psychological significance"* (Rogers, 1965). These distressing life experiences may include but are not limited to the following: being unheard, being unappreciated, not fitting in, misplacement, not getting needs met in relationships, distorted perception of one's self, discrimination, or oppression.

These recurring life experiences are central issues warranting the group's exploration. Indeed, most members feel a sense of relief to be able to talk about their reactive emotions to people and events in their lives, especially when others can relate.

Primary Emotions and Life Experiences Associated With Them

As members continue to open up and the leader continues to listen, in time, other emotions will emerge.

Primary Emotions. These other emotions seem to be buried in the deeper layers of the onion and hold even more charged energy. These are called *primary emotions* (Greenburg, 2008; Greenburg & Pascual-Leone, 2006; Johnson, 2004). Primary emotions are kept submerged because they bring on an overwhelming sense of *vulnerability* when exposed (Greenburg, 2008; Greenburg & Pascual-Leone, 2006; Johnson, 2004). Examples may include a sense of unworthiness, loneliness, shame, or being flawed.

Life Experiences Associated With Them. These primary emotions are often connected to certain *life experiences* that *carry even more "psychological significance"* (Rogers, 1965). They may include but are not limited to the following: abandonment, being unwanted, a sense of being flawed, a sense of unworthiness, basic trust being broken, betrayal, or loss of self.

Since the underlying themes associated with the primary emotions are often abstract, we the leaders really must *quiet our minds*, listening carefully to grasp the matters buried in members' sharing.

These deeply rooted life experiences must be processed to reach resolutions. However, most members will not volunteer to talk about them unless they are provided with a special environment where they unequivocally feel safe and accepted.

METHODS OF WORKING ON
MULTIPLE MEMBER CONCERNS SIMULTANEOUSLY

The method proposed in this chapter requires that we listen mindfully to find something psychologically significant that warrants group exploration. As if to reward our patience, different common threads will naturally and reliably emerge in members' stories, like waves coming to shore.

This section presents the steps of working on multiple member concerns simultaneously in an unstructured session. Leadership skills are simplified for educational purposes, rendering them linear, but actual application is not.

Open the Floor to Generate Spontaneous Sharing

If this is a new group, you can encourage members to use their anxiety and uncertainty, provoked by the unstructured setting, to enhance awareness of how they are with others:

Thank you for your *check-ins*. Now we are going to move on to the unstructured portion of our session. You have the freedom to decide what you want to make out of it. If you feel anxious, not knowing what to say or what's going to happen, it is totally normal. You can sit with it as you observe how the session goes, or you can *express your anxiety* to get it off your chest.

After this, try to provide *a natural continuity from the check-in*.

Example 1:

I noticed that during the check-in, several of you expressed that you are experiencing stress in your lives. As we move on to the bulk of our session, I encourage you to take some group time to explore these stressors. Of course, if you have expressed stress in your life but *did not mention it during check-in*, you are encouraged to ask for group time also. Lastly, if you want to hear more from some specific members, do please tell them so. Who would like to start?

Example 2:

At this time, we would like to open the floor. Please speak only when you feel moved. Silence is OK, but we also encourage you to take initiative to share one of the following:

(1) anything that you have wanted to say to anyone in the group but have not gotten the chance to do so;

(2) any reactions that you've written in your reflective journal that you would like to share with the group;

(3) any desire that you have to get to know more about a specific member;

(4) anything you think can help us work together to reach the group goal; or of course,

(5) any stressful events in your lives.

If you have any one of these, please feel free to bring it to the table for the group to explore. OK. The floor is open. Who would like to start?

Don't Tackle the First Presented Issue Immediately

Once the first member starts talking, be mindful of the following "don'ts" lest they dwindle the power of a group:

- Don't immediately jump the gun to process this first member's issues.
- Don't slip into the mode of working with one member for an extended period of time.
- Don't feel responsible for solving the member's specific presenting problems.

An exception would be if a member is feeling especially emotional or vulnerable after sharing very personal experiences, he or she may need other members to rally around him or her to validate his or her pain and struggle. If the group has not spontaneously done this, you might facilitate the group to do so. This will solidify the group as a safe environment.

Engage as Many Members as Possible, Using Themes

Avoiding the "don'ts" listed above, you move to the next step—focus on encouraging members to relate to the issue just shared. Warmly affirm it whenever any member takes courage to self-disclose. If the group is new, and members have not learned how to participate spontaneously, you may use a prompt to encourage participation,

[To the group] Some of you seem to be quite affected by Julie's story.

I wonder, *what reactions were stirred in you* when you listened to Julie describe her struggle?

While a few members are relating to one another back and forth, *your job is to listen mindfully*. Sooner or later, you might spot a common thread that you can use to invite the rest of the group to join the conversation:

[To the group] From what a few members just shared, it seems like *feeling unheard* is a particularly painful experience. I wonder, for the rest of the group, whether this feeling of being unheard [repeating the key words] has ever come up in your life as well?

Keep Listening and Keep Engaging the Group With Common Themes

This theme may or may not spark heightened group discussion. If it doesn't, it is all right. Just continue to listen while members are talking; you may spot another theme to try out. Keep in mind you may need to repeat this a few times.

In time, you may spot something deeper that you can spin out again to the rest of the group:

Just this moment, I seem to hear a sense of *being unwanted* among the experiences that many of you are sharing. I wonder, *what memories come up for you* surrounding the theme of *being unwanted* [repeating the key phrase]?

Again, detach yourself from the outcome of this theme that you just offered to the group. Eventually, as you keep listening and keep engaging the group, something dynamic will emerge. The result? A deep and intimate space will open up between members—a place they could not have arrived at alone.

Allow the Dialectic Tension to Do Its Work

When working on multiple member concerns, we need to allow the dialectic tension to do its work. Dialectics is a creative process in which two opposing forces interact. Hegel, the German philosopher, teaches us how to arrive at the truth by a dialectic line of reasoning by stating a thesis and then developing a contradictory antithesis (Bhaskar, 2008). Surprisingly, arising from the interaction of the two opposing forces comes a new position, a synthesis that unexpectedly solves the argument being discussed (Corey, 2017; Rizvi, Steffel, & Carson-Wong, 2013; Sommers-Flanagan & Sommers-Flanagan, 2015).

For example, in one unstructured group, Dahi talked about his 7-year relationship in which his needs were not being met. He told the group he wanted to let go of this relationship but found himself returning to it again and again. Several members also shared similar experiences. Through this sharing, a theme, *fear of aloneness,* came into view.

The group, responding to the leader's invitation to share their experiences surrounding this theme, enjoyed a fervent dialogue on how the fear of aloneness urges them to cling to relationships.

Later, a radically opposite theme, *fear of being hurt,* emerged. Again, the leader invited members to share around this theme. Several members shared how this fear of hurt has driven them to be *alone* by totally cutting people off.

As such, the dialectical tension between two interacting forces puts the group on its toes, giving rise to an engaging and mesmerizing session. To arrive at a synthesis—a new position, if you will—the leader invites the group to reflect further:

> [To the group] So there are two opposing sides of your stories: one is to stay in a relationship where your needs are unmet due to fear of being alone; another is to cut people off when disappointed due to fear of being hurt again. Both of these ways of being in relationships are driven by our fear. I really enjoy the tension that is created by these two opposing themes. It seems that due to fear, we develop different strategies to cope with it, and, yet, no matter which strategy we choose, we always end up feeling trapped. I wonder, after exploring these two opposing themes, what new coping strategies could you adopt that would be more nourishing and wholesome ways of being in relationships?

In this process of working on multiple member concerns simultaneously, the leader's job is to facilitate the members to express themselves in ways that are liberating to their true selves. The process may seem unpredictable; the end results, however, spell heightened self-awareness for the members and intense motivation to be the best of who they are. The group's patience and trust in the process completely pay off.

LOW-INTENSITY HERE-AND-NOW DISCLOSURE

Self-disclosure surrounding common themes tends to involve members' life experiences outside the group; therefore they are called *there-and-then disclosure* (Leszcz, 1992). This kind of disclosure helps group members understand each other's worlds, enabling them to give empathy and support to one another. However, if the group members want to really enter each other's experiential worlds, members will eventually need to progress to *here-and-now disclosure*.

In the here-and-now disclosure, a member reveals his or her first-hand experiences within the group and his or her direct experiences with other members of the group. This type of disclosure perks the group up, working to foster intimacy and authenticity among the group members.

This chapter introduces techniques for low-intensity here-and-now disclosure, appropriate for the earlier stages of most types of groups. Chapter 11 will cover techniques for higher levels of intensity, reserved primarily for experiential groups in their mature stage of development.

Invite Member Disclosure of Reactions Toward Historical Incidents Inside the Group

To make members' self-disclosure more pertinent and interesting to the group, the leader may facilitate members to reveal how they have reacted to certain historical incidents in the group. With this technique, you *shift* the conversation *from* discussions about *life events outside the group* toward historical *incidents inside the group*. This invites the mildest here-and-now disclosure. For example,

Julie, you said that you feel exploited every time you trust someone or reveal yourself. I wonder, *has there ever been a time in this group* when you have experienced this feeling?

Janet, you have claimed that people discriminate against you in your school. I wonder, *has there been a time or an incident in this group* when you felt rejected or ignored?

Encourage Disclosure of Members' "Now" Experiences "Here" in the Group

Another low-intensity self-disclosure involves members disclosing their in-group experiences. This step often has group members perk up instantly. To do this, you turn members' disclosures on life events outside the group into ones on direct experiences within the group. Consider the following examples:

Kayra, thank you for talking about the trust issues that you have long struggled with in your life. Would you tell us *what it is like for you* to talk about yourself *here in the group*?

Barbara, you said that you feel strongly sometimes when people cut you off. *Do you feel cut off by the group right now?*

Bill, how did *you* feel about *my* interrupting you *just now* to stop you from giving advice to Don?

Rita, in the past, it has not been safe enough for you to share this vulnerable side of yourself, but today you choose to do so. I wonder: what happened in the group, or in your feelings toward the group, today, that allowed you to do this?

[To the group] The topic of feeling unheard came up a moment ago. I just want to stop for a moment and ask, *Has anyone here ever felt unheard in this group?* Has anyone in this group *felt unheard by another member* of this group? Or has anyone in this group *felt unheard by me*?

[To the group] It is refreshing to see Sasha speak up freely today as compared to the way she stayed in the background in the past few sessions. I wonder, *what* do you see *is happening in today's session* that makes it easy for Sasha to be herself?

Invite Disclosure of Feelings Toward Other Group Members

To get the group more emotionally involved, you may ask the group members to state *how they feel toward a specific member* at a critical point.

Here, you are not aiming to draw out empathy from the group. You are not trying to have members validate other members' feelings. Rather, you are trying to guide the members to reveal *their own* personal reactions toward one another.

> [To the group] I wonder, after listening to Mark's profound sharing, how do *you feel toward Mark* at this moment? I am curious not about how you relate to Mark or how you think Mark might be feeling but how you *feel* toward Mark.

If, by misunderstanding, a group member responds with a reflection of Mark's feelings, just gently steer her to disclose her feelings *toward* Mark. For example,

> Etana, thank you for acknowledging Mark's feeling. Right now, instead of focusing on Mark's feeling, I am actually more interested in hearing how *you* feel *toward* Mark after listening to his profound sharing. Would you tell Mark about how you feel toward him in this moment?

Encourage Disclosure of Reactions Toward the Group as a Whole

Members usually have strong feelings toward the group, similar to those harbored toward their first group: their family of origin. Asking members to talk about their feelings toward the group can bring strong emotions to the forefront for exploration. To do this, the leader moves the group discussion from outside events to feelings toward the group itself. For example,

> [To the group] Even though Brenda said that she just wants support from the group, the group keeps going back, again and again, to try to solve her problem. [turning to Brenda] Brenda, *how do you feel toward the group* regarding this behavior?

Prompt Members to Respond to Another Member's Here-and-Now Disclosure

If a member, Jenna, says that she is worried about taking too much time from the group, you, as the leader, can *invite the rest of the group to respond to Jenna's disclosure*:

[To the group] I wonder, would any of you like to respond to Jenna's fear of taking up too much of the group's time? How does her fear match or not match *with your experience of her in the group*? Please speak directly to Jenna.

If another member, Jeff, says that he is afraid of being judged, you can *invite the rest of the group to respond to Jeff's disclosure*:

[To the group] I wonder, after hearing Jeff's anxiety, what would you like to say to Jeff regarding his fear of being judged in this group? How does judgment or the lack of it play a role *in your relationship with him*? Please speak directly to Jeff.

These above-illustrated techniques of *low-intensity here-and-now disclosure* should perk the group up, allowing much intimacy and authenticity among the group members.

BABY STEPS TOWARD HERE-AND-NOW FEEDBACK

As members self-disclose on either life events outside the group or on direct experiences inside the group, members will soon run into a chance to receive feedback—feedback on how they come across to others in the group. This is called *here-and-now feedback*.

The here-and-now techniques are spread out over various chapters. This chapter will introduce *the baby steps* to take toward implementing the *here-and-now feedback*. Chapter 10 will go into the intermediate steps, leaving Chapters 11 and 12 to methodically cover the advanced steps.

The Functions of Here-and-Now Feedback

A here-and-now feedback calls attention to a member's interpersonal style as it occurs right here, right now, in front of the group. Feedback itself, like a mirror, gives the receiver a chance for *reality testing* (Corey, 2017; Dewane, 2006). It reflects back directly to the member his or her interpersonal patterns and relational strengths. This is why the there-and-then feedback, featured in Chapter 7 for semistructured groups, seems pale in comparison.

Rather than relying on the leader to give here-and-now feedback, the group is better off if it takes up this responsibility itself, as most members prefer feedback *from their fellow members* as opposed to from the leader (Corey, 2017; Toth & Erwin, 1998; Yalom & Leszcz, 2005).

It is important to note that it is not just the receiver who benefits from the feedback, it is also the *giver*. To offer a here-and-now feedback, the contributor must sort through his or her own reactions and then decide on how to deliver feedback in the most sensitive and honest way. This act of self-reflection, along with the boost in self-esteem that comes from altruistically giving, is how the giver of the feedback paradoxically *receives by giving*.

Invite Here-and-Now Feedback
Based on Recurrent Reactions

A here-and-now feedback is actually a special type of self-disclosure, not about one's life experiences but about one's *recurring* feelings and reactions toward a specific member or to the group as a whole. Candidates for such disclosure may include those recurrent reactions—amazement, boredom, anger, respect, closeness, disappointment, distance, powerlessness, irritation, and so on—toward a specific member or to the group as a whole.

When delivered in an honest and caring way, this kind of here-and-now feedback helps the receivers see how their interpersonal styles affect others. Members, however, may not venture into this kind of here-and-now feedback unless prompted by the leader. Consider the following examples of how to encourage members to put these recurrent feelings into words.

Example 1:

> [To the group] I sense some reactions going on in the group. I wonder *what the group is feeling at this moment.* If you have felt a certain way more than twice, I invite you to *trust your feelings* and *try to express them in a way that is easy for others to hear.* [pause for the group to comprehend these words] Would anyone in the group like to share some *feelings that you have had in the group but are unsure of how to express them?*

Example 2:

> [To the group] For the last several minutes, we have been discussing "safe" issues, but I sense that some of you have *feelings about one another* in the group that you are not openly discussing. I know it's not easy, but let's try to take some time to talk about *these feelings about one another* that are difficult to share.

Example 3:

> Jane, you gave the group permission in the first session to offer feedback to you whenever they observed combative behavior so as to help you reach your stated goal of finding peace. Has that changed? If not, would you be open to hearing feedback from the group now? [Jane nods] [turn to the group] Okay, would anyone in the group like to share some *feelings that you have had* when you see Jane's combative behavior in the group?

Seek Consensual Validation for a Here-and-Now Feedback

A here-and-now feedback, coming from the giver's subjective experiences of another member, is far from objective. For the benefit of the receiver, the leader might want to check with the rest of the group about whether the giver's subjective experiences also reflect others' experiences. This act of checking is called *consensual validation* (Dewane, 2006; Marmarosh & Tasca, 2013; Yalom & Leszcz, 2005) previously presented in Chapter 7.

Consensual validation gives both the giver and the receiver a reference point, against which both sides can assess the validity of the feedback. Consider the following examples:

Example 1:

> [To the group] Kevin just took some risks to share how he feels alienated and frustrated by Bill's tendency to intellectualize and deflect. Do any of you experience something similar to what Kevin experienced?

Example 2:

> [To the group] Jenika just said that she could sense a simmering anger inside Oleg from day one, and she feels threatened that his anger may go off at any moment. I wonder, do the rest of you feel threatened by Oleg's anger, or do you have a different experience of Oleg's anger?

Encourage Members to Request Here-and-Now Feedback

Some members could truly benefit from here-and-now feedback from the group but simply do not know that they can actually ask for it. Here is how a leader can prompt them to take such a courageous action:

Pat, you said you don't know why people tend to take you for granted. Since you have been in the group for awhile, perhaps you can ask people in this group how they see you stepping into this reality. [Pat nods] Okay, please use your own words, and ask the group.

Jenika, you said that you have transcended your anger toward your mother's and your father's self-centeredness but cannot understand why Oleg's presence in the group still triggers intense distrust in you. Perhaps you can ask people in this group how they see you in regard to this. Would you like to ask them about it?

Connect the Here-and-Now Feedback to Members' Outside Lives

The ultimate purpose of a here-and-now feedback is to help members transfer their in-group insights to their outside-group behaviors. To support this transference, the leader can use prompts to help members connect the dots:

First,

Pat, now that you've gained perspectives about how your sole focus on others in the group, without revealing much of yourself, can set up other members to take you for granted, would you please reflect on how this very behavior pattern may cause people in your personal life to do the same?

Much later,

That's very perceptive of you, Pat, to see the very same pattern played out with your spouse and your children. So, the question is, what are you going to do with this new realization?

MAKING MEANINGS OUT OF DIFFICULT LIFE EXPERIENCES

Sharing difficult personal experiences and receiving here-and-now feedback from the group can do something remarkable for members—it takes them to a reflective state where they see their lives with a rare sense of clarity. In that clarity, they see this: through years of life struggles, they triumph; out of the struggles, they emerge in the company of a human spirit alive with ingenuity and purpose—just like through years of fermentation, grapes triumph and yield a wine awash with exquisite aroma and taste.

The Unmet Needs That Drive Coping Strategies

To cope with painful emotions, people often adopt certain coping methods (Greenburg, Korman, & Paivio, 2002), including wearing masks, building walls, hiding one's true self, denying, blaming, complaining, reacting with passive aggressiveness, being overly confrontational, overaccommodating, placating, people-pleasing, escaping into social media, food, shopping, substances, sex, work, and so on.

Through rounds and rounds of the group's feedback, members arrive at a place of honesty and clarity about these coping strategies. For example, they come to reflect on the needs that drive them to use these coping strategies. In other words, behavior patterns have served certain functions for them (Gonzalez & Prihoda, 2007; Hammond & Marmarosh, 2011).

Often, the original coping behaviors or thought patterns came to exist to meet certain unmet needs, such as the need for safety, recognition, a sense of belonging, acceptance, love, or so on. Looking at their coping behaviors through this lens of unmet needs creates an "aha" moment for members: Even their maladaptive behaviors carry special meanings.

Out of Hardship Comes Inner Strength and Resourcefulness

Through session after session of group feedback, members also come to realize that they actually have a resilience and resourcefulness that they have previously ignored. Out of the hardships endured, something stupendous has emerged (see Chapter 1), just like out of the high-pressure process of cleaving, shaping, rounding, grinding, and polishing, a diamond emerges from a rough molten rock, so brilliant that it refracts and reflects light.

Through the group's discussion, it becomes clear that members' struggles and pain do not wither their lives but actually bring that brilliant crystal out, revealing their true inner beauty and their high purposes. This philosophy of meaning-making is akin to strength-based therapy (Seligman & Csikszentmihalyi, 2000; Wolin & Wolin, 2010).

Reclaiming One's Own Voice

Through their self-disclosure and received feedback, members often arrive at a point where they start to reclaim their own voices. It is a touching phenomenon to witness.

Before entering the group, many members have long practiced a habit of suppressing their voice. Perhaps a part of them felt unwelcomed as a child; perhaps they learned to hide a certain attribute shamed by those around them; perhaps they were overwhelmed by countless demands and expectations; perhaps they were frightened by trauma. . . . In any case, experiences like these started to lock away their true inner voices. After years of self-censoring, stress, anger, and resentment inevitably started to scream inside, leaving their sense of self-worth emaciated.

As the group gets going and as the here-and-now feedback works its magic, members cannot help but challenge each other to be real rather than be right, to stop managing other people's feelings, to be clear and direct about what they want, to say what they need with respect, and to say "no" instead of "no problem." The hard work toward authenticity creates a ripple effect in their personal lives.

More and more, they are able to take risks to speak their truths and be authentic with their loved ones or their associates, saying something to the effect of the following:

This doesn't feel right for me.

I'm feeling uncomfortable about the loud voice I hear. I want to leave early.

I need to take time for myself right now.

Would you repeat what you just said? I am not sure I understand it.

In sum, the group experience is a meaning-making process. Out of this process, members often find their true selves.

INTERVENTION TECHNIQUES FOR
UNSTRUCTURED GROUPS—BASIC LEVEL

The freedom and ambiguity of the unstructured session allow for various types of member behaviors to show up. All can be tackled with ease by using *the basic level of intervention techniques* if the group is still in its tender age. This section presents a few of the common kinds of scenarios and their accompanying interventions.

If Someone Gives a Canned Response

When hearing members using canned statements to respond to others, you might want to intervene to draw out more authentic inner reactions:

Jim, would you be more specific about what you mean when you say, "I understand how that feels"?

If Someone Rambles

When someone has a pattern of rambling, the group rarely has the courage to stop that person, especially in the early stage of group development. You as a leader may intervene by saying the following:

Bogdana, thank you for your sharing! [look away from Bogdana and toward the rest of the group] I am also interested in hearing what others have to say about the experience of *isolation*. Who else would like to share your experiences?

Deal With Monopolizing Behaviors

Those who are extroverted may unknowingly monopolize, taking up the entire time talking about their experiences. Those who are quiet, shy, or introverted might be left without room to say anything.

If the group is mature enough to go to the advanced level, you can use process illumination to bring insight into this dynamic (Chapters 11 and 12). If the group is still trying to establish trust, then you can use redirection to intervene:

Thank you, Stella, Leslie, and Nicole for sharing. [look away from the three talkative members and toward the quieter ones of the group] I am interested in hearing from those of you who have not had a chance to share your experiences of using social media to escape from your inner self. [turn to the group] Would anyone in the group like to *invite someone* to share a bit?

Handle a Member With a Pattern of Always Jumping in First

Some members deal with their anxiety in the unstructured group by quickly and frequently jumping in to relate to just about anything after someone else has just said something. This kind of anxiety-driven behavior can take away others' chances of responding. Though feeling frustrated, other members often feel that they are not in the position to point it out.

One way to deal with this it to *make this anxious member a helper*. That is, you can ask this member to *help invite others to participate*.

Cezar, thank you for being the first to respond as usual! It takes a lot of courage to jump in like that. I do also want to see that other members get a chance to be the first to respond so that they can practice their initiation skills. *Would you help me notice who in the group might have been waiting to participate?* And *would you help* me *invite him or her to join in?*

Manage Disruptive Behaviors

As mentioned, the unstructured group is an environment where members' maladaptive behaviors may organically sprout. Examples may include provocative statements, arguing, being disrespectful, and so on.

The best way to deal with disruptive behaviors is to engage the whole group to provide feedback to the person. Consider these examples:

[To the group] *Whitney was just at a turning point in reaching her deep emotions when Dragos started to ask her a series of questions.* I wonder how the group responds to the timing of this questioning? [Handling disruptive manners.]

[To the group] I see some strong reactions in the group when Caesar said to Maureen, "I have trouble feeling empathy for you." I wonder whether some of you would like to put your reaction into words. Anyone want to try? [Handling provocative manners.]

[To the group] Let's stop for a moment. When Andy (a member with autism spectrum disorder) made that comment to Emily (a member with a self-esteem issue), I saw some strong reactions in the group. I would like the group to speak up about how you think Andy's comment may have come across to Emily and how this might have an impact on Emily's self-esteem? [Handling disrespectful comment to another.]

[To the group] Let's stop for a moment. I see that the heated discussion between Lois and Domingo is about to reach its boiling point. I wonder what the rest of the group sees is going on between Lois and Domingo? Where, do you think, each of them is coming from? [Handling arguments or conflicts.]

Deal With Prolonged Silence

If a group is mature enough, we may examine the meanings and impacts of a prolonged silence (See "process illumination" in Chapters 11 and 12).

If a group is still tender, we can encourage members to share what they are feeling in the ambiguity:

[After the group has been sitting in silence] Right now, I am sensing some tension. I am wondering whether any of you would be comfortable sharing with the group what was on your mind as we were sitting in silence?

[To the group] I sense some reactions in the group not being openly expressed. *If you have had any feelings or reactions toward any member or the group as a whole, I encourage you to openly share them so that we can learn from each other.* [Pause, and let the group take the responsibility to start. If there is silence, let the silence linger a bit longer.]

Please note that, due to space limitation, we can only present the scenarios and interventions above. For more, please review Chapter 4 for basic intervention techniques, especially redirecting, refocusing, and correcting.

In conclusion, if you conduct the unstructured group session in a way that nurtures focused and intimate discussions, your members are likely to leave the session feeling *energized, connected, lifted,* and *alive.* A new sense of compassion and purpose will fill their hearts. Often, deeper insight and forgotten resources will emerge from within, and members will find new and creative resolutions to their problems. A sense of spirituality also often prevails as members go deep to explore the meanings of their existences.

∞∞∞

In closing: The *unstructured* group interaction is the engine that harnesses the group's therapeutic power. However, accompanied with the freedom of the unstructured interaction comes a sense of anxiety and uncertainty. To ease that anxiety while boosting the effectiveness and the depth of the group, the leader can elect to work on multiple member concerns simultaneously.

Finding a theme among various members' stories and turning it into a focal point of group exploration is like "mining gold." And you are likely to find your gold nuggets in reactive emotions and primary emotions.

In this search for the gold, the leader can, slowly and surely, introduce members to low-intensity here-and-now disclosure, help them take *baby steps* toward the *here-and-now feedback, and* work with them to extract meanings from life's struggles.

A CASE IN POINT

The fifth session was this group's first unstructured session. Through the following snippets of reflective journal entries, we can catch a glimpse of how the common threads work through the session. There is no coverage of the here-and-now feedback in the journal entries here as they will come up in later chapters.

The Leader's Narrative Session Notes

Tonight was our first unstructured session. It provided a wonderful venue for sharing deeply emotional and painful stories. After the session was opened, two themes came to light:

- The felt burden to protect the emotions of others
- The feeling of unworthiness

Members felt safe enough to take risks and allowed themselves to show vulnerability, which created a deep and powerful session. The processing of these two themes allowed multiple members to open up. *The vulnerability and courage seemed infectious* as one member's opening up led to others revealing deeper parts of themselves. Connections between members deepened because of the incredible courage and vulnerability of the members.

Toby—"The Smelly Kid" and His Hoarder Mom. Out of all the members, Toby made the biggest strides by tackling his goal of overcoming the fear of rejection. He was able to let others in, and he really surprised me with his ability to rise above his fear and share the powerful and painful story of where he was from. Toby shared that his mom is a hoarder, that he had had no clean clothes to wear, that he was "the smelly kid," and that he was ridiculed and bullied throughout his school years.

Shame. He experienced a deep sense of *shame* about who he was. Since he rejected this part of himself, his self-rejection leads him to assume that others will not be receptive to him either.

Group's Acceptance of Toby. It amazed me to see every group member give Toby powerful input about his sharing. For example, Lexia shared with Toby that she feels so much more connected to him after hearing his story. Charlie shared that he fully accepts Toby with no judgment, and that this piece of new knowledge about Toby only makes Charlie feel more connected to him. I felt a deep sense of group connection and compassion for Toby.

From Group Acceptance to Self-Acceptance. I hope this support helped him realize that he is worthy of deep connection with others. I also wonder, with continued vulnerability and opening up, whether Toby might feel more confident that he can start to accept who he is outside of the group. I felt deep pride for Toby in the leap that he took tonight in moving toward his goal.

Various Member Reflections

Member Reflection 1:
   At one point Brooke said to Toby,

   No wonder you have been disconnected from others, *your mother literally built a fortress around you.*

As Brooke said that, I could see an emotional reaction in Toby. I also saw it in many other members, including myself.

Even though I had known Toby's history, I have never felt as close to him as I did after Brooke said this. I literally visualized him trapped in a fortress, wanting to stay inside where it was "safe" and, at the same time, wanting to escape. I felt the urge to hug the "little Toby" in that moment.

It seemed that in light of his feelings of *shame*, the positive responses from the group, including my own, which described his *resiliency*, might have been a healing experience for him.

I, for one, felt much closer to Toby after our first unstructured session this past Monday night.

Member Reflection 2:

> The unstructured setup worked really well because it allowed conversations to flow more freely and allowed many group members to dig deeper into certain issues, providing a new perspective into their lives, like what was happening with Charlie and Toby.
>
> It also allowed for a great connection to be formed between Kate, Brooke, and Lexia regarding *alcoholics, parents,* and *divorce*.

Member Reflection 3:

> One thing that stood out to me in the fifth session (our first unstructured session) was how beautiful the group is. It's beautiful how *one thought or feeling strikes another and opens new passageways*, and when one can't find words, the group is there. This left me feeling so *energized* and *alive* the entire week.

AN OVERVIEW OF THE FLOW AND TIME FRAME OF A BASIC LEVEL UNSTRUCTURED SESSION

This section provides you with an overview of a basic unstructured session. Please remember, a table can never do justice to the richness and complexity of interaction in a live group.

Table 8.1   An Overview of the Flow and Time Frame of a
Soft-Landing Unstructured Session

A. Opening the session (10 minutes)

-Relaxation exercise (optional)

-Check-in: Members sharing lingering feelings and picking an interpersonal skill for practice during the session

B. Opening the floor for unstructured discussion (65 minutes)

-Facilitate sharing of presenting problems, validation, and feedback

-Pick the first layer of common theme (listening carefully to key phrases) from the stories shared by members

-Engage multiple members to share on this first layer of common theme; facilitate mutual validation and feedback

-Mine to a deeper theme, or work on two opposing themes; facilitate mutual validation and feedback

-Reflecting on and extracting meanings from coping strategies for life difficulties that members shared

(All along, the leader facilitates, intervenes, participates, and maximizes member engagement, keeping members' interpersonal characteristics in the mind)

C. Closing the session (10 minutes)

-Announcing the closing

-Checking-out

-Reminder

EXERCISES

Scenarios for Your Practice

1. During the initial check-in, Leslie expressed feeling resentment and frustration about her mother-in-law intruding into her life too much. She wishes her husband would do something about it. Krista shared about her new boyfriend and her frustration that she gives and gives and gets very little in return. She wonders when he is going to step up and do for

her the way she does for him. Gus shared his frustration about his mother meddling and prying into his private life. He wishes she would stop but doesn't want to hurt her feelings. What common theme/themes might be derived and brought forward for group discussion and processing?

2. Given the scenarios previously mentioned above, frustration could be seen as a more reactive or secondary emotion. What might be a primary emotion or deeper emotion that has yet to be identified or expressed?

3. Jim is usually the first responder within the group and readily shares about himself. In fact, he has an uncanny ability to personalize almost every issue mentioned by other members. What might be the deeper issue here for Jim, and how can you bring that forward in a way that the entire group might be able to relate?

4. Anna has shared a particular issue that she has struggled with for a very long time. She was extremely vulnerable and actually became quite emotional when she shared. The group was very responsive to her. Members began asking question after question in hopes of "figuring out" how Anna might deal with her issue. They offered many suggestions, all of which Anna tried valiantly to respond to. In spite of all the feedback, Anna continued to be distraught and uneasy with what was occurring in the group. Was the group effective in their interaction with Anna? Why, or why not? If not, please state how the group might have validated Anna more effectively? To take this scenario a step further, how might you, as the counselor, intervene so that not only Anna benefits but also the entire group?

5. Lou constantly holds back his emotions and almost maintains a bit of a "poker face" when he expresses himself. On the other hand, Rosemary is a big bundle of raw emotion and readily cries in response to just about everything. While these two may seem polar opposites, what might be a common theme between these two individuals that might also be common to the entire group and therefore useful for processing?

Self-Reflection

1. More often than not, the reason we recognize issues in others is because the same issues also exist, on some level, in us. Have you ever observed issues in your immediate circle of influence that actually resemble your own?

2. Think back to a time when you felt really frustrated with or angry at someone; what might really be the deeper issue? In other words, where might you have felt hurt? Where might you have felt unloved?

3. So often, even the most extroverted of people have trouble giving voice to their true feelings. Are there instances in your life where you were not able to truly express yourself and speak your "truth" in situations? Give examples. As a clinician, how might you model authentic expression of thoughts and ideas?

4. Generally speaking, one can only take a person as far as they have gone themselves. What are you doing to further your investigation of your own internal world?

5. Boundaries and the lack thereof is a common theme amongst people. Often we say "yes" when we really mean "no." Can you think back to times when you said yes to a person or situation when you really wanted to say no? How might boundaries be pertinent for you as a clinician?

CHAPTER 9

WORKING WITH UNSPOKEN TENSION AND OPEN CONFLICT

Embarking on the journey into the unstructured or experiential mode, a group will sooner or later come upon a new rite of passage—tension and conflict. Some beginning group leaders feel threatened in the face of this tension and conflict; others even take it personally, believing it a proof of their personal failure as a leader. It is no wonder when interviewing graduate students about their experience in group leadership training, Ohrt, Ener, Porter, and Young (2014) found a consistent theme: *an overwhelming anxiety about managing conflict within the group.* Sadly, this fear of conflict sends many prospective therapists running for the exit from leading groups.

To address this anxiety, this chapter presents concepts and methods of handling the two types of group conflict: (1) unspoken tension and (2) open conflict. Equipped with this knowledge and skills, beginning group leaders can start to build their therapeutic muscles as they learn to face conflict head on, taking, so to speak, the bull by the horns.

THE TRANSITION STAGE AND MEMBER DISSATISFACTION

The Transition/Storming Stage of Group Development

The transition stage—the second stage of group development—can come about as early as the second session in unstructured groups (and a bit later in structured ones). Characterized by *projections, tension,* and *conflict,* the inherent competition and power struggles in this stage can wreak havoc on a young group (Corey & Corey, 2014).

Running parallel to *the adolescence period* of a human life, this stage of a group can overwhelm us with its *unpredictable and volatile qualities.* As parents of adolescents know all too well, their teens' *struggle for independence and self-identity* can create much sound and fury. This is why you may hear the transition stage also referred to as the *storming* stage (Tuckman, 1965).

Suppressed Feelings Producing Disappointment

Once having passed the initial forming stage, a group often shakes off its sense of innocence and promise, plummeting into a stage of *relative dissatisfaction* (Lacoursiere, 1980) by reason of a number of issues:

- Perceived untrustworthiness of other members
- Perceived lack of competence in the leader
- Serious self-doubt about being able to change

In one way or another, members may feel that the group is not turning out quite like they had hoped.

Yalom and Leszcz (2005) reason that, early in the forming stage, members' yearning for acceptance is so strong that they often *turn their back on their own feelings* for the sake of group cohesiveness. Once the group hits the transition stage, however, members begin to feel *disappointed* for having held back their own feelings.

Struggle for Control

Our need for control stands as one of the three universal human needs (Schutz, 1958). Once the need for inclusion has been satisfied, the need for control activates itself. The dissatisfaction in the transition stage has a great deal to do with every member struggling to meet this need of control. Every member scrambles to keep in check how much to expose themselves, how much to influence, and how much to be influenced.

When preoccupied with the need for control, members may act out various tactics of behaviors:

- Aggression
- Scapegoating
- Silence
- Storytelling
- The pursuit of secondary gratification

These indirect displays of control create unspoken tension.

Power Imbalance

The power in a group seldom distributes equally. As with the need for control, power displays come in various shades of indirect behaviors:

- Dominating by speaking louder or responding quicker
- Interrupting by changing topics, talking over others, or spoiling a critical emotional moment with a joke or an irrelevant comment
- Withholding by not revealing thoughts and feelings

Seldom are these power imbalance issues openly commented on, thus becoming another source of unspoken tension.

Differences in Shades of Openness

Perceived differences in shades of openness can also provoke tension (Ferguson & Peterson, 2015). Usually, the extroverts cannot wait to jump in and take the floor, whereas the introverts wait anxiously on the fringes, unable to get a word in edgewise.

Not realizing that introverts struggle to get a foothold in the conversation, the extroverts perceive the quieter people as not willing to open up; the introverts see the extroverts as domineering. Both sides feel frustrated, taking the different shades of openness from the other side as a threat. This, unsurprisingly, leads to tension and conflicts.

With this in mind, the leader might want to ask members to discuss how long it typically takes for them to trust new people and what factors slow them down in opening up.

Mind Reading as a Source of Misunderstanding

The filters developed from our past experiences accompany us and influence how we interact with others wherever we go (Heitler, 1993). In a group, for example, someone with a strong personality may be read by another member as an authoritarian or even an abusive figure, even if the association is completely unfounded. The phenomenon of misinterpretation kicks in fairly early in the group, as demonstrated in Jill's journal entry below:

When we started our second session, I felt fairly open and able to share. But after I made one comment to another member, I sensed that she didn't value or appreciate what I had to say.

This feeling was based on her facial expression and the fact that she didn't say anything back to me. I felt really hurt and immediately began to withdraw. For the rest of the session, I felt alienated from the group, even though I rationally knew I was overreacting.

At first, I got caught up in thinking that she didn't like me and that's why she acted that way. Then I realized that this member probably did not mean it, but it was too late: Her lack of reaction had already set off all these other emotional reactions that I could not rationalize.

I also was surprised by my physiological reaction of a headache. I did not feel able to share this with the group at the time because I don't feel trusting enough yet to be honest with feelings.

The other thing I didn't expect was that I recognized this pattern within myself in relationship to my extended family. I know that this is exactly how I felt as a child and even as an adult when relating to my dad's side of the family.

I am surprised that I am having such strong reactions to these memories or patterns related to my extended family. Today's session has brought up some extremely painful memories for me. I would never have thought that this would have been brought up for me so early in the group.

Please note that some group members might not be as reflective as Jill and therefore are not quite aware of how they project their unresolved inner conflicts onto others (Daniel & Gordon, 1996; Ogden, 1979; Yalom & Leszcz, 2005).

CULTURE/DIVERSITY FACTORS AND UNSPOKEN TENSION

Other factors that cause unspoken tension in the group have to do with cultural differences and diversity issues. Members can feel threatened by differences, real or perceived, in values, beliefs, communication styles, mannerisms, or cultural backgrounds. These differences can breed anxiety and negative projections.

Cultural Differences Regarding Rates of Verbal Expression

Group members with differing cultural and ethnic backgrounds often have their own rates of communication (Halverson & Cuellar, 1999). For example,

Native Americans and Mexican Americans tend to have lower *rates of verbal expression*. They tend to express their feelings and thoughts in rather reserved and indirect ways (Shen, Sanchez, & Huang, 1984).

Members of the dominant culture, who value open expression of feelings and thoughts, may judge this low rate of verbal expression as resistance or aloofness. This inevitably creates misunderstanding and tension.

Culturally Bound Behaviors: Another Source of Misunderstanding

Many of our behaviors are culturally bound. For example, behaviors related to the concept of time/punctuality, openness/emotional expression, and the sharing of personal issues outside the family, are very much culturally bound. *Misinterpretation* occurs when a member assumes that another member shares the same norms and values.

Here are some examples of misunderstanding and misinterpretation that almost inevitably happen in culturally diverse groups:

- A lack of punctuality in a member from a culture laid back in terms of time may be interpreted as irresponsibility by other members who come from cultures that place a high value on punctuality (Hall, 1989; Kluckhohn & Strodtbeck, 1976).
- Members from cultures that encourage openness and self-expression may not appreciate the reservation of members whose cultures teach them to keep feelings and reactions to themselves (Hofstede, Hofstede, & Minkov, 2010).
- Blunt behaviors may be construed by one member as purely honest, yet by another as thoughtlessly rude.
- Face-saving behaviors may be construed as thoughtful and mature by some members, yet avoidant and deceitful by others.

Misinterpreting Culturally Bound Responses to Disagreement as Malicious

Culture often shapes the way people respond to disagreement. If people mistake the culturally bound responses to disagreement as having a malicious intention, it will surely brew tension. There exist two culturally bound ways of dealing with disagreement:

Western and Individualistically Oriented Cultures. These tend to focus on the outcome of the event. This *orientation toward outcome* propels them to take actions that seek to preserve self-esteem as well as gain individual power and status in the group. They will *defend* their own positions and *disagree with passion* when circumstances warrant it. For members of individualistic cultures, *the action of defending oneself reflects self-respect.*

Collectivistic Cultures. These, on the other hand, may focus more on the *process* of working through the disagreement. Whatever action they take to settle discord is likely to be geared toward *promoting harmony* within the group and *preserving* the dignity or *"face"* of people in the group.

In collective cultures, it is a norm for their members to try to *avoid expressing their disagreement* or to find someone to *mediate* the dispute. In the latter, it is usually an elder who helps both parties find a *compromise*, offer apologies, or set up a private time to *address the issue* (Shen et al., 1984; Ting-Toomey, 1999; Ting-Toomey & Oetzel, 2001). This effort to reach harmony is often so elaborate that it can be seen as *an art form* all of its own.

Given these two distinct culturally sanctioned responses for disagreement, it is of no surprise that one might mistake the other's intention as malicious, even though each is only doing what has been taught by his or her culture.

Minimizing Others' Experiences of Subjugation

Diversity factors in the group can also be a source of distrust and tension. Diversity includes such aspects of human difference as socioeconomic status, educational attainment, language, gender, disability, and sexual orientation.

Members of *the dominant groups* often find it difficult to understand the subjugation that many minority members have endured in their lives. The experiences of oppression presented by minority members may simply be glossed over by those from the dominant/privileged background (Ting-Toomey & Oetzel, 2001).

For example, if a gay member of the group alludes to discriminatory experiences at work, some group members may attribute the problem to the individual in question. Instead of acknowledging the pain and injustice experienced by this member. Members from *the dominant groups* may say something like, "Perhaps you are just a bit too sensitive about that."

The anguish of being glossed over within the group is devastating because it reminds the minority person of the chilling realities they experience in society at large. Furthermore, as each distressing personal experience is *invalidated*, these minority members become even more reluctant to disclose significant issues. As you can see, insensitivity to diversity issues, however unintentional, can impede an atmosphere of openness and tolerance in the group.

The Subtle Dynamics of Power Imbalance Among Culturally Different Members

Both culture and diversity factors can contribute to *power differentials* within the group, further adding to the tensions and impasses (Ting-Toomey & Oetzel, 2001). However, the power dynamics are likely to be subtle, and one can only observe the imbalance when the dynamics are in action.

We encourage leaders to pay special attention to the following signs of power imbalance among culturally different members as suggested by Conyne (1998):

- Certain values held by diverse group members clashing with preferred group behaviors
- Members of differing backgrounds expressing disagreements in *indirect* ways
- Members of diverse backgrounds being *interrupted, cut off, or avoided* when sharing their issues within the group
- Diverse group members not being invited to participate in the conflict-resolution process
- The group skirting around culturally sensitive topics, such as issues of ethnicity
- Certain members conveying a tone of *superiority* about their own preferences while expressing *contempt* for the approaches of others

OPTIONS FOR MANAGING UNSPOKEN TENSION

Though intensely felt, unspoken tension is not typically talked about aloud. Instead, the group will fall into an unproductive silence. Ironically, this silence will only make the tension that much more difficult to ignore. Anxiety will rise, and members may struggle to break the silence with offhanded comments, stilted humor, or nervous nonverbal behavior. So, the question is, how can you, the leader, help your members deal with the tension they so intensely feel but are so desperately trying to suppress?

Members' Indirect Ways of Dealing With Tension

Members rarely voice out loud the tension they feel due to the dread of negative consequences. Essentially, there are two fears (Champe & Rubel, 2012) that keep members' personal reactions, disagreement, insecurities, or perceptions sealed shut:

- Fear of hurting one another
- Fear of being rejected

Well-mannered as they try to appear, their *nonverbal clues,* alas, betray them (Osbeck, 2001). These nonverbal clues may turn up in the following fashions:

- Withholding comment
- Avoiding eye contact (and other telling facial expressions)
- Positioning outside the circle of the group

Avoidance may turn up in *more subtle behaviors* (Agazarian & Simon, 1967), including the following:

- Griping about issues that have little connection to the group
- Joke telling that pulls the group away from moments of intensity
- Chit-chatting about people or events outside the group that wastes group time
- Making ambiguous statements that keep others guessing

These indirect ways obviously do not serve to get members' needs met.

How to Embrace Tension as a Change Agent for Groups

What is a more honest and direct way of dealing with tension? Embrace its force. When welcomed, tension has the power to motivate members to take risks and to cross the bridge "between the superficial conversations of the first stage and the more direct expression of feelings in the later stages" (McClure, Miller, & Russo, 1992, p. 268).

Often, we have witnessed that the tension at this stage of a group will build to such an extent that it fires members up to speak out about the truth of their reactions. And all of a sudden, a slow group comes alive, teeming with spontaneity and authenticity.

Kraus, DeEsch, and Geroski (2001) are right on target to assert that tension and conflict, when embraced, can serve as *a change agent* in the group.

For the general tension in the group, a leader needs to think through strategies for helping the group embrace it and turn it into a change agent. As you read the following strategies, you will notice that you can actually use the stage of the group as a guidepost for determining which option you might put into action.

1st Option: Postpone It

If a group is just beginning, the leader may choose to postpone dealing with the tension simmering in the group. Instead, the leader may focus on fulfilling members' need for inclusion, on instilling hope, and on building a sense of universality. In choosing to postpone looking into underlying group tension, the leader is not avoiding dealing with conflict but buying time for the group to develop the necessary maturity to deal with it (Kormanski, 1982, 1999).

2nd Option: Have Members Communicate Their Worries About Bringing Up Issues

If the fears stated by Champe and Rubel (2012) are causing the unspoken tension, leaders ought to encourage members to express their worries of bringing up such issues:

[To the group] I can sense some tension in the room, and I sense that there are many things that members want to bring up but are afraid of the consequences of doing so. I wonder whether we could spend some time exploring *what you are worried about* when you think of *bringing something up?*

3rd Option: Illuminate the Process

Rising tension cannot be left unaddressed for too long. The key to addressing it hinges on grasping the meta-messages in members' communication. Bateson (as cited in Perlmutter & Hatfield, 1980) noted that all communications include certain kinds of *metamessages*. Only when the metamessage is brought to the forefront can the door to true intimacy be unlocked (Marshak & Katz, 1999; Perlmutter & Hatfield, 1980).

You can use *process illumination* (Yalom & Leszcz, 2005) to bring the metamessages of tension to the forefront. This skill sheds light on members' patterns of interpersonal behaviors that cause the tension (Swogger, 1981).

Chapter 12 will detail various techniques of process illumination. For now, we will just give you a few examples for illustration purpose.

> Jeff, I heard *the frustration in your voice* when you gave feedback to Noel. [using the nonverbal as a clue] I wonder what it is about Noel that makes you feel frustrated. [inviting *decoding of the metamessage*]

> [To the group] I notice *we are off to a slow start.* [using subtle behaviors as clues] I wonder *what has brought about this heavy silence.* [inviting illumination of the group dynamics]

> [To the group] Let's stop for a moment. Something has just happened between Mitch, Charlie, Thomas, and Dane. There is tension so thick you could cut it with a knife. What do you sense is causing it to happen?

> [To the group] Right now I sense a great deal of tension in the room. I have felt this tension since Jane started talking. I wonder how you make sense of this tension and what Jane has just said?

4th Option: Use Reflective Writing as a Tool

As a last resort, you can use reflective writing to manage tension. Firstly, you may use *narrative session notes* (see Chapter 15) to provide observation and feedback without the pressure of having to sort things out on the spot. Secondly, you may encourage members to write *reflective journal entries* (see Chapter 15 as well) after each session and report back to the group in the following session. These methods give members the space and time they may need to address group tension.

The following options pertain more to how to manage tension among culturally different members.

5th Option: Use Common Goals to Transcend Cultural Differences

A culturally diverse group can bridge gaps and work through sensitive issues together by looking for *common goals* that will transcend individual and cultural differences (Ting-Toomey & Oetzel, 2001). To this end, the leader might say,

[To the group] There seems to be a lot of tension here. Let's slow down for a moment and recall the common goals in our group. I recall that *a goal shared by many of our members is to improve communication with others who are different from us.* Let's look back and reflect on how we have been doing so far in our efforts to improve communication with others different from us.

6th Option: Have the Group Practice Culturally Sensitive Listening Skills

Minority members with experiences of subjugation often find it difficult to speak of their pain; those without experiences of oppression also find it difficult to listen because they feel guilty that they are *lacking* such experiences (Comacho, 2001; McGoldrick & Giordano, 2005).

The members speaking need to feel heard those listening, while not need to feel guilty. To meet the needs of both sides, the leader can ask the listeners to *acknowledge the pain* expressed. This action may seem small, yet it contains the power to bridge the rift created by differences. With their pain acknowledged, members who experience subjugation will feel heard and accepted, their sense of shame reduced (Comacho, 2001; Ting-Toomey & Oetzel, 2001). Those acknowledging the pain, the listeners, will feel that they have given something of worth to the sharing members. To accomplish this, the leader may say,

[To the group] Barry has just shared with us some very painful experiences.

Although his experiences are difficult for some of us to take in, it would be helpful for Barry right now if several of us could acknowledge some of the struggles he just shared or some of the feelings he has been suffering from in these experiences. Who would like to start?

7th Option: Bridge Various Culture and Diversity Gaps

If you notice that members of different backgrounds seem unable to openly disagree or that they express their disagreements in indirect ways, you may bring it to the group attention:

[To the group] Let's stop for a moment. I understand that we carry into this group a wide variety of ways of responding to disagreement; some are more direct whereas others are more roundabout. I want everybody to know that there is no right or wrong way to disagree. But it is important that you clearly state what your preferred ways of communicating disagreement are so that others can respect your choice.

If you observe that the free-flowing expression promoted in the group clashes with some culturally sanctioned way of expressing emotions, you may say,

[To the group] I know that in the group we tend to advocate the free sharing of emotions and reactions. Yet I also know that some of you come from homes and communities that are more reserved in the expression of feelings and emotions. If this is the case for you, I'd like you to share what it has been like to come to this group.

People from some diverse backgrounds tend to pause longer before going on to their next thought. If you notice that these members are getting cut off or are being overlooked, it might be because other members of the dominant group lack the understanding of the difference in rhythm in communication. You may address this issue by saying,

[To the group] I noticed that a couple of times when Arturo stopped talking, he actually hadn't quite finished his sharing. People from some cultural backgrounds, like that of Arturo's, take longer pauses in between their thoughts. I wonder whether the group can honor these members' need for longer pauses in expressing themselves by not immediately jumping in.

If you notice that certain members convey a tone of superiority about their own views while expressing contempt for those of the minorities, you may say something like the following:

George, I noticed that you seem very certain about your view that we ought to break off from a relationship when it's frustrating. You are so certain of your position that you start to belittle the views expressed by Arturo, Li, and Sanjay. Would you be willing to slow down and recognize some of their comments?

**MEMBER NEGATIVE
TRANSFERENCE TO THE LEADER**

Though being the leader, the group therapist is, nevertheless, a part of the group; his or her presence will undoubtedly elicit a plethora of reactions from the members. These reactions will also assuredly include negative transferences. Some negative transference has to do with members' families of origin; with others, it relates to members' genuine reaction to the leader's incompetent behaviors or inappropriate attitudes. This section covers the phenomenon of member transference.

Transference Distortion

Members bring to the group their own unique developmental histories and filters, especially from their families of origin. These cognitive filters are called "transference distortions" (Yalom & Leszcz, 2005, p. 21). These histories and filters are particularly prone to be activated by the dynamics of a group that, being so similar to those of a family, often puts the leader in the position of *the parent* and members as the children.

Due to this, most clients perceive the therapist *incorrectly*. Any *unresolved issues* from members' relationships *with their parents* can evoke strong reactions toward the leader, especially when they sense any hints of leader imperfection. Any issues related to *a past authority figure* may play themselves out with the group leaders.

This transference distortion may play itself out in the form of

- making outright critical or sarcastic remarks to or about the leader,
- refusing to participate in group discussions,
- rolling their eyes in the dismissal of the leader's ideas, and
- complaining about group rules.

Just a side note: Somewhere along the line, the effects of member's birth order (Salmon, 2003) may start to kick in: The youngest expects the leader to lavish attention on him or her or the middle child is quick to feel ignored, and the oldest child feels left to manage on his or her own. You can decide on your own whether birth order might have any relevance to transference distortions occurring in your group.

Negativity to the Leader Based on Legitimate Concerns

Sometimes members respond to the leader negatively because they actually observe some negative traits or behaviors in the leader's actions, such as

- a poor attitude,
- incompetence,
- playing favorites, and
- unprofessional behaviors.

Leaders who have not been through proper training and supervision are most susceptible to the above behaviors.

METHODS OF HANDLING NEGATIVE MEMBER TRANSFERENCE

Allow Transferences to Fully Play Themselves Out

Dealing successfully with a negative transference ultimately depends upon whether or not the member can gain insight into what he or she is really reacting to (Gelso, Hill, & Kivlighan, 1991). The most effective way to accomplish this is to allow transferences to fully play themselves out, without taking it too personally.

Once the negative reactions play themselves out, you can facilitate the group to explore the essence of the member's reactions (see Chapter 12). The group's observations and feedback have more weight than yours in providing the said member with insights into how his or her attitude toward you, the leader, relate to certain unfinished business from the past.

You do need a great deal of patience and willingness to deal with transference, but it will pay off. When worked through, transference can become a pathway to new change for members. As Alexander (in Alexander & French, 1980) states,

> Re-experiencing the old, unsettled conflict but with a new ending is the secret of every penetrating therapeutic result. Only the actual experience of a new solution, in the transference situation or in his everyday life, gives the patient the conviction that a new solution is possible and induces him to give up the old neurotic patterns. (p. 338)

Below are some viable options for handling transference:

Treat All Members as Equally Acceptable

You can limit negative transference to a certain extent by watching out for the fact that *members are especially sensitive to any hint of favoritism*. If you can treat all members as being equally lovable and acceptable in your eyes, this unconditional acceptance might help keep negative transference at bay.

Invite the Member to Share His or Her Perspective

If a member is hostile toward you, you might want to express your here-and-now thoughts and feelings openly and authentically. For example,

Dale, I am a little taken aback hearing your frustration toward me. I do apologize if I have said or done anything to offend you.

After sharing your here-and-now thoughts and feelings, you may invite the member to share what he is upset about:

Would you please help me understand exactly what I said or did today or in past sessions that made you feel so irritated?

Ned, I am sensing that you are upset with me right now. [acknowledging the member's feeling] I want you to know that I value your presence in this group and the unique perspective that you bring here. [pause] I am very interested in hearing what your concern is about me.

Seek a Reality Check, a Consensual Validation

When being challenged or criticized, you may be tempted to defend yourself; this is understandable. The best way to handle member criticism, however, is to defuse it with nondefensiveness and with curiosity.

Your curiosity will motivate you to sort out whether a member's negativity arises from transference distortion or an authentic response to your real issues. To get your answer, you can intervene with a *reality check* or a *consensual validation* (Mahon & Flores, 1993; Morran, Stockton, Cline, & Teed 1998). You may say,

[To the group] I would like to get some feedback from the group. Whenever I share my observations, Jason always challenges me or rolls his eyes. How do the rest of you see this?

[To the group] Joe said that I play favorites in the group and that I especially favor Ron. I wonder whether other members of the group have observed this? Your input will help me realize if I do have a favoritism problem. And it will give me a chance to change so that I can better serve the group. Would anyone like to share some observations regarding this?

If the group's consensual validation reveals serious limitations on your part, then take action to seek supervision and personal development.

Increase Your Level of Transparency

Increasing your degree of transparency helps decrease members' negative transference toward you (Yalom & Leszcz, 2005). You bump up transparency by gradually revealing, when appropriate, more of yourself—your motives, feelings, life experiences, and especially your *here-and-now reactions* (See the section on "Leader Self-Disclosure" below).

Such sharing can help members look at you more realistically and to deconstruct their distortions about you. Sharing the narrative session notes (see Chapter 15) with all members can also increase your transparency and defuse negative transference.

LEADERS' OWN COUNTERTRANSFERENCE AND HOW TO HANDLE IT

Whenever we feel our buttons being pushed by clients; whenever we react, consciously or unconsciously, to clients; and whenever these reactions reflect our values, biases, or past experiences, we are undergoing a countertransference (Gillem, 1999).

Having a countertransference to a client does not necessarily spell trouble, but failing to recognize it does. As Yalom and Leszcz (2005) state, "an inability to perceive countertransference responses, to recognize personal distortions and blind spots, or to use one's own feelings and fantasies in one's work, will limit the effectiveness of any therapist" (p. 559).

This section details types of countertransference and how to handle them.

Deal With Objective Countertransference

There exist two types of countertransference responses: objective counter-transference and subjective countertransference (Vannicelli, 2001). We will discuss the former first.

When you emotionally react to *a client's experiences*, and your reaction *has nothing to do with your own* conflicts and issues, an *objective countertransference* is happening. For example, an alcoholic client, who feels useless and inadequate, lashes out and accuses you of failing to make him or her better. Rather than taking this accusation personally and becoming defensive, *you feel useless and inadequate* as if *resonating with this alcoholic client's core issues* (Vannicelli, 2001). This is *objective countertransference*. The client wants you to feel how *he or she* feels.

An objective countertransference, when untangled, can actually help us to understand clients' inner experiences on a personal level. With that understanding, we can share an "empathic response to the client's feelings" (Clarkson & Nuttall, 2000, p. 371).

The best way to share your empathic response is through *disclosing the feelings brought out in you*:

> Jason, I hear how you succumb frequently to the allure of alcohol and suffer broken relationships as a result. *I can sense how inadequate and useless you feel.* [an empathic response to the member's feelings] *Personally, I am feeling a similar sense of inadequacy and uselessness in me as well.* [disclosing personal feelings] The journey of recovering can feel like climbing Everest; it is taxing and at the same time, strengthening. I see your strengths as evidenced by the fact that you come to the group, session after session persistently. It really speaks of your strength as well as your desire to change. [Focusing on the strengths.]

Handle Subjective Countertransference

On the other hand, when your emotional reaction to a client has something to do with *your own past and personal experiences or with your own conflicts and issues*, a classic form of *countertransference* is happening—a *subjective countertransference*, in truth. A beginning leader reflects on his subjective countertransference:

Ali had been waiting to tell his own story. When Eve stepped ahead of him to share hers, Ali challenged her by asking, "Do you have an ability to be alone?" When this dynamic happened, I, the leader, saw it and wanted to address it, but I held back due to the countertransference that I experienced at the moment. *I felt Ali's aggression viscerally, but I avoided addressing it. I reacted with the very same coping pattern I used to survive the difficult experiences in my early life.*

A subjective countertransference does not make you an ineffective group leader. In fact, it gives you "one of the most important tools for the therapist's work, providing insight into the patient's inner world" (Richards, 2000, p. 332).

So how can we put this tool to work in group counseling? Literature suggests we *disclose our subjective countertransference* to the client. Doing so gives the client an opportunity to discover how we experience him or her and how his or her behavior has an impact on us (Casement, 2014; Clarkson & Nuttall, 2000).

Of course, not all countertransference reactions are appropriate for disclosing; some are best left alone, saved for private processing in supervision and personal therapy. Others, when disclosed properly, can enlighten members about their interpersonal patterns.

Consider the following example where a group leader self-discloses his subjective countertransference to a member:

Tim, I have noticed that you frequently make arguments just to be in opposition to what other members are saying. You also do this with me in the group. Although I can appreciate this behavior as a trait of your independent thinking, *I am finding myself reacting to your defiance with an increased sense of frustration and with a need to keep you at a distance.* [leader self-disclosing subjective countertransference reactions] Although I have my own past experiences that might contribute to my own need to keep my distance when facing your opposition, I do wonder if my reaction to your antagonistic way of behaving might not be unique. Indeed, I wonder if *other people in your life* have reacted just the same as I have but have chosen to walk away without ever telling you why.

GUIDELINES FOR LEADER SELF-DISCLOSURE

Though leader self-disclosure plays a significant role in cracking the difficult dynamics and countertransference issues, it is not hazard free. This section proposes guidelines for how to exercise caution when using it.

To Disclose or Not to Disclose, That Is the Question

Before taking the risk of self-disclosing, the leader must weigh the pros and cons. In terms of the pros, literature abounds in references to how the therapist's self-disclosure might benefit the therapy process (Beiman, 2013; Rogers, 2007; Ziv-Howe, 2011). Some examples include the following:

- Strengthening the therapeutic bond
- Giving a sense of normality to members' experiences
- Reducing the power differential between therapist and group members
- Instilling a sense of hope in clients and reducing shame
- Increasing leader transparency, thus reducing the likelihood of *transference*
- Enlightening members as to how others in their lives might experience them.

On the other hand, plentiful suggestions in the literature (Howe, 2011; LoFrisco, 2012) point to the disadvantages of therapist self-disclosure:

- Clients can become too comfortable with you, viewing you as a friend instead of a professional group leader.
- Poorly timed or inadequately delivered self-disclosure can lead to distrust. Clients may question your motives or see you as getting too involved.
- Clients may feel that you are not listening and are more focused on your own interests instead of those of the group's.
- Clients may feel like the therapist is impaired, questioning the therapist's ability to help.
- The focus of need and care may shift from the client to the therapist.

With evidence for and against self-disclosure, what are group leaders to do? Thankfully, there is something else to be discussed below that we would need to take into account before we arrive at a decision.

Boundary Crossing and Boundary Violation Issues

This something else is the issue of boundaries—an issue that beginning group leaders struggle getting a handle on, especially in regard to the difference between a boundary crossing and a boundary violation.

Boundary Crossing. A group therapist's self-disclosure always borders on *boundary crossing* (Gutheil & Gabbard, 2008). What is boundary crossing?

Giving a supportive hug to a client in grief, attending a client's wedding, or accepting gifts from a client at the time of termination—all of these behaviors are considered boundary crossings because they *digress from the standard therapeutic stance* but, nevertheless, are *harmless, nonexploitative, and supportive of the client's work.*

In the group setting, when a group leader uses self-disclosure to help the group, he or she is crossing the boundary between the leader and the members. To remain *boundary-conscious,* most effective group leaders limit their disclosure to contents that can only benefit the clients.

Boundary Violation. In contrast, a therapist enters into a *boundary violation* (Gutheil & Gabbard, 2008) when engaging in an exploitative relationship with a client. This exploitation can harm the client. For example, if your self-disclosure is for *your own* benefit, is burdening group members with unnecessary information, or is getting you into a role reversal where your members start to take care of *you*—then you are violating boundaries (Gutheil & Gabbard, 2008). Group leaders must do everything they can to avoid stepping into the danger zone of boundary violation.

Guidelines for Leader Self-Disclosure

Given the above considerations, we suggest that we leaders adhere to the following guidelines for self-disclosure to avoid engaging in boundary violations:

- *Avoid being even slightly self-indulgent in our self-disclosures.*
- Make our self-disclosure *brief:* say what we need to say, and say it in the most concise manner possible.
- *Limit our disclosure to only the contents that benefit the client.*
- Choose *here-and-now disclosure* above all.
- Make your "self" a reliable and accurate instrument through supervision and personal therapy.

If asked to name the type of leader self-disclosure that benefits the group the most, it would have to be *impact-disclosure* (Gutheil, 2010), also called here-and-now disclosure. In impact-disclosure, you, as a leader, reveal a persistent feeling that a member's behavior pattern has repeatedly elicited in you. The skill of impact-disclosure is covered in the section of "Intermediate Steps Toward the Here-and-Now" in Chapter 10.

Having the power to deal the client a big jolt, impact disclosure must be used judiciously. We should only disclose those here-and-now feelings that the member has the capacity to handle (Kiesler, 1988).

We also need to make sure that our "self"—the instrument of therapy—"be as reliable and accurate as possible" (Yalom & Leszcz, 2005, p. 174). When our here-and-now reactions become too intense, our internal data tend to become unreliable. It is at these junctures that it becomes imperative to refrain from disclosing our here-and-now reactions and to instead use supervision or personal therapy as a safe and trusting forum to explore our countertransference and possible blocks.

THE PARADOX OF OPEN CONFLICTS

Open conflicts can trigger a great deal of emotional distress and yet, paradoxically, it can also contribute to the creativity, growth, and cohesiveness of a group. Viewing open conflict as a sign of increased trust and heightened risk taking among members, you can put your fears of group conflict to rest and start to look for ways of harnessing its power.

The Emotional Distress of Open Conflicts

Open conflicts are often associated with images of conquering or of being conquered, of family members cutting themselves off from one another, sometimes for decades—images that provoke *distress* and *fear*.

The signs of an open conflict are palpable, evident in the tone of voice and in the expression in the eyes, body language, and breathing patterns. Hearts beat fast as the adrenaline rushes. Facing such open conflict, most people react with a stress response because their past experiences with open conflict have been anything but constructive.

Emotional Hijack: The Fight-or-Flight Response

When conflict arises, people naturally fall back on the fight-or-flight stress reaction (Fishbane, 2014), a state in which they are hijacked by their emotions. The fight-or-flight response can be categorized into the following *four maladaptive modes* of coping (Seaward, 2015). The first two modes belong to the flight response, while the latter two, the fight response:

- Withdrawal: by sidestepping the conflict, remaining silent, or even walking out. Withdrawal only breeds more resentment or prolonged hostility; therefore it is a maladaptive coping.
- Surrender: by giving in to the will of others. Habitually using this strategy to manage conflict tends to make one feel like a victim, hampering one's self-esteem.
- Hostile aggression: by yelling, pounding fists, or throwing objects across the room. Aggressive behaviors such as these seldom resolve any conflict but only serve to worsen the tension, fear, and hostility between people.
- Persuasion: by trying to change others' beliefs, attitudes, views, decisions, or behaviors so as to win in a conflict. The one who tries to persuade never wants to hear the voice of the other side.

Conflict as a Dialectical and Creative Force

If not facilitated, open conflicts can cause tremendous emotional distress for the group resulting in defensive behaviors and hostility as well as damage to the group's sense of trust. If facilitated properly, however, these conflicts can actually contribute to creativity and growth.

The wonderful views available in the Himalayas emerge from the conflict between tectonic plates. Through the clash of these plates, the land was pushed higher and higher toward the sky: a beautiful transformation.

Likewise, the water of the Nile River sometimes conflicts with the land as when spring rains bring inundating floods to river valleys. Out of this clash come the life-giving soils deposited on the land, bringing rich sustenance to nurture the crops.

In the same vein, interpersonal conflict creates something new and otherwise unreachable in relationships. Unfortunately, a *dualistic* view of conflict rules our society, where people fight to assert who is right and who is wrong. Will a *dialectical* view of conflict be given a chance one day, to galvanize the creative potential of all participants involved in a conflict (Fox, 2000)?

We hope so. If group leaders guide members to see that conflict is but a pathway toward greater growth, deeper intimacy, and clearer boundaries (Kottler, 1996), that out of conflicts may come something new and good, then and only then will open conflict become a beneficial force that can help shatter those unconstructive, entrenched patterns (Lewin, 2008).

The Absence of Conflict—An Impairment to Group Development

To reach its highest potential, the group must help its members see this: Beneath the exterior frustration and anger expressed during the conflict there actually hides *fear* or *hurt*. From what we have observed, a conflict puts members in a spot where they cannot help but reveal more and more of themselves in an effort to clarify their positions. As more information is revealed, each member comes to understand more deeply the experiential worlds of other members. Resolving conflict will thus help members have empathy for the vulnerability hidden underneath tough or hostile exteriors.

In short, conflict, along with its resolution, is such a critical component to the interpersonal learning in the group that it's no wonder Yalom goes so far as to assert that *the absence of conflict* can actually impair a group's development (Yalom & Leszcz, 2005).

SEVEN STEPS OF CONFLICT RESOLUTION

The safe and supportive atmosphere of the group gives members an ideal setting to learn and experience conflict resolution. The method of conflict resolution proposed in this chapter gives leaders a toolkit with which open conflict can be worked out constructively.

1st Principle: Pull Members out of the State of Emotional Hijack

The first principle of conflict resolution is to pull those involved out of the state of emotional hijack. During the open conflict, as we discussed previously, our brains usually short circuit, sending us into the state of "emotional hijack." When this occurs, neither party has the capacity to hear the other person, nor to introspect.

At this juncture, any attempt, including persuasion, modeling, or skill training, will fail to get the parties involved to listen to each other or to become introspective. To get people to hear each other, we need to get them out of their short circuit. But how?

2nd Principle: Validate Their Feelings and Views

The answer lies in the second principle: The best way to free people from their states of emotional hijack is to affirm that their feelings and perspectives make sense. When validated, people in conflict tend to be able to get out of the short circuit and regain their ability for introspection and mutual listening.

Validation works. It works because underneath the open conflict often hide certain unexpressed disappointments and resentments that can be traced back to previous encounters. Beneath the defensive, combative, bullying, hostile, or alienating exteriors there conceal certain feelings of betrayal, hurt, abandonment, neglect, or rejection that have been with the person since a tender age—feelings that crave being recognized.

We cannot fix the past, but we can validate the present—we can validate the feelings and views still churning inside the person. Additionally, if we can help members see beyond the exterior of their rival and look into the internal pain that he or she suffers, the grips of the conflict often soften.

Yalom and Leszcz (2005) stress that once a member appreciates how the aspects of an opponent's earlier life have contributed to his or her current behaviors and stance, the member is often able to see how the opponent's behaviors and position not only make sense but also may even appear right. The group then is able to search for a caring, empathic, and sensitive way to provide understanding and acknowledgment to the person in need.

Below, we propose a seven-step method of conflict resolution, born out of our clinical experiences and firmly rooted in the above two principles—a method that has been refined throughout the years and has proven to work well consistently in resolving conflicts within a couple of sessions, if not one.

1st Step: Recognize the Signs!
Stop Conflict Before It Gets out of Hand!

The group's success in resolving open conflict relies heavily on the leaders' ability to recognize the signs of rising tension. The pitch of members' voices alone may not be the best indication of a conflict. Some members become loud when they are excited or enthusiastic.

Rather, the following signals are more reliable in indicating that some members' emotions have reached a certain threshold and some form of aggression is present:

- Tense or twitching muscles
- Staring at the other or lacking eye contact
- Closed defensive postures
- Shallow breathing
- Clenched fists
- Use of four-letter words

Group members typically can sense the emotional intensity of these signals, and the group, including the leader, is likely to feel overwhelmed.

But you, as the leader, must quickly recover from the stress reaction and take action immediately. First, check the faces and bodies of members in front of you to understand how they are reacting to what's going on. Then, take action to stop the conflict before it gets out of hand:

[To the whole group] Okay, we all see the heated tension in the room right now. We need to devote some time to resolve this conflict. So, let's stop here and give our priority to the issue between Alice and Dale.

2nd Step: Invite Dialogue

In an open conflict, each party often believes that he or she is right, and the other is wrong. Each often stops listening to the other and sometimes even misinterprets what the other has just said (Yalom & Leszcz, 2005). Anger and frustration thus smolder, and communication breaks down.

At this moment, it is not a good idea to invite unrestrained expression of anger. Instead, a better option would be to invite a *dialogue* (Seaward, 2015). Since broken trust is at the heart of all conflicts, a dialogue may work to restore trust back to the relationship as the views, perceptions, and beliefs of both sides are given a chance to be heard (Deutsch & Kraus, 1962).

To invite both parties for a dialogue, the leader may say something like the following:

[To the parties involved] Alice and Dale, I hear that both of you feel irritated by what the other just said to you, but I'm not sure whether either of you is hearing the other. So, I would like both of you to *take turns* to describe where your feelings and views are coming from. Please describe what you see, what you believe, and how you take it all in. Okay. Alice, would you go first, then we'll go to Dale.

3rd Step: Engage the Group to Offer Validation

As the involved parties begin a dialogue, their feelings and perspectives may start to become clear to the group but not to each other as they are still too tense to clearly hear the other's feelings and assumptions.

So, what you can do is engage the group to give both parties validation and affirmation. This helps them feel heard and affirmed, thus paving the way for them to later be able to resolve the disparities.

There are two possible ways of offering validation:

1. Validating the feelings and the sources of the feelings,

    [To the group] Alice and Dale are still trying to straighten out this issue between them. I wonder, can the rest of you share your understanding of the following: *what each of them might be feeling and assuming,* and *where these reactions are coming from*? Please speak directly to Alice and Dale.

2. Validating the emotional impacts or the coping strategies,

    [To the group] If you were Alice and just heard Dale say to you that he doesn't care about what you say to him and what you said is totally irrelevant, how would that impact on you? [This is a validation for Alice and a here-and-now feedback to Dale as well. See Chapters 10, 11, and 12 for details on here-and-now feedback.]

    [To the group] And if you were Dale and if you had historically shut off emotions to deal with intense feelings, what might you do to protect yourself from being flooded by Alice's intense emotions? [This is a validation for Dale and a here-and-now feedback to Alice as well.]

4th Step: Facilitate Self-Reflection

After both parties have received validation from the group, they will become calmer, more able to see things from both perspectives, and more capable of engaging their higher brain to reflect on the context of their conflict.

For conflicts to be successfully resolved, the personal context of the conflict must be identified and examined (Kleinberg, 2000). That means each party needs to *reflect on the triggers* contributing to the conflict as well as the *meaning* the conflict holds for them.

This kind of self-examination should not take place until both parties have felt heard and validated by the group. Following is a prompt that you might use to invite reflections from those involved parties after having received validation from the group:

> Alice and Dale, I can sense both of you feel a bit more understood and relaxed now. I would like to invite you to share what might have been *the triggers* that led you to become so emotionally charged and reactive. When you are ready, Alice and Dale, one of you can go first.

5th Step: Restructure the Interaction

When both parties are able to own up to the triggers that set them off, the leader needs to *listen vigilantly for any phrases or words that show an opening for reconciliation.* These are words that convey *a better understanding of the self and the other, an apology,* and *a wish to connect.*

Watch especially for changes in nonverbal cues. When eyes are softer, and the body is leaning slightly forward, the individuals are showing that trust has come back.

Usually, these new positions are conveyed indirectly. But we want to take it one step further—we want the two parties to *convey their new positions directly to each other.* To this aim, you will need to set up a new, restructured interaction between the two. Consider these examples:

> Dale, I am happy to hear you say a few things: First, your conflict with Alice was triggered by your sense that she dislikes you. Second, you know what you said could be extremely hurtful. Third, you only have a good intention toward Alice now that you feel understood. Since you only said these things to the group, not to Alice directly, would you be willing to please say these things again but this time directly to Alice?
>
> Alice, Dale just opened his heart to you. How do you respond to what Dale just said to you?
>
> Dale, how does it feel to express yourself in this way to Alice?

In the same way, you will invite Alice to express her new perspective directly to Dale.

6th Step: Transfer the Here-and-Now Learning to Clients' Outside Lives

To maximize members' ability to transfer what they have learned *within the group* to their outside lives, you can prompt the two parties to reflect on what they are going to take away from the experience and how they will apply this new learning to their personal lives:

> Alice, thank you for your hard work tonight. I remember you talked about your difficulty in expressing anger with your partner. From tonight's experience with Dale, I wonder if there is anything you *might be able to apply to your interactions with your partner at home?*
>
> Dale, thank you for your hard work as well. You have talked about how you tend to cut people off and stop seeing them if the relationship does not go as you would like it to go. From tonight's experience, *how might your new ability to express your heartfelt feelings and to apologize be carried to your personal life outside the group?*

7th Step: Invite a Whole-Group Processing

Systems theory (Getz, 2002) teaches us that the actions of one or two members can influence the rest of the group. This systemic perspective calls for whole-group processing to examine the impact that the conflict and its resolution have on the group:

> [To the whole group] Now that Alice and Dale have shared their newly gained awareness and have reconnected with one other, I'd like to invite the rest of the group to share your thoughts and feelings about how our group worked on resolving the conflict in this session. How did you personally experience the conflict? What did you learn about yourself and others in working through today's conflict? This will bring closure to tonight's intense experience. Who would like to start?

For a case example of confliction resolution, please refer to Cases in Point near the end of this chapter.

THE GROUP LEADER'S SELF-CARE

There is a saying, "If you don't fill up your tank, then you have to put all your energy into pushing your own car." Under stressful conditions, such as tension and conflicts in the group, those leaders lacking self-care habits may become disheartened or even disillusioned. This section highlights the importance and the practice of self-care for group leaders.

The Importance of Remaining Centered and Grounded

One has to stay centered and grounded to maintain a clear perspective (Heider, 2015) in the midst of emotionally charged tension and conflicts. When centered, we experience the following benefits:

- No erratic acts of others can throw us off balance.
- We do not get drawn into triangulation with members trying to sway us to take sides.
- We instead see those emotional tugs of war as opportunities for members to explore their patterns of relating with others.
- We see the tide of emotion from members as a signal that they need increased awareness in that specific area of life.

Our personal work will partially determine our capability to remain centered in dealing with tension and conflict within a group. The more we are aware of what drives us, the less likely we are to be caught by surprise when hot issues arise in a group (Secemsky, Ahlman, & Robbins, 1999). If our internal issues are not worked through sufficiently in our own lives, these issues can be easily triggered during group conflict. It is, therefore, imperative that we continue our personal growth work throughout our professional career.

Believe in the Therapeutic Process

Working with a group's tension and conflict requires that we trust people's capacity to change. It requires that we see chaos as only transitory, as having the power to give birth to a surprising new order. It asks that we accept members' difficult behaviors, not as symptoms of their dysfunctions but as their desperate, erratic efforts to break out of an ill-fitting, outdated mold.

It is imperative to remember that the smallest progress made by group members, especially by inpatient clients or substance abusers, is, in itself, big. If we can see small as big, then we will be in a better place to walk with our groups through the journey of conflicts and resolutions.

Use Supervision to Get Ourselves out of the Way

Successful group work requires that leaders learn to be *detached from outcomes* and be more engaged in the process of the present. Our egoistic minds sometimes have the tendency to become invested in particular outcomes, and the more insecure our egoistic minds are, the more obsessed we will be with these outcomes. As we get our egos out of the way, we become a better instrument in the work that we do (see Chapter 2).

If you cannot do this by yourself, then consulting with your colleagues and mentors can often shed light on your situation. It is imperative to use supervision to help with processing the transference and countertransference that may occur (see previous sections of this chapter) while you are working with tension and conflict in a group.

Establish a Firm Habit of Self-Care

Kottler and Englar-Carlson (2010) indicate that burnout is "the single most common personal consequence of practicing therapy" (p. 180), and it is during the transition/storming stage that we are most at risk. We can avail ourselves of the many options to restore our emotional health, including individual counseling, group counseling, journaling, art therapy, music therapy, meditation, yoga, and so on. All of these bring a disciplined *self-reflection* to our lives, nurturing a greater degree of wholeness through increased consciousness.

Here are some down-to-earth activities to prevent burnout from happening, and the best part is that they cost not a penny:

- Respect your own limit: Avoid taking on extra work-related responsibilities if you are feeling overwhelmed or spread too thin.
- Respect your needs for personal renewal through personal therapy, exercise, proper sleep, and solitude in nature.

- Do something that does not involve intellectual activities. Use your hands and your body: Take up a new hobby or revisit one that you enjoyed in your past. Whether your passion is unicycling, basketball, rollerblading, painting, writing, cooking, gardening, playing with your pets, knitting, or so on, make sure you have time to do what you love.
- Let fun have a place in your life: Read some nonclinical literature. Learn or read just for fun. Keep your entertainment light-hearted. Watch funny movies or television shows to bring you back to a good mood.
- Make time for family and friends: Whether you are married with children, single, or somewhere in between, quality connection with loved ones is important. Schedule downtime with those close to you. Connect with others when you are not in the therapist role. *It is also crucial to develop friendships outside of the counseling/therapy community.* These are the people with whom you can escape to for a movie or a drink when stressed. With these *lay-friends*, you can *get away from the serious topics of counseling and people's problems*, thus *creating a cleansing space for yourself.*

∞∞

In closing: Embarking on the journey into the unstructured or experiential mode, a group will sooner or later come upon tension and conflict—an important rite of passage for a group's development. When welcomed, tension has the power to motivate members to take risks and to cross the bridge "between the superficial conversations of the first stage and the more direct expression of feelings in the later stages" (McClure et al., 1992, p. 268).

Helping members to embrace tensions and conflicts, the leaders also gain wisdom on how to deal successfully with negative transferences from members, how to manage countertransferences from themselves, and how to center and ground themselves in the midst of dealing with emotionally charged interpersonal processes. They start to build their therapeutic muscles as they learn to face conflict head-on, taking, so to speak, the bull by the horns.

CASES IN POINT

Case 1: Managing the Open Conflict Between Sue and Loretta (Fifth Session)

It was the fifth session of a 12-session group. The session started as usual with a check-in. Group members looked calm, relaxed, and enthusiastic for the session to start. What happened that night was something that took the group by surprise.

The Conflict. During the check-in, a conflict arose between Sue and Loretta. Sue said she was thinking of quitting the group because she was angry and hurt by something Loretta said at the end of the previous session. As she expressed her anger, Sue's face became stern, her eyes intense, and her voice fluctuated. Loretta met Sue's confrontation with a similar intensity of emotions.

The Group Stunned. The confrontation between Sue and Loretta soon led to high-flying emotions in the group. Many members were stunned by the intensity of Sue's reaction. Few had picked up on how Sue felt toward Loretta's comment in the previous session. As the tension rose, the group felt paralyzed.

Stopping the Check-In. It was obvious that if the conflict was not attended to by the entire group, it could cause a serious rift within the group. Therefore, the leader informed the group that they would stop the check-in and allow both Sue and Loretta adequate time to air their feelings and work through the conflict. The leader said,

> [To the group] OK. What happened between Sue and Loretta is very important. Let's stop our check-in for the moment and give our priority to resolving this issue.

The Enactment of Roles Played in Their Families of Origin. Sue came from an alcoholic family where she was hurt repetitively by the insensitive comments of her family. Loretta came from a family where her parents constantly battled, leaving Loretta feeling powerless despite her frequent protests against their behavior. Sue and Loretta locked horns with each other when *the roles* they played in their families of origin *were enacted in the here-and-now context* of the group.

The comment that Loretta had made in the previous session, while seeming innocent to other members, had triggered Sue's feelings of being ostracized and criticized. Loretta had, in a way, filled the role of Sue's critical family of origin through her confrontational comment to Sue. On the other hand, the intensity of Sue's reaction during the check-in triggered Loretta's feeling of powerlessness that was so familiar from her family of origin.

The Leader Facilitating Desperately Needed Validation. As Sue and Loretta were trying to resolve this friction, both of them seemed to repeat, in a circular manner, the points they desperately wanted to get across. The leader noticed this and realized that each party needed a sense of validation from the other. *But validation is difficult to come by when emotions are overpowering cognitive processing.* The leader, therefore, steered the group to validate both members' experiences by saying,

> [To the group] I can imagine how vulnerable and stressed both Sue and Loretta are feeling right now in trying to straighten out this conflict between them. I would like to invite the rest of the group members to share your understanding of this event. What I think would be most helpful is for you all to share how you understand the way both Sue and Loretta might be experiencing this event and how these reactions make sense. Who'd like to start?

This intervention brought the group together to help both Sue and Loretta feel heard, validated, and affirmed regarding their feelings and positions.

A Sense of Relief. It was a successful intervention, the conflict between Sue and Loretta was resolved, and the tension in the room gave way to a sense of relief. The icing on the cake was when Sue and Loretta hugged each other at the end of the session, which indicated they no longer had hard feelings toward each other.

Members' Reflective Entries Regarding the Conflict and Its Resolution. Following are snippets of some group members' reflective journal entries:

Loretta

This session was a real breakthrough for me because it showed me how processing issues openly in the group can provide multiple viewpoints. This process gave me much insight into how I am perceived by others. Many in the group showed compassion for me and told me that I was courageous. They were careful to protect me as they empathized with Sue's pain.

Through the group processing, I now know that talking nondefensively can work to resolve the conflict, and I think I am now willing to confront someone if I am truly convinced that it can help him or her. Also, the importance of being genuine became obvious to me tonight when Sue searched my face endlessly for the "truth" of my feelings for her. I feel so fortunate to be so personally involved with tonight's experience; those strong emotions I felt helped me more fully understand the interpersonal processes. My hope is that in the future I will never again lose sight of the person I am responding to and I will endeavor to keep in touch with the emotions that he or she carries. All along in this group, I have been struggling with what my role is in my own issues. Now I am somewhat satisfied.

Sue

Group Session 5 was very surprising for me because I did not know that my issue would surface in the group. I had many lingering feelings about the fourth session. I was angry because I felt criticized by Loretta at the end of the session. What I wanted at the end of our previous session was reassurance that I had done a better job in carrying out the interpersonal skill that I said I wanted to practice during the session. But what I got from Loretta was the opposite. It was like she sideswiped me. There was nowhere to go with the feelings that were triggered in me. The timing of the confrontation was inappropriate because it was near the check-out. I had to sit with my confusion, anger, and hurt all week.

As a result of the processing facilitated by the leader, Loretta said that she felt very ashamed of what she said to me. She said that she had caught herself on more than one occasion being critical in her responses toward others.

It feels like once you are in the group process, you are caught in a spider's web, and there is no escaping what will transpire!

Kim

This group session was very interesting for me. I first felt apprehensive when it was Sue's turn to check in with her reaction from our previous session. I wondered what she was going to say and was afraid she would be angry. Anger has always been a difficult emotion for me to both feel and to deal with when it is from others.

When Sue, in fact, started to express her anger, my heart started pounding, and my breathing got shallow. If the anger had been directed at me, I would have gotten paralyzed with fear. I would have been unable to respond and would have shut down completely until it seemed safe again. When someone is angry with me, I tend to feel shame because I take it to mean that I have caused them harm and therefore must be a terrible, thoughtless person.

Lately, though, I have been working on owning my own anger and using it as an indication that one of my boundaries has been crossed and then deciding what to do to maintain/restore my boundary. This has helped me to feel more in control of my anger and use it as a source of power rather than seeing it as something scary about to take over me.

Julie

When Loretta burst out with her response to Sue at the end of the session, I felt like the air had been knocked out of me because I knew how painful it would be for Sue; however, at the same time, I felt admiration for Loretta because she was being honest and rising to the request.

I think this fifth session was very healing for both Loretta and Sue. They both seemed to feel a lot of gratitude when we as a group took the time to understand where each other's reactions were coming from. I was so fascinated by what other people had to say and by what they thought about what had happened that I just found myself leaning forward to listen to everyone. I was also interested in how Sue and Loretta responded to what everyone else was saying. I was very relieved to see both of them relax a lot as they heard the group members offer validation and show understanding and acceptance of each of their points of view.

Lisa

During the session, I was impressed by how the conflict between Sue and Loretta was resolved. It was truly a productive process that I admire. But my feelings came flooding up when I was barely out of the driveway and on my way home. I felt a deep sadness that, all too often, my husband and I don't resolve things the way that Sue and Loretta were guided to do tonight. I felt sad also that often I just retreat or try to go my own way when I feel frustrated by my husband, and thus our communication diminishes.

Sam

I thought it was fascinating to watch Sue and Loretta fight. They both started out so angry and hostile and yet ended the evening being relaxed, friendly, and laughing. They seemed to come full circle within the 90-minute session.

It was interesting to me that although Loretta continually states that she does not like confrontation, she actually provoked a confrontation by making the initial remark to Sue at the end of our previous session and then rose to Sue's confrontation immediately in this week's session.

It was also interesting that though Sue's fear is being ostracized from the group, she actually initiated an interaction that had the real potential of forcing the group to cut her off. The group had to make a choice this evening regarding Sue: to come to her defense and include her fully in the group or to side with Loretta and confirm Sue's worst fears that the group would reject her.

I thought the group handled the situation beautifully by supporting both women and rejecting neither one. At the end, Jim innocently provided the comic relief that we all needed. This session showed beyond doubt the value of humor to defuse tension in the group. When it is genuine and not meant to make fun of anyone, humor can be a wonderful tension reliever. I am so glad we had it tonight.

Case 2: Managing Tension Crossing Two Sessions (the Seventh and Eighth Sessions)

This is a conflict that happened near the end of the seventh session; therefore it did not get resolved until the group came back in the eighth session. Following are the key points of the conflict in the seventh session:

Eleshia's Insight About Big Words Such as **Drugs.** In this unstructured session, Joseph responded to a confrontation from another member by admitting that he relies on speaking with large words to feel like he is worthy of attention; he said doing this is kind of like a drug for him at times. Eleshia appreciated Joseph's disclosure, adding that her brother also uses big words as "drugs" for the purpose of avoiding closeness with people. It is indeed quite an insightful analogy, and her concerns about her brother were felt by the group.

However, Henson heard the word *drug* and misunderstood what Eleshia said. With sternness, he said that he did not appreciate how Eleshia put Joseph's behavior in the same category as drug abuse.

Eleshia Feeling Hurt by Henson's Misunderstanding. Eleshia was shocked and hurt by what Henson said. Coming from a family where she is constantly a caretaker because of her father's substance abuse issue, Eleshia was especially sensitive to being unappreciated and judged. Eleshia explained that she didn't come up with the word *drug* on her own; she took it from Joseph's own words. As Eleshia explained herself, she began to cry. Other group members started to speak up at this point in defense of Eleshia.

Why the Word **Drug** *Was a Trigger for Henson.* The attention then stayed with Henson for a while because many members in the group felt like they didn't know Henson well and would like him to talk a bit more about himself. Ginger, Sala, and Sabrina all prompted him to share more about why the word *drug* was a trigger for him and whether it had anything to do with his daughter's suicide attempt. Henson did open up a bit. The group felt closer to him and told him so.

Ted Confronting the Group Members About Their Interactions With Henson. This, however, sparked a reaction in Ted. Ted told the group that he felt like Henson was forced to share about his private life for the benefit of the other members' curiosity. He deemed this kind of motivation as disrespectful to Henson.

Group Members Triggered by Ted's Accusation. Hearing Ted's accusation about the group's motivation, Sala was triggered and got very angry. Ginger was also triggered because she felt that her own wish to understand Henson was coming from a genuine wish to know him better. She was livid that her contribution was unappreciated. Eleshia also expressed her resentment toward Ted for writing off Henson's sharing with the group as being forced.

Sabrina Honestly Confronting Ted's Wall of Superiority. As these interactions were happening, Sabrina was shaking her head and showing a strong facial expression. When invited by one of the leaders to share her observation, Sabrina told Ted that sometimes she feels like Ted is an outsider looking in, like he is always judging the group. Sabrina told him that she felt resentful because while she and other members lay bare their hearts and their vulnerability in every session, Ted wore a mask of superiority and only shared part of himself.

The group really appreciated how Sabrina put their experiences with Ted into these piercing insights. However, after her comments, Sabrina beat herself up for exposing herself once more. She said she was trying not to be the crusader in other people's battles but felt pushed into that role once again, and she hated herself for doing that.

Ted Rejecting the Feedback, Ensuring a Conflict With the Group. Ted did not budge at all. Indeed, he told the women in the room that it is their decision if they want to feel resentful or judged—that's up to them how they want to feel. This rigid response did not sit well with the group. The conflict between Ted and the group, especially between Ted and Sabrina, thickened. However, Session 7 ran out of time, and the group had to wait until the eighth session to process the conflict.

∞∞

During the week, group members mulled over their feelings from the session and reflected in their journal entries. Ted e-mailed the leader his journal entries and asked for feedback. The leader just encouraged Ted to share with the group exactly what he wrote in his reflection.

When they came back, there was a different atmosphere. The following are the key points of Session 8.

Ted Checked-In With More Vulnerability and Emotional Connection. Ted really set the tone for more cohesive and intimate connection to occur. He was the first to share after the check-ins, and he did so with such vulnerability and emotional connection. Suffice it to say that up until Session 8, Ted had come across as superior in his assessments and indeed seemed to hide behind this wall of superiority. Surprisingly, he readily acknowledged this in his sharing.

Yet, when he began sharing, a very tender, emotionally present and expressive man began to emerge. For the first time, Ted was full blown in tears and shared his heart with the group. Group members all bore witness to this powerful and sensitive person.

The group was visibly affected and indeed readily responded respectfully and lovingly to Ted when he asked for feedback. And much to his credit, Ted was able to hear the feedback and take it in.

Ted Disclosing His Relationship With His Brother. Light was definitely shed on some fairly dark places within Ted when he was able to connect his superior way of being within the group to how he bullied his little brother . . . to the point where his brother ended up not wanting much to do with him. He was on the outside with respect to his brother, much the same way he has been on the outside with respect to the group. He masks his pain through by evaluating other's issues, excluding himself from that assessment.

This was a moving disclosure for all group members to witness because most of us can easily fall prey to analyzing others rather than looking at ourselves. Ted's bravery in examining himself in the group paved the way for the rest of the group members to be able to deeply look at their own behavior patterns.

Sabrina Examining Her Own Pattern of Devaluing Herself. Encouraged by Ted's expressive vulnerability, Sabrina was able to almost immediately reflect on her pattern of diminishing and devaluing her opinions and emotions. The tears began flooding out. She was experiencing guilt, shame, and even a great deal of confusion having spoken her mind about Ted. In short, she second-guessed herself and her instincts. What was most devastating was that Sabrina felt like no one could handle her emotions and all of the trauma that she had gone through.

Leader Facilitating Feedback to Sabrina. At this juncture, the leader asked the group, "Sabrina just said that no one in her life can handle her emotions. I wonder who in this group feels they can handle her emotions and expressions and who cannot?"

The group gave Sabrina warm support and acceptance. Perhaps the most meaningful feedback that Sabrina received was from Ted himself.

Ted's Powerful Feedback to Sabrina. Ted admitted he was at times perplexed, confused, and indeed frustrated by Sabrina's vacillating back and forth with whether or not her feelings and thoughts were valid. This was an illuminating idea for Sabrina because it showed her that she actually set the stage for rejection of her emotional expression because that's what she actually does to herself. The rest of the world was just following her lead. This pattern was instilled in her by her family, which, Sabrina admits, tends to view her as overly sensitive, therefore invalidating her experiences and feelings.

Increased Intimacy After the Conflict Resolution. There were also a lot of "I-thou" disclosures or impact disclosures in the session that were so much more effective for the group than story-telling. The group members became very close as a result of this change.

Members' Reflective Entries Regarding the Resolution. Following are snippets of some group members' reflective journal entries:

Sabrina

I was dreading coming to the eighth session tonight. I seemed unable to rein in my emotions, and that isn't like me; I'm usually really good at wearing a mask. The lingering tension between Ted and me from our previous session seemed palpable.

To my surprise, after the check-in, Ted jump started the session right away by sharing that his limbs were a bit shaky when he had left the previous session, and his stomach was in knots all week. He said that he struggled to sleep that night and had lots of uncomfortable realizations throughout the week as he thought through what had occurred.

In our previous session, Joseph did give Ted feedback about his distancing himself from the group. Ted told the group that Joseph's feedback had struck a chord and prompted his self-reflection. He then dove deeper.

He disclosed that the feeling he had leaving the previous session was indeed a familiar one—one that reminded him of his past animosities with his brother. He was in tears as he talked about the shame that he felt about how rough he treated his brother and how it has ruined their relationship.

This is a side to him that was completely absent in previous sessions. I just melted when he melted. My compassion for him when he was open was equally as strong as my anger toward him when he was closed off.

As he talked openly about his lingering feelings and connected them to previous events in his life, I felt all of my anger with him lift, and I told him so. Tears came spilling out of my eyes; I couldn't hold them back.

Later, I asked the group members to give me feedback about the level of harshness that I suspected I had with Ted last week and about how the members react to my emotionality. They gave me a lot of insights and support. But it was the feedback from Ted that was the easiest to let in.

Ted stated that my emotions did feel messy and somewhat dramatic to him, and that it did overwhelm him, and he wanted to go away. But it was not really the messiness of my emotions but the pattern of "pull and push" between "demanding" others to listen to me and then beating myself up for it that really pushed him away. I'm not sure if I latched on to it because it was from Ted or because it was the hardest to hear so I deemed it the truest.

I'm a bit overwhelmed by the amount of introspection that this new experience with Ted is bestowing upon me. I know it will be very valuable to my own healing. I feel really lucky to have this group. We laugh, we cry, we support, we argue, and we forgive.

I look forward to next week to continue the progress that we've made so far.

Ted

After brief check-ins, I began the eighth session by sharing my lingering feelings and thoughts from the previous session. I felt vulnerable as I talked about how it had had a powerful impact on me. I became emotional while disclosing this to the group, especially when I got to the part about how it hurt me when my little brother stopped wanting to hang out as we got older.

During my disclosure, Sabrina once again began crying. When she was calmer, we talked a bit about the energy and conflict between us. She also shared that she often feels like people cannot handle her strong emotions and difficult story. I was honest with her about how I didn't know if I could, in fact, handle it. I told her that her emotions feel messy and somewhat dramatic to me, and that it overwhelms me, and I want to go away.

During my feedback to Sabrina, I was clear with her and the group that part of this is my own issue, my own trouble with intimacy, especially the messy, unflattering kind of intimacy.

I later gave her another piece of feedback about how there are times when she just lets her sharing flow naturally, without the pull and push, and in these moments, I actually don't feel the urge to withdraw. But it is the times when she is second-guessing herself and speaking out loud a harsh internal dialogue of self-judgment and self-hatred that I tend to feel like I need to move away from her.

Sabrina appreciated this honest feedback from me and said it helped her realize that it is her own judgments of herself that tell others how to treat her. It seemed like an "A-ha!" moment for her.

I felt relieved that I was finally able to handle things with Sabrina. I felt calm and was in a good space to give her feedback, unlike in previous sessions when my frustrations with her were boiling over, and I was afraid I might say something cruel or hurtful to her if I was to give her honest feedback.

The group also gave me some positive feedback that made me feel redeemed. I felt like I was more open and vulnerable and exposed a part of myself previously hidden. I felt better understood. I realize that perhaps my feeling of being "in the wrong" with the group previously might have come from my own internalized judgment of myself as being "a difficult person to be around" at times.

I hope that as the group continues, my internalized judgment of myself will be diminished, and I will start to embrace the softer parts of me that the group is starting to see.

Ginger

I think our group has connected more because of the trials we experienced in Sessions 7 and 8. As the Hawaiians say, "No rain, no rainbows." Everyone walked out of Session 8 with enlightening insight.

Sala

Probably because there has been a resolution to the intense and heated prior session, I feel our group is growing just like how a relationship grows: In the beginning, there is some rapport building; then there are some deeply rooted pains revealed; then there are some fights and arguments; then the resolutions; and then comes the understanding and cohesion, and finally, lightness, humor, and laughter.

Joseph

Seeing conflicts being worked through in the group has instilled in me the hope that actualization of peace with my father is possible, despite the intrinsic differences in our personalities and modes of relating. I hope that one day my relationship with my father will reach the level of cohesion that our group has.

Tim

I was deeply touched and moved by Ted's display of emotion and his ability to connect to that emotion. This really touched a "hot button" in me: I deeply long to be privy to a man's (or more specifically my father's) internal world.

Also, Ted gave me some feedback about how he experiences me. Ted said that my deeply felt desire for emotional connection with him and other men in the group, and moreover, my anger contained within that desire, felt more like a demand than just a desire to connect. This really, really resonated and made sense to me.

I could easily recall the countless instances of rage that have welled up within me in my pursuit of a relationship with my father. Unfortunately, no matter how I hard I tried, pressed the issue, cajoled, begged, or demanded . . . my father was not and is not interested in being in any sort of a relationship with me. This is the crux of what I project onto most men.

This awareness is invaluable to me and my relationships with men. All of this illustrates the notion that how we behave in life outside of the group experience is also how we behave within the group experience. As Jon Kabat-Zinn's book on mindfulness states, "Wherever you go, there you are."

The very nature of human beings is the quest for inclusion, safety, and intimacy. Our quest sometimes comes out sideways, and that is exactly what was happening in the seventh and the eighth sessions. I am grateful to have witnessed it in others and myself. I felt very proud of everyone for being so present and so available for one another. As I contemplate on this, it makes me want to cry, albeit with happy tears.

Ted Again (3 Weeks Later, After Session 11)

A brief insight came to me in the moment when the group was giving Miquel feedback about living on his own and fully discovering who he is as a person so that he will be less defensive or combative with his reactive family regarding his sexual orientation.

I realized that I had sort of the opposite problem as some of the people who are struggling to set boundaries (Sabrina, Miquel, Eleshia). I am so fiercely independent and clear about my boundaries. I am very wary of neediness and dependence.

While I know that dependence is often an unhealthy thing, it is also true that in order to be in a deep, intimate romantic relationship, one must surrender some of his or her independence. Of course, being codependent is unhealthy, but at the same time, *I take the need to be independent too far and keep my partners at an arm's length at times, fearful of feeling attached and vulnerable.*

EXERCISES

Scenarios for Your Practice

1. In the fourth meeting of a group, Joshua looks at you and states, "You are just like my dad, expecting me to be a clone of you instead of who I really am." What is possibly happening here? How might you want to address this within the group, and especially with Joshua?

2. In a personal growth group, Wayne looks at Martha and states, "You cannot scare me with your short hair and your heavy shoes. I know your kind. I know people like you just want to put others down." What type of process is at play here? What would you do to de-escalate the situation? What might you say?

3. You are meeting with a group that includes two members from the Middle East and one member from Asia. The group is focused on increasing personal communication skills and awareness. In the third session, Myra emphatically states, "Non-Christians are untrustworthy sinners. They should all become Christian if they are going to stay in this country." What are some of your options as the group leader for responding to Myra?

4. In a group meeting, after a brief heated exchange with Martha, Gertrude turns fully away from Martha and, facing Patty, says (with a little smile and nudge), "Do you believe that she's actually saying this stuff? I'm sure that you agree with me that she's dead wrong." How would you respond?

5. In the third meeting of a personal growth group, Jill, with a scowl on her face, says, "Glen, you try to act like you're best friends with everybody in the group, like you're so sincere. You're such a fake!" What are your options for intervention?

6. A strong disagreement has occurred in the group just a few minutes before the end of the session. You suggest that the group table the discussion until the next meeting because of lack of time to explore the issue. In a sharp tone, Tony objects: "Wait a minute. I'm not going to let you weasel out of this. Before we leave here tonight, I need to know that you all agree that my view prevails." What are your choices for responding before you leave this session? What are your choices for responding when you begin the following session?

7. As the group moves into the final half hour of its third meeting, you have a sense that group members have mentally checked out. You are aware that this drop in energy seems to have hit the group just after Verla very obliquely contrasted her view of the growth process with Hugo's. What are some of your options at this point for helping the group identify what is actually happening?

8. David, who has been a bit emotionally removed from the group up to this point, looks at Reggie, who originates from Alabama and who has been quite active in the group, and says: "Do you actually expect

anyone to consider your suggestions seriously when you state them with such a drawl?" As the group leader, what issue would you want to highlight? How might you engage the group to address this dynamic?

9. Marvin divorced his wife, who recently came out as a lesbian. During group, he addresses Willis, who is gay, as follows: "I don't think you get the picture here. There are two sexes, forming the cornerstone of our society, which will soon fall apart if undermined by you people." What is the underlying issue? How would you engage the group in addressing it?

10. During the fourth session of a group for interpersonal skills development, you notice that Wayne is starting to tease and mock Bhavani about his foreign accent, although he always does it with a big smile. Bhavani looks a little annoyed by this but does not say anything. As the leader, how might you work on this issue from a diversity perspective?

Self-Reflection

1. What have been your experiences with conflict? Have most of them been harmful and destructive, or have you had some personal experiences with conflict that resulted in positive outcomes? What factors contributed to the resulting outcomes? What were your contributions to the outcomes?

2. What approaches to dealing with conflict were most prevalent in your family of origin? Do you find yourself continuing to use these approaches in your own day-to-day conflicts? If not, what influenced you most to incorporate different approaches to conflict?

3. What transformative activities do you engage in to promote your personal growth and increase your level of self-understanding?

4. In your personal life, what signs do you look for to help you recognize the covert conflict with your family and friends? How do you act once you are aware that covert conflict is present?

5. As a developing group leader, how can you ascertain when you might be expressing countertransference or projecting onto group members?

6. What is your own level of awareness, knowledge, and skill in working with diverse individuals? What is the range and depth of your personal experience in building relationships with others of different cultures, ethnicities, sexual orientation, socioeconomic level, educational attainment, age, and ability/disability? How do such factors influence your views of diverse members?

7. What personal experiences have you had in shifting worldviews in order to "live in more than one world" as members of many nonprivileged groups have done?

CHAPTER 10

TAKING RISKS IN COMMUNICATION

Having just passed the transition/storming stage but not yet arrived at the working stage, the group readily enters the "interim" of the *norming stage* (Tuckman, 1965; Tuckman & Jensen, 1977). The norming stage *bridges* the there-and-then focus in the early sessions to that of the here-and-now coming soon. This chapter focuses on leadership skills and techniques that help members *cross this bridge*.

THE NORMING STAGE OF THE GROUP

The *norming stage* is one of intense preparation (Tuckman, 1965; Tuckman & Jensen, 1977) for the hard work of here-and-now—the birthing of members' inner transformation. This intense preparation will land the group at a high level of cohesiveness and intimacy to which the early stages paled in comparison.

Group Cohesiveness and the Norming Stage of the Group

Much like *young adulthood* of human life, *intimacy* becomes a critical developmental task in the norming stage of a group (Zarrett & Eccles, 2006). Intimacy is the precursor of *group cohesiveness*.

Boiled down, group cohesiveness is the sense of "we" or the solidarity that binds the group together through thick and thin (Schutz, 1958; Weber, 1999). Up until now, leaders have invested a great deal of energy in building and maintaining group bonding through pregroup preparation, careful member screening, using structured communication topics, and working on common themes. All of these efforts will pay off in cultivating group cohesiveness.

As the group moves to the norming stage, group cohesiveness becomes even more crucial.

The Needs for Affection/Brotherly Love

The *need for affection* (Schutz, 1958) tends to surface once *the needs for inclusion and control* have been sufficiently met. This occurs in the norming stage of a group when group cohesiveness kicks in.

In a group setting, *affection* relates to the degree of *brotherly love and caring* that members need from one another. Affection, as Bemak and Epp (1996) so wisely state, "is a powerful therapeutic tool that can aid in the transition of group clients from a pattern of failed or unhealthy love relationships to a greater understanding of love's reality" (1996, p. 125).

Members are able to feel affection and brotherly love when they get to a point where they can give and receive caring words, gestures, acceptance, and compassionate behaviors in an unprompted manner. Those who *have yet to* experience solid *peer acceptance in their childhood and adolescent years especially crave this kind of brotherly love and affection* (Rogers, 2003). When the need for affection is met, a shift occurs: Members begin to take more risks in their personal disclosure as well as in the feedback they give to one another.

A Disguised Blessing: The Confrontation That Deepens Self-Disclosure

Do not be misled into thinking that members only communicate supportive and validating comments to one another in a cohesive group. In reality, confrontation happens from time to time during the norming stage of a group.

Though feared by many group members, confrontation can actually *enhance self-disclosure in the group* when expressed as a corrective feedback and can result in mutual understanding. The reason is that when challenged by confrontation, people typically disclose more in an effort to clarify their own positions and reveal their different points of view. Through this disclosure, members tend to find that their differences can co-exist and even enrich each other. Thus, the tension created by confrontation and corrective feedback is really a disguised blessing.

Increased Sense of Ownership of the Group

As the norming stage moves forward, and group cohesiveness solidifies, an increased sense of ownership of the group starts to emerge. Typical behaviors that show an increased sense of group ownership (Yalom & Leszcz, 2005) include the following:

- Trying harder to influence other group members
- More openness to being influenced by other members
- Listening to and accepting of others without judgment
- Experiencing greater security and relief from tension in the group
- Participating more readily in group interaction
- Greater disclosure
- Protecting the group norms and exerting more pressure on individuals who deviate from the norms
- Less susceptibility to disruption when a member terminates prematurely

INTIMACY, COHESIVENESS, AND HIGH-QUALITY COMMUNICATION

Group cohesiveness, like any type of intimacy, hinges on high-quality communication. This section discusses what it takes to achieve a high-quality level of communication in the group.

Three Levels of Low-Quality Communication: The Prework Level

Interpersonal closeness ensues when the parties involved take risks in being open and vulnerable. The classic Hill Interaction Matrix (Hill, 1965) classifies five levels of risk-taking in communication: responsive, conventional, assertive, speculative, and confrontive (Agazarian & Simon, 1967; Hill, 1965).

The first three levels represent low-quality levels of communication, which Hill labels as the *prework* level of communication. People within these three levels stay on *safe and less personal topics*, often waiting until others prove themselves trustworthy before diving into something more personal. The three levels are as follows:

- **Responsive:** *Passively letting others do all the talking, taking* no initiative to reveal anything about the self.

- **Conventional:** Talking only on *the content level,* revealing minimal personal *information.*
- **Assertive:** Assertively taking the floor to talk, yet not revealing too much of the self, remaining safe and self-protective.

Two Levels of High-Quality Communication: The Work Level

The next two levels represent the most personal, truth-telling, and high-quality communication styles, which Hill labels as the *work level* of communication. They are as follows:

- **Speculative:** Willing to *reflect* and *speculate* out loud about issues and internal experiences of their own, as well as those of others' upon being invited to do so.
- **Confrontive:** Willing *to take risks to express the truths of their internal experiences* and *to offer feedback and reactions to others* even when doing so stirs apprehension.

It's safe to say that within the norming stage, the group aspires to arrive at the *speculative and confrontive* levels of communication. To arrive at this state of group health, members will have to deepen their self-disclosure and take risks in feedback-giving—the major topics of this chapter.

Johari Window Profile: Effect of Self-Disclosure and Feedback

Our willingness and ability to *make ourselves vulnerable* epitomize our greatest strength and, as Brown (2015) asserts, our depth of connection with others. Yet, many of us shy away from a state of vulnerability. We mistake it as a sign of weakness, especially when it has to do with revealing our inner self. We choose to stay away from in-depth self-disclosure. As a result, our low self-disclosure leads to misunderstanding and loneliness, even when greater understanding and bonding is what our goal is.

In the same vein, our openness to feedback is our greatest courage. Through feedback, we become aware of the impact our behaviors have on others. Many people in our society don't have the opportunity to receive honest feedback. As a result, low-level feedback leads to our low self-awareness even though we desire to know how we come across to others.

- *Johari window.* A "Johari window" (Luft, 2000, Yalom 2009) illustrates the very effects that self-disclosure and feedback have on people's state of health, before and after group therapy.
- *Before entering the group.* As shown in Figure 10.1, before people enter group therapy, their Johari window profile shows *a large area of unconscious (unknown) self* (in the fourth, lower right, quadrant). The bigger the unconscious part is, the less a person is aware of the impact his or her behaviors have on others. And the more a person is unconscious of his or her behavioral options, the more the person views himself or herself as *powerless* prey to others.

The upper left, the first quadrant of Figure 10.1, displays *a small area of the open part of self*, typical for people prior to entering group therapy. With a small open area of the self, they may feel unseen, invisible, misunderstood, and thus *lonely* and unsupported.

As such, this profile (in Figure 10.1) shows a *small open area* with *a large unconscious area*. This usually indicates that a person is suffering from *low self-awareness* and *low levels of intimacy*—an individual *in great need of psychological help*.

Figure 10.1   Johari Window Profile—Before Entering the Group

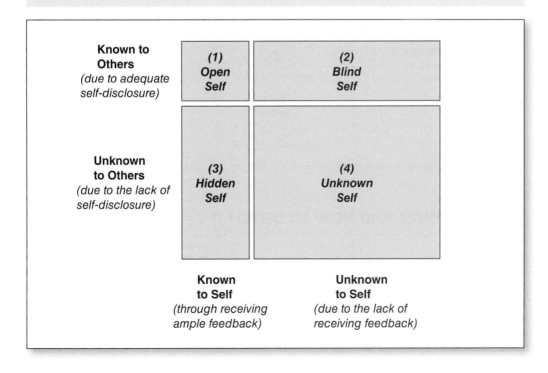

- *After completing group therapy.* As shown in Figure 10.2, after completing group therapy, people usually have a Johari window profile that shows *a reduced fourth quadrant* (unknown self) and an increased first quadrant. What contributes to this dramatic change? The following sections try to answer this question.

Figure 10.2 Johari Window Profile—After Successful Group Experiences

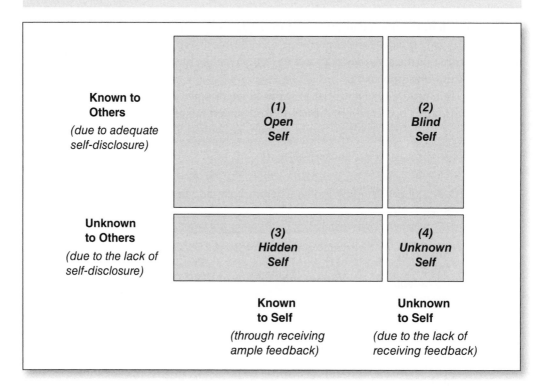

SELF-DISCLOSURE AND HOW TO DEEPEN IT

Increasing our open area and decreasing our unknown area (see Figure 10.2 above) in our Johari window profile requires a deepening of self-disclosure. This section focuses on the barriers that prevent members from a more personal disclosure and how to overcome these barriers.

1st Barrier: Pseudo Self-Disclosure— Storytelling or Secret-Telling

According *to social penetration theory*, the deeper the self-disclosure, the greater the level of intimacy will be (Doyle, 2004). Yet, many barriers exist that block people from disclosing on a more personal and meaningful level.

The first barrier to a more personal and meaningful self-disclosure is a tendency to talk about things irrelevant to the concern at hand or telling stories on the surface level, called *pseudo-self-disclosures* (Rains, Brunner, & Oman, 2016). This type of superfluous or irrelevant self-disclosure is touched upon in Chapter 7. We will go into more detail here.

Self-disclosure doesn't actually involve pseudo-self-disclosure or telling one's dark secrets. Pierce and Baldwin (1990) articulate this by pointing out what self-disclosure is not about. They state,

Appropriate self-disclosure is *not* revealing one's innermost secrets and digging into one's past, it is *not* expressing every fleeting reaction toward others, it is *not* telling stories about oneself, and it is *not* letting group pressure dictate the limits of one's privacy. (p. 152)

Irrelevant and superficial, pseudo-self-disclosure only slows the group down and causes frustration. If it continues, the group needs to give here-and-now feedback (see next section) to those unwilling to disclose their authentic self. It is only at this juncture that the group starts to move toward serious work.

2nd Barrier: Nondisclosure

The second barrier is no disclosure. Paranoid that their disclosures will be negatively evaluated, people use a number of devices to avoid revealing themselves, such as

- asking advice,
- using the editorial "we," and
- changing the subject.

Such avoidance tactics can create alienation for these types of members.

Solutions for 1st and 2nd Barriers: Facilitating Self-Disclosure at a Heart Level

To form connections in the group, a member's self-disclosure must come from the heart. Though simple to some, speaking from the heart can be tricky for those who like to stay in their own heads, speak in abstract or intellectual language, or for those who like to rehearse everything they plan to say.

Following is a reflection from a member, Charon, on how his tendency to disclosure from the head has an impact on the group dynamics:

> I have to wonder how much of the tension in our session was due to my input in the group. I know that I am not a highly emotional or warm person. Perhaps if I had come more from the heart rather than from the head, our group would have bonded more.

To speak from the heart requires that we get in touch with our feelings, allowing what moves us inside to guide what we share—even if what's inside does not make much sense at the moment. In doing so, we make room for surprises or chaos as well as room for insights or "aha" experiences.

To speak from the heart also requires that we speak from that emotional place touched by human conditions, such as

- current struggles,
- unresolved personal issues,
- fears and expectations,
- sorrows and joys,
- a sense of inadequacy or self-doubt,
- inspiration and hope, or
- strengths and weaknesses.

Disclosing from the heart is what helps us overcome the 1st and 2nd barriers discussed above.

To get the group to this emotional place, the leader can use prompts to guide the group to a more personal level of self-disclosure. For example, when members tell their long-winded stories without revealing much of any feelings or inner reactions, the leader may intervene by saying,

> Julie, I am very interested in hearing about these stories because they help the group get a sense of what your life has been like. However, please help us see how what you just described connects to your present struggle.

Some group members many need encouragement in taking a measured risk in candid disclosure. The leader can provide an educational moment without sounding preachy:

Julie, I know it is not easy to open up to other people. It does take some risk to open up. Even so, as we let others in, we are less likely to be misunderstood. As we become less mysterious, we are less likely to become the target onto which people project their own feelings and assumptions. Most importantly, as we take measured steps to share things at an intimate level, we are more likely to get the support and care we so desire. Does this make sense to you?

3rd Barrier: There-and-Then Disclosure—Important but Limited

The third barrier is *there-and-then disclosure,* or a *vertical disclosure* (Leszcz, 1992)—a disclosure stuck in stories about life events from the past or outside the group. Often cathartic, *the telling of there-and-then stories* can prove therapeutic, especially when others listen with attention and empathy. For that reason, *the group ought to allow members to tell their there-and-then stories in an unhurried fashion.*

Unfortunately, there-and-then disclosure lacks the power to animate the group. In fact, if left to continue on and on, it can render the group listless, checked-out, or even disintegrated (Slavin, 1993).

Solutions for 3rd Barrier: Facilitating Here-and-Now Disclosure

Given the limitations inherent in there-and-then disclosure, members must eventually move away from it and into something more immediate and applicable for the group. Therein lies the here-and-now disclosure.

There is an array of ways in which leaders can help members reach the here-and-now disclosure. In Chapter 8, we presented ways of facilitating members to *low-intensity* here-and-now disclosure. In a later section of this chapter, we will cover *medium-intensity* here-and-now disclosure, which is *impact disclosure* (the second intermedium step toward the here-and-now). Chapter 11 will present *high-intensity* here-and-now disclosure.

Respecting Individual Pace

Self-disclosure must be voluntary. Some areas of a person's life are better off left private; others, left delayed. Each member's readiness differs, and we must respect their unique pace. If a group pushes a member for deeper self-disclosure before he or she is ready, the leader must intervene:

[To the group] There are obviously some things that Julie does not yet feel like sharing. Although most of us are eager to understand more about Julie and what Julie feels about the group, Julie does not feel comfortable enough yet. So, let's respect her pace for now.

Jerome, I sense the group is eager to know exactly what made you decide to leave home at such an early age. However, you don't need to give in to group pressure. You are the only one who can judge for yourself when and how much to disclose.

FEEDBACK-GIVING AND HOW TO MAXIMIZE ITS POWER

To *increase our open area and decrease our unknown* area (see Figure 10.2) in the Johari window profile, we have to receive honest and caring feedback. This section focuses on the concepts of feedback and how to maximize its power in group work.

Through Feedback, We See Ourselves as Others See Us

The power of feedback lies in its ability to help members understand how their own behaviors impact others. Feedback, asserts Yalom (2009) in his book *The Gift of Therapy*, helps us see:

- how our behaviors are viewed by others,
- how our behaviors make others feel,
- how our behaviors influence others' interactions with us, and
- how our own self-esteem is influenced by the way others interact with us.

Yalom (2009) continues: "It is through feedback that the patients become better witnesses to their own behavior and learn to appreciate the impact of their behavior upon the feelings of others" (p. 119).

Feedback as a Tool for Reality Testing

Boiled down, feedback is a tool for *reality testing* (Corey & Corey, 2014; Dewane, 2006), helping us check the validity of our assumptions and interpretations of the interpersonal reality. As we all know, we are often held hostage by our own exaggerated imagination of what others think of us. Feedback helps us see our reality as what it really is, rather than what we imagine or fear it to be.

Seeing our reality from the perspective of others allows us to drop our blinders; a new awareness begins to sink in—alas, our problems are not simply caused by the actions of other people or external factors; we are in fact the co-creators of our own reality.

Feedback That Zooms In on Interpersonal Patterns

For feedback to be a reality-testing tool, it needs to bring a person's outdated interpersonal patterns to his or her attention. This comes as a surprise to many members because they come to group counseling to "cure" whatever symptoms that concern them—stress, anxiety, depression, sleep disturbance, relationship problems, eating disturbance, weight issues, health issues, career dissatisfaction, and so on.

In truth, groups cannot cure anyone's symptoms. Symptoms are merely the end products of an underlying behavioral pattern (interpersonal and maladaptive) that perpetuates the symptoms.

Yalom and Leszcz (2005) indicate that the first step of group therapy is to translate a member's symptoms into ineffective interpersonal behavior patterns and coping mechanisms. These maladaptive interpersonal coping patterns function as the root of the symptoms. Once the root is removed, the symptoms dissipate.

For example, Bruno came to the group due to his symptom of depression. In the group, it became obvious that he employs a coping pattern of discounting his true feelings, trying overly hard to please others, and not honoring his own needs. These patterns feed on his depression. Bruno was surprised when the group brought these patterns to his attention. Confronted by his truth, Bruno started to change, and his depression lifted.

All You Have to Know Is Already Within the Group

Why are members unable to hide their interpersonal patterns from the eye of the group? The answer to this is because the group is a *social microcosm*

(Yalom & Lescz, 2005) where, sooner or later, masks will come off; bona fide interpersonal styles will surface—the cat is out of the bag, so to speak. Therefore, all you have to know is already within the group.

Some members may argue that the group is an *artificial setting,* and that they act differently outside the group. This argument serves to *devalue* the group's feedback when in fact, it may have hit something close to home.

For example, in the first session, Ana presented a problem regarding a complaint frequented by her family members that she is cold to them. As the group continued, it became apparent that she either holds back her reactions to others or keeps her own counsel.

In the eighth session, the group finally gave Ana feedback about how they tried to get to know her, yet were perpetually up against a brick wall. Ana brushed the feedback off, saying that she did not feel a need to open up to others in the group because the group was an *artificial* environment.

To her surprise, the group members did not take the bait. The members easily pointed out to Ana that her very act of *devaluing* the group truly replicates her behavior pattern of pushing people away in her own life. Their firm stance was essential in turning things around because Ana became an active participant after that.

Watch Out for Two Types of Poor Feedback

Two factors may lead to poor feedback, making the recipient feel as if he or she is under attack. Watch out for them:

- *Feedback without a preceding empathy.* At times, group members become overzealous in helping each other. As soon as a member finishes telling his or her story, the group nails down his or her self-defeating behavior patterns, completely skipping the necessary step for offering empathy first. As you can imagine, the group's effort is met with defensiveness as the receiver feels "attacked."

Even though the feedback may be valid, without a preceding empathy, the person who receives it may feel "attacked." The leader must make sure that sufficient empathy is offered first to buffer the jolt coming from corrective feedback.

- *Feedback starting with the "you" statement.* A feedback starting with a "you" statement will strike as accusatory or as blaming. This kind of finger-pointing will most certainly shut the recipient down or at least invite defensiveness.

To Facilitate a Useful Feedback—Make It a Self-Disclosure

Useful feedback starts with the *"I" language* versus the finger-pointing style of "you" language. In using "I" language, *the person* providing feedback *is*, in a sense, *owning up to and disclosing* how he or she experiences the recipient's patterned behaviors in the group. Giving this kind of feedback will certainly grab the recipient's attention.

So, to facilitate a useful feedback, the leader needs to have a member make the feedback a self-disclosure, or so-called *impact disclosure* (to be covered in the next section).

If a member gives feedback starting with "you" language, the leader may redirect him to disclose his experience by using "I" statements:

Don, thank you for sharing your perceptions regarding Niki. To help Niki understand, would you please repeat your message, but this time change the "you" language to "I" language. Please deliver your message in a way as if you are actually disclosing your personal experience of Niki in the group by speaking directly to her. For example, you may fill in the blanks in the following sentence "I may be wrong, but I feel _____ whenever you _____." Would you like to try that, Don?

Redirect It When a Feedback Comes Off Indirect or Evasive

Sometimes members try to tone down the intensity of their feedback by turning it into *a question or an intellectual comment.* This kind of *indirect or evasive feedback* lacks the power of reality testing. If this happens, you as the leader can guide the individual giving the feedback to make it more self-revealing. Consider the following examples:

Example 1: A member, Nina, was making intellectual comments rather than taking the risk to share her reactions toward a member. You may redirect by saying:

Nina, please share how Julie's personal style comes across to you and how you feel toward her, rather than how you think.

Example 2: Another member, Marcy, frames her feedback into questions to make it less personal. You may redirect by saying,

Marcy, I noticed that you have asked two questions of Julie. I sense that hidden in each question is something you really wanted to say. Would you share your reactions for what they really are, rather than as a series of questions?

INTERMEDIATE STEPS TOWARD THE HERE-AND-NOW

This section starts to take intermediate steps to the most electrifying actions of a group—the here-and-now—a kind of candid communication wherein members talk openly about how they experience one another inside the group, a kind of truthful communication that increases *intimacy* and *transparency* in the room, getting members to *the pot of gold at the end of the rainbow*.

Here-and-now leadership skills are spread in four locations in this text:

- Chapter 8 introduces *the first baby step* suitable for early stage of a group.
- Chapter 10 (this section) covers *intermediate steps* fitting for the norming stage
- Chapters 11 and 12 expound the *most advanced steps* apt for the working stage.

This section presents *three intermediate steps*. Though less intense than the advanced steps, the following three intermediate steps can elicit strong emotions in the group. Only when trust has reached an adequate level should a leader apply them in the group.

1st Step: "I-Thou" Relationship Disclosure

The first intermediate step involves having members disclose their feelings that have surfaced within the relationships of the group. This is called an *"I-thou" relationship disclosure.*

- *I-Thou.* According to the Vienna philosopher Martin Buber (1937/2003), "I-thou" relationships epitomize the highest level of human communication. In it, the "I" of the person engages in an in-depth personal exchange with the other person—the *thou* (Watson, 2006). The polar opposite of the "I-thou" relationship is the *"I-it"* relationship (Buber, 1952) where the other person is treated as an object or a target for rational analysis.

- *"I-thou" relationship disclosure.* In the group setting, *an "I-thou" relationship disclosure* ensues when a member communicates how he or she feels *toward* (not about) the other member when he or she has a direct encounter with the person in the group—even if he or she has to get out of his or her comfort zone to verbalize it. This disclosure also includes expressing positive feelings *toward* the other in the most congruent and transparent way (Knox, Wiggins, Murphy, & Cooper, 2012). "I-thou" relationship disclosure can bring a deep richness to each member's encounter with the other.

To clarify, in "I-thou" relationship disclosure, "what is important is not that one discloses oneself, but that one discloses something important in the context of the relationship with others" (Yalom & Leszcz, 2005, p. 134). This criterion is what proves to be the most difficult for members.

Many members can usually rise to the challenge of talking about their feelings toward *someone not present in the group* but coil at the thought of directly disclosing their feelings toward *someone in the group—someone in front of them.*

A little help from the leader will go a long way in bringing out this kind of I-thou relationship disclosure in the group:

(1) Initial step:

Julie, you said you struggled with a sense of insignificance while growing up. *How do you feel about sharing this in front of the group today?*

Jeff, how do you feel as you tell the group about your porn addiction? How do you feel toward the group right now? How do you anticipate they will respond?

(2) Later step:

Suppose Julie and Jeff share their here-and-now feelings with the group. You can then *invite the rest of the group to share their "I-thou" experience with these two members:*

[To the group] As you listen to Julie expressing her fear of taking too much time from the group, I wonder, how do you *experience Julie* right here in our group? How do *you experience her taking too much or too little of "your" time? What do you wish your relationship with Julie to be*? When you are ready, please speak directly to Julie.

[To the group] I wonder, after hearing Jeff's anxiety, what would you like to say to Jeff regarding his fear of being judged? How do you judge or not judge him as you see him right in front of you? Please speak directly to Jeff.

2nd Step: Impact Disclosure

The second intermediate step involves *impact disclosure* (Kiesler, 1982b; McCarthy & Betz, 1978), also called *self-involving disclosure*. In this disclosure, a member reveals how he or she is personally impacted by another member's behavior. For example, feeling closer or distant, inspired or disconnected, touched or pushed away, connected or rejected, or so on. Impact disclosure is basically *a here-and-now feedback* (see the third step) because it serves two functions: It is a self-disclosure and also a feedback. When making an impact disclosure or self-involving disclosure, a person often has to experience the following to make it effective:

- Feeling *vulnerable* for disclosing his or her own inner reactions
- *Confronting* his or her own feelings and telling the truth as it is
- Wanting to use sensitive and caring language to increase the recipient's receptivity (Kiesler, 1982b)

How does impact disclosure as feedback differ from uninvolved feedback? Consider the following comparison:

- *Uninvolved feedback*: Though insightful in his feedback, Tim removes himself from the picture when giving feedback, rendering his feedback detached and less effective:

  [From Tim] Joseph, I may be wrong, but I notice that whenever you share, there are a lot of academic words. Even when you talk about your feelings, the way you intellectualize them makes it sounds like you don't have any feelings around it. [Tim focusing only on Joseph's behavior pattern without disclosing how it has an impact on Tim, himself.]

- *Impact disclosure as a feedback*: Here, Tim allows himself to be transparent when giving feedback and thus makes what he has to say an attention grabber:

  [From Tim] Joseph, I so really, really, want to connect to you, [starting off with a caring language] but *I feel lost* whenever I hear you talk in such a verbose way, with a lot of big intellectual words. [impact disclosure] Even when you talk about your feelings, I feel like I am missing out something about you because of the way you intellectualize them. Truth be told, even though I really want to, I cannot understand, not to say connect with, your feelings. [impact disclosure again] I am frustrated with myself for continuously missing out on you. [more impact disclosure]

3rd Step: Here-and-Now Feedback: Three Essential Components

The third intermediate step toward immediacy is here-and-now feedback. Please note, here-and-now disclosure is identical to impact disclosure, just with a different name—both serve as feedback and self-disclosure.

Here-and-now feedback is the most robust tool for reality testing in the sense that the person who gives the feedback has to disclose *how he or she experiences the other*—how he or she feels closer, shut out, or feels disconnected in his or her *direct encounter* with another member at the very moment.

When giving here-and-now feedback, remember this principle: Package the feedback in a way that feels *caring and acceptable* to the receiver. To this end, a here-and-now feedback needs to contain *three components*, as proposed by Leszcz (1992):

- An emotional component on the part of the giver
- A relationship component between the giver and the recipient
- A risk component in disclosing the above two

Consider the following example of how Alison gave a here-and-now feedback to June:

June, I don't know whether I should share this. [a risk component] I want to know what is alive within you; I want to know what you are actually thinking and feeling. [two relationship components] When you put so much focus on telling the stories of how your colleagues accused you of things that you didn't do, and you leave out any of your own feelings and reflections, I find myself frustrated [an emotional component] because I struggle to feel connected to you. I really want to connect with you, but I am having difficulty with it! [another relationship component]

Here-and-now feedback is best implemented when a sufficient level of trust and safety is established within the group, as it has the capability to stir up strong emotions.

Methods of Facilitating Here-and-Now Feedback

Giving here-and-now feedback requires tactics. To meet this criterion, members need a leader to navigate them to the path of success. Below are four examples showing how a leader does just that. The key is to simply ask the group members how they *experience* the recipient *firsthand*, with *regard to the theme that the recipient is discussing*:

Example 1: With regard to a member who has experienced mild depression

> [To the group] It seems apparent that Julie *takes on the responsibility for everything that goes wrong in her relationships*. [sum up the theme] Have any of you seen *this behavior pattern* manifested *within our group*? If so, *what impact* does it have *on your relationship with her*? [here-and-now feedback]

Example 2: With regard to a member who has had an issue with low self-esteem

> [To the group] From Al's story, it seems as though he often *discounts his true feelings* when interacting with people in his life. [sum up the theme] I wonder if any of you ever found Al *doing that with you*? [here-and-now focused feedback] If you have, please share your experience with Al.

Example 3: With regard to a member who has had issues with control

> [To the group] Debbie is obviously concerned with her seemingly fanatical need to maintain control in her relationships. [sum up the theme] Have any of you *seen this pattern in her when she interacts with you in the group*?

Example 4: With regard to a member who has had consistent difficulty in relationships

> [To the group] As you listen to Bill, do you see any parallels between how he acts *with you* in the group and how, as he told us, he struggles with his relationships? [connect to the theme]

Validate Both Givers and Receivers of Here-and-Now Feedback

It takes a great deal of courage to give as well as receive here-and-now feedback. For the individuals giving the feedback, they have to *expose their personal perceptions, impressions, and reactions* in front of the group. For the people receiving, they may feel ill-prepared to receive such stimulating feedback.

The leader must recognize the risks and the vulnerability felt on both ends. Tread lightly and with caution. Remember that the receiver and the giver both need validation during this process. Consider the following examples:

Example 1: Validating the person *giving* here-and-now feedback

> [To the group] Kevin just took a risk in sharing how he feels alienated and frustrated by Bill's tendency to intellectualize and deflect. Have any of you experienced something similar to Kevin's experience?

Example 2: Validating the person *receiving* here-and-now feedback

> Bill, I can understand how difficult it must be to receive feedback from the group members about how they feel toward your ways of pushing people away via intellectualization and deflection. I wonder how this feedback sits with you? Does it fit your general self-perception, or does it only fit some *parts* of you? (Note that incorporating "some parts" in your prompt allows the receiver to be more receptive.)

A Member's Reflection on Receiving Here-and-Now Feedback

When giving here-and-now feedback, some members intuitively mix supportive feedback with corrective feedback in an effort to strike a balance. As a result, here-and-now feedback can be corrective on one hand and radically accepting and heart-warming on the other.

The following passage comes from a member, Matt. His journal entry provides a reflection on receiving honest here-and-now feedback from the group:

> It was something I had been wondering about for a long time, so tonight I decided to ask the group how I came across to them. I was left

feeling overwhelmed with the input I received from the group. Virtually everything they shared had at least some truth about me in it, but I also imagined some members' own issues coming into play. Perhaps the most important feedback for me to hear was not about what others have found difficult around me, but that they still like about me despite those difficulties. When people began to focus on showing me unconditional acceptance, I soaked it all in; it was the most important part of the session for me. The unfortunate thing was that the session was running out of time, and I was left hungry for more.

LEADER PARTICIPATION IN HERE-AND-NOW FEEDBACK AND IMPACT DISCLOSURE

As a part of the group, the leader has his or her own perceptions and reactions to events occurring in the group. It would not serve the group well if the leader were to remain quiet, keeping his or her true self concealed behind a mask. Unfortunately, most new leaders tend to err on the side of caution, making fewer disclosures than what is therapeutic for the group.

Chapter 9 covered the guidelines for leaders' self-disclosure and highlighted this point: In the early stage of a group, if given at the right time, therapist self-disclosure can alleviate feelings of isolation and despair in clients. This section will specify guidelines and principles of an extraordinary form of therapist self-disclosure—impact disclosure—which also serves as a compelling form of feedback—here-and-now feedback.

Functions of Leader Here-and-Now Feedback and Impact Disclosure

If there is one reason that can convince leaders to participate in impact disclosure, it is this: "The most essential intervention in interpersonal communication therapy occurs when therapists provide *meta-communicative feedback* that labels *the interpersonal impacts* they thematically experience" (Kiesler & Van Denburg, 1993, p. 5).

Identical to here-and-now feedback, metacommunicative feedback assists the recipient in seeing how the ways in which they communicate have an impact on others. Boiled down, it is the same as an impact disclosure.

Your Green Lights to Use Impact Disclosure

Before making an impact disclosure, you, as a leader, need to get in touch with your own inner reactions and answer the following two questions:

Is there a consistency in my reaction to a specific member who has a repetitive pattern?

Do my reactions to this members' specific pattern seem to mirror those of the people in the member's life outside the group?

If both answers are positive, then take them as your green lights to use impact disclosure. Your impact disclosure will serve the group well because it

- helps members gain *awareness* about their interpersonal effect;
- serves as a model of transparency for the group; and
- allows, you, the leader to feel more confident, alive, real, and engaged with the group.

Perhaps related to these reasons, *group leaders who make impact disclosures are rated as significantly more expert and significantly more trustworthy* (McCarthy & Betzs, 1978).

Package Your Here-and-Now Feedback With Support and Care

According to Kiesler (1988), in *impact disclosure*, leaders reveal their inner reactions (such as feelings, thoughts, fantasies, and action tendencies) directly evoked by members' recurrent behavioral styles.

To increase the effectiveness of your impact disclosure, you must ensure that your reactions do not come out as anger, dislike, boredom, or frustration. Impact disclosure of such reactions does not come across as sensitive and caring (Kiesler, 1982b).

Package your impact disclosure with support and care so that it is received well by the member (Leszcz, 1992).

Example 1:

Jamie had been guarded in the past, and in this session, she finally opened up. Seizing the opportunity, the leader gave her the following here-and-now feedback:

Jamie, *I felt closer* to you when you revealed this very vulnerable and open part of yourself to the group. I feel I have come to know you on a much more intimate level. I believe that when you feel safe enough to show this part of you to people outside the group, they may feel drawn to you like the group does today. [impact disclosure, plus connecting here-and-now to there-and-then]

Example 2:

In the past, Helen relied on the leader to invite her to talk. During this particular session, the leader decided that it was time to give Helen a nudge with here-and-now feedback:

Helen, I appreciate that you come to group every week. However, I am a bit worried that you are silent during most of the sessions, unless invited to speak. As much as I want to help you and have helped you, I decided to resist bringing you into today's discussion. I know that by continually bringing you into the group, I am taking away the power of doing something that you can do for yourself. I don't want to take your power away. It will be much better if you can initiate participation on your own. [This disclosure also served as feedback about the client's style within the group.]

Example 3:

Ellen was crying, but her emotions did not match her stories. The feelings seemed inauthentic to the group. This was not the first time Ellen showed dramatic emotions. As the frequency of these occurrences began to accumulate, members began tuning her out. This particular time, though, group members felt overly frustrated with Ellen. The session came to a stalemate.

Seeing this happen, the leader gently addressed the issue with a here-and-now feedback (impact disclosure) and invited the group to join in as well:

Ellen, thank you for sharing. I am taken aback by one thing. I want to understand what's bothering you, but for some reason, I don't feel the emotions behind the tears. In all honesty, I am feeling lost here. [turn to the group] I wonder, does anyone else in the group feel the same way?

Such disclosure from the leader is likely to give other members permission to comment on the way they experience Ellen, without fear of appearing insensitive.

Example 4:

Maria was telling a painful story with a smile on her face, which really baffled the group. The leader stepped in to make an impact disclosure:

> Maria! Thank you for sharing such a painful experience. As I listened to you, I noticed that you smiled the entire time you were talking about your pain. I felt perplexed. [turn to the group] I wonder whether other members feel the same way.

Other examples:

> Julie, there are times when I see that you want to be close to others and really care for others [supportive process comment], but there are other times, like today, when I see you as rather aloof and almost critical of others. When this happens, *I feel disconnected* from you. [corrective impact disclosure] What do you know about this part of you? And how does it benefit or disserve you? [examine the function]

> Mark, I respect the tremendous strength it must have taken for you to endure the pain of abuse you suffered during your childhood. [supportive process comment] At the same time, *I was taken aback* by the lack of emotion in your face and the flat tone of your voice when you shared your story. [corrective impact disclosure] I wonder if how the way you tell your story might create distance between you and others. [link to the outside world]

> Wayne, you contribute very actively whenever the women in our group talk about their relationship issues. [supportive process comment] At the same time, I sense that something seems to deeply get under your skin whenever men-women issues come up. Frankly, *I have been concerned* and have been waiting for you to raise this issue on your own. [corrective impact disclosure] I wonder, are you aware of this reaction? Do you see how it might push women away? [link to the outside world]

As a word of caution, although leader impact-disclosure is important, do not overwhelm the group prematurely (Leszcz, 1992). This is especially important in the early stages of group where the leader needs to provide structure and set appropriate norms. The best time for a leader's impact disclosure is when the group is mature and group cohesiveness is well established.

A Case in Point: The Group's Impact Disclosure to Julie

A group member, Julie, presents an issue of performance anxiety in the first session. Yet, what is most evident in the group is her tendency toward perfectionism. To manage her anxiety, she is often the first to talk, leading other members to feel annoyed. In addition, her body language is always so tense that it sends out a message for others to stay away and rubs other members the wrong way. Unfortunately, no members of the group are willing to take risks in giving her honest feedback.

The Leader's Impact Disclosure to Julie. Finally, an opportunity appeared for the leader to share her impact disclosure with Julie. The leader delivered it in this way:

Julie, I find that you are always ready with a response to help with an issue or problem at hand. Yet, I find myself puzzled by the uneasiness I feel when I talk with you. I find it difficult to be as humorous with you as I am with other members. I feel as though you are trying so hard to be on target, to be correct, to be perfect all the time in your actions within the group. Perhaps this desire to be perfect is connected to the performance anxiety that you originally presented as your long-term issue?

The leader's impact disclosure led other members to offer their own impact disclosures as well. Following are two examples of impact disclosure from members:

Kelly

Julie, I often feel protective of you because your mannerisms and the way you go about doing things remind me of my grandmother. I was taught to be frightened of her and to be on my best behavior around her. She was a woman who was respected and feared. I was always taught to wear my best clothes around her and to stay at a safe distance. As a consequence, I never really got to know her. In the same way, I feel like I'm not able to get to know you; it's as if there is a veil covering who you really are.

Sara

Julie, I find you good at speaking from your heart and choosing your words effectively. Yet, as I listened, I saw your body tighten up as you sat on the edge of the chair, and your eyes fell upon your hands holding your glasses. This makes me feel protective of you. I have tried previously to give you some feedback, but I didn't feel heard. You have a way of deflecting what I try to say. I am struggling as I tell you this because I don't know whether this will cause conflict between the two of us.

Julie Starting to See Others' Needs and Relax. These impact disclosures created an "aha" experience for Julie. As someone often unaware of how she comes across to others, Julie finally started to see others' needs through the honest feedback provided. She started to relax and feel less of a need to be fixated on being right.

SEVEN PRINCIPLES OF CONSTRUCTIVE CONFRONTATION

According to Hill's Interaction Matrix (1965), *the confrontive level* of communication signifies the highest level of group interaction. In its true sense, confrontation means taking risks in expressing one's truths or one's views in a constructive manner. Unfortunately, many people mistake criticism, antagonism, or verbal attacks as confrontation. On top of that, confrontation, in most people's experience, only results in tension, conflict, hurt, or withdrawal. It's no wonder that just hearing the word *confrontation* would suffice to invoke tremendous anxiety.

Essentially, these negative effects stem mostly from poor delivery. To avoid negative effects, confrontation needs to be delivered constructively. Delivery should be in the form of a *challenge* and a *feedback*—in the form of inviting one another to *examine the discrepancies* between words and actions or between actions and long-term interest. This kind of *constructive confrontation* leads to the highest level of honest interaction.

This section proposes seven principles of delivering a constructive confrontation—a sensitive and constructive manner of challenging each other in the group that has proven effective over decades of our personal experiences.

Confrontation/Corrective Feedback—The Catalyst of Change

Boiled down, confrontation is a *corrective feedback*—opposite to supportive feedback. While it is easier to get the recipients to appreciate supportive feedback, it is the corrective feedback that drives them to the self-examination, helping them become aware of their unproductive behavior, and providing them with the drive for change. As Toth and Erwin (1998) state, "Corrective feedback provides information about a group member's behaviors that interfere with his or her interpersonal relations or that have other negative consequences" (p. 295).

Simply speaking, confrontation is telling one's own truth with regard to another person. It has nothing to do with right and wrong. It is not attacking or criticizing. It is simply taking a risk in telling one's own truth *in a caring and sensitive way* with regard to the other person.

Given this, confrontation actually serves as a *catalyst for change*. The recipient becomes more aware of his or her interaction with others, more willing to adopt new ways, and more likely to increase his or her interpersonal effectiveness in the end. The following is a personal reflection from a member, Jack, on the impact of receiving confrontation in the group:

> Having someone tell you, face to face, that they have a concern with you is so rare in our culture that I felt mostly unprepared for it. I accepted it and thought about where it might have been coming from. This experience pushes me beyond my comfort zone to the edge of growth. I am finding this experience enlightening and very rewarding.

Fear of Confronting or Being Confronted

Many members find it unnerving to confront others who display unproductive behaviors, such as dominating the group or telling others what they should or should not do. The fear of confrontation may be related to one of the following reasons:

- *Fear of failure.* Confrontation is a high-level interpersonal skill. Without properly learning the skill, the message can be lost in the course of *poor delivery*.
- *Fear of destruction.* Members' past experiences with confrontation were often damaging to relationships due to lack of skill.
- *Fear of punishment.* People worry about becoming the target of retaliation as a result of confrontation.

When people shy away from confronting others due to the above reasons, they also have to bear the consequences of their avoidance strategy. Consequences can include the following:

- The same problem persisting
- Frustration and powerlessness intensifying
- Resentment building up, leading to distance
- Misunderstanding increasing

Members find it just as unnerving when their behaviors are confronted. The fear of being confronted centers around the fear of facing what one doesn't want to know, fear of being embarrassed, fear of being criticized, fear of being disapproved, fear of being rejected, and so on.

These fears might be irrational, but they are very real for the person.

Principles of Constructive Confrontation

If done following certain principles and in good timing, confrontation does not need to be feared. The first key to success is good *timing*. *The only good time for confrontation is during the middle and later stages* of the group (Toth & Erwin, 1998). Leaders should withhold the group from getting into heavy duty confrontation when still in the beginning stages.

The second key to success is following the principles of constructive confrontation. In the following, we propose seven principles of constructive confrontation that have proven to be effective in our group leadership experiences:

- Own up to one's own part in the equation.
- Give a positive comment prior to making a negative comment.
- Avoid "you" statements.
- Describe specific behaviors. Do not make personality judgments.
- Tell the receiver how you feel, rather than what you think.
- Avoid asking questions.
- Avoid sarcasm.

Since educating and providing information is a therapeutic factor in group therapy (Waldo, 1985; Yalom & Leszcz, 2005), leaders can maximize members' chance of success with confrontation by sharing these principles with them.

In the following, we explain and provide examples for each specific principle.

Principle 1: Owning Up to One's Own Part in the Equation

When our corrective feedback focuses solely on how the other person is making us feel, we are missing out on *how we play a part in the dynamics*.

This kind of one-track focused feedback has a connotation of blame. To amend this, we must first own up to how we contribute to the situation that has evoked an undesirable feeling in us.

For example, Jen has long been intimidated by a monopolizing member, Michael. In this particular session, Jen finally had the courage to confront him after having felt frustrated with him for several months. To make sure that her corrective feedback was well received, Jen thoughtfully prepared and sensitively delivered her confrontation:

> Michael, this is not easy for me to say, but I am going to try. I have wanted to say this but haven't quite had the courage to say it. I feel invisible and powerless whenever you take charge of the group. Especially when you chime in quickly to respond to whatever is going on in the group and don't give the quieter members a chance. So many times I wish you had noticed the other members who wanted to share. [describing the specific behaviors that impact her] I guess *I myself also play a part in this feeling of invisibility and powerlessness.* I have been struggling with a sense of *feeling unworthy* since I was very little; speaking up has always been difficult for me. So here in the group, just the same, *I feel as if my opinions and input do not matter.* So, when you took charge of the group, leaving no chance for others to step up, my difficulty with speaking up just got worse. [Owning up to the part that she plays in the dance.]

Michael was dumbstruck by the confrontation. Up until now, he wasn't aware that his quick and frequent responses were preventing others from sharing. Michael ended up appreciating Jen's confrontation. What made it easy for Michael to absorb everything was that Jen owned up to her part in the equation. Afterward, Michael began to change; he became more considerate of others' needs.

The experience of successful confrontation toward Michael simultaneously boosted Jen's self-esteem. She started to come out of her shell, taking measured risk-taking more frequently, both in the group and in her life.

Principle 2: Compliment First, and Then Challenge

The second rule of thumb is to *avoid causing the recipient to become defensive.* In confrontation, it is not just honesty that counts but *honesty expressed in a tolerable way for the receiver.*

To adhere to this principle, each confrontation must include two components: "First a stroke then a kick," to borrow the language from Salvador Minuchin (Nichols, 2016). A stroke is a *compliment and an acknowledgment* of the other person's strength. A kick is *an honest expression, a challenge*, on how the maladaptive behaviors impact others. The sequence of these components is what matters. Reverse the sequence, and it loses its function. As a structural family therapist, Minuchin always complimented his family clients first before he delivered his challenge on their dysfunctional interaction patterns. In applying this principle, the confrontation won't come across as a nasty accusation. Consider the following examples:

> Claire, I appreciate your willingness to participate and talk about yourself. [compliment] However, I am concerned that I have heard very little from several others in the group, and I would like to hear from them as well. [a challenge, almost too subtle]

> Mark, I know you work very hard trying to figure out why most women are put off by you. You figured out that the way you relate to people in general is very different from the way you relate to most women. You are very articulate about what model of communication is most effective in each interpersonal relating. [a compliment] Yet, I am afraid that the very way you theorize yourself without revealing your inner feelings may make it difficult for others, especially women, to feel close to you. [a challenge]

Principle 3: Avoiding "You" Statements

A "you" statement, such as "*You make me* feel agitated, Kelly," will set the confrontation on the wrong track for two reasons. First, starting a statement with "you" is like sticking out your index finger and pointing out the faults of the other person. This causes the listener to feel defensive. Second, the phrase "make me" implies a blaming attitude, suggesting that others are responsible for our feelings.

When combined, the "you" and the "make me" create a surefire formula to put the receiver in a defensive position. Unfortunately, the phrase "you make me . . ." has become so ingrained in our daily language that few recognize its destructive effect.

In order to make confrontation constructive, we need to change the "you" statement into an "I" statement:

Kelly, I *appreciate* your contributions to the group. [start with the positive] *Sometimes, I feel agitated when* you keep talking and prevent other members from speaking. [the corrective feedback] [The use of "I" language is similar to impact disclosure.]

Principle 4: Describing Specific Behaviors and Avoiding Personality Judgments

You can feel the destructive effects of using personality judgment in the following examples of confrontation:

Why do *you* have to be *so domineering*, Peter?

Peter, *you* are *so self-centered! You* get what you want here and leave nothing for others.

Examples of what not to do are evident:

- "You" language
- "Why" language
- Judgments about the receiver's personality traits

A confrontation involving these negatives will invite defensiveness or hurt. The alternative is to *describe the behaviors* as the target of change.

Example 1: A constructive confrontation with specific behavior description

Jim, I appreciate what you have to offer in the group. I do want to say one thing. Quite a few times when our group was just starting to experience a deep emotional connection and a point of awakening, you jumped right in to say something totally irrelevant, completely taking away the thrilling connection. [describing the behavior] I don't know whether you have noticed it or not, but it really took away the feelings that I was experiencing at those important moments. I have really felt frustrated about it. [describing the impact]

Example 2: A constructive confrontation with specific behavior description

Pete, I appreciate your contribution to the group. I appreciate your ability to verbalize what's on your mind and your ability to be assertive about what you want. [positive feedback] The only thing is that every group session seems to be occupied with your agenda. [describing specific behavior] The group gets accustomed to you taking the floor. I certainly feel relieved when someone like you is willing to kick start the discussion, yet I also feel frustrated that other members are not given the opportunity to take initiative. [describing the impact: self-involving disclosure]

Principle 5: Trying to Avoid Questions and Principle 6: Describing Your Feelings, Rather Than Your Thinking

Some people use *questions* in an effort to *disguise their confrontation*. See the following two examples of confrontation disguised as questions:

Sue, how many times have you caused people to shy away from you by giving too much too soon?

Brenda, is it safe for you to reveal so much about yourself so quickly? Do you think that it might scare some people off?

The use of questions, as an indirect confrontation, often *causes the receivers to go to their head level, rationalizing their behaviors*. Such questions only turn the interaction into mere intellectualization and self-defensiveness.

Instead of asking questions, *make a statement*. Even more helpful *is to make a statement of feelings, not thoughts*. When hearing our thoughts, receivers are inclined to want to explain and reason their behaviors. When hearing our feelings, the receivers tend to be more receptive.

Here is an example of confrontation that does not hide behind a question but describes the behaviors and added feelings into the mix:

Brenda, you have shared yourself more openly than anyone else in the group. [a compliment] And now, in our third session, you have begun to explore your sexuality. [describing the behavior] Frankly, *I feel concerned* when someone moves that fast. Also, *I am worried* that other group members might feel pressured to match your level of disclosure. [making feeling statements]

Principle 7: Avoiding Sarcasm and Cynicism

Sarcasm is almost a staple in our daily life. For example, "Whoa, Dale! You really know how to be honest!" Such sarcasm and cynicism are meant as an indirect way to confront others' undesirable behaviors. Yet, they tend to end up stirring resistance in the receiver. A more conducive way to confront someone is to describe the behaviors:

> Dale, there is something significant going on between you and Jean. I see tears in Jean's eyes. She seems to be feeling very hurt. I respect your honesty [a compliment] when you told her that her choice of relationships is dumb and self-destructive, yet your opinion was given with little emotion. [describing observation] I find myself feeling extremely upset on Jean's behalf. [adding feelings to the mix]

HOW TO DEAL WITH POOR CONFRONTATION

As the group gets into this type of corrective feedback, *confrontation without tact* is likely to occur. People in our society and in the group, in particular, are seldom well versed in the principles of constructive confrontation. When poor confrontation happens, the group is likely to feel inundated and confused as to how to ease the tension. At this juncture, the responsibility of repairing the damage falls squarely on the shoulders of the leader. How to amend the damage?

Acknowledge Feelings Evoked by Tactless Confrontation

The first thing to do is to acknowledge the receiver's feelings. The person who is on the receiving end of a tactless confrontation may feel any of the following reactions: hurt, offended, annoyed, shut down, humiliated, or ashamed. These feelings need to be acknowledged in order for the damage to be repaired:

> Jean, you look irritated with what Tom just said.

> Lorena, it seems that what Issa just said was very difficult for you to hear. You almost feel that you are being lectured. Is that correct?

Reshape a Tactless Confrontation Into a Sensitive One

To amend a tactless confrontation, you also need to coach the giver in restating the message in a more sensitive way. Most confrontations stem from good intentions; the contributor is caring enough to want to help the recipient change, but the lack of tact inhibits his or her goal.

Coach the contributor by asking him or her to restate the message but in a way that is easier for the recipient to absorb:

> Tom and Dale, it sounds like both of you really care about Jean and want her to know that she is not making the best choices in her life. Yet, it seems that what you said was difficult for Jean to hear. Would you be willing to try and restate your comment in a different way? Perhaps, starting with an "I" statement instead of a "you" statement will make it easier for Jean to hear your message. Would you like to try that?

> Issa, it sounds like you care deeply for Lorena and want her to make the best choices in life. Yet, the way in which you said it was difficult for Lorena to hear. Would you please try to make your point again, but this time, speak from personal experience? Would you like to try that?

Ensure a Sense of Safety When Confrontation Gets Uncomfortable

There may be times when the much-needed confrontation goes beyond a place of comfort for some members, especially those coming from a background where direct communication is not embraced. In these incidences, the leader should encourage the group members to talk about how they feel about the confrontation and how to ensure that everyone feels safe.

For example, during a session, Tim tried to confront Henson for being emotionally closed. Other members followed suit and offered their observations. The reality was that Henson had missed a session and was merely having difficulty catching up with the group progress. The confrontation from Tim and other members was naturally ill-received and caused Henson to become defensive while causing Tim to become frustrated.

Tensions began to mount within the group. A couple of members felt uncomfortable about the tension and pointed out that Henson appeared "attacked" or "judged."

Upon hearing these charged words, the leader stopped the group and asked members to discuss *the issue of safety* with regard to the uncomfortable confrontation:

> [To the group] I am impressed with the risks that many of you have taken in sharing your reactions and observations with each other. As a

result, a lot of hidden feelings and assumptions emerged in our discussion. However, I am concerned that a couple of you felt as if Henson was "attacked" during the exchange. I would like the group to discuss *what needs to happen so that everyone in the group can feel safe and still allow group members to speak their truths.* Let's hear from everyone since this determines how our group can move forward. Who would like to start?

A consensus was then reached in which all members agreed to respect each other's boundaries and at the same time appreciate the honest input of others. The effect of this discussion was reflected in a member's journal:

I am glad that we were able to talk civilly about how to make sure everyone felt safe enough to do the kind of honest sharing needed in the group. Even though I feel safe in the group, I am glad we had this conversation; I definitely feel like everyone was a little more relaxed afterward.

GROUP MEMBERS' REFLECTION ON CONFRONTATION

The following are the reflections by group members that demonstrate the psychological inner working of members confronting or being confronted:

(1) Lori

My goal in the group was to be able to confront people without fear or embarrassment when their negative actions had an impact on me. My goal remained the same throughout our group life, but my motivation changed. Originally, my motivation was to tell the most difficult person in my life (my sister) how her unpleasant behavior affects myself and others. But now, she is no longer my motivation. Now I am my motivation. I have discovered that I feel liberated when I speak what is in my heart and on my mind. It is very therapeutic as long as it is done tactfully, the way I learned to do in the group.

My Past Experiences With Confrontation. Before this group, I had some bad experiences with confronting. I thought I was simply being honest with others, but my comments were not readily accepted. After many disappointments, I just closed myself down. If anything, I only focused on "pleasant" things. This is how I came into our group. I recall during many earlier sessions wanting to share some personal reactions toward others but shying away from it due to my fear of being retaliated against. I really was afraid.

The Turning Point. During one group session, the leader told me that I write excellent reflections, full of insights and authentic reactions, but that I disconnect from my feelings when in the group. She encouraged me to allow my emotions to surface and speak to others as I did in my reflective journal.

My first response to her comment was resentment. I resented her because her comments penetrated my soul. But that was the turning point for me. Later I knew why the leader's comments affected me so strongly. They were 100% true, and I had never acknowledged them to myself.

A Transformation. After that realization, a transformation took place in me. I felt determined and motivated to practice my skill of confrontation. I was still afraid of being retaliated against, but then I was even more afraid of staying the same.

I took enormous steps in practicing the skill of confrontation in the eighth session. My progress grew by leaps and bounds when I confronted Rose. I continued to make huge strides when Eve presented her issue. Since then, I have felt more empowered with each passing session. I feel very confident about myself. I don't worry or become anxious when I am experiencing a negative feeling toward someone's behaviors and need to speak my truth.

This group experience broke through my old facade. It allowed me to make improvements on my connection with others. It has helped me become a stronger and more truthful person.

(2) Joseph

Today's session was a big surprise for me. Tim challenged me to examine and reflect on my tendency toward rigidity and obfuscation in my response style. My reflexive response was to defend my propensity for sounding verbose. But one thing I have learned from our group is the way in which interpersonal pathologies appear in the spontaneity of group interaction.

Tim's commentary on my interpersonal pattern actually illuminated a truth about myself that I needed to hear. I now realize that my tendency toward profundity and verbosity is a defense mechanism that inhibits my capacity for authenticity and spontaneity. My response style tends to degenerate into sterile intellectualism that may come off as stilted and stultifying. Knowing this, I now feel an immense relief that I can be myself without hiding behind a facade of intellectualism. This was a cathartic moment for me.

The Group's Feedback About My Strident Intellectualism. I also heard from the rest of the group members that they want to get to know the real, deep-down version of me. They feel that my interpersonal pattern obscures normal communication between myself and others in the group. I have a habit of trying to elicit respect and reverence from others by resorting to strident intellectualism. Initially, this communication style was adaptive. I derived a sense of euphoria and "intoxication" from sounding professorial and intellectual.

After hearing consistent feedback from Tim, Sabrina, and Ella, I now know that this habitual pattern of communication is maladaptive and maladjusted to my current situation. I need to relinquish this facade of intellect and open up emotionally and verbally to others in the group.

Honest Confrontation Has Liberated Me. Prior to this moment of being confronted, I was in this impermeable fortress, unwilling to experiment and cultivate a new style of communication. Now I feel liberated from obscurity and isolation. I feel I am now a vital part of the group, thanks to Tim and the group's honest and direct feedback.

I feel that confrontation directed toward me has disencumbered me. I feel that in this session I have reached the antechamber and vestibule of change. I am forever grateful to Tim and the group for their challenge and their invitation to get acquainted with the real me.

COACHING MEMBERS TO REQUEST AND RECEIVE FEEDBACK

Coaching Members to Request Feedback

When members do not know how they come across to others or how their interpersonal style impacts others, you can invite them to request feedback from the group.

Kelly, there are many people who know you very well in this room. Why don't you ask them about how they experience you, pushy or not? Okay, go ahead and ask!

June, it will be helpful if you ask the group for feedback about your interpersonal style. You can say to the group, "I would like to know what I do that puts people off"?

Enhancing Ability to Listen to Feedback

The ability to hear feedback is directly related to one's self-esteem. People with a higher self-concept typically have a greater ability to accept and integrate corrective feedback (Kivlighan, 1985) and vice versa. Since not all people have the same capacity for feedback, teaching members how to hear feedback with openness is essential work for the leader.

A major barrier in receiving feedback is a tendency for the receivers to want to immediately respond or explain away the reasons behind their behavior. Such reactivity prevents them from fully hearing what others have to say.

In this incidence, the leader needs to intervene by asking the receiver to listen before responding:

Example 1: With a member wanting to reply to feedback immediately

Julie, when people give you feedback, it would be more productive if you could listen reflectively without rehearsing how you are going to reply. After most members get the chance to share their feedback with you, then it would be fitting to hear your reactions to the feedback.

Example 2: With a member rejecting feedback immediately

Tom, the feedback given to you by many members seems to be consistent. It would be helpful if you would take them seriously, considering the validity and the significance of the message. Sitting with this feedback for the week will allow you to have a greater understanding of what you are going to do with this new self-knowledge.

Enhancing Ability to Mull Over Feedback

To help members differentiate between unhelpful and helpful feedback, the leader may ask the receiver to identify what feedback (members and leaders) was most helpful and what feedback caught them by surprise:

Julie, several members, including me, have given you some strong reactions. *What is your reaction to our comments?*

Peter, which of the comments you just heard struck you the most?

Jane, this week I have seen you listening to the group with less arguing. You have even said "thank you" twice. I wonder whose comments have been particularly helpful in silencing your anger, allowing you to hear them.

Jake, you've received some fairly direct feedback from the group. How are you putting together these remarks for yourself?

∞∞

In closing: As the group enters the "interim" of the *norming stage,* group cohesiveness and intimacy becomes the apple of the eyes. It, however, challenges the group to advance to the *speculative and confrontive* levels of communication. To this state of group health, members will have to deepen their self-disclosure and take risks in feedback-giving.

Intermediate steps to the here-and-now—here-and-now feedback and impact disclosure—are instrumental in increasing *intimacy* and *transparency* in the room. When packaged with support and care, these here-and-now communication tools will get members to the pot of gold at the end of the rainbow.

CASES IN POINT

Case 1: Kelly (Fifth Session)

Kelly's original presenting problem was her tendency to act as if everything was okay when in fact, it was not. Therefore, her goal was to have the ability to be herself as she desired.

In the fifth session of her group, Kelly presented a personal issue. The issue was originally presented as a career decision-making struggle. Kelly explained to the group how she was torn between completing her graduate program and pursuing a long-standing dream of stand-up comedy. As she talked about stand-up comedy, her face lit up, even glowed. Excitement and enthusiasm were present in her voice. But Kelly felt tremendous pressure to live up to the unreasonable expectations of her family members who also constantly judge her choices. Many times she said, "I made another screwed-up decision."

Hiding the Pain. As Kelly spoke, she hid her pain behind a smile. Her speech was rapid and upbeat. Several times, she used the word "*closet*" to reference the place she retreated to lick her wounds.

Here-and-Now Feedback. Seeing Kelly's pattern, the leader asked the group to take a risk and give *here-and-now focused feedback* by linking their first-hand experience of Kelly in the group to their perceptions about Kelly's struggles in life. The leader said,

[To the group] While I was listening to Kelly's stories, I noticed that she used the word *closet* several times to describe her struggle. She also smiled and laughed a lot throughout. I wonder, how does the group experience Kelly at this moment, in this room? How might your experience of her run parallel with the way she copes with the outside world? When you are ready, please talk directly to Kelly.

Members Speak Up. The following are members' here-and-now disclosures to Kelly:

Lori:

I experienced you as a person who hides behind the closet of smiling and laughing while telling a story that is painful in nature.

Peter:

Your main emotional energy seemed to be a rush of excitement, but I wondered what was beneath it. I like your way of communicating, but I guess there is more beyond the smiling, joking, and fast talking that you showed to the group. By keeping the band of emotions so narrow, it was limiting to *me*. It was as though you were controlling not just your emotions but also *mine*.

Rose:

I experienced you like a clown who is laughing on the outside, yet crying on the inside. It seems to tie into the stand-up comedy, where you can continue to laugh and not show the side of yourself that is hurting.

Floodgates of Tears. At this point, the floodgates opened; Kelly's smile gave way to tears upon hearing the words "my family." She then revealed her sexual orientation as a lesbian and her subsequent pain over the lack of acceptance by her family and society in general. She described feeling shame when walking down the street with her female companion.

As she exposed this part of herself, Kelly's overly enthusiastic persona faded away; she became more calm and vulnerable. The group was elated to see this side of her and began to feel much closer to her than before.

Snippets of Members' Reflective Journals

- Peter's reflection:

  I felt very connected to Kelly, and I told her so. I felt that I really shared myself with Kelly. I empathized with her, and I challenged her in ways that were not always easy for me. I felt that Kelly saw herself in our session today. It wasn't until after the session that I fully understood the connection between Kelly's need to joke and laugh for her parents and her need to be an entertainer.

- Eve's reflection:

  I'm not sure what it was about this session, but I had great difficulty moving on from my feelings of overwhelming sadness. I cried all the way to the parking lot. Although I have tried to figure out what happened and why the session affected me that way, I haven't reached any conclusion. I felt that Peter was so insightful in being able to make the most poignant statements to Kelly. I remember at one point Lori and I looked at each other and said, "Wow!"

- Kelly's reflection on Session 5:

  This was an extremely helpful session for me. I learned a lot about how I don't present my true self to people, but rather I just show enthusiasm and a smiling face. I was aware that I do that sometimes but was not aware of the extent of it. I certainly was *not aware that people could tell or that they felt limited in their experiences with me*. It was a bit uncomfortable for me to be given all this feedback at once. But it was such powerful feedback. Because of this, I would like to try to not be afraid of showing my authentic self around people.

  I have a different sexual orientation from everyone in the room, and I have a radically different home life than people in the group. Growing up, I learned to pretend that everything was okay and wonderful because that was how I could get people to accept me. I think that is why I started crying in the session. I will say that I have experienced a lot of abuse, and I really feel as if I was a person who didn't have the freedom and privilege to be herself. At the same time, I feel that my background has made me a very strong and aware person. To be honest, I often look at people and think that I have a lot more experience in life because I have been through a lot. Some people will take who I am and see it as someone who must be crazy. For example, my family thinks I am crazy. I, therefore, am very scared about the notion of really showing myself to people.

However, now I feel I want to start being myself.

- Other reflection from Kelly, one month later, right before the termination of the group:

   I presented my personal issue, and I was struggling with my career path. In that session, through the feedback of my fellow members, I learned that I am constantly hiding who I really am from others. I was hiding many things and trying to be the person that I thought people wanted me to be. I was trying to hide the fact that I was a lesbian, without really understanding what it was or what it meant. I was hiding the fact that different relatives had abused me because I was afraid I would shame my family by telling the truth. I had hidden behind a smiling face for so long that I didn't even realize I was doing this. It had already served its purpose, but I continued to do it.

   Not Ashamed Anymore. In the group, I learned that I hide from people. Now I feel I can make a choice about whether to hide behind a smile or to be myself. This revelation has taken my path in life to a new height. *I have been writing a great deal of stand-up comedy,* and for the first time in my life, I am not ashamed of my work.

   Finding My Voice. In addition, I have been able to really talk about myself and my life and am *starting to find my voice as a comedian.* Three months ago, I would not have been able to talk about *being a Latino, Jewish lesbian while on stage.* Now I can.

   I Wish the Group Could Run for Another 3 Months. In the group, I have been challenged to be myself and to stop hiding. I know that is why people keep their distance from me. I have always had a hard time getting close to people beyond a superficial level. I never understood why until now. My challenge to myself now is to let people in. I wish the group could run for another 3 months so that I could continue to work on this skill. I hope to take what I have learned and apply it to my everyday life.

Case 2: Mindy

Mindy's original presenting problem had to do with a deteriorating relationship with her husband. Her goal was to improve her methods of handling problems with him. Mindy had come from an alcoholic family where she received very little nurturing. In the group, she tends to be the one who "takes on" everything: a caregiver who feels responsible for everything. When she is unable to exert control over things as a caretaker, she gets defensive, as demonstrated by her conflict with Anna (the incident is illustrated in Chapter 12).

Lied to by Her Alcoholic Parents Again. In the sixth session, Mindy presented an issue of a recent event where she got extremely upset. Her parents were supposed to go to Iowa to visit her brother and his family. Unfortunately, her parents' drinking overshadowed their obligation to family. Once again, they made up an excuse as to why they were unable to go and subsequently let Mindy's brother down, causing a great deal of disappointment. Mindy is most troubled by her inability to distinguish between what is true and what is a lie in what her parents tell her. So often there is a grain of truth to their stories.

The External Focus Sank the Group. As the group listened to Mindy's story, members were supportive and considerate. Yet, the stories were completely focused on Mindy's parents and their behaviors. After a while, the group's energy began to sink.

The Leader Took a Risk to Facilitate a Here-and-Now Feedback. At this juncture, the leader sensed that something needed to be done to revitalize the group. *Here-and-now focused feedback* is precisely what the group needed. Although risky to shift the focus from complaining about external events to communicating to the person in the room, it was the right time to do so. The leader said,

> [To the group] It seems that Mindy feels supported by the group's understanding of what she has gone through. At this point, I would like the group to tell Mindy *how you experience her first-hand in the group.*

This intervention brought the group discussion from an outside focus toward something more relevant—the members' subjective experience of Mindy. The discussion turned out to be a very enlightening experience for the group and for Mindy.

One Step Further—Connection-Focused Feedback. Later, the leader asked the group to take one step further and give Mindy *connection-focused feedback.* The leader said,

> [To the group] Okay, let's take this another step further to see whether we can give Mindy some additional insight. My question is, what connection

do you see between Mindy's experience with her parents and her current difficulties with her husband?

The Group Points Out the Heart of the Issue. The group pointed out that not being able to count on her parents due to their alcoholism led Mindy to have her roles prematurely reversed—she became the caregiver of her parents at a young age. Her lack of parental guidance as a child is most likely related to her fear of intimacy with her husband—she is *afraid of getting too close.* This connection between Mindy's experience with her parents and her issues with her husband was enlightening for Mindy to hear, as she had never made the connection between the two.

Other Members Coming Out of the Dark. Near the end of the session, the leader invited all of the group members to share their reactions to the session. Many members shared that they, too, came from alcoholic families. Most striking among them was Keith's revelation that he too came from an alcoholic home and attended Al-Anon. It was drastically different from past sessions where he painted a picture of having a perfect family.

Mindy's life story certainly caused members to begin thinking about their own history and to understand how their families of origin have impacted their lives.

Snippets of Members' Reflective Journals

Jenny

I empathized with Mindy. *I too grew up in an alcoholic home,* and it is where I learned that my father was not someone who could follow through with commitments. I learned at an early age not to trust or depend on men. It is an issue that I continue to work on to this day.

Mindy touched on the fact that she did not like to feel vulnerable, and I too could relate to this. I keep myself at a distance when intimate with my husband. *I subconsciously think that if I don't give myself completely, I will not get emotionally hurt or rejected.*

This is something I continue to work on as well. I am making progress, and I shared this with Mindy during group. After listening to Mindy, I realized how far I have come in my self-actualization. I am becoming healthier in my relationship with my husband.

Thinking about Keith's behavior and the way he lives his life, I realize that *self-denial is common for many of us who grew up in an alcoholic home*. I was glad that Keith opened up and shared this information with the group.

Keith

I have a tendency to withhold my true feelings and to not ask what I really want to know. Often times I catch myself not being as forthright as I could be at the moment. By the end of the session, when we shared how we reacted to the session, I have to say, I was speechless, and it was hard for me to describe.

At that moment, I realized that the reason I have a problem expressing how I feel is because I grew up in an alcoholic family. I have emotionally detached myself from my own true feelings surrounding the subject. So, when I was asked how I felt, my mind drew a blank. I conveyed this to the group.

I expressed to Mindy that I was very much in tune with her message and her feelings. When it came to my own feelings, though, that was another story. I came to the group tonight to work on a skill but ended up realizing a personal issue that I plan to share for the next session.

Anna (Who Was Often Seen by Members as Cold and Aloof in the Group)

When wrapping up the group, Mia said that she often wondered where I was during the session. I thought about this statement a lot and realized that I had not let people in about my internal state.

I was in extreme pain for the entire session. I had a severe illness as a child. Well, that illness is a *chronic bowel disorder*, and I will always have it. In February, I had a surgery. Since then, I have been ill off and on. When I was a teenager, *I resolved not to complain to others about my chronic pain* because I felt strongly that people receded from me and perceived me differently when they knew about my health.

However, now I realize that my way of dealing with pain may have become self-defeating. *While I was determined to be quiet, it came across to others as being disengaged or cold.* I should perhaps rethink my nondisclosure strategy and take some risks in letting people know what is going on with me.

Mindy

When the leader talked about how the group "experienced" me, I was a bit apprehensive. Yet, because of the bond I have with my group members, I did not feel threatened.

Keith commented that he feels I am a giver, but that maybe I'm not as comfortable receiving care as I am giving it to others. That's pretty much in line with how I am. I often feel guilty when others do things for me and am constantly "keeping score." This is something my husband always chides me for.

Mia stated that I seem strong on the outside, but inside there is a sensitive and vulnerable little girl. I felt this was right on. I feel this way a lot. I have always been an extremely sensitive person and feel myself regressing when I get very upset about something. Although living and working in New York has helped me develop a thicker skin, there are obviously still times when I feel like that oversensitive little girl.

The most important part of the session for me was when the group was asked to identify the underlying connection between the issue with my parents and the difficulties in my marriage. A connection was made between the loss I experienced due to my parents' alcoholism and my fear of intimacy with my husband. It was an enlightening thing to hear as this association has never come to my attention before.

Not being able to count on my parents is a huge disappointment for me, and it hurts to know that I cannot really go to them for anything. My parents can't be there for me. Instead, my brothers and I are their caregivers. My parents can hardly remember to ask what is going on in our lives. They are so busy complaining about all their ailments, which then serve as their excuse to keep drinking. This relates to my fear of intimacy and what I am currently experiencing in my relationship with my husband.

Subconsciously, I reason that if I am too close to people and they leave, I will get hurt just as I have been hurt by my parents. The abandonment I experience might be either in the emotional or physical sense or both. This is beyond what I can handle, and I would fall apart.

I feel like we entered a new territory when the group made the connection between my parents' alcoholism and my fear of intimacy. The group really went deeper than we had ever been before. I appreciated everyone's honesty and directness. It was so helpful for me to hear those connections being stated out loud.

EXERCISES

Scenarios for Your Practice

1. During a session of an interpersonal skills building group, Emily makes the following statement: "I really don't feel like saying much about myself." As the group leader, how might you handle this in a way that encourages greater self-disclosure and also shows respect for Emily's right to choose her own pace of disclosure?

2. During the seventh session of a group for interpersonal skills development, you realize that you are becoming a little frustrated and distant toward Jamie. Sometimes she does not respond to the issues you raise but instead quickly changes direction and asks another group member about an issue raised in a previous session. How might you effectively disclose what you are experiencing?

3. Ricardo talks about his relationships and how he feels that people retreat from him, and his response is to chase them more aggressively. He says he doesn't know how this cycle started or how to break free of it. He looks directly at you and asks, "You are the expert here. What should I do when people run away from me?" What might be a helpful response that you, as the group facilitator, could make?

4. As the group begins, William states, "I usually prefer to be an observer in groups. I feel that I learn so much watching the interactions of others." What are some key issues associated with this type of stance? What are your options as a group leader for handling this situation?

5. You become aware that Jim continues to question Phil about the factors that played into his decision to quit his job and how Phil's family has responded to that decision. Although you are aware that the discussion may be of some benefit to Phil, you are also aware of your own feelings of discomfort with this exchange, especially with Jim asking several very pointed questions of Phil. What might you want to say to Jim or ask of him?

6. Curtis opens a session with a long and detailed description of a disagreement he had with his mother over the weekend. You become aware that he is asking for validation from you and the group. You are also aware that there may be some parallels between what is happening in the group and what happens to Curtis outside the group. How would you choose to help Curtis become aware of this?

7. In a support group for caregivers, Josephine has been very attentive to other members and supportive of their issues. Although Josephine has asked for nothing from others in the group, you recall that she entered the group partly at the urging of her adult son. He feels she does not take any time for herself and is concerned about this. How would you help Josephine see this possible connection?

Self-Reflection

1. Think of your own level of awareness as represented by the Johari window. What relative sizes would you assign for each of the windows? Would they all be the same size, or would some be larger than others? If they would be of different sizes, which windows would be larger?

2. What methods do you tend to use in your life to increase the size of the Johari window area that is labeled "known to others, but not to self"?

3. Do you have any strategies or approaches in your life for decreasing the size of the area that is "unknown to self"?

4. What type of self-disclosure do you think is most appropriate for a group leader? To what extent might you expect group members to meet your level of risk-taking and self-disclosure?

CHAPTER 11

ADVANCED STEPS INTO THE HERE-AND-NOW

Once starting to take greater risks in self-disclosure and feedback, the group rapidly gains momentum and moves ahead into a breathtaking terrain—the here-and-now.

Though most compatible with unstructured groups in their "working stage," the here-and-now method can benefit many other groups and settings. Indeed, small doses of the here-and-now can actually be used in the early stages of a counseling group and even in psychoeducational groups or mandated groups. The key lies in choosing a level of intensity that suits your group's needs and capabilities.

In an effort to cover all levels of here-and-now intensity, Chapter 8 presented some *baby steps* toward the here-and-now; Chapter 10, the *intermediate steps;* and now in Chapters 11 and 12, the *advanced steps.* And even at the advanced level, the here-and-now techniques further partition into several levels of intensity. The hope is that your success with the less intense techniques will embolden you to apply those of higher intensity if it so suits the needs of your group.

THE WORKING STAGE AND UNSTRUCTURED GROUPS—ADVANCED LEVEL

Sometimes called the the *production stage* (Lacoursiere, 1980) or the *performing stage* (Tuckman, 1965), *the working stage* (Corey & Corey, 2014)—the fourth stage—of a group starts when the group reaches the *halfway point* of its life span. At that time, a seismic shift in group energy happens, demanding a more advanced level of leadership skills since the basic leadership skills no longer suffice to meet the group's needs. This section depicts this major shift and how to meet the group needs at this new stage.

Trust, Honesty, Productivity, and Humor

Running parallel to the stage of adulthood, the working stage is the period in a group's life when it is finally geared up for the most intense form of interpersonal learning. In contrast to the prior stage (the norming stage, Chapter 10), *speculative* and *confrontive* levels of member-to-member communication (Hill, 1965) now reign the working stage.

It is a time when the strong trust slowly built up over the previous three stages starts to free members up to take even more risks in traversing the unknown of the here-and-now, like a ship sailing into uncharted waters.

The working stage brings excitement to both the leader and the members as they can now rigorously pursue those interpersonal dynamics previously put aside in favor of establishing group function and norms. The group can now afford to target those unprocessed perceptions and relationship issues that have been going on beneath the surface since day one.

Advancing successfully through this working stage, the group will harvest greater levels of trust, intimacy, self-disclosure, feedback, confrontation, and, most importantly, humor.

Yes, humor. You will definitely hear a lot more hearty laughter at the absurdity of our own human conditions. Humor is a barometer, telling us that the group is well into its working stage.

If a group has passed the halfway mark of its life span and still feels like it has not yet reached the maturity and productivity of the working stage, you might want to look into any unresolved issues, carried over from previous stages, that may be stalling the group's progress.

Member Autonomy and Self-Initiation

The working stage is a time when members finally gain a sense of *autonomy* by *initiating their own communication* without relying on the leader's guidance. It is a time when *less is more—the less the group relies on the leader, the more vivacious and confident it becomes.*

As the members become more and more active, you, the leader, can delegate more and more control to them, leaving you with more energy to address those crucial here-and-now issues floating on the fringe.

Members as Cofacilitators and Guardians of the Group Goal

The newly gained sense of *autonomy* can invigorate members to take on the role of *cofacilitators* of the group process. Only when all members take equal responsibility for acting as *cofacilitators* can the group become a true community wherein all commit themselves to monitoring the group's functioning and progress as well as the growth and well-being of everyone involved.

Establishing an agreed upon *group goal*, outside of individuals' personal goals, can go a long way in heartening members to act as cofacilitators. Consider the examples below:

[To the group] Before we start our group processing, let's decide on a collective group goal for our group to work on for the rest of our group's life. With a clear shared vision of what we as a group are willing to commit to, our group may reach its highest potential. Let's have a go-around, in no particular order, and have each of you voice your view about what our group could be.

Later,

If I may condense all of your voices into one sentence, it sounds like you guys all want to speak from your hearts without self-censoring, to be open to feedback and to give honest feedback generously. Does this sound about right?

Much later,

Now that we have solidified our group goal, from now on, each of you will be the cofacilitator to help our group reach this goal. Being the cofacilitator, each of you has *the responsibility* and *the authority* to voice whatever the group needs to take care of in an effort to reach our desired final destination. I hope everyone will keep this group goal and your cofacilitator role in mind as we adventure into the rest of our group time together.

Step in and Initiate a Process
Discussion When Members Cannot Cofacilitate

There will come a time when something happens in the group that is beyond members' capacity to cofacilitate and to resolve it. This kind of phenomenon is bound to happen more and more in the working stage. Leszcz (1992) explains:

> As initial anxiety and social politeness diminish, the group becomes a social microcosm and interpersonal laboratory in which members behave and interact, as they typically do in their outside world, reproducing their characteristic maladaptive interpersonal style. (p. 50)

At such a juncture, when someone plays out his or her behavior pattern in the group is exactly the time when the leader must step in to do what the members cannot.

For example, a verbal member, César, has dominated the floor for quite a while, and no one in the group has the capacity to comment on this dynamic. Seeing this, the leader intercedes to get the group to look at this interpersonal event:

> [To the group] I wonder, what do you see is going on here?

And later,

> [To the group] You guys are making great strides in acknowledging your reactions to César's taking over the floor! Now I want to ask another question: *What is stopping you from sharing your reactions honestly? What is the reason that you allowed this one-person show to last for so long?*

A Comparison of Advanced Versus Basic Leadership

Exemplified above is an example of an advanced level of leadership. How does it differ from that of a basic level? Below we provide a side-by-side comparison of how an advanced-versus basic-level leadership would handle an identical scenario.

The Scenario. A member, Cindy, told the group a regretful recent life event. Luis, another member, jumped in to ask her a series of questions. One or two members then chimed in to relate their own stories, which unfortunately wandered off into completely unrelated topics. Following this, Cindy was completely silent.

Basic Leadership Focusing on Content and Rapport. Should the group be in the early stage, the leader would focus on *the content level*—Cindy's stressful *life experiences*—and on building *a safe environment* where everyone has a chance to feel heard and understood. With these two focuses in mind, the leader would be thinking of the following questions:

- How does Cindy feel in this stressful life event?
- Beneath all his questions, what is Luis really trying to say to Cindy?
- How can I, the leader, help Luis rephrase his questions so that Cindy can hear Luis's true message?
- How can I redirect the group to offer empathy and validation so that Cindy does not feel alone and uncared for?

Based on these considerations, the leader might do any of the following:

Luis, I heard you ask a series of questions to Cindy. Behind your questions, there seems to be something you wanted to say. Would you like to state what you want to say to Cindy directly instead of putting it in a series of questions?

[To the group] Can anyone imagine what it is like for Cindy to undergo such a betrayal and abandonment by a person she thought she could trust with her life?

[To the group] From the stories shared by Cindy, there seems to be a sense of "I'm too intense, or I'm too much of this or that for others." I wonder whether this "I'm too much of this or that for others' strikes a chord for you?

The above-listed leadership skills represent the bare bones of a basic level group facilitation.

Advanced Leadership Focusing on Interpersonal Processes. In the working stage of the group, rather than focus on the content level or on highlighting a supportive environment in the group, the leader will zoom in on *interpersonal processes between members*. With this focus in mind, the leader might be thinking of the following questions:

- How does Luis's questioning style shut Cindy down?
- Does Luis recognize how his questioning style has an impact on others?
- For those members who used self-referencing to try to show support for Cindy, do they recognize that their self-referencing is actually contributing to Cindy feeling invisible?

- How does Cindy's silence in this moment resemble her silence and lack of voice in her personal life?
- How does the lack of support that Cindy got from the group resemble the lack of support in her early life?
- What is going on inside the minds of the rest of the members as they see Cindy being ignored? What stops them from saying something about it?
- How do I feel about all of these unspoken dynamics? Do I trust the group process enough to tackle immediacy issues, to take the bull by the horns?

With these questions in mind, the leader will do something at the advanced level to pursue the meanings behind these behaviors. This and the following chapters present methods for unearthing these meanings.

A New Paradigm and a Unique Responsibility

As illustrated above, when we focus on what happens at the interpersonal level, we open our eyes to an entirely new vista of the group. To adjust our eyes to these new views, we must make a radical shift in our counseling and therapy paradigm. Going beyond *the content* level of *verbal presentation*, we must hone in on the *unspoken messages* at the *process level* of the group.

And if there is one thing that members cannot do by themselves at the working stage, it is this: They cannot elevate themselves above the group to address the immediacy issues happening within the group. Members instinctively stand by an unspoken social rule of not commenting on the interpersonal process, and anyone who violates it risks being perceived as acting superior and becoming the target of resentment.

Given this, the responsibility of addressing the immediacy and interpersonal process issues falls squarely on the shoulders of the leaders.

THE HERE-AND-NOW METHOD AND THE PROCESS LEVEL OF COMMUNICATION

A powerful therapeutic concept, the here-and-now was originated by Jacob Levy Moreno (1978), an Austrian American psychotherapist who was a leading pioneer of group psychotherapy. Moreno was a bona fide legend for his ability to guide clients to re-enact and work through their unfinished past business in the present moment of the group. Taking delight in Moreno's ability to do this,

Yalom refined the concept, coining it the *here-and-now method* (Yalom, 1983; Yalom & Leszcz, 2005).

This method has inspired many therapists, including us (the authors), to concoct various therapeutic intervention strategies in an effort to move the therapeutic encounter in the group to a more intense, present-centered place. This section depicts the fascinating concept and method of the here-and-now.

"Content" Level of Communication Transmits Only 35% of Message

To understand the concept of the here-and-now, we must understand two levels of communication: the content level and the process level.

Content refers to the *words, stories, and life events* verbalized in the group. Focusing on the content level of communication will only help us pick up less than 35% of the messages (Pease & Pease, 2006) of the communication in the group. Consider the following scenario:

Mary:	I am angry with my sister for not sharing the responsibility of taking care of my parents. But she is an alcoholic and cannot even take care of herself.
John:	Why do you let her get away with this? Being an alcoholic is just an excuse.
Mary:	[looks distressed and feels compelled to defend herself]
John:	[gets nervous and tries harder and harder to convince Mary of her self-defeating behavior]
Other members:	[feel frustrated about the argument between Mary and John, yet feel hesitant to say anything]

Given this scenario, if the leader focuses on what Mary said, what happened between her and her sister and its accompanying distress, the leader will probably try to get the group, and especially John, to help Mary feel supported, mostly by giving her affirmation, information, resources, wisdom, and support. Doing so will ignore the other 65% of the messages transmitted in the interpersonal context—a choice that will only take the group so far.

"Process" Level of Communication Transmits 65% of Message

The other 65% (Pease & Pease, 2006) of the message transmitted back and forth in the above exchange is called the "process" level of communication (Yalom, 2009; Yalom & Leszcz, 2005). It includes reactions, attitudes, communication patterns, relational styles, nonverbal cues, tones, facial expressions, and so on. These kinds of communication, although unstated and hard to pinpoint, have a powerful and visceral impact on the people involved.

Take the previous scenario. The dynamics felt instinctively by everybody in the room may include the following:

- John's way of communicating, including *advice-giving, confrontation, and accusation*
- Mary's feelings of being *unheard and unaccepted* by John. She might be triggered to become defensive in the next moment.
- John's lack of awareness of how his communication style has an unpleasant impact on others
- The sense of *powerlessness* felt by the group

Felt in the body but not talked about openly, these unstated dynamics lead to most of the interpersonal misunderstandings and difficulties in people's lives. Not confined just to the group setting, these kinds of interpersonal difficulties can, indeed, happen in workplace relationships, between family members, between couples, and in intimate relationships.

Relentlessly Pursue the Meanings of the Process Level of Communication

Unearthing the meanings of the process level of communication gives an extra oomph to any form of therapy, but for group therapy with the here-and-now focus, it gives blood and oxygen. As Kiesler and Van Denburg (1993) point out, all other jobs of the leader pale in comparison to the job of helping the group get how their own metacommunication messages come across to others.

Being the crux of group counseling and therapy, this job of meaning decoding has inspired our profession to conjure up numerous terms to describe it: *process observation, process exploration, process commenting, process illumination,* and *process examination.*

Observed by an outsider, effective leaders' work in a group may seem effortless, yet *their minds are constantly alert, relentlessly tracking the process level of communication within the room.* Sensing any dynamics going on below the surface, the effective leader will lead the group to *catch these elusive dynamics in action,* in an effort to shed light on the meanings and the impacts of these dynamics.

This relentless quest to shed light on the process level of interpersonal communication is rather *atypical, unusual, and,* indeed, *precious.* During our daily interactions with people, seldom will others listen carefully to what we say without impatiently interrupting us with their own views. And rarely do others carefully track our messages, or read between the lines, to detect the personal implications of our oftentimes convoluted stories.

Hence, it truly surprises a member when others in the group share with him or her how they interpret his or her behaviors, letting him or her know the impacts, positive or negative, that the behaviors have on them. It is a cherished find for many members.

Integrate the "Task" and the "Process" Aspects of Group Work

Though starting to put increased focus on the "process" aspect of group work, the group never veers away from working on *its primary task*—helping members to achieve their goals. Instead, the "process" aspect slowly interweaves with the "task" aspect, as the group moves back and forth between these two areas of focus.

Thus, anyone who presents a life stressor will receive the group's attention just like in the early stages of the group, and the sense of acceptance and cohesion never cease to nurture the group. It is when certain dynamics emerge during the group interaction warranting process exploration that the leader will step in and take action to examine them.

Working on both the task and the process aspects, simultaneously, may feel overwhelming at first; eventually, though, your brain will start to incorporate these two different perspectives into your awareness. It will eventually feel like the most natural thing in the world to integrate the there-and-then and the here-and-now, like knitting threads of colorful yarn into one beautiful strand.

Embrace Members' Doubts or Anxiety

Members may perceive the here-and-now focus as irrelevant to their personal goals of working through their life difficulties. Soon, however, their doubts subside. They will begin to see how their here-and-now relational styles faithfully reflect their relational styles *outside* the group. They will realize that what happens at the process level *within the group* is real—these here-and-now events have tremendous power in revealing how they function in interpersonal contexts.

Fearing becoming the center of the group's process examination, members may feel like deer caught in the headlights, anxious or surprised, not knowing what to predict or anticipate. You can channel this anticipated anxiety by using a prompt to invite members to *talk openly about their anxiety* of the process level of communication. It is only when members embrace their own anxiety, and when they perceive the group as safe and trustworthy, will they accept the value of diving into the here-and-now encounter. Consider the following prompt:

> [To the group] I can sense some hesitancy or anxiety floating around the room right now. Perhaps we could spend some time talking about what concerns or anxiety you might have about looking at our interpersonal styles in the here-and-now. Who would like to start?

Another anxiety that members experience has to do with their fear of having nothing to talk about that is worthy of the here-and-now exploration. This kind of anxiety can be turned into an opportunity for a different type of check-in. For example,

> [To the group] We would like to start with a more adventurous kind of check-in. During this check-in, please tell the group *what you have wanted to say but haven't yet had the courage to.*

Following the check-in, you might ask a member to expand upon what she said:

> Stephanie, during the check-in, you said that last session had stirred up a lot of strong emotions in you, reminiscent of the way you often react to your siblings. Would you like to expand a bit on that? [using Stephanie's emotions as a springboard for group interaction]

Alternatively, if a group is ready to take the necessary initiative, you can ask members to speak when they feel so moved, allowing any silence to linger:

> [To the group] Our floor is completely open. Whoever feels moved to say anything, please take the liberty of jumping in.

THE HERE-AND-NOW METHOD: THE TWO TIERS

The here-and-now method actually consists of *two tiers* (Yalom & Leszcz, 2005):

- Affect stimulation (experiencing the emotions)
- Process illumination (examining the process)

These two tiers form *a continuous, circular action* in a fluid process. The two tiers are *not cut-and-dried or linear*. As Yalom and Leszcz (2005) stated well, "Therapy is a continuous sequence of experiencing and then examining the process" (p. 34). It is only for educational purposes that we separate these two procedures.

It Takes Two Tiers to Boost Neural Plasticity

Working on these two tiers is exactly what it takes to facilitate *neural plasticity*. As proposed by Cozolino (2010), neural plasticity happens when the following conditions are met:

- A safe and trusting relationship has been established.
- There is the presence of moderate levels of stress.
- Emotion and cognition are both activated.
- New meanings have been co-constructed for the clients' life stories.

Without a doubt, the two tiers in the here-and-now method involve all the required conditions for neural plasticity.

First Tier: Stimulate Group Affects—"Stir the Pot"

A group can achieve a moderate level of emotional animation through a procedure called "*here-and-now activation*" or "*here-and-now disclosure*" (Yalom & Leszcz, 2005). In this text, we call it "*stirring the pot*" just to make it a bit more visual.

When used properly and with the right timing, the technique of stirring-the-pot can embolden members to disclose emotions stuffed beneath the surface, providing an eye-opening experience for all involved, as reflected by the following comment by a group member:

As we begin to delve further into our unstructured sessions, and as *the pot continues to be stirred, the group is becoming more interesting and worthwhile.*

See the following method of how a leader stirs the pot to bring the group into the here-and-now:

A group member, Jim, has been going off on a tangent about some infuriating events in his life involving various people. Feeling bored by his rambling and by his excessive fixation on details, the group begins to tune him out. Seeing the group starting to check out, the leader steps in to stir the pot:

> [To the group] From what I am hearing, it seems that *Jim is telling us that he has difficulty sharing his anger with others.* [borrow Jim's words] I wonder, *with whom in the group* do you think Jim would feel safe expressing his anger, and *with whom in the group* is he likely to suppress it? [first tier of here-and-now; leader trying to *shift focus of conversation toward people inside group*]

Causing somewhat of a commotion, this here-and-now technique sparked emotions in the group, resulting in a much-heated discussion. During this heated discussion, certain interpersonal dynamics came out organically, and it was time to move to the second tier of this technique.

Second Tier: Illuminate the Meanings Hidden in the Interpersonal Process

With its ability to touch and stir up emotions in many members, the here-and-now technique must be carried to completion. Don't just hit and run. Rather, make sure that everyone affected by the here-and-now activation has a chance to explore and examine the *meanings* of the event for them.

That is where the second tier, *process illumination,* kicks in. This is the tool that decodes the meanings of the following interpersonal processes:

- The group or individual behavior patterns happening in the moment
- The functions that these interpersonal patterns serve in this particular moment
- The ways these interpersonal patterns have an impact on members of the group
- The ways the here-and-now reflects members' unresolved past issues or interpersonal difficulties outside the group

Process illumination, itself a *cognitive reflection,* helps members make sense of what's going on inside of them. It serves as a *meaning-making* device through which members come to understand *the meaning and implications* behind their emotions and the behaviors. During process illumination, as Yalom and Leszcz (2005) so succinctly put it, the group "performs a self-reflective loop and examines the here-and-now behavior that has just occurred" (p. 142).

Let's continue with the above case of Jim. After the leader stirred the pot, a heated discussion—about which person in the group Jim would feel safe enough with to express his anger and with which person Jim would suppress his anger—ensues, bringing to surface various buried feelings and reactions. Some people smiled, Anne got upset, and Charlie started to tell a story.

To unravel the meanings of all these reactions, the leader stopped the group and asked members to comment on what was going on according to their observations:

> [To the group] I may be wrong, but I sense that some important things have been happening in the last 5 minutes. I wonder, what do you see is going on here? And why? [second tier of here-and-now; leader trying to illuminate the meanings of aroused behaviors]

For Charlie's benefit, the leader followed up with a further process illumination:

> Charlie, the group seems to say that you have a tendency to use your storytelling to pull the group's attention away from any tension happening in our group. They pointed out that when Anne got upset just a moment ago, you changed the focus to something else, perhaps trying to reduce her emotional upset. I wonder, when you do that, how does it have an impact on Anne and on the group? [second tier of here-and-now; leader trying to illuminate the impact of the aroused behaviors]

The leader wrapped up the process illumination with Charlie by saying,

> [To the group] It seems that Charlie is becoming more aware of how this rescuing behavior has an impact on all involved. I wonder whether any of you see any connection between Charlie's need for rescuing others and his feeling of helplessness as a child when he witnessed his sister being abused and was not believed when he told his parents about it? [second tier of here-and-now; leader trying to illuminate the connection between the present and the past]

For Anne's benefit, the leader followed up with the following process illumination:

> [To the group] It seems that Anne is reacting strongly to the group feedback about her being the person in the group to whom Jim might have difficulty expressing his anger. How are you experiencing Anne right now? And why are you feeling the way? [second tier of here-and-now; leader trying to illuminate the impact of the aroused behaviors]

Later,

> Anne, I wonder what you get from the group's feedback for you? How does it sit with you? What feedback fits with the way you see yourself, and what does not fit? [second tier of here-and-now; leader trying to illuminate the perception of the member receiving feedback]

The above illustrated here-and-now technique gives you some idea of how the first tier starts the emotional experiencing, and the second tier finishes the cognitive reflection loop.

KEY TO THE HERE-AND-NOW METHOD: ZIGZAGGING THE HOT SEAT

Being the center of here-and-now processing is such an intense experience that many of our group members call it the "hot seat." When on the hot seat for too long (more than 20 minutes), members start to feel flooded. As you can well imagine, a person typically needs to take a breather to recover and to reflect after being on the hot seat for a while. To accomplish this, you can shift the group's attention to others whose emotions and behaviors also have been aroused. We call this transferring back and forth of the hot seat "zigzagging."

What Do You Zigzag and When to Do It

As a *nonlinear* way of here-and-now processing, "zigzagging" has nothing to do with a disorganized discussion or a haphazard change of topics. Rather, it depicts the tempo and the movement of *moving the hot seat from member to member*.

A question that frequently comes up is, when can I best zigzag to the next person for here-and-now processing? From our experiences, the following markers present ripe opportunities for zigzagging.

Zigzagging Marker 1: When Someone's Interpersonal Style Is Stirring Up Group Reactions

Whenever a member's *interpersonal pattern* shows up, provoking *charged reactions* in others, you can zigzag the group processing to that person without delay. Don't fret over not finishing up with the previous member—you can always go back to revisit the member whose topic has been interrupted.

To zigzag in this case, you may say,

[To the group] As Ted told Sabrina—that it is her decision if she wants to feel resentful toward what he said, that it's up to her how she wants to feel, and that he won't change a thing—I saw strong reactions in the group. I would like to invite the group to tell Ted directly what you were reacting to in that moment. [second tier processing. The group is already reacting, there is no need to go to the first tier for a dose of affect stimulation]

Zigzagging Marker 2: When You Hear Loaded Words

Whenever you hear *loaded words* from a member, grab the moment, and zigzag the hot seat to that member, asking him to expand on it.

For example, the spotlight has been on Cathy for a short while, and now you hear *some charged words* from Diana. You could zigzag seamlessly to Diana:

"Diana, in your response to Cathy just now, you said that *you know exactly what it feels like to be always hiding.* [recap the loaded phrase] Would you please say more about that? What parts of yourself do you need to hide, and from whom in the group do you have to hide?" [a combination of the first tier and the second tier]

Zigzagging Marker 3: When the Group Attention Lingers Too Long on a Member

Sandra has been on the hot seat for awhile, but the group seems stuck with her, not knowing how to peel its attention away from her and shift to other members. Sandra expresses that she wishes other people would speak, so therefore, she does not dominate the floor.

You take the hint from Sandra and get ready to zigzag the hot seat to some other members who need the group's attention:

[Smiling and nodding to Sandra] Sandra, thank you for noticing other people's needs for group attention! I wonder from whom in the group do you wish to hear more and why? [The leader uses an opening to zigzag the hot-seat to someone else.]

Let's say that Sandra names three *quieter members*, Rosie, Kate, and Mary. You can then shift the focus to them:

Rosie, Kate, and Mary, many members nodded their heads when they heard Sandra expressing her desire to know more about you three. How would you respond to this? [This naturally draws the quieter members to open up more.]

THE PRINCIPLES OF ENGAGING THE FIRST TIER: STIMULATING GROUP AFFECTS

For organizational purposes, the remainder of this chapter will focus on just the first tier, leaving Chapter 12 to cover the second. This section reviews the principles of using the first tier of the here-and-now method—affect stimulation (stirring the pot).

1st: No Need to Engage the First Tier When the Group Is Already Reacting

The first principle of engaging the group in the here-and-now is this: You don't always need to start with the first tier. If the group's emotions are already heated up, stimulating group affects by stirring the pot is *not necessary*.

Indeed, most of the time you don't need to stir the pot because *the group has a number of built-in mechanisms that will organically stir up members' emotions* (Yalom & Leszcz, 2005). These built-in mechanisms may include but are not limited to the following:

- Competition
- Projection
- Distortions

- Sibling rivalry
- Members playing out the roles they took on in their family of origin, and so on

As any of these inherent elements kicks into action, members will emotionally and viscerally react to one another. At this moment, the leader can skip the first tier and jump directly to the second tier (next chapter) to illuminate the meanings of what's going on.

2nd: "Stirring the Pot" to Permit Suppressed Inner Reactions to Break the Surface

That said, circumstances exist where you do need to use the first tier of the here and now to fan the flames of group energy. These circumstances mostly have to do with members internally reacting to others' interpersonal patterns while outwardly concealing these reactions. In a society where we prize above all images of being strong and rational, it is no surprise that members deem it weak to display their emotions.

Fearing being judged as such, many people will go out of their way to employ tactics to avoid experiencing emotions—for example, suppressing them, deflecting them, dodging them, masking them, ignoring them, denying them, intellectualizing about them, or so on.

For example, when someone is dominating the group, group members might employ the tactic of suppression. Even when seething with anger on the inside, they might appear peaceful and agreeable on the outside. Hence, the second principle of the here-and-now involves giving suppressed inner reactions a chance to break the surface.

When given a chance via the first tier of the here-and-now, those core materials locked inside get to come up to meet the light of the day and benefit from group exploration and examination. This focus on here-and-now truly "energizes group members, heightens their interest, and often evokes insightful responses" (Ferencik, 1991, p. 169).

3rd: Don't Be Afraid of Stirring Group Affects

The third principle is this: Don't let fear block you from stirring group emotions. You will do good to the group when you stir the pot. As stated previously, for neuroplastic processes to happen, members need to experience a moderate level of emotions (Cozolino, 2010).

Many new group leaders shy away from the here-and-now method due to their fear of stirring up members' censored emotions. If only they could see past their fear and recognize the benefits of group affect stimulation! Yes, the first tier will definitely bring submerged, dormant emotions to the surface, but this gives the group opportunities to talk about things *long left unspeakable*. In so doing, it ignites the fuse of group aliveness; members will sit up straighter, lean forward, and maintain alert and focused eye contact. Even in moments of silence, the focus is so alive, you can almost hear a pin drop.

4th: Follow It Up With Process Illumination

The fourth principle is that the second tier should follow the first tier to complete the here-and-now loop.

As we explained previously, the second tier removes members' blinders, enabling them to see who they are in an interpersonal context. This meaning-making must be an integral part of group work, and we should not leave our members in a state of emotional arousal without helping them make sense of it.

BEHAVIORAL MARKERS FOR GROUP AFFECT STIMULATION

This question frequently comes up: What *signs* do I look for that tell me that it's time for me to go to the first tier to stimulate group affects? To answer this question, this section provides several behavioral markers that tell you when it's time to stir the pot.

Stirring the Pot Marker 1: Excessive Niceness and Politeness

The first behavioral marker has to do with excessive niceness and politeness among members even when the group has already passed its early stages. As stated previously, external pleasant exchanges do not necessarily reflect people's internal reactions. Due to social conditioning, they prefer to appear nice and polite—maybe too nice to be true.

A group displaying such excessive niceness and politeness often becomes lethargic and lifeless. The longer members mask their feelings, the harder it becomes for them to interact with one another on an authentic level. Therefore, when you see excessive niceness and politeness during the working stage of the group, go stir the pot.

Stirring the Pot Marker 2: Excessive Storytelling

The second behavioral marker involves excessive storytelling. Excessive storytelling keeps the group stuck on the *content* level of communication, stripping the group of any sense of immediacy. Slife and Lanyon (1991) indicate that any type of therapy that lacks immediacy will become sterile.

To be clear, members do need to talk about their stressful or problematic life events. This kind of there-and-then disclosure (Leszcz, 1992) helps group members understand each other's world, enabling them to give empathy and support to one another. Time is well spent in this manner.

But when stories of there-and-then events go on and on in the group, problems will happen—sessions will become stuck, and members will soon find themselves tuning out. Take this as your green light to step in with a here-and-now activation.

Stirring the Pot Marker 3: Excessive Agreement—Group Collusion

The third marker concerns *excessive agreement* among group members. This is called *group collusion*. Comparing it to the tension and conflicts of the transition stage, group collusion in the working stage doesn't sound too bad, does it? However, by colluding to ignore critical events and sweep them under the rug, members are unconsciously avoiding their *primary tasks* while chasing after the bait of certain *secondary gratifications* (Gladding, 2015; Shields, 1999). Common secondary gratifications may include being popular, being liked, a sense of coziness, a secure position in the group, avoidance of conflict or confrontation, or so on.

For instance, a member might excessively agree with others in the group in order to gain popularity but does so at the expense of being truthful to his or her own feelings. This behavior represents a type of regression toward self-protectiveness, distracting the member from working on his or her primary goals and ultimately, from personal transformation. Seeing this marker, you can go ahead with the first tier of the here-and-now.

Stirring the Pot Marker 4: Other Signs That the Group Needs You to Stir Affects

Other signs signaling that the group is becoming removed and bored—and is in need of a here-and-now stimulation—may include the following:

- Members wriggling in their seats
- Emotions of group members flattened
- Group interaction staying at the intellectual level
- Group hitting a wall in trying to help a member
- Members remaining externally focused

These signs indicate that the group members are having a hard time interacting with one another in a meaningful and authentic manner. The group is becoming stagnant. When you see these signs, you know that you need to stir things up to bring the group into the here-and-now.

Choose the Right Dose of Here-and-Now Activation

With these behavioral markers in mind, you can choose how much of a dose of here-and-now solution you want to give to your group. As stated in the opening of this chapter, leaders don't need to wait until they have a process group or when a group enters the working stage to lead the group into the here-and-now.

Whether you have experiential groups, psychoeducational groups, or even mandated groups, small doses of here-and-now solutions can boost members' self-awareness as well as the group's sense of aliveness. The key is in choosing a proper level of intensity, one that suits your group.

In the sections that follow, we present here-and-now oriented leadership techniques, ranked by the level of their intensity. You can pick and choose whatever level suits the specific needs of your session.

(I) MEDIUM-INTENSITY STIMULATION: MEMBERS SETTING HERE-AND-NOW SESSION GOALS

Chapter 8 in this text introduced the low-intensity stimulation techniques suitable for most groups in their early stages to become acquainted with an intimate level of communication. Please review Chapter 8 if you are seeking some mild *affect stimulation techniques* to bring more buzz to your group.

To kickstart this presentation of a series of advanced here-and-now techniques, this section presents medium-intensity here-and-now activation techniques.

Here-and-Now Oriented Session Goals

More synergistic with the mature stages of a group, the here-and-now oriented session goals reshape members' goals to become *more interpersonal and more immediate* (Kivlighan & Jauquet, 1990). This resonates with Ferencik (1991), who asserts that "External issues must first be transformed into the here-and-now in order for the group to work on them" (p. 170).

In re-orienting members' goals to the here-and-now, the leader adds zing to the group atmosphere and stimulates the group to a heightened state of emotions.

How to Reshape Members' Goals to Become Here-and-Now Oriented

Below we present a few examples of how to reshape members' goals to become more here-and-now oriented.

Example 1:

Member: I would like to practice speaking up more openly.

Leader: With whom *in this group* do you need to practice speaking up more openly?

Member: Well, I would like to practice expressing myself more openly *toward Kelly* [another member] regarding my feeling unheard whenever I try to tell her how her behaviors affect me in the group.

Example 2:

Member: I would like to practice becoming more honest in my conversations with people.

Leader: Has there been any event *in the group* where you wish you had been able to speak more honestly?

Member: Yes, many times *in the group* I only say positive things to placate other members even when I feel the opposite. In this session, I would like to work on honestly expressing my feelings even when I feel uncomfortable or even when I disagree with something that happens in the group.

Example 3:

Member: I would like to practice being more assertive.

Leader: With whom *in this group* would you like to become more assertive?

Example 4:

Member: I would like to practice speaking more of how I feel.

Leader: What kinds of feelings have you had *in this group* that you would like to speak up more about?

(II) HIGH-INTENSITY STIMULATION: REVEALING IN-GROUP PERCEPTIONS

Group members' *interpersonal perceptions* pack the richest data that you can ask for in a group. One way to access these rich data is to stimulate group affects by having members reveal their perceptions about *people within the group*. Through zigzagging of the hot seat, the group will bustle with a high level of engagement.

Since this high-intensity here-and-now technique can arouse strong emotions, it should be applied with prudence. Use it only when group trust reaches adequate levels, and make sure to follow it up with process illumination (second tier).

First Tier: Members Disclosing Perceptions About Others in the Group

In this step, you heat up the immediacy by moving the focus of the conversation from people in a member's life outside the group to *the people within the group*. Remember to draw out both the positive and the negative side of member perceptions so that you are striking a balance.

The Case of Lisa. The group has been discussing some there-and-then events nonchalantly and for quite a while now. Sensing a need to nudge the group into the here-and-now, the leader looked for an opportunity. After Lisa talked about her fear of disapproval from her family, the leader grabbed a chance to do so:

[To the group] Lisa has talked extensively about her *fears of disapproval from people in her life*. I wonder whether we could shift the focus just a bit. If you were to make a wild guess, *from whom in the group* is Lisa likely to anticipate disapproval? And *from whom in the group* is Lisa likely to anticipate approval? [the first tier of here-and-now activation; moving from outside focus to inside focus]

A member, Susan, jumped in and disclosed that Dale would be the one within the group from whom Lisa would most likely sense disapproval. The group became silent. The leader then followed up on Susan's disclosure by turning to the group to seek more data:

Thank you, Susan. [turning to the group] I wonder how the rest of the group responds to what Susan just said. Does anyone else feel the same way as Susan does? [prompt seeking consensual validation]

Two Other Examples. Following are two other examples of how to steer the group toward disclosing their *perceptions about others inside the group*:

[To the group] Kim has been coming to the group for about seven meetings and has been unable to share with us *due to fear of judgment*. I wonder if the group can guess *from whom in this group* does Kim fear judgment? And *from whom in this group* does Kim feel accepted? [the first tier; use only in the working stage, and should be followed later by second tier process illumination]

[To the group] Kelly said that, in her daily life, she tends to *feel responsible for others' feelings. For whom in the group* do you guess Kelly is most likely to feel responsible, and *for whom*, the least?

Second Tier: Process Illumination

Once here-and-now disclosures kick into action, some members may become defensive; others may try to smooth things over; still others may try to reduce the intensity by changing the subject to outside events.

Whatever members do, the ways in which they respond to the heated emotions and conversations often mirror their interpersonal patterns outside the group. The group must explore and reflect on these responding and reactive patterns, examining their meanings. Though the second tier (process illumination) will be covered in next chapter, for the purpose of highlighting the continuity between the first and the second tiers, we underscore it again here.

Let's continue with *the case of Lisa*. When Susan disclosed that Dale would be the one within the group from whom Lisa would most likely sense disapproval, two other members provided similar observations. At that juncture, Dale became defensive and began to rationalize his behaviors.

Sensing that Dale was in direct conflict with the three members, another member, Jane, the peacemaker of the group, broke into the conversation and indirectly tried to diffuse the tension.

It is obvious that *multiple processes have emerged during this event*. Not only was Dale's pattern enacted, but Jane's interpersonal pattern also added another wrinkle to the dynamics. Both processes require illumination. At this point, the leader may pose a process question to the group:

> [To the group] Let's stop for a moment here. It looks like there are two important dynamics going on here. Let's talk about what you saw in Dale's reaction to the feedback, and what you saw going on with Jane's reaction. [multiple process illuminations]

Zigzag the Hot Seat

As the group gains insights through the process discussion, it may organically zigzag the hot seat to other members. If this does not happen, the leader ensures it does.

Let's go back to the case of Lisa. Once the group finished the discussion on Dale and Jane, the group did not know how to move on. To remedy this and to engage even more members in the process discussion, the leader used a prompt to shift the spotlight to other members:

> [To the group] Has anyone else ever sensed disapproval from another in the group? [zigzagging the hot seat away from Dale and Jane and onto others]

Deal With Reluctance

Suppose that the group was *unresponsive* to your first-tiered question (from whom in the group might Lisa anticipate disapproval). What then? Rather than pressing the group to respond, you might want to consider if it is simply an issue of *timing* or *readiness*.

If the group has not reached a solid level of trust, you can expect members to be reluctant to get too personal. In this case, stay clear of overstimulating the group with here-and-now activation lest members feel unsafe. Instead, you could work with the member (Lisa) and look at the general pattern of her issue, without bringing up the immediacy issue.

If, however, the group is well into the working stage and has reached an adequate level of trust, then *the unresponsiveness is a very meaningful dynamic in and of itself.* You may go directly to it to shine a light on the factors causing the resistance:

[To the group] Dead silence. Hmmm . . . I wonder what is going on here. What is stopping you from speaking? [processing reluctance of group]

(III) EVEN HIGHER-INTENSITY STIMULATION: HYPOTHETICAL ROLE ENACTMENT

To crank the level of intensity up a notch, you can have members enact hypothetical roles in the group. This technique is both an affect-stimulation and a process illumination.

Enactment is a technique frequently used in psychodrama (see Chapter 13 for more concepts and illustrations). But, in hypothetical role enactment, members have to project their here-and-now perceptions/reactions to a hypothetical situation. This technique can stir up highly intense emotions, but at the same time, it can also feel *playful.* It gives members the chance to talk about their reactions to one another normally about issues that are *difficult or awkward to talk about.*

To Start, Observe Your Own Reactions and Those of Members

Before kicking this high-intensity stimulation into action, observe your own internal experiences. Notice what kinds of reactions you have while listening to members talking. For example, you notice that you are reacting to the domineering style of a member, Alvaro, as he interacts with other members. You may first think to yourself,

Well, am I the only one who *feels ticked off* by Alvaro's domineering style? How often does he steal the floor with no consideration of others' needs to talk? How is this domineering style related to his problems in his inter-personal relationships?

After that, you then further ponder to yourself,

Hmm . . . so how is the group reacting to Alvaro's domineering style of talking? Do they see the connection to the problems that Alvaro has in his relationships outside the group? Do members feel put off by his behavior? Do they feel frustrated or resentful, but lack the opportunity to express it?

First Tier: Initiating Here-and-Now Feedback via Enacting a Hypothetical Role

Having contemplated the parallel between your own and members' reactions, you are ready to kick off the intervention. You have two choices to help Alvaro see his interpersonal impact clearly: via a low-key here-and-now feedback or via an intense hypothetical role enactment.

A Low-Key Here-and-Now Feedback. To initiate a mild and gentle here-and-now feedback, you may say,

All of you have known Alvaro for a few weeks now. I wonder, through your own experiences in the group, what do you know about Alvaro that he might not know about himself?

But this low-key feedback *lacks the subtlety and playfulness of the hypothetical role enactment* below.

An Intense Hypothetical Role Enactment. So, you opt for the hypothetical enactment technique here, allowing your members to speak more honestly about their reactions to one another. *Through the disguise of the hypothetical role,* members often *chuckle and are free and playful in divulging their first-hand experience with a specific member.* You may say,

[To the group] Alvaro has expressed that he is having many problems in relationships at work. Maybe the group can help Alvaro gain fresh per-spectives by *imagining if* you were Alvaro's hypothetical coworker. After spending all day with Alvaro at work, what would you be saying to your-self at the end of the day? How would you feel toward him? [the first tier, stirring the pot using hypothetical role enactment]

Second Tier: Connecting Here-and-Now to There-and-Then

After members disclose their reactions and perceptions in the hypothetical situation, the leader may try to help the person in the hot seat to connect what goes on in the group with what goes on in the outside world.

Alvaro, I wonder *if* there might be people in your life who feel the same way as the group members feel toward you; that is, *if* people at your work might respect your intelligence and desire to help people yet interpret your take-charge style as being domineering and controlling, all because they don't get to know your underlying fear of appearing inadequate? [the second tier; using process illumination to elucidate parallel process]

More Examples of Hypothetical Role Enactment

Example 1:

First tier:

[To the group] Marcia has expressed that she experiences a great deal of stress in relationships with men in her life. To help her see things in a new light, I would like the group to *imagine if* you were to go out on *a date* with Marcia. What would you say to yourself after the date? What would you feel? [the first tier: stirring the pot using role-taking]

Second tier:

Marcia, *perhaps* there are people in your life who feel the same way as the group members did toward you; that is, *perhaps* there are people who are attracted to you and want to get close to you but who sense your mistrust and aloofness and, therefore, feel pushed away. Your fear of closeness pushes these potential suitors away. [the second tier: process illumination—illuminating parallel process]

Example 2:

[To the group] *If* you were to have a conflict with Anika, what do you *imagine* would be your visceral experiences?

Example 3:

> [To the group] "It is now 6:00, and we still have half an hour left. *Imagine if* it were already 6:45, and you had left the session and were on your way home, what would you be feeling about group today?" [Members enacted this hypothetical situation and were invited to talk more openly about their reactions to the session.]

Examples 2 and 3 would need to be followed up with process illumination to make the exercise complete.

(IV) HIGHEST-INTENSITY STIMULATION: HYPOTHETICAL GRADING

In its highest-intensity level, this here-and-now activation prompts members to disclose their reactions and perceptions about themselves and others via *hypothetically having them "grade" one another's effort in the group.*

Of course, this technique does not aim to have members actually grade each other. Rather, it intends to provoke members to disclose their perceptions of themselves and others. The reactions, stirred up by this activation, are ripe for exploration and have the potential to bring a lot of awareness to the group members.

Though this technique does not intend to evaluate, it might still touch on a *sensitive spot* or *anxiety that members have about evaluation.* Hence, it is regarded as having the highest intensity of all affect-stimulation techniques. Please proceed with care and thoughtfulness:

> Mateo, *if* you were to grade the work done in this group, what grade, in your imagination, would you deserve for your own work, and what grade would you give to each individual in the group, and why? [Use this technique only in the working stage and only if you can follow it up with process illumination.]

Through hypothetical grading, various interpersonal dynamics will indubitably emerge calling for the need to proceed to process illumination, as we have emphasized repeatedly.

∞∞

In closing: Once starting to take greater risks in self-disclosure and feedback, the group rapidly gains momentum and moves ahead into a breathtaking terrain—the here-and-now. To adjust our eyes to this entirely new vista, we must make a radical shift in our counseling and therapy paradigm. Going beyond *the content* level of *verbal presentation*, we must hone in on the *unspoken messages* at the *process level* of the group.

The here-and-now method actually consists of *two tiers* that form *a continuous, circular action* in a fluid process. To be sure, the leader does not always start with the first tier; only once certain behavioral markers arise does the leader get the green light to stir the pot.

Armed with a series of advanced here-and-now techniques (from medium-intensity to highest-intensity), you have the tools now should you feel a need to crank up a notch the intensity level of group affects. Geared up with the markers telling you when to stir the pot and when to zigzag the hot seat, you have the method now to get your group to bustle with a high level of engagement, organically filled with rich metacommunication messages, ripe for the group to hunt for their hidden meanings via the second tier of the here-and-now, explored in the next chapter.

CASES IN POINT

Case 1: Mary

Fear of abandonment and isolation plagues Mary's mind. Her father, an alcoholic, used to hit Mary's mother, and there seemed to be a *parallel pattern* in Mary's own marriage: Mary's ex-husband drank a lot, verbally abused her, and had chased her around the house trying to hit her.

Though Mary got out of the marriage, she was haunted by grief because her ex-husband and his new wife were living in the house that Mary and her ex still owned together, and her ex had adopted the child of his new wife.

Mary had suffered four miscarriages while she was married to her ex, resulting in a great deal of grief and loss. In her mind, Mary was convinced that *due to her difficulty in having babies, men would find her undesirable.* She was afraid that she would be excluded from happiness and would live in loneliness.

As Mary talked, the leader sensed that Mary's sense of inadequacy for not being able to have children had distorted her view about her self-worth as a woman. She had been so inundated with her losses and struggles that she had lost sight of her true qualities.

Although group members tried to give her different perspectives, Mary seemed to take no refuge in their words. At this moment, the leader decided to initiate a hypothetical role enactment:

[To the group] *If* you went out on a date with Mary, and you had just come home from the date, what kinds of thoughts or reflections might you have about the date with Mary?

Everyone in the group responded with extremely positive comments about Mary. They said she was funny, attractive, intelligent, insightful, considerate, witty, a good dancer, and so on. Every member stated that he or she would want to see Mary again.

This role enactment exercise made Mary laugh and, at the same time, forced her, in a good way, to listen to the many assets that she had forgotten she had.

After the session, Mary wrote the following in her reflective journal about the influence of this experience:

> I must admit that the exercise on "how would you feel if you just came back from a date with Mary" was pretty interesting and strange to hear at the same time. It felt weird hearing members say such nice things about me.
>
> Perhaps the one comment that left me thinking the most was Keith's. I recall him repeating to me that there were a lot of good men out there, like him, who would appreciate a good woman. It seemed a hidden message somehow because he repeated it as if trying to tell me something.
>
> I didn't anticipate that people would say such wonderful things about me even though they have only known me for a short time. This group has shown me some of my qualities so visible to others yet unrecognized by myself. It is so heartwarming! It makes me feel I am okay as a person, even though I have felt so miserable in my life. I really appreciate gaining this new perspective on myself.

Case 2: Dianne

The case of Dianne is one that gives us affirmation that, given the proper conditions, the human spirit will always triumph.

Dianne had proved to be a difficult person for the group to get along with. People had been feeling on edge with her yet had not known what to do with their feelings. During the seventh session, Dianne presented her difficulty in her relationships at home and at work.

The group members expressed their empathy to her, yet no one had the guts to tell her how she came across to the members. The group felt stuck because their empathy could not do a thing to provide the reality check that Dianne so badly needed.

Sensing that the group was unable to gain any traction, the leader realized that she had to do something to move the group into high gear (remember, members are not in the position to do that). So, the leader took the risk to initiate a hypothetical role enactment:

[To the group] Please use your first-hand experience with Dianne to answer the following hypothetical question: *If* you were to spend 24 hours with Dianne, when the day was over, and you were back at home, what thoughts might you have about your experience with Dianne?

The group responded to this question with honest disclosure about their reactions. After that, the group processed more to connect what happened inside the group with Dianne's relationships outside the group.

It was a powerful session for the group, and especially for Dianne. This is captured in her reflection following the group:

I have just arrived home from the group after probably one of the most intense 90 minutes of my life. There was a lot of truth-telling, and it was very difficult to take in. I have been struggling with my issues of judgment and anger for a very long time. I have been very angry at the world, family, friends, and coworkers, all of them never seem to live up to my standards of what it means to be a moral, humane person.

The group process tonight has changed me forever. I received consistent feedback from seven members—so consistent that I couldn't easily dismiss it. The essence of the feedback is that it wouldn't be easy to spend 24 hours with me!

When Linda told me that she would not enjoy how competitive I am, something penetrated the hard shell of my anger. It brought me back to the pattern I had with my siblings in my childhood. It was painful for me to realize how this pattern still haunts my life.

What is paradoxical about tonight's session is that I have never felt more loved and respected than I did tonight. Everyone took a risk to help me see the reality of myself as it is, all in an effort to help me grow to my full potential. There wasn't any bullshit. That is what I found most refreshing. Compassionate honesty is very powerful.

AN OVERVIEW OF AN UNSTRUCTURED SESSION WITH A HERE-AND-NOW FOCUS

This section provides you with an overview of an unstructured session with a here-and-now focus. Please remember, a table can never do justice to the richness of the flow of a live group session where multiple actions and circular interactions often occur simultaneously at any given moment.

Table 11.1   An Overview of an Unstructured Session with a Here-and-Now Focus

A. Opening the session (10 minutes)

   -Relaxation exercise (optional)

   -Check-in: Members sharing lingering feelings, progress, and personal realizations

B. Starting unstructured discussion (65 minutes)

   -Opening the floor of the unstructured session

   -Members starting to share and respond to one another with validation and feedback

   -Using common themes to get more members engaged simultaneously

   -Stirring the pot when needed to shift attention from there-and-then stories to here-and-now direct experiencing (the first tier—group affect stimulation)

   -Examining any interpersonal dynamics or behavioral patterns occurring in the heat of the moment (the second tier—process illumination)

   -Transferring (or zigzagging) the here-and-now processing gradually from one member to another and yet another

   -Shifting back and forth between here-and-now experiences and there-and-then stories

C. Closing the session (10 minutes)

   -Announcing the time for closing

   -Checking-out

   -Reminder

EXERCISES

Scenarios for Your Practice

1. Rocky admits to the group that he greatly fears what other people think of him, but that he cannot bring himself to ask others what they think for fear of being devastated by their response. Upon hearing this, the group members are totally frozen. They are stuck. What are some options for handling this situation?

2. In the sixth session of an interpersonal learning group, Wayne shares that, "At my work evaluation meeting today, my boss told me that I'm not relating well with my coworkers. I don't know what he's talking about. I'm always teasing the people I work with, and I always have a good laugh. Maybe it's some kind of political correctness thing. I just don't know how to figure it out." As a group leader, how might you respond to this statement?

3. Rolf states to the group, "You know, I tried out several of the suggestions that this group gave to me last week in dealing with my boss to show him that I can demonstrate personal initiative. He didn't like the ideas at all, and he looked at me like I was way out of line. What should I do now?"

   Take a look at the possible interpersonal dynamics involved, both at the individual and group level. How might you choose to address the issue with the group?

4. As the fourth session of a personal growth group begins, the energy seems low. Members are sharing what they would like to explore for that session, but no one sounds especially invested in the issues they are raising. Jill continues the round of discussion by intellectualizing,

   > I am just learning so many tips on how to deal with situations here.

   > I get to hear what others have faced and learn how to handle those situations. I'm sure it will save me from a lot of trouble someday. It's so good for me to just observe in here.

   What do you sense is happening in this group? What does Jill's comment suggest about the depth of involvement that group members are experiencing with one another? Give an example of an intervening statement or question that you might make to move the group more fully into the here-and-now.

5. Gary and Cathy have spent about 10 minutes in the group discussing the pros and cons of whether office workers should bring donuts to work in the mornings. You notice that other group members have been shifting around in their seats for a while but are not offering any significant verbal input. What might this situation suggest to you about the current state of the group's dynamics? How might you intervene in order to change the level of interaction?

6. Zinnia shared the following in the group:

> I usually feel overlooked for my contributions at the agency where I work. I put a lot of work into a grant application for which we were able to get a sizable amount of funding. We are now able to offer some very good programs as a result. Yet, no one took notice. It was just like everyone thought it was no big deal. Others seem to get a lot of recognition for what they do, but what I do is not often acknowledged. I guess it's not really that important. . . .

How might you choose to address this issue in terms of the here-and-now of the group? How might you encourage group interaction around this issue?

7. Bart responds to Zinnia's lead (see Question 6).

He says, "At least you're not getting negative attention. It seems like, for me, I only hear about the bad things I do. It's always been that way, going back to my childhood; my older and younger sisters always got heaps of praise for their accomplishments, and I was some kind of 'bad boy.' Maybe I should just carry out my fantasy of getting a motorcycle and hitting the road."

What options do you have for responding to Bart? If his statement came right after Zinnia's, should you ignore his statement and turn your attention back to Zinnia? Alternatively, might there be some way for you to bring the issues together so the group could address both at once?

Self-Reflection

1. How do you recognize potential hot-seat issues? In terms of your own emotional self-awareness, what helps you to sort out what could be an important aspect to explore versus something that is truly your "own stuff" and not especially relevant to your particular group?

2. What do you feel physically and emotionally when you are bored in a group interaction? Conversely, what do you feel physically and emotionally when you are engaged and find something interesting or moving when in a group?

3. Consider recent relationships in which you've been involved and the development of trust and understanding within those relationships. What types of incidents occurred to help move those relationships toward a deeper level? Can you recall some specific examples? What happened, and what occurred afterward? Are there any lessons that you can take from these experiences to apply toward working with group members struggling to improve their relationships?

4. What are some of your primary concerns about "stirring the pot" within a group? How might you deal with each of these concerns?

5. Consider key "I-thou" relationships that have thrived in your life. What aspects tell you that these relationships are especially alive? Are these factors that you can actively promote among group members?

6. How do you feel about working in a "zigzag" fashion within a group? If you prefer to work from a more linear or analytical perspective, how might you balance that approach with working in a zigzag fashion with a group?

CHAPTER 12

PROCESS ILLUMINATION

Group dynamics, in our view, encompass all of the group's interpersonal processes. They are the group's unique constellation of behavioral patterns—a constellation constantly in a state of flux. They are, as well, the group's driving force, thrusting it forward, if not backward. As such, group dynamics are almost the "holy grail" of group counseling—earnestly pursued by all devoted group therapists.

This chapter picks up where Chapter 11 left off, striving to illustrate the second tier of the advanced level here-and-now method—*process illumination*. In its relentless pursuit of the meanings of the process level of communication, this chapter rallies a multitude of techniques to shed light on this enigmatic object of interest—the group dynamics.

PROCESS ILLUMINATION AND CHANGE

The Elusive Nature of Process Illumination

Lacking a succinct definition, the concepts of process illumination often elude many beginning group leaders. Yalom and Leszcz (2005) admit, "It is not easy to discuss, in a systematic way, the actual practice of process illumination. How can one propose crisp, basic guidelines for a procedure of such complexity and range, such delicate timing, so many linguistic nuances?" (p. 178).

Nevertheless, we will try to depict this highly complex, abstract, broad, and powerful concept by looking at it from various different but equally important angles. All of the angles hopefully will come together to form a holistic picture of what process illumination is.

The Gift of Process Illumination

Process illumination can create an experience unlike anything else. When a group catches someone's interpersonal style in the act, so to speak, it is electrifying to witness and experience.

Though it might shock the person at the center of the process illumination, if done with sensitivity and prior support, as well as at an appropriate time, this here-and-now method can open space for members to arrive at new realizations, breaking ground for therapeutic work to come. Such an experience is indeed a gift. One member, Lou, reflected in her journal on this experience:

Without this group, I would not have known that I unconsciously change the conversation when I become emotional. I did not really expect people in this group to tap into my issues. It was a tumultuous, yet pleasant, surprise. It was tumultuous because people in this group started seeing my vulnerabilities but pleasant because it shows that people really accept me for who I am as a person.

The Trajectory of a Critical Incident: Process Illumination and Self-Discovery

Change often begins with self-awareness and self-discovery. In the group, members' self-discovery arrives after going through a "critical incident" (Yalom & Leszcz, 2005). Each critical incident may differ, however; all of them follow a similar path. For educational purposes, we will risk oversimplification by outlining that path:

- A member, say, Talisha, is actively interacting with the group in her usual way.
- Either organically or through an affect stimulation technique used by the leader, something in Talisha is triggered (this part is the here-and-now activation, the *first tier*).
- As a reaction to the trigger, Talisha's interpersonal pattern surfaces, and the group viscerally reacts to Talisha's reactivity pattern, but no one dares to say anything.
- The leader recognizes all of the above as they occur and prompts the group to give here-and-now feedback (an impact disclosure) to Talisha (this part is the process illumination, *the second tier*).
- Talisha gains awareness and insight into the causes of her trigger as well as the impact her interpersonal pattern has on others (this part is the self-discovery).
- Motivated by the group's support and her own new awareness, Talisha starts to change the way she interprets or assumes things as well as the way she deals with her emotions within the group (this part is the here-and-now transformation).

- Talisha carries her new behavior over to her own life outside the group (this finally is the there-and-then transformation).

The above picture delineates a common trajectory that a member goes through to arrive at self-discovery and change.

Process Illumination and a Sense of Psychological Visibility

Though nerve-wracking, process illumination gives people a sense of being seen—a rarely found gift. Underlying many people's developmental problems, insecurities, and inadequacies in relationships lie the agony of feeling invisible. For many, healing often begins when they reclaim those unrecognized qualities in their personality and psyches.

In the group, there exists a precious "mirror" through which members are enabled to see their inner beings and their interpersonal beings. This mirror represents the group members' perceptions about what goes on in the here-and-now.

When the group offers a perception resonating with a member's deepest and unexpressed vision of who he or she is, this member will feel *psychologically visible*. The member will have a sense of *finally being seen* by others, and with this will come a newfound sense of freedom.

Receiving group insight to the depth of this level, this member will have a high probability of becoming aware of his or her unrecognized capabilities, latent potentialities, and character traits that never before surfaced to such a level of explicit recognition.

Increased psychological visibility leads to an expansion of the member's consciousness, helping him or her deepen contact with his or her own psychological self. Integration becomes possible as the member begins to heal internal psychological splits. From this more unified self, the member finally has free access to his or her inner light and love—his or her true nature.

WAYS TO RECOGNIZE GROUP PROCESSES

"It is NOT easy to tell the beginning therapist how to recognize process . . . beginning students who observe [group] meetings find them [the dynamics] far less meaningful, complex, and interesting than do the experienced therapists" (Yalom & Leszcz, 2005, p. 159).

Yalom's lament echoes the moans from many educators of beginning group therapists. Is there any way to help therapists-in-training recognize the process? This section proposes several ways for you to take a crack at the mystery of how to recognize group processes as they happen.

Constantly Ask Yourself the Meaning and the Significance of What's Going On

First, develop a habit of questioning the meaning and significance of an individual's or group's dynamics. To do this, you constantly question, in your mind, why the dynamics are the way they are:

"What is going on here? What does all this *mean*?"

We, leaders, must "assume that every communication has meaning and salience within the individual's interpersonal schema until proven otherwise" (Yalom & Leszcz, 2005, p. 167). When looking for what dynamics to pursue, pay special attention to members' *emotional reactivity* inside the group.

It is only when we finally understand the meaning and the significance of members' reactivity patterns that we will truly comprehend the nature of members' issues in their lives outside the group.

What Hot Buttons Are Likely to Be Pushed? Get Familiarized With Sensitive Areas

Whenever we put a group of people together for a period of time, sooner or later people's buttons will be pushed. So secondly, familiarize yourself with people's sensitive areas. Hetzel, Barton, and Davenport (1994) found that people usually have four areas of sensitivity: *intimacy, control, power*, and *competition*. When pushed, these hot buttons can fuel intense reactivity.

- *Intimacy.* The button of *intimacy* gets pushed fairly early on in the group. All of us harbor an inner conflict between our instinct to protect ourselves and our desire for emotional intimacy. Eventually, we have to decide how much to let ourselves be vulnerable and how much to protect ourselves.
- When we get right down to it, what really gets activated with the intimacy button is our *fear of vulnerability*. As Brown (2015) states, "the level to which we protect ourselves from being vulnerable is a measure of our fear and disconnection" (p. 2). This fear of vulnerability can cause some members to speak abstractly and intellectually, while others distance themselves and withdraw from the rest.

- *Control. Control* involves a need to maintain things within a tolerable level of predictability and security. This need stands against potential change.
- *Power. Power* involves a desire to have *influence over others. Power is* taking control from the personal level into the interpersonal level.
- *Competition. Competition* occurs as people "vie for" limited resources so as to maintain personal control and interpersonal power. Competition can take many forms. As Hetzel et al. (1994) observe, some members attempt to compete with others "by relating an even more painful or embarrassing incident, by offering advice, or by attempting to solve a particular dilemma" (p. 58).

When these four buttons (intimacy, control, power, and competition) get pushed, members may not openly talk about it, as they are trained in this society not to talk about things that "hit too close to home," but you will definitely see some reactions and changes in the interpersonal dynamics of the group. These change of dynamics are signs that the group needs us to carry out a process illumination.

Keep an Eye on Those Roles
Easily Enacted Between Members

Group members tend to carry *the roles they played in their early lives* into their adult relationships. These roles are often reactivated, not by the leader stirring anything, but just by members interacting with other members of the group.

When people reactivate, in the present moment, the role that they played in their family of origin, their reactivation is call *enactment* (Ferencik, 1991; Moreno, 1978; Woodward, 2004). Following are some of the *roles* that you need to familiarize yourself with as they can easily get enacted in the group:

Problem solver	Achiever	Peacemaker
Therapist	People pleaser	Hero/Heroine
Caretaker	Mediator	Placator (rescuer)
Observer/spectator	Scapegoat	Lost child
Troublemaker	Talker	Boss
Parentified child	Perfectionist	Entertainer
Surrogate father	Clown	Victim
Rationalist	Rebel	

Once roles are enacted, members tend to lock horns with one another. For example, Kyle's "rescuer" role locks horns with Kenan's "scapegoat" or "lost child" role. This demonstrates the reciprocal nature of interpersonal enactment. As Ferencik (1991) indicates, when roles are enacted, a whole set of expectations and assumptions attached to a role will be promulgated, causing all involved parties to display certain behaviors and receive certain responses from the others. Subsequent responses proceed from prior ones.

A group provides the most fertile soil for interpersonal enactment to happen. A member describes this phenomenon well in her journal: "It feels like once you are in the group process, you are caught in a spider's web; there is no escaping what will transpire." The third way to take a crack at the group processes is to keep an eye on these roles and see how they get enacted between members.

The Elephant in the Room

The elephant in the room represents certain kinds of troublesome behaviors that go on right in front of everybody's eyes with no one daring to address them. In the following, Ferencik (1991) provides some examples of these kinds of unsettling interpersonal dynamics:

- Certain members identify with each other and interact in a manner that excludes the rest the group.
- Two alcohol abusers support each other in their denial.
- Two depressed members reinforce each other's belief in helplessness and in the group's ineffectiveness.
- Members of the same gender or age form coalitions.

Other types of elephants in the room may include the following dynamics that no one in the group dares to address:

- Members engaging in a power struggle
- Members getting upset with each other
- Leaders being attacked verbally
- Members falling asleep

Group members seldom articulate these troublesome behaviors for what they are because, as Ferencik (1991) points out, when behaviors have established their patterns over a period of time, their effects are insidious and their manners difficult to pinpoint.

As the leader, you need to develop a sharp eye for those sticky behaviors that members dare not address. Unfortunately, many new leaders fail to develop this capacity. It is no surprise that Yalom (1983) laments: "Over and over again, I have observed wonderfully ripe therapeutic plums spoiling on the tree because of the inability of the therapists to focus on interaction" (p. 23).

The Case of Mindy and Anna: Mutual Enactment

The case of Mindy and Anna might help you see the interpersonal process in a more concrete picture.

Anna's Social Inadequacy. Anna entered the group stating that, as a very shy person, she often did not initiate greetings to others. Although Anna was capable of one-to-one deep conversation, she felt inadequate in social groups where interactions are more spontaneous and require one to be more active in reaching out. She found herself with no friends outside of her immediate family. It was no surprise to hear that the goal Anna set for herself in the group was to improve her interpersonal relationships.

Anna's Stoic Family and Her Decision to Hide a Chronic Illness. Later in the group, Anna also revealed two critical pieces of information: First, she came from a family that was very stoic; as a result, she had inherited a cold and distant look.

Second, she had been suffering from a chronic illness, but she had decided at an early age not to disclose to others the physical pain that she had to endure every waking hour. This decision was based on painful experiences from a childhood of being excluded and discriminated against after disclosing her chronic condition.

These two pieces of information helped members understand why she looked so stern and seldom seemed to be emotionally present. Therefore, no one really took her mannerisms personally—except Mindy

Mindy's Alcoholic Family and Her Sensitivity to Peer Rejection. Mindy (who appeared in the case illustration in Chapter 10) came from an alcoholic family where she received very little nurturing, and this upbringing had made her very sensitive to rejection. On top of this, she had many painful childhood memories of being rejected by her peers. These wounds of *peer rejection* never healed, and they exerted influence in Mindy's encounters with others in her adult life. Until coming to the group, their influence had remained hidden from Mindy.

The Enactment Between Mindy and Anna. When Mindy encountered Anna in the group, she reached out to Anna in an attempt to build a friendship. In response, Mindy received only Anna's stern look and distance.

Immediately, Mindy took these cues personally, enacting her intense feeling of hurt and anger—her painful past was being relived with Anna in the here-and-now of the group! As a result, Mindy's reactions to Anna often seemed out of proportion, especially when compared to the reactions coming from other group members.

Process Illumination for Mindy. The leader recognized that Mindy might have enacted certain unresolved issues in her interaction with Anna and invited Mindy to see whether she could make a connection between the here-and-now and the there-and-then.

After the group's illumination and Mindy's personal reflection, Mindy started to associate her reactions with her childhood rejection. Once these experiences were connected, Mindy had an "aha" experience and started to change. The group members gave Mindy their affirmation for her new realization.

Anna Suspecting a Clique Between the Group and Mindy. As the group was giving Mindy affirming feedback, Anna took it as an indication that they were forming a clique that excluded her. It made sense that Anna's past experience of being excluded and discriminated against when she revealed her chronic conditions understandably would make her particularly sensitive to any signs of possible discrimination, and this sensitivity was enacted in the group. She felt as if people were conspiring against her.

Process Illumination for Anna. As the leader recognized what was going on process-wise for Anna, she invited the group to share their here-and-now observations, giving the group a chance to illuminate and correct Anna's interpersonal distortion. Slowly, Anna started to unveil her chronic condition and family stoicism.

As Anna started to come out from the dark, Mindy also started to share her childhood pain, which helped Anna deeply connect to her. The case of Mindy and Anna had a happy ending, as indicated in their reflective journals.

Anna

The group had a great impact on me, as I was able to see myself through the eyes of others. And through them, I see those aspects of my personal style that I want to further work on—my being stoic and somewhat unresponsive to others. The critical event in the group was Mindy's reaction to my comment about her. This reaction made me become aware of my impact on others. I used to have a distorted perception of myself: *I used to think that people didn't notice my stoic and sometimes shy behavior.*

But the group let me know through their honest comments that they at times take this pattern of behavior personally. This feedback is very valuable for me in terms of addressing my social-emotional goal.

Mindy

I need to be aware of the personal filter through which I take in everything that Anna says. I did not know, on a conscious level, that I was still carrying around those childhood experiences and the hurt associated with them.

I was relieved when Anna stated that some of the stoicism that she displays is a result of her upbringing and physical pain. Now I can tell myself that the cause of her coldness was external, that is, not because of her dislike of me.

I think the idea of a personal filter is a really important thing for me to remember from now on. It has been enlightening for me to realize the extent to which I still carry around the strong thoughts and emotions surrounding my past experiences. And I am happy that I went through all of this, if only for that revelation.

TIPS FOR PROCESS ILLUMINATION

To elucidate a group's interpersonal process—complex, circular, and interdependent—and turn it into a therapeutic instrument is a skill often beyond the reach of untrained group workers. And even after a period of training, you may still question whether you have a knack for it. This section aims to boost your confidence by providing a few tips that have proven beneficial for many beginners.

Dare to Put Members on the Hot Seat—You Are Giving Them a Gift

Many new group leaders shy away from putting members on the hot seat, worrying about provoking intense emotions in members and then having to handle those emotions—a fear very common in our society. Paradoxically, rather than harm, putting people on the hot seat can actually do them good. Though the here-and-now experience can unnerve members, it also rewards them with new learning and reveals for them new paths of action.

The simple fact is *people begin to change only when they begin to feel uncomfortable.*

By putting process illumination into action, your members will receive honest here-and-now feedback. Through this, you are giving your group the best chance for *reality-testing* and correcting any distortions that are not serving them well. New realizations will empower members to make more conscious choices in their lives. Through this, you are giving your member a precious gift.

Don't Do for Them What They Can Do Themselves

Many new leaders ask, "If we want to help a member change, why don't we just go ahead and tell the member the distortions we have observed? Why do we need to painstakingly prompt the group to offer their process comments?" This is a great question. Our experience teaches us that it is better to ask members to do what they can do themselves.

First of all, your process prompt allows members to own up to what they see, how they feel, and what they react to in the group interaction. The leader does not need to take it upon himself or herself to point out or interpret what is happening in the group; all the leader needs to do is to create an opening for the *members* to do this themselves.

Second, insight coming from members is usually better received and is typically experienced as more powerful and on target than insight coming from the leader.

Zigzag the Spotlight Among Multiple Interpersonal Dynamics

Rarely will members' interpersonal dynamics play themselves out in a one-at-a-time fashion; in reality, multiple interpersonal dynamics can set themselves off simultaneously during a here-and-now group processing.

For example, Akio, who is on the hot seat, might deflect the spotlight by talking over another member, Ba Tu, while yet another member, Chet, who has been holding grudges against Akio, might use this opportunity to confront Akio. Still another member, Hisoka, who often plays the rescuer role in the group, might be trying to downplay the confrontation, and so on.

These dynamics and a lot more can happen simultaneously.

When this happens, the hot seat will need to zigzag to those members who show their reactivity patterns. Circumnavigating the hot seat around will reward the group with an alive and engaging exchange—one that doesn't let any members off the hook.

Let the Reactivity "Markers" Guide Your Zigzagging

One question often asked by new group leaders is, "Among all the complex dynamics within a group session, which direction should I zigzag the hot seat to?"

From our experience, the spotlight of process illumination goes to members manifesting their *reactive patterns* or *intense emotions* in the present moment. These we call *the reactivity markers*.

When you spot a reactivity marker, *seize the moment* to take stock of what is causing the intense reactions and what it means to the person.

Here are some examples of the reactivity markers that you might want to be on the lookout for:

Getting defensive	Lashing out in anger
Blaming	Domineering
Intellectualizing	Negative out-looking
Rescuing	Yes-butting
Deflecting	Avoiding
Shutting down	Excessive people-pleasing
Excessive accommodating	Intense emotions

Create a "Corrective Emotional Experience" for Those Who Suffer Deep Pain

Though we need to zigzag the hot seat to include multiple dynamics, when a member's suffering and deep pain come to the forefront, we need to stay with him or her a bit longer before zigzagging again—long enough to allow the member to benefit from a *corrective emotional experience* (Alexander & French, 1980; Khantzian, 2001; Yalom & Leszcz, 2005).

First coined by Franz Alexander (Alexander & French, 1980), a Hungarian psychotherapist, the term *corrective emotional experience* has since been held, among counselors and therapists, as the key to client change and transformation (Gaylin, 2000). Research in interpersonal neurobiology has also garnered strong support for this conviction: When provided with an *emotional meaningful experience*, the human brain grows new neural connections; *in the presence of emotional and interpersonal interactions*, the brain cells grow new pathways; when fed with new ways of interaction in relationships, the person will experience profound change on the behavioral level (Cozolino, 2016; Doidge, 2014; Makinson & Young, 2012; Siegel, 2015).

To create a corrective emotional experience for the member, the group has to offer the person exactly what he or she *was deprived of* in his or her earlier experiences *and is deprived of* in his or her current world. In other words, the group needs to do the opposite of what usually happens in the member's personal life.

Sometimes, members instinctually know how to create a corrective emotional experience for the person in need; most of the time, however, they need an artful nudge from the leader. In Chapter 13 (Using Psychodrama for Unresolved Pain), we propose an experiential method through which a leader can guide the group to provide *healing* and *restorative* experiences for a member who suffers deep pain.

Watch Closely the Dynamics of "Subgroups" or "Whole-Groups"

As we keep tabs on individual members' reactivity markers, we also need to watch closely the behavioral and reactive patterns of "subgroups" and even "the group as a whole."

- *Dynamics of the group as a whole.* As a rule of thumb, issues such as *trust issues, group collusion, or group avoidance*, tend to have the potential to threaten the functioning of the entire group; hence, they always take priority over any individual issues.
- *Subgroup dynamics.* Issues such as *triangulation* and *cliques rescuing each other* belong to subgroup issues. If spotted, they *must also take priority over individual issues as well.*

Here is an example of subgroup dynamics interwoven with whole-group dynamics. In the eighth session of a group, three interpersonal processes happened all at once, encased all together like Russian dolls.

Mitch, who had difficulty being true to his own feelings, finally took the risk of confronting Charlie about his using drinking in dealing with the tension in his life. Thomas and Dane, who are both Charlie's friends, jumped in right away to dismiss anything that Mitch said. As this happened, thick tension arose, pulsating in the air, yet the rest of the group acted as if nothing had happened. Mitch did not raise his eyes again.

In this example, the three dynamics transpired:

(1) Mitch took the risk to do something unusual.

(2) A clique colluded to protect one of its affiliates by dismissing Mitch.

(3) The group went into its avoidance mode, abandoning Mitch to feel even more alone and powerless, resulting in him retreating back into his shell; this, in turn, enables Charlie's self-defeating behavior (using drinking to deal with tension in his life) to continue.

Which immediacy issue would you go after first? Since the tensest issue should be addressed first, we suggest the following order: the group, the colluding three, and then Mitch.

The method of applying process illumination to these three layers of dynamics will be illuminated in a later section, "Process Illumination Technique (IV): Explore the Meanings of Behaviors Engaged by 'Dyads,' 'Triads,' or 'the Group as a Whole.'"

Interweave the Two Tiers Into a Fluid Process

Alternating between the first tier of emotion stimulation and the second tier of process illumination is a fluid, ever-evolving process. It is anything but cut-and-dried. Yalom (2009) states, "Effective group counseling and therapy consist of an alternating sequence: *evocation and experiencing* of affects followed by *analysis and integration* of affect" (p. 71).

In practice, the group alternates, back and forth, between the first tier and the second in a seamless manner. It is only for educational purposes that we differentiate between the two tiers. In doing so, we are risking the possibility of making the process appear linear. But, as pointed out above, the boundary between here-and-now emotion stimulation and process illumination is anything but concrete. Emotional experiences often subtly interlace with process observations and vice versa.

For example, a group might be processing certain dynamics, and suddenly something stirs other new emotions. The newly emerged emotions call for a new wave of process illumination, which may stir yet more new dynamics in the group. One cannot tell exactly when the group shifts from here-and-now experiencing to process illumination. Again, it works in a fluid process.

Such interlacing of the two tiers is reflected in Peter's and Heather's reflective journals.

Peter

I will always remember this week's session when almost everyone was in the "hot seat." It was so funny, full of suspense and surprises, literally better than most movies. Through the here-and-now method, many hidden truths were suddenly revealed: Eve and Lori had been hiding their negative reaction to Heather and Rose. And Heather and Rose, in turn, had been trying to hide their negative reaction to my long-winded verbal expression.

And my reaction to Lori's comments was, "What? Who's been disrespecting me? I know it's that damned Rose! And Heather, too!" Sara laughed so hard at this that I thought she'd fall off her chair.

Then Kelly put the icing on the cake by announcing that she was angry with the leader, and she was so sick of me being the favorite member. She thought that I get so much attention just because I am a man!

This session was really great. It definitely is a springboard toward future growth.

Heather

I will forever remember my feeling of being in the "hot seat." After Lori confronted Rose and me about rolling our eyes and acting rude to Peter, I was embarrassed and felt like a kid being caught red-handed.

But it gave me insight into myself and the way I kept my emotions hidden and end up showing them like an open book, especially through my facial expressions. My rolling of eyes is never meant to hurt anyone, but now I know it comes across to others and has an impact on them. I also know how one would feel being put in the hot seat.

Analyze Members' Avoidance of the Here-and-Now

While some members take pleasure in the richness and aliveness of the here-and-now experience, others find themselves recoiling when provoked by heightened emotions. They hasten to bring the temperature down as if to put out a fire.

For example, Kathy, a member, has just stated that some people in the group have a tendency to intellectualize. As the group is just beginning to discuss this sensitive issue, another member, Chuck, shifts the conversation to something completely irrelevant, taking the group away from the immediacy issues at hand. Ironically, Chuck does not even see he is doing that! It seemed so natural to him to bring up a new topic, to ask a new question, or to talk about something arising on the horizon of his mind. As such, a potential moment for exploring critical interpersonal processes disappeared into thin air. The group members feel let down but cannot figure out why this is so.

Seeing Chuck's avoidance of the here-and-now and seeing its impact on the group, the leader calmly and assertively brings the group back to the lost moment in an effort to analyze the meaning of this avoidance behavior:

[To the group] We were just beginning to address a difficult issue in the group, and suddenly we are talking about a totally unrelated topic. I wonder, what do you observe is going on here? [prompting the group to analyze the avoidance behavior without explicitly spelling out for the members what the leader has seen]

If the group is in its early stages, obviously you will just redirect (a basic intervention technique, see Chapter 4) the group back on track. However, the technique of redirection pales—by comparison with the here-and-now method—in generating intensity and fails to illuminate the meaning of Chuck's avoidance behavior. See for yourself how the technique of redirection differs from the process illumination just presented above:

[To the group] I noticed that we got *sidetracked* just now. Let's go back to the statement Kathy made, a few minutes ago, about some people in this group having the tendency to intellectualize. I notice there were some strong reactions toward what Kathy was saying, so let's stay with the intellectualizing issue a bit longer even if it feels a bit intense. [redirecting back to the original process discussion but completely failing to address Chuck's avoidance behavior]

Words of caution: Though the here-and-now method acts literally like a powerhouse for interpersonal learning, its use must arise from sound clinical judgment and a strong sense of timing. Catching people in the act will make people "feel naked," so to speak. If used without first establishing a sense of deep trust, people can become defensive or shut down. Therefore, the use of redirecting does have its place for handling undesirable behaviors when the group is in its early stage.

THE FIVE COMPONENTS OF PROCESS ILLUMINATION: THE LEADER'S COURSE OF ACTION

It takes a complex course of action for a leader to carry out process illumination—a course of action that involves several components, all happening simultaneously. For educational purposes, we will dissect this method into five steps, all from a leader's point of view.

#1: Notice Your Here-and-Now Reaction and Its There-and-Then Parallel

When a charged incident occurs, you first step back and attend to what is happening *in you*—how you are *being pulled into and affected by* the emotional field of the incident. Simultaneously, you consider whether the way the member conducts himself or herself within the group *ties in with* the member's relational world at large and whether the way you react to his or her style might run parallel to that of people in the member's life. A found resemblance will ensure that your reaction does not come from your own subjective countertransference (see Chapter 9).

For example, when a member, Marcy, is rambling on end, and the group is not saying anything, your internal thinking may go like this:

Well, I am sensing that the group is hitting a brick wall, and I am more and more bored with the way Marcy goes on tangents without showing any feelings or connections to anything. I wonder, *What does this mean? Is it about me or is it about the way she talks? Do my reactions run parallel to the way people react to her in her life?*

#2: Speculate on the Group's Reactions at the Moment

Simultaneously, you turn your focus to and speculate on what is going on between Marcy and the rest of the group, taking into consideration the history of the group up to this point:

Hmm . . . and how is the group reacting to this style of storytelling? Do they see any connection between the stories and goal that she said she wanted to work on? Do they resist her style? Do their minds wander? Do they, like me, feel the boredom and the frustration of getting shut out by her style?

Notice that at this phase, your internal processing remains private and unspoken. All you are doing is taking in the interpersonal data.

#3: Invite the Group Members to Speak Directly About Their Reactions

When you have confirmed, through body language observation, that the group is reacting to Marcy, albeit silently, you start to almost concurrently formulate a here-and-now intervention. Since the group is already reacting, you can skip the first tier and go directly to the second. You invite members to speak openly and directly to the specific member about what is being evoked in them that they are keeping inside:

> [To the group] "Let's stop for a moment. I am seeing *some* strong reactions while Marcy is talking. I wonder what this tension is about. Does anyone want to start? And please speak to Marcy directly." [Note: *You do not spell out your own observation and speculation of the member's pattern. Rather, you let the group do their own work by allowing them to own up to and articulate their own observations and reactions.*]

The above here-and-now intervention is vague on purpose—to allow members to come to their own observations and articulation. But if you are aiming for a clearer delivery of the same intervention, you may try the following:

> [To the group] I would like the group to shift gears a little bit. I wonder, *how do you personally experience Marcy* right now as you listen to her talking about her issues? How do you feel *toward her*? I am not asking about how you feel toward her problems or how she feels in her problems. But I am asking about how you feel *toward her way of telling her stories*. When you are ready, please speak directly to Marcy.

Suppose a group member, John, responds,

> Marcy, your stories are very colourful, and I appreciate the drama in them, but I have been waiting to hear what your stories have to do with your current struggles and your personal work in the group. I am not seeing it, and I feel lost. Frankly, the more I hear you talk, the more I feel detached. So, I don't know.

At this point, you do not need to agree or disagree with what John has said. What you need to do is just to thank him and continue with an invitation for other members to speak.

> Thank you, John, for your openness. [turning to other members] For the rest of you in the group, how do you feel toward Marcy and her way of telling her stories?

Another member, Susan, may comment,

> Yes, I always feel something about you, Marcy, but I haven't been able to put my finger on it. Today when I listen to you, though, it becomes more and more clear. It is like I want to get close to you, but I'm never able to cross your wall. It is like you really don't want people to get to know you or something.

Again, you only need to thank Susan and then persist in your invitation to the group until the dynamics have been fully explored:

> Thank you, Susan. [turning to the group] Anyone else?

This relentless pursuit of the meaning hidden under a specific incident marks the third component of the leader's course of action.

#4: Zigzag Process Illuminations to Multiple Members

As you pursue the meaning of Marcy's behavior pattern and the impact it has on the group, other members' interpersonal styles may surface. For instance, as the group focuses on Marcy, she starts to protect her vulnerability by shifting the focus of the conversation on other members. Seeing this, another member, Ellen, who has struggled for a long time trying to be more assertive, worked up the courage to tell Marcy how she just deflected what the group was trying to tell her.

At that moment, the *tension* between Ellen and Marcy arises, but no one in the group dares to address the issue. At this juncture, another member, Mike, who often takes on the peacemaker role, jumped in to rescue Marcy by telling a story of his own, totally irrelevant to the dynamics at hand.

The group's heightened energy was dissipated as a result, and a moment of honest interaction between Ellen and Marcy was sidestepped.

In this above scenario, four dynamics were happening simultaneously:

(1) Ellen made huge progress by taking a great risk for the first time in the group, sharing what she observed in Marcy and refusing to let the group feedback be deflected.

(2) Marcy's discomfort led her to resort to her familiar coping mechanism of deflecting and escaping.

(3) The tension between Marcy and Ellen prompted the group members to react in their own habitual ways.

(4) Mike's inability to tolerate anxiety propelled him to enact his role of the peacemaker. In doing so, he took the moment of truth-telling away from the group.

All of these dynamics are equally important to explore and examine. When faced with multiple dynamics going on at the same time, the leader needs to zigzag the hot seat, one dynamic at a time to cover all the bases. This is the fourth component of a leader's course of action in process illumination.

Since the tension between Ellen and Marcy is pulsating in the room, it is the dynamic that should be explored first.

[To the group] Let's stop for a moment. I sensed some rising tension in the group that has not been resolved. Let's go back to the interaction 5 minutes ago between Marcy and Ellen. What do you see was going on between them? And what blocked all of you from speaking up about your truth? [process illuminations]

Later,

[To the group] Thanks, everybody for your feedback to Marcy. How about Mike? What do you see was going on between Mike and the group? How did you personally experience Mike at that moment? [process illuminations]

Much later,

[To the group] Ellen has struggled to be more assertive in the group. Just in this session, Ellen took a great risk to tell her truth about how she experienced Marcy. How did you experience Ellen at that moment when she took a risk to be assertive for the first time in the group? What do you know about her that she might not know about herself? [process illuminations]

#5: Link the Here-and-Now Back to the There-and-Then

In this last component, the leader directs the group to make the connection between the group's here-and-now occurrences and members' there-and-then lives. It always amazes us to hear the group members share how what happens in the here-and-now of the group really runs *parallel with* or *corresponds to* what happens in the there-and-then outside the group.

Individuals' "inside of group" interpersonal patterns are often *a social microcosm* (Yalom & Leszcz, 2005) of the interpersonal fields of their outside lives at large. Indeed, we can take this one step further by saying *everything that members want to know about others' perceptions of them is amassed inside the here-and-now of the group.*

This makes the group a perfect *interpersonal learning laboratory* (Leszcz, 1992) where members can see their own interpersonal pulls on others and vice versa.

The leader, thus, decided to make *a process comment* to help Marcy connect her here-and-now issue with the there-and-then issue of her outside life:

> Marcy, what most members have been trying to say is that they want to but seem unable to get close to you. I remember that the very issue you presented in the first group session was your inability to build a close relationship with people in your life. I think the feedback that members gave you a moment ago may give you some valuable perspective as to why people in your world out there feel pushed away by you.

In the same token, you might proceed to help Mike gain insight into how his immediacy issues are closely linked to his outside world behaviors.

PROCESS ILLUMINATION TECHNIQUE (I): GO AFTER REACTIVITY MARKERS

After becoming familiar with the five components of the leader's course of action in process illumination, it's time to get down to the nitty-gritty—the techniques. The *first technique is to go after the reactivity markers.*

What Are Reactivity Markers?

As we briefly touched upon earlier, reactivity itself means a knee-jerk emotional response NOT mediated by the consciousness. This emotional response, immediate and reactive, shoots up when one's sensitive issue is triggered. Accompanying the emotional response are some visible signs or behaviors (the reactivity markers we listed earlier), signaling that certain highly sensitive and significant issues have been stirred.

In more dense language, Leszcz (1992) helps to explain this concept with the following statement:

Intense emotional heat that seems "out of proportion" with the objective situation is often *a very useful signal* that some core interpersonal vicissitude that reflects on the individual *sense of self* has been touched. Through its *hyperactivity*, it serves as a marker for central issues. (p. 57)

Be Hawk Alert! Look Out for Reactivity Markers

Since these reactivity markers are trying to signal to us that certain highly sensitive and significant issues have been stirred, we have to be hawk alert, looking out for these markers. But how to do it? Reactivity markers may become manifest in the form of

- *facial expressions,*
- *verbal or nonverbal behaviors, and*
- *outward behaviors.*

When someone's sensitive part of the self is touched, common outward behavior markers may include the following: getting defensive, lashing out in anger, deflecting, shutting down, and so on. Please review examples of reactivity markers listed in the previous section to help you increase your ability to recognize them.

When any such reactive markers show up, the group will have emotional reactions. As we sense the heat, there is no need to stir the pot (the first tier). But rather, we can go right into the second tier to inquire about the meaning of members' emotional reactions and the behavioral patterns of the person who has provoked them.

The following process illuminations cover the *three arenas* in which emotional reactivity markers tend to heat up: (1) member-to-member relationships, (2) member-to-leader relationships, and (3) mass group relationships.

Pursue Reactive Behaviors in Member-to-Member Relationships

[To the group] I would like the group to stop for a moment. Something very important has just happened in the group. What do you see was going on *between Helen* [the offended] *and Jim*? [process illumination]

Follow-up:

> Thank you for sharing, Tom. [turning to the rest of the group] I would like to hear more from the rest of you about your observation of the incident *between Helen and Jim*. Does anyone else want to contribute? [process illumination continued]
>
> [To the group] I wonder, have any of you had the same experience with Jim that Helen encountered today? How does this make it difficult for you to reveal yourselves? [further process illumination] Jim, what do you see is the effect of your behavior on others? Does this occur in other life situations? [illuminating parallel process]

Other examples include the following:

> [To the group] I would like to call a time-out for the group. The exchange *between Jessie, Tom, and Diana* has been going on for more than 10 minutes and seems to be going nowhere. I sense a lot of strong feelings in the room. I would like the group to respond to this question: What do you see has been going on in the last 10 minutes?
>
> [To the group] *Jim and Steve* have been conversing with each other for awhile now, and I notice something unsaid building up in the group. I wonder, what do you observe is going on here?

The process question should be extended to the rest of the group as many times as necessary so that all members have a chance to share their observations.

Examine Reactive Behaviors in Member-to-Leader Relationships

Previously, during the storming stage of the group, the skills presented in Chapter 9 (working on tension and conflict) would have sufficed for dealing with challenging dynamics between members and leaders. Here, in the working stage, process illumination becomes the best tool for dealing with difficult dynamics between a member and a leader. For example,

> Jessie, as you said that to Mary, *I also heard some of your feelings toward me*. Would you be willing to talk a bit about these feelings so I can better understand what is happening between you and me?

Later,

> [To the group] How does the rest of the group feel about what happened between Jessie and me?

Much later,

> Jessie, I now understand these feelings of inadequacy and fear of disapproval that you feel toward me. I really appreciate your trust in me and the group by sharing these sensitive feelings. I will certainly keep what you shared in mind in my interactions with the group and you. I do want to encourage you to reflect on whether you might have similar feelings toward the authority figures in your world outside the group. I wonder whether they might actually approve of who you are as a person and yet might be perceived as disapproving of you?

Explore Reactive Behaviors of the Group as a Whole

Competition for dominance abounds in group dynamics. Similar to *sibling rivalry, the dynamics of* competition for dominance surface as members struggle with one another to establish a pecking order within the group. When you, as a leader, see this marker, it oftentimes serves the group to shine a light on it:

> [To the group] I wonder why it is always Jean who reveals first and the most. Why does the group let her carry the burden of the entire meeting? [process illumination]

Later,

> [To the group] All of you seem to have noticed this. What has stopped you from acting on your observations? Why does the group look to me, the leader, to do what all of you are capable of doing? [even further illumination]

Another example:

> [To the group] I notice that this is becoming a discussion exclusively between Jane, Patrick, and Nancy, while the rest of the group is sitting silently. I wonder, how do the rest of you see this, and why are you letting it happen this way?

PROCESS ILLUMINATION TECHNIQUE (II): UNCOVERING HIDDEN MEANINGS

A group really starts to plug into its power when it pursues the meanings of members' unspoken dynamics (Lieberman, Yalom, & Miles, 1974). From our experiences, the secret codes for cracking these unspoken dynamics can often be found in

- nonverbal cues in members' actions,
- unexpressed emotions and reactions in members' behaviors, and
- unchecked perceptions or assumptions that become apparent in members' verbal expressions.

Leszcz (1992) explains it well: "Each action or behavior by each member of the group *has meaning* and the therapist's task is to help all members *pursue this significance*" (p. 57). This section presents ways to decode these hidden meanings.

Hold off on Revealing Your Own Interpretation. Let the Group Do the Cracking

All here-and-now techniques, in a sense, aim to crack the significance and meaning of unspoken dynamics. To crack them, the leader first formulates hunches in his or her mind but *without jumping the gun to interpret them out loud*. Rather, the leader *turns to members, inviting them* to *decipher together the meaning of the unexplained actions or behaviors*.

Once again, don't do for members what they can do for themselves. So, keep your own interpretation and hunches to yourself, turn to members, and invite them to speculate about the meanings. In so doing, you delegate to the group the responsibility of interpreting what is going on. As a result, they may gain a sense of self-agency and self-empowerment.

Meanings of behaviors may not expose themselves within a single incident, so try NOT to expect the full yield within one occurrence.

Following are *four types* of *unspoken dynamics* containing meanings and messages that merit process illumination. These behaviors include (1) puzzling group behaviors, (2) nonverbal behaviors, (3) omitted behaviors, and (4) the influence from the absent members.

Crack the Codes of Puzzling Group Behaviors

When spotting a puzzling group behavior, you may ask the group members what they make out of it:

[To the group] Right now I sense a great deal of tension in the room. I have felt this tension since Jane started talking. I wonder how you make sense of what Jane just said and what triggered this tension. [process illumination]

[To the group] I feel puzzled about the session and wonder whether the group is avoiding something. If so, why? [process illumination]

[To the group] I see that half an hour has gone by, but something seems to be going on here that is keeping us stuck. I would like to ask, can any of you identify what may be going on that is causing us to spin our wheels? [process illumination]

Decipher the Implication of Nonverbal Behaviors

About 65% of communication in groups takes place through nonverbal means (Burgoon et al., 1993; Pease & Pease, 2006), and these nonverbal behaviors tell more truth than do verbal ones. Indeed, Gazda (1989) suggests that we have more faith in the nonverbal should we come across any incongruence between the verbal and nonverbal.

In the group, nonverbal behaviors leak out messages that the conscious mind tries to conceal, making for a rich reservoir of data, available for the group to interpret and make meaning of.

The following nonverbal cues, as suggested by Yalom and Leszcz (2005), might warrant the group's exploration and speculation:

- Who chooses to sit where?
- Which members sit together?
- Who chooses to sit close to the leader, and who sits far away?
- Who sits near the door?
- Who comes to the meeting on time?
- Who is habitually late?
- Who looks at whom when speaking?

- Who looks at his or her watch?
- Who slouches in his or her seat?
- Who yawns?
- Who has his or her coat on?
- How quickly do the group members enter the room?
- How do they leave the room?
- How and when do members' postures shift?

In addition to the list above, don't forget about *tones of voice* and *facial expressions;* they contain rich data for uncovering meanings.

To invite the group to make an interpretation of nonverbal behaviors, you may try any of the following:

> [To the group] I wonder, what impressions do you get from Maria's nonverbal messages as she tells us her painful stories? Did you see anything in her nonverbal behavior that might be incongruent with her verbal expression? [third step of process illumination]

> Steve, I heard anger *in your voice* when you gave feedback to Noel. I wonder, what is it about Noel that makes you feel angry? [third step of process illumination]

> [To the group] I am not sure what is going on in our meeting today, but I do see some unusual things. For example, Jack has been quiet, Lee has moved his chair back about 3 feet, and Karen has been glancing at me for the past few minutes. What ideas do all of you have about these things?

The following comes from a reflective journal entry by Maria (the person in the first example) after listening to the group's interpretation of her incongruence:

> The most helpful feedback that I received was when I was told by Keith that *I related my painful story with a constant smile on my face.* How can I expect anyone to understand what is going on inside of me when my nonverbal behavior indicates that everything is fine? *I did not know I was smiling all the time until Keith said that.* Now I know what I have to do.

Decode the Meanings of Omitted Behaviors

That which is omitted in the group actually has a strong presence, drawing the group energy to it ever more. Omitted behaviors could include the following:

- Certain topics that are never talked about
- A specific person never giving feedback to another specific person
- A specific member never being confronted
- A particular member never being supported

When noticing any of these voids, you may invite your members to interpret the meanings behind what is not happening:

[To the group] I wonder, what is the underlying reason why Mary is *never* confronted? [process illumination]

[To the group] I am curious why Dean is *never* supported. Would anyone in the group like to share your observation? [process illumination]

Decipher the Influence of an Absent Member

Paradoxically, the influence from a member, positive or negative, speaks most clearly when that very member misses the session. Perhaps it is harder to heed the influence that a member is having on others when the group is busy interacting with the specific member. Surprisingly, when this given member skips the session, the group suddenly feels a change in its energy.

The leader may bring this change to the table for the group members to examine, helping them realize the impact that the member has on the group:

[To the group] Everyone seems more alive today than in past sessions. Even Kim, who has been quiet, has blossomed with animated self-expression today. *I wonder, what is it about today's session that makes the difference?* [starting a process illumination]

Later,

[To the group] What you have discussed today about the impact of Dale's behaviors on the group is very important. I am not surprised that the impact actually speaks louder when Dale is absent. I think Dale needs to be aware of these discussions about him. Therefore, we will need to bring this up with him when he returns next week. [further comment]

Another example,

> [To the group] Today everyone seems to feel helpless and threatened by the responsibility of making the group run. I wonder, *what is it about today that makes the difference?*

PROCESS ILLUMINATION TECHNIQUE (III): MAKE THE INVISIBLE VISIBLE

Bring Members' Blind Spots to Awareness

Through group interaction, each member's characteristic interpersonal style—his or her blind spot, so to speak—becomes visible to others in due course. For example, a member who resists engagement may think that he is not showing anything about himself. But his characteristic *defense against intimacy* actually speaks louder than he could have ever realized. Indeed, this defense goes back to his personal style of relating. And everyone in the group can see it—except him.

Examples of blind spots may include members' defenses used for handling challenges in the areas of conflict, power, and belonging. It is up to the leader to illuminate these blind spots so as to help the person increase awareness of how they co-create their own interpersonal realities. For example,

> [To the group] It seems that Labon still could not understand why Crisanna got so upset when he said to her that her reactions were her own problems and were totally irrelevant to him. If you were Crisanna, how would Labon's way of responding have an impact on you? [illuminating Labon's blind spot about the impact his dismissive style of communication has on others]

Make Inner Qualities Visible—Fostering a Sense of Psychological Visibility

The deepest, unexpressed, and hidden qualities of who we are often remain unrecognized by us *until accurately articulated by others.* Then, *a warm sense of psychological visibility washes over us, awakening our true self.*

Process illumination makes that happen: It gives members a sense of finally being seen by others, of finally being appreciated, of the capabilities, latent potentialities, and character traits never before being acknowledged or accepted. This sense of psychological visibility can heal many of our developmental problems, insecurities, and inadequacies in relationships.

To make members' inner qualities visible, consider the following process illumination:

[To the group] It would be especially helpful if the group could tell Peter something you see in him that Peter probably doesn't already see in himself. [the second tier, illuminating unrecognized traits]

[To the group] I wonder what the group knows about Mary that she might not know about herself. [second tier]

[To the group] I sense that members are experiencing a lot of emotions that are related to Shelly at this moment. It will be most helpful to Shelly if any of you can try out the following sentence, saying it directly to Shelly: "Shelly, when you . . . , I feel. . . . [second tier]

A reflective journal entry from a group member, Kathy, demonstrates how process illumination at this level brings about a sense of psychological visibility:

A powerful moment for me in the group tonight was when Sue reflected that I give generously to the group; however, I have never asked anything from the group. I felt awakened in hearing it. Later on, the leader asked me, "If there is one thing you could request from the group, what would it be?" Just for a moment, I stuck my turtle head out of its shell, so to speak, but didn't actually trust that my needs would be fulfilled. But when the group actually tried to meet my request of being appreciated just for "my being" instead of "my doing," I was very touched. All of a sudden, I had hope.

This little girl inside me has always felt unworthy or ashamed of myself; I feared that others who see the true me will abandon me. How I long for being loved just because I exist. Through tonight's group, I realized that I don't have to do anything to be valued by others; just my presence is enough—enough to make people desire a chance to get to know me further.

Still now as I write this, tears well up in my eyes due to a sense of awe and grace. I never thought people would see me and get me. Their way of seeing me allows me to see myself in a way that I never have before. The group session had a great healing impact, not only on my interpersonal relationship patterns but also on my intrapersonal patterns as well.

PROCESS ILLUMINATION TECHNIQUE (IV): EXPLORE THE MEANINGS OF BEHAVIORS ENGAGED BY "DYADS," "TRIADS," OR "THE GROUP AS A WHOLE"

When a group gets stuck, it is time to examine the group dynamics—a "dyad," "triad," or "the group itself" might have unconsciously engaged in unproductive dynamics. Though *subtle,* these dynamics have the power to stagnate the group. Recall the earlier example in this chapter:

(1) Mitch taking a risk to confront Charlie's drinking

(2) Charlie's clique colluding to dismiss Mitch

(3) The group remaining silent as if nothing happened

Faced with multiple dynamics surfacing all at once, the leader shall *deal with the tensest dynamics first*. In this case, it would be *in the order of the group, the colluding three, and then Mitch.* This section presents the techniques for how to illuminate these dynamics.

Illuminate the Meanings of Behaviors Engaged by "the Group as a Whole"

As a whole, the group can engage in unproductive behaviors, including but not limited to the following:

- Remaining on the surface (chit-chatting)
- Saying nothing when some tension is building up
- Avoiding addressing the elephant in the room
- Depending on a dominant member or the leader to get the group rolling
- Ignoring leaders' questions or comments
- Talking about something in a roundabout, indirect manner
- Establishing a take-turn format
- Slipping into the problem-solving mode
- Spending too much time on the very first person who speaks up
- Competing for who has the most dramatic story

Since the group as a whole is not likely to be aware of what the members collectively are doing, leaders need to create an opportunity to explore the meaning of these behaviors and to look into the *function* of these group dynamics—how are they serving the group? Consider the following examples:

First,

> [To the whole group] Let's stop for a moment. Something has just happened between Mitch, Charlie, Thomas, and Dane. The tension in the air is thick, *yet the rest of the group members have said nothing.* We need to look at what happened that caused this tension. But before that, I first would like to ask the group, what do you sense is going on at the group level? Why do the members not say anything?

Later,

> [To the whole group] Thank you, everyone, for admitting that as a group, you were using an avoidance strategy as a collective effort to ease your anxiety about the tension and conflict in the room. Can we talk about what impact this avoidant group behavior might have on individual group members? And what alternatives might be possible for us to ease the anxiety and, at the same time, get to the bottom of the tension and conflict?

Interpret the Meanings of "Dyad" or "Triad" Behaviors

"Dyad" or "triad" dynamics may include but are not limited to the following:

- Colluding
- Rescuing each other

To interpret the meanings of these "dyad" or "triad" dynamics, consider the following examples:

First,

> [To the whole group] Now that we are on the same page about how we can stay emotionally present when tension arises, let's look at the tension we all have sensed. What did you observe happened *when Mitch tried to confront Charlie's drinking*? What did Charlie, Thomas, and Dane do? And *why* did they do it? And how did it have an impact on others? [illuminating the dynamics of a triad]

Later,

> [To the subgroup] Thomas and Dane, is the group's observation on target?

Much later,

> [To the subgroup] It makes sense that when you saw your friend Charlie being challenged by Mitch, you wanted to give him a hand to help him out. Your desire to protect him came from a place of caring. However, I wonder whether this rescuing behavior is actually helping Charlie or whether it is derailing him from achieving his goal of developing emotional intimacy with people in his life? And what could you do as friends to help him in a different way that better serves his goals?

Finally, picking up the individual dynamics for processing,

> [Back to the group] Mitch took the risk of doing something unusual, that is, he confronted Charlie, but things did not turn out as he was hoping, and since then he has kept his head down and has not spoken a word. I wonder, if you were Mitch, what might your withdrawal be trying to convey?

> OK. I appreciate the group's recognition that Mitch was feeling let down when he most needed the group's back. I also appreciate the fact that Thomas, Dane, and Charlie also owned up to the impact of their behavior on Mitch. [summarizing the processing]

> [Turn to Mitch] Mitch, how do you respond to the comments from the members? What else needs to happen for you and the group to move forward?

PROCESS ILLUMINATION TECHNIQUE (V): LINK HERE-AND-NOW TO THERE-AND-THEN

The final touch of process illumination is to *link the here-and-now to the there-and-then*. As mentioned, how people behave in the group mirrors how they behave in their interpersonal fields outside the group—think of the group as *a live example* of the interpersonal field in which that member exists.

Given this, experienced leaders take every opportunity to link here-and-now process comments to members' outside worlds. In so doing, the leaders help members see the *parallel occurrences* between the two worlds, increasing their awareness of both strengths and blind spots. Without this last step of process illumination, member awareness may not be complete. See the following examples:

Julie, I wonder if there might be *people in your life* who feel the same way toward you as *the group members* do. That is, are there people who are attracted to you and want to get close to you but who sense your aloofness and misinterpret your fear of closeness as snobbishness? [process illumination]

Mark, I understand these ambivalent *feelings* you have *toward me* within our group. I cannot help but also wonder if you might have similar *feelings toward the authority figures in your past* that remain unresolved. Perhaps you might want to get in touch with these issues. [process illumination]

Dale, I wonder if *others in your life* might feel the same way as *the group members* do when you focus on negative aspects of others? I wonder what disadvantages this behavior brings you? Do you pay a price for it? [process illumination]

El, you said that you don't know why you are always attracted to aggressive women. And I have seen you, for the past 15 minutes, lock horns with Kathy, who assertively engages you with her questions. But in locking horns with Kathy, you have forgotten about the rest of the group. Many members of the group have been trying to get your attention but have failed. *I am struck by the parallel between what has happened here in the group and what happens in your relationships with women in your life.* I wonder if there may be nice "nonaggressive" women waiting on the fringe for you if you look around, but because you are so busy engaging with the ones with the loudest voices, you are unable to notice those nice, quiet women. [process illumination]

∞∞

In closing: Group dynamics are almost the "holy grail" of group counseling—earnestly pursued by all devoted group therapists. To hunt for the meaning hidden within this enigmatic object of interest—this highly complex, abstract, broad, and powerful phenomenon—we need to look into the way members *enact* the roles they play in their personal lives within the group.

To this aim, we keep ourselves hawk alert, looking out for *the reactivity markers.* As we see them, we *seize the moment* to decode these hidden meanings, to bring each member's characteristic interpersonal style into their consciousness or to examine the unproductive dynamics involved in a "dyad," "triad," or "the group as a whole." As we do so, we take stock of what is causing the intense reactions and what it means to the person.

In this relentless pursuit of the meanings of the process level of communication, we have a multitude of techniques to shed light on this enigmatic object of interest—the group dynamics.

A CASE IN POINT

The Case of Jean

Declining to Take Group Time. During the check-in of the eighth session, a member, Jean, shared briefly with the group an event that happened at work, earlier in the day, that made her feel as if no one cares for her. Historically, Jean had not really shared very much of her life with the group, although she had given other group members a lot of support and insight. Given that, the leader asked if she would like to take some group time to explore her feelings. Jean politely declined, saying that the event was really not that important.

As the unstructured session continued, however, Jean indirectly related to one member, Tom, and once again mentioned her feeling of *invisibility*.

Stirring the Pot—Moving From Outside Focus to Inside Focus. Seeing this as an opening, the leader asked Jean,

Jean, is there any time in the group when you feel invisible and find it difficult to fit in? [the first tier—moving from outside focus to inside focus]

Jean's face turned red. She obviously felt put on the spot, but she held herself together very well and admitted that, yes, she often felt invisible and unimportant *in the group,* just as she had always felt in her family. In response to Jean's honesty, the group members' ears perked up, and members started to extend warm words to her, affirming her for her valuable contributions. This made Jean feel more connected to the group.

Further Stirring the Pot. The leader sensed that there were still some core issues not yet touched upon. So, the leader took things one step further by using the stir-the-pot method:

[To the group] I would like to ask everybody here in the group, with whom in the group do you think Jean is likely to experience a sense of invisibility and with whom in the group is Jean more likely to feel validated and affirmed? [still the first tier of here-and-now]

The group became *fully animated* by this question. Two members of the group admitted that they probably had made Jean feel invalidated at some point in the group, and they apologized for that. The group also pointed out that Tom and Lisa were the two whom Jean would feel supported by.

Zigzagging. At some point, the hot seat was zigzagged to two other members, who then became the center of group discussion for a while because of their charged exchanges. The group quickly moved away from Jean and on to the new dynamics at hand.

Sitting quietly in her chair all the while, Jean looked like she was deep in her own thoughts as if she wanted to say something but couldn't quite do it. The group members had gotten so involved with the other two members who had more dramatic expressions that they had forgotten about the fact that Jean's issue was still unfinished.

Illuminating Jean's Invisibility in the Here-and-Now. Sensing that Jean's "button of invisibility" was being pushed once again, right here, right now, in the group, and that she was starting to retreat into herself (her characteristic interpersonal style), the leader got the group to *loop back* to Jean by saying,

[To the group] I wonder what the group imagines Jean to be feeling right now in the group.

Group Feedback on Jean's Mixed Signals. The members immediately realized that they had just recreated Jean's experience of "no one really cares about me." The group members reflected on that and gave feedback to Jean about how they received mixed signals from her at the beginning of the session and simply misread her true desire.

Jean opened up and said that she felt guilty taking group time and that she did not feel worthy of others' attention, and this was why she gave out mixed signals. Another member responded to Jean's sense of guilt and told her how important she was to him and that she deserved to get what she needed from the group.

Staying Longer at a Critical Point. Upon hearing these comments, tears flooded Jean's eyes. Something had happened inside of her. Sensing that this was a *critical point* for Jean, and that she needed the group to *stay a bit longer with her feeling,* the leader asked the group,

[To the group] Can any of you guess what Jean's tears are trying to say? And how do Jean's tears influence you? [the second tier here-and-now; to illuminate underlying meanings of aroused emotions and, at the same time, allow for a possible corrective emotional experience]

At this, members responded affectionately to Jean, unanimously saying that they felt close to her and were very happy to see her let her emotions show because they had often wondered about her and were concerned that she had been keeping her feelings to herself.

Corrective Emotional Experience for Jean With the Group. The group members' affectionate responses and warm acceptance were exactly the opposite of her earlier experience. The experience was healing and restored a sense of hope in Jean. Jean had a *corrective emotional experience* in the group in that session.

For the first time in her life, Jean felt totally free to be herself because she saw that people in the group truly cared about her, accepting her feelings and needs. For the first time in her life, she did not need to hide behind a facade of polite tranquility. Also, *for the first time, she "got it"; she realized that she sent out mixed signals that served only to defeat her own needs.* This experience became the landmark for Jean's personal growth.

EXERCISES

Scenarios for Your Practice

1. During the sixth session of a group for laid-off workers, you become aware that in the group Joe and Bill frequently support one another's statements but seldom comment when others speak. For many sessions, you have noticed them exchanging smiles and smirks when no one else in the group is smiling. You have a growing suspicion that they are forming a strong dyadic subgroup at the exclusion of the others. What are your options for dealing with this dynamic?

2. Lena relates to the group her personal experience with racism, saying that she feels strongly that it was a critical factor in her brother's death as a young adult. Tex (who has been asked by his employer to join this group to increase his interpersonal sensitivity) asks in response, "While I'm sorry for your brother's death, aren't you just dredging up the ancient history of slavery to say that it's racially motivated?" How might you work with this dynamic as it arises in the moment?

3. In a general personal growth group, you become aware that Martin tends to adopt a posture that appears to be physically quite tense and that he often seems to offer judgments about situations that other members describe. You also notice that he fails to connect with any other

members on a feeling level. When fellow group member Joe states that he has decided to get a divorce, Martin begins grilling him about whether Joe's efforts to keep the marriage intact have been strong enough. How would you choose to handle this dynamic?

4. It is the fifth session of a support group. As she has done in each of the past two sessions, June immediately starts the session by launching into a recitation of her difficult experiences during the past week. You realize that you have not heard much from about five of the other eight members. Only Augie has been able to get in much airtime over June. What issues are involved here? What would you do to handle the dynamics at hand?

5. Frowning a bit, Joe says to Martin, "I wasn't asking that you evaluate or even agree with my decision to get a divorce. After agonizing about this decision for a very long time, I only wanted to share the pain and difficulty of it with others here." Martin responds defensively, "Well, I strongly believe that you will never feel good about making a bad decision." What are the processes involved, and how would you choose to address them?

6. You are facilitating a support group for people going through a divorce. During your initial introduction to the group members, one of the members asks you very sternly, "If you haven't been divorced yourself, how can you possibly help us?" What underlying issues are at the heart of this type of confrontation? What are some possible responses you could make to address these underlying issues?

7. Chloe tells the group, "You know, last night I found this great group on the Internet where I can say all I want to say without interruption, unlike what usually happens in *this* group whenever I want to say something." As the leader of this group, how would you respond?

Self-Reflection

1. Think back to any instances in which you felt like you were in the hot seat. How did you react? What feelings arose for you? Did your relationship to others who were involved change as a result? Overall, did you experience a positive outcome? How might this experience affect your approach to dealing with hot seat issues in groups that you will lead?

2. In your family of origin, how were intense emotions handled? Were they often ignored, deflected, or resolved in some significant way? Depending on how your family responded, how did this affect your past and current tendencies to respond in certain ways to intense relationship issues?

3. Can you recall a situation from your family of origin or with friends in which you suddenly became aware of an elephant in the room that others were failing to mention? What was it like for you to be in this situation where some problem became very obvious, yet no one seemed to want to acknowledge it? How did you react at the time? Was there any long-term influence on you as a result of this experience?

4. Of the four hot buttons of intimacy, power, competition, and control, which button are you most susceptible to having pushed? That is, which of these topics is likely to be the most difficult for you to handle without losing your cool or shutting down emotionally?

CHAPTER 13

USING PSYCHODRAMA FOR UNRESOLVED PAIN

There may come a time when a group member divulges an unresolved pain and loss, and the here-and-now method is inadequate to heal it. Using their instincts, group members will often stay in an empathic mode with the person. This results in the group spending the entire session trying to soothe the person's pain and loss, regretfully leading to a lack of deep work. Facing this unique challenge, the leader needs an alternative method to optimize the group functioning, and simultaneously, expediting the healing for the person in pain.

Enter psychodrama.

As a type of experiential therapy, *psychodrama* uses deep action methods to explore and work through issues identified by clients. Though a full-out psychodrama is best conducted by a *psychodrama* director (a therapist trained in this method), small doses of psychodrama can be put into practice by a beginning group therapist. This chapter proposes just this kind of small-dose psychodrama technique. Used properly, a small dosage of these solutions can speed up the healing process for those suffering from unresolved pain, disenfranchised loss, trauma, and trapped emotions.

THE POWER OF PSYCHODRAMA IN THERAPY

In sharp contrast to talk therapy, psychodrama uses an *action method* to do therapy (Dayton, 1994). Powerful, flexible, and adaptable to all treatment settings, it reaches the zenith of all experiential therapies. Psychodrama can be traced back to the early work of Jacob L. Moreno (1946), the founder of psychodrama (Hagedorn & Hirshhorn, 2009). Though replete with action-oriented techniques, psychodrama is greater than the sum of a combination of techniques. We need to understand the principles and concepts behind the techniques so that we can properly transpose them to a group counseling setting.

Liberated Self-Expression and Heightened Awareness

Experiential methods, like psychodrama, fuel the power of therapy by setting clients free from experiential avoidance and suppression, plunging them into a liberating kind of self-expression unimagined by the clients (Bannister, 2003; Casson, 2004; Longo, 2004; Moreno, 2005). Such energy can certainly liven up a sluggish or deadlocked group.

For example, Dayton (2005) finds that experiential techniques work effectively in helping members deal with addiction-related losses and grief, providing opportunities for the addict to develop heightened self-awareness and personal empowerment.

Corrective Emotional Experiences and a Sense of Closure

Psychodrama techniques create opportunities for group members to do, say, or hear in the *here-*and-*now,* what they could not do, say, or hear in the there-and-then (Dayton, 1994). Therefore, in a sense, psychodrama uses actions to provide for clients' *corrective emotional experiences* (Alexander & French, 1946; Yalom & Leszcz, 2005).

Through corrective emotional experiences, *members are given the very thing that their lives failed to give them*—interpreting and experiencing the past emotional event in new ways, integrating the compartmentalized or disowned emotions into their whole being. This corrective experience not only brings *a sense of closure* to an unspeakable pain but also achieves *emotional integration.*

Enactment and the Shift Between the Experiencing Ego and the Observing Ego

A key therapeutic agent in psychodrama, enactment puts an emotional event into action (Keats & Sabharwal, 2008; Paré, Bondy, & Malhotra, 2006; Westwood, Keats, & Wilensky, 2003). Moreno (1978) often uses *enactment* to bring clients' interactional difficulties into the session. Applied in the group setting, reenactment brings the past to the present, allowing members to work through unfinished business in a favorable way (Ferencik, 1991). Applied in individual therapy, enactment—as with the empty chair technique—brings clients' *internalized figures* (that they have in their minds) into the here-and-now, allowing clients to reconstruct their "encounters" in a therapeutic way (Chen & Giblin, 2018).

During enactment, members shift back and forth between a state of the "experiencing ego" and a state of the "observing ego" (Kellermann, 1979). When in the state of *the experiencing ego,* the member feels and senses what is occurring in his or her mind and body at each present moment, whereas, in the state of the observing ego, he or she *reflects on* the meanings associated with the sensations and reactions. We can say that the observing ego represents our rational adult self, while the experiencing ego represents the sensitive child self.

Once the enactment completes, the clients are free to transfer the skills and insights that they gained through the here-and-now, to the there-and-then of their lives (Woodward, 2004). This is in keeping with the tenet of group counseling and therapy.

BASIC CONCEPTS OF PSYCHODRAMA APPLICABLE TO GROUP PRACTICE

Group therapists can easily integrate many basic psychodrama methods into regular group sessions. It often amazes us how much more creative and effective our sessions become even when a simple psychodrama technique is applied to a group session. This section presents some basic concepts of psychodrama (Dayton, 1994; 2005; Karp, Holmes, & Tauvon, 2005; Pines, 1986) applicable to group counseling. Later sections will provide detailed case examples to illustrate how to implement these concepts in group therapy.

The Protagonist (the Presenting Member, the Main Player)

In their interaction with others, group members often bring their *internalized significant figures and family systems,* as in the way of transferences (Kernberg, 1995; Roisman, Madsen, Hennighausen, Sroufe, & Collins, 2001). Through enactment, members not only experience the internalized interpersonal system in the here-and-now but also undergo a therapeutic breakthrough. The member, to whom the enactment surrounds, is the *protagonist.* In a group, two or more people might engage as *coprotagonists* to work through conflicts or experience something new. On occasion, the group therapist will take on a coprotagonist role to explore certain transference dynamics or deal with a challenge.

The Double (the Inner Self or Different Voice of the Presenting Member)

During enactment, a few group members can take on the role of *the protagonist's double*—the protagonist's "inner self," a dream figure, a wiser and older self, or an emerging new self. Under skillful facilitation, the double can explicitly express the emerging voice or the voice that the protagonist has repressed.

Our group members like to use the term *alter ego* (another side of oneself; a second self) for the double. Since it makes sense to them, we often go along with it. The double has proven to be a powerful psychodrama technique through which the healing of unresolved pain can take place.

The Auxiliary (Other Participating Members) and the Reformed Auxiliary

Under skillful facilitation, members who play an auxiliary or a reformed auxiliary have the capacity to communicate a new level of understanding and empathy to the protagonist that goes beyond words. What is the auxiliary? And what is the reformed auxiliary?

- The *auxiliary* refers to a member who enacts the role of *someone* in the protagonist's life—*a family member, friend, supervisor, or some other person*. Of course, the auxiliary might also portray *different roles within the mind of the protagonist*—for instance *the bully, the vulnerable child,* or so on.

Auxiliaries often are able to raise very intuitive and insightful points that might never have occurred to the group facilitator. This supports Moreno's contention that, in group therapy, every member becomes *the agent of healing* for other members.

- The *reformed auxiliary* is another useful concept in healing unresolved pain. The reformed auxiliary takes on the role of the internalized other—the significant figure from the member's past who got internalized in the member's mind. With proper facilitation, the reformed auxiliaries have the capacity to hear and validate what the protagonist (the presenter) has endured. Their abilities to hear and validate the protagonist often bring healing to the injuries or losses long suffered.

Please keep in mind that when working with traumatized members, it is recommended that you enact the reformed auxiliary, instead of the auxiliary, so as to avoid retraumatizing the presenting member.

The Director (the Group Facilitator)

The *director*—the group leader—facilitates the enactment of a member's internalized interpersonal dynamics in the group. The director facilitates when the protagonist needs to try on a different role or when the supporting players (auxiliaries) need to portray some internalized significant figures.

A good director should be "person-centered"—keep the needs of the protagonist (main player) top of mind—so that he or she directs the enactment in a way that meets the needs of the protagonist, rather than imposing any assumption or frame of reference on the main player.

The Audience at Large (the Group Itself)

The audience at large—the group itself—provides an emotional space where a sense of intensified reality can be felt by the main player enacting his or her issues.

The group itself acts as *a reality check* because the more people who have seen and heard the member's expression, the less likely the member is to retreat behind habitual defenses. The audience (the group) is of maximum use when providing feedback during processing.

MAXIMIZING THE GROUP'S HEALING POWER WITH PSYCHODRAMA TECHNIQUES

In individual therapy, the Gestalt approach uses psychodrama in the form of *monodrama* (Dayton, 1994; 2005) wherein the individual client plays all parts, and the dialogue is with "the empty chair" (Chen & Giblin, 2018). While the empty chair technique can certainly expose how clients project their own perceptions onto their internalized significant others, it lacks the added dynamics that can be experienced by having multiple auxiliaries (or reformed auxiliaries) *portray the internalized others.*

To be fair, monodrama has the power to help clients shift back and forth between a state of the "experiencing ego" and a state of the "observing ego" (Kellermann, 1979). However, it does not have the same level of enthusiasm that comes with the vivid encounter of several reformed *auxiliaries* or with *coprotagonists*, enacting the internalized others.

Group therapists can adopt numerous basic psychodrama techniques to provide meaningful and healing encounters for members, without having to go through the intense formal training of becoming a certified psychodramatist (Dayton, 2005; Karp et al., 2005; Pines, 1986). Due to space limitation, this chapter will focus on demonstrating two psychodrama techniques:

- Reformed auxiliaries
- The doubles

Case Scenario 1: Jeff

Jeff presented a history of being bullied during his early life. The effect of this painful event continues to haunt him to this day. As he told the group about his experience, his voice quivered, his hands trembled, and he reported that his heart was pounding.

During this particular session, Jeff spoke of how he hated soccer as a child because he was tortured by his teammates. Adding insult to injury, his coach and the parents of his teammates joined forces to scold him for his less than perfect performances. He was able to rationalize why his teammates acted like jerks, but he could not understand why the adults also treated him, to use Jeff's words, "like shit." He thought that he must be truly worthless to deserve such treatment.

Setting Up the Enactment of the Reformed Auxiliaries

The group members had compassion for Jeff's unresolved pain and suffering, yet they felt at a loss for how to help him heal from it. The leader decided to engage the group with the psychodrama technique, by enacting the reformed auxiliary:

[To the whole group] Jeff has suffered from the humiliation of bullying long enough. I wonder whether we can try something to help him release his pain. I wonder who among you might want to *take on the roles* of the bullying kids, the coach, or the bullying parents? If you do, please use your imagination, put yourself in the role, and say something with emotions, something from the heart—*something that Jeff needs to hear but never did*. When you are ready, please speak to Jeff directly.

The Reformed Auxiliaries Speak

Upon the leader's direction, many members jumped in to participate in the enactment. The following are the words of the reformed auxiliaries, verbatim:

Ginger enacting the role of a reformed bully parent:

Jeff, I am so sorry. All I was thinking about was winning, and I did not even see the little boy who I was yelling at. If a parent had spoken to my kid the way I spoke to you, I would have punched him. I forgot the purpose of soccer, which is to teach teamwork and how to support each other. I acted the exact opposite. I was sorry the moment I said those horrible words, and I was so embarrassed when I got home, but I never had the courage to apologize. Now that you brought it up, you have given me another opportunity to say how sorry I am. Thank you for being strong enough to talk about it today. I am so sorry that I was an adult bully. I am so sorry that you have carried this pain with you all these years, and I am the cause of that pain. I hope that you can accept my apology.

Sabrina enacting the role of a reformed coach:

Jeff, I want you to know that I behaved selfishly as a coach, and all that I wanted was to win. Winning was more important than a child's soul, a child's well-being. As a coach, it is my job to foster an environment where a child can grow—not just win the game. I was so focused on winning that I failed you. I failed to see the little soul inside you that was hurting. I failed to stop a parent from behaving in a completely unreasonable and unacceptable way. It was my job to step in, and I didn't. I wronged you, and for that, I am so, so sorry. If I could have known how much damage I was doing at the time, I would never have said those things or acted in ways that hurt you and failed to protect you. I wish I could go back and change that; you didn't deserve it. You were a child.

Tim enacting the role of one of the bully kids:

Jeff, I'm so sorry for the way I treated you, for the way we all treated you. I just wanted to be one of the guys, to belong. Somehow, for some reason, I don't remember or maybe for no reason at all, we picked you to be the scapegoat. We all played; we could have won together or lost together, but we blamed you so that we didn't look bad—it was so much easier, but it was chicken shit. We didn't have the balls to be a team. I just want you to know that it wasn't you—it was me, it was us, and I'm sorry.

Jerome enacting the role of one of the bully kids:

Jeff, I'm so sorry for what I said. I said it because I wanted to be like everyone else, and I don't feel good about myself. I wanted security, and I found it in going along with the crowd. I felt very afraid and insecure. I want to make amends and be your friend.

Tabu enacting the role of one of the bully kids:

Jeff, man, I'm really sorry for being such a dick to you on the team. Playing soccer is supposed to be a fun and happy time, but I helped make it a hellish experience for you. I had some stuff going on with myself; I didn't feel very confident or like myself much back then. And I took my frustration out on you. I'm sorry, Jeff, for the pain and embarrassment I caused you.

The Impact of the Psychodrama on Jeff

It was a powerful experience for everybody and especially for Jeff. At home, Jeff had a quiet moment to reflect on the impact the psychodrama had on him, which he recorded in his journal and shared with the group in a later session:

I was feeling really nervous right after sharing the part about how the parents made fun of me; I noticed that my voice cracked a little, and I felt somewhat embarrassed and wanted to hide. When other group members enacted the role of the coach, the parents, and my teammates, I was all over the place emotionally.

Initially, I felt a surge of anger. I harbored so much anger against my coach, the teammates, and parents that I didn't feel like forgiving them; I kept thinking, "You have wronged me. You have hurt me more than you can possibly imagine. Why should I forgive you?"

However, I noticed a switch with my emotions when Ginger was taking on the role of one of the parents. Ginger said something along the lines of, "I got carried away, and I'm so ashamed and sorry for what I did to you." At that moment, it was as if all of the anger I've harbored over the years started to melt away. I felt the sincerity of the apology, and it made me feel lighter and calm.

I remember thinking at that moment that I have let these people affect me for far too long and that I gave them way too much power over me. I started to see that I needed to let go of my anger with these people, for it did not benefit me in any way.

I was also touched by Tabu taking on the role of my teammates. Tabu mentioned that he only mocked me because he had his own issues to deal with and that he was taking his frustration out on me. This moment somehow struck me and left me speechless. I hated the kid that Tabu portrayed the most, but after hearing Tabu, I started to pity him and actually had empathy for him as well.

Collectively, I felt touched by everyone who enacted a role for me. Part of me wanted to say "thank you" to each of the group members, but I felt somewhat embarrassed since I have never had so much focus on me during the group. That being said, I felt closer and a stronger bond with everyone in the group. I truly felt touched by everyone's efforts to resolve my pain; I don't think I'll ever be able to thank them enough. It was a difficult experience to go through, especially since I'm not used to being the focus of group, but it was necessary. From this experience, I feel that I can trust other people and that I can start to let my guard down more.

Case Scenario 2: Sami

Sami presented her life-long struggle with her brother. In a nutshell, Sami has taken care of her ailing parents since she was a child—an incredibly time-intensive sacrifice that took a toll on her energy and robbed her of her childhood. Her brother always smirked and laughed at her as if she was nothing. He even accused her of having an ulterior motive for taking care of their parents. He claimed that even though he was not educated, he could see why Sami did what she did. He said he knew her intentions. At this, Sami felt deeply hurt and judged. This was devastating to Sami.

Sami was obviously in pain. She talked on and off over several sessions about this unfinished business with her brother. She even labeled it as trauma for her. But the way she presented her stories was with a coy smile on her face, explaining away everything she said and talking in circles.

The group asked Sami what she would like to say to her brother if she got a chance, but she seemed uneasy, not knowing what to say. Her conflicting thoughts and emotions were all jumbled. She just continued her way of explaining and talking in circles. You could see that other group members in the room started to feel disengaged, tuned-out, or bored.

Setting Up the Enactment of the Doubles

Knowing that Sami is from a culture where direct communication is not the norm, the leader sensed that Sami might need some help from the group in dislodging her "traumatic" experience with her brother and to experience something new and healing.

The leader decided that it was time to invite group members to take on the role of Sami's double in an effort to help her express her hidden feelings:

[To the whole group] It seems that Sami would benefit from expressing her suppressed feelings toward her brother so that a sense of justice can shine in her heart again. But the culture that she comes from has prohibited her from expressing those feelings. I wonder whether some of you could take on the role of Sami's doubles? Please speak on Sami's behalf and give a voice to those feelings. When you are ready, please stand beside Sami and touch her shoulder as you speak.

The Doubles Speak

Ginger enacted the role of Sami's double, and with emotion, she spoke to her brother:

I don't know why you complain about what I am doing. I am doing my best, and although I would love you to help me, I do not expect that. I do, however, expect you to support me with kindness. It hurts me when you laugh at what is happening in our family. It infuriates me when you smirk. It is almost as if you are happy to see our parents in pain. I would love for you to help me and guide me, but you chose not to, so I am only able to do what I know.

As Ginger spoke, she was partly channeling the emotions that she felt toward her recently deceased sister. She did an incredible job of speaking from the heart to Sami's brother. Sami immediately became emotional and covered her face as the tears flowed. Terri and Tim also spoke on behalf of Sami, as she continued to cry.

Terri enacted the role of Sami's double:

Azad, I know you have a different way of handling things than I do, but I wish you would have just asked me if I needed anything or if I needed your help. Just knowing that you cared would have helped me so much with taking care of our parents. Instead, you would just smirk and laugh and discredit my work. I'm so upset that you would ever question my motivation behind taking care of our parents. I can't believe you would think that I just wanted their money or house. I was taking care of them because they are our parents, and I love them.

Tim enacted the role of Sami's double:

Azad, I am sooooo angry at you . . . so hurt. I don't know how you could possibly think that I have any other motive to care for our parents other than love. How dare you question me! And where were you when I needed help? Nowhere to be found! You left me all alone with them. I had no one to turn to. Instead, you just smirked at them as if you didn't care. How could you?!

The Impact of the Psychodrama on Sami and Group Members

Ginger wrote in her journal:

I was excited to see that Terri offered her voice to Sami because I knew in a sense that Terri was talking to her own brother who has a similar attitude. I was actually talking to my sister. I felt that the group spoke what Sami was truly feeling inside. I saw Sami break down and succumb to those feelings that she has long pushed away. It was a beautiful sight.

Terri wrote in her journal:

I felt very motivated to speak as Sami's double because I knew there were also things I needed to say to my brother. By giving Sami the language she needed to stand up to her brother, I also gathered the language I needed to speak with my brother about our past with our dad. It was very therapeutic for me and I actually imagined my brother standing in front of me as I was speaking as Sami's double.

I believe Sami really needed this because, during this activity, she broke down in tears. I believe she was so moved by what I, Tim, and Ginger said. She needed to hear all of it. She needed to hear the words herself. She needed to imagine it and experience it for herself. I think before this enactment, Sami could never imagine speaking honestly from her heart to her brother, let alone come up with the language for it. I believe that after this activity, it changed Sami's perspective. She has made a small step toward coming to terms with what happened between her and her brother.

This enactment really helped me because I honestly never thought about my brother when it came to my relationship with my dad and how I felt stuck in the middle with my mom and dad's fighting. I just naturally took on that role of being the caretaker and being there for my mom when she was upset about my dad. I never even thought twice about where my brother was or why he wasn't there for my mom like I was.

After Sami spoke about how unfair it felt that she had to take care of everything and her brother did not, it somewhat hit me. Where was my brother during this time? Where is he now? Why does he not seem bothered or fazed by what my dad did to our family? Does he not care? Why did he never ask how I was doing or feeling? Why did he never ask if I needed help? As Sami was speaking about this, it kind of bothered me. All these thoughts started bubbling up that I had never even thought about before. I got somewhat angry with my brother. I was in the same boat with Sami; there was no way I would ever speak to my brother about it. My brother and I barely speak, to begin with, so speaking to him about something so heavy would make me nervous and uncomfortable.

Before the group, I felt like no one would understand how I was feeling if they didn't have a father who was a drug addict and alcoholic. I now see that people can go through different situations but still find ways to connect. Like Sami and I, even though her dad was not a drug addict, she and I have experienced similar feelings, even though our situations are so different. This is what I love about the group. This really is the power of group for me.

Finally, this is what Sami wrote in her journal:

While Ginger, Tim, and Terri were speaking to my brother as my doubles, I literally felt that they were speaking what I feel in my heart. I cried so hard that I had to use my hands to cover my face. I have never cried like this before on this issue. Perhaps it is because, at that moment, I felt understood for the first time in my life regarding this issue. I felt heard and touched. My emotions and feeling have never been understood with such a depth before. Never. Those three members touched my heart, my soul, and so I just could not contain my emotions.

I have some deep anger and hurt that I have never expressed. I have bottled them up inside. My past experiences with my brother, his ways, and his behaviors, had affected me so deeply that I wasn't able to forget. Those were things I was unable to explain to others, but they did hurt me so deep down.

But as Ginger, Tim, and Terri were speaking to my brother as my doubles, I was able to cry and grieve. I was grieving for myself. I really imagined as if I was saying all that to him, and through saying it, I could grieve.

Although I can't change my brother's behavior, his mentality, or his thoughts, I am able to grieve now and have some peace with my past. With it, I will be able to take him as he is and not let him hurt me anymore. This experience has been a powerful therapy for me; that is why I felt so lighthearted the next morning.

Case Scenario 3: Gina

Gina told the group about two heart-wrenching events: First, her unresolved grief surfaced each time she ran into the daughter of the man who killed her father in a car accident, and second, her grief overwhelmed her whenever she felt again the crude treatment that her relatives gave to her family, after her father's death.

In Gina's case, feedback was not what she needed for emotional healing; what she needed was something else. She needed to close the wounds. To achieve this, the leader asked the group to do the following to help Gina develop a new perspective:

[To the group] We can clearly see that Gina is carrying around an unbearable pain.

She is repeatedly hurt by the cold attitudes of the people who killed her father. In addition to losing her father, she also lost her relatives, who treated her family's grief in a heartless, uncaring way. There are so many feelings of anger, hurt, pain, and sadness that prevent Gina from moving on. At this moment, I would like all of you *to imagine that you are Gina's father, and you are in this room now, seeing your daughter's pain. What would you say to your daughter so that she can resolve this intolerable pain and move on with her life?* Please take a moment to reflect on what you would say. When you are ready, please speak to directly to Gina.

Due to space limitations, we will not include examples of what members said to Gina in the role of the double.

Allowing Members to Express Newly Surfaced Feelings

To complete the experience of emotional integration, the leader may ask a member to express any feelings that surfaced. It can be done through journaling or in-group expression.

A DETAILED CASE

Case Scenario of Joe—Unresolved Traumas

- Presenting problem: Anxiety and panic attack

Joe's original presenting problem was an acute anxiety that he had been unable to shake. In the ninth session, Joe decided to pursue his anxiety issue in the group in the hopes that the group would be able to help ease his anxiety.

Joe shared with the group that approximately 2 years ago, he suffered a panic attack at work and ended up in the emergency room. After that, he sought individual counseling and continued to suffer minor bouts of panic. From time to time, he found himself losing control of his emotions, particularly nostalgia, sentimentality, and melancholy.

- September 11: The trigger

The September 11th terrorist attack, which happened a few months before Joe joined the group, had triggered major anxiety and agitation at his job and in his personal life. It stirred up traumatic memories and feelings from a tragic school shooting that occurred when he was a teen.

- **The past trauma**

In that shooting, numerous children died but several classrooms of other children were led to safety by an unwitting hero—Joe. Still at a tender age, Joe managed to execute extraordinary and unthinkable actions to lead them to safety.

When he went home, his mother not only did not acknowledge his actions but reprimanded him for not finding his sister early enough. His father watched by the side, failing to defend Joe against his mother. Joe felt a mixture of hurt and sadness because he received no acknowledgment from his parents either for the traumatic event he endured or for his actions of saving other kids.

- **Retraumatization**

The 9/11 attack brought retraumatization for Joe. He became emotional and reactive, even harsh with a colleague who wouldn't allow anyone to talk about 9/11. Without knowing Joe's PTSD, Joe's supervisor reprimanded him for the emotional display and subsequently threatened him with a demotion.

- **A theme of abandonment**

Joe went on to disclose more pain in his adult life with regard to addiction, losing friends, being abandoned by his significant other, and his unconventional lifestyle practice. As Joe told his stories, a theme of emotional abandonment seemed to run through his life. He felt abandoned by his parents who were emotionally unavailable to him. Indeed, as a kid, he was forced by his father to take on a caretaking role of his ailing mother.

This caretaking dynamic had been repeated in Joe's failed marriages. He has always been the caretaker and never received the nurturance of being taken care of. When he hit bottom as an addict, his friends, who enjoyed the substance use together with him, vanished into thin air, nowhere to be found to support him on his road to recovery. And of course, he had felt abandoned by his supervisor at work.

All of these abandonment and betrayal issues combined to create an undercurrent of anxiety in him that could surface at any time, and Joe was terrified of having more panic attacks.

- **The group trying to help Joe heal his deep pain**

As Joe told his stories in a raw and messy way, group members sensed a deep anguish within him; a churning tide of pain, sorrow, suffering, and torment.

Many members of the group found it grueling to listen to his stories. They did not know what to do with all the information Joe laid out to the group. They did not know which issue to remedy first. Furthermore, Joe seemed to clearly recognize the pattern of abandonment in his life. He had tremendous insight into his childhood trauma and how it continued to influence his current life. Additional insight was not what he needed.

So how could the group help? The group worked hard to provide Joe with empathy. They reflected the fear and vulnerability Joe was feeling inside. Yet, any empathy they gave seemed feeble in light of the massive suffering that Joe continued to carry with him.

Setting Up the Enactment of the Reformed Auxiliaries

The group was beginning to feel anxious, and a sense of powerlessness pervaded the air. At this moment, the leader (Mei) asked the group to do a psychodrama experiential exercise to provide Joe with some emotional healing and integration:

[To the group] "Joe has talked about a long history of abandonment and betrayal by his supervisor, family, and friends since an early age. In light of the panic attacks that he has been experiencing, I wonder whether we as a group could try out an exercise with Joe. I'd like to see if each of you could choose a role from one of the persons (either his supervisor, father, mother, ex-wife, or friend) who abandoned or betrayed Joe in some way. As you take on that role, please say something to Joe that your heart wants him to hear so that healing can begin. [pause] When you are ready, please jump in and speak directly to Joe."

The Reformed Auxiliaries in Action

Everyone in the group took on the role of a specific person who had let Joe down at some time in his life and apologized to Joe. Due to space limitation, we will skip the examples of what the members said to Joe in their roles of being the reformed auxiliaries.

Many members had tears in their eyes as they enacted the role they picked. After each member offered a heartfelt apology, there was a moment of deep silence. A sense of spirituality and emotional connection pulsated in the room.

The Impact of Psychodrama on Joe

Joe was visibly emotional. His face got flushed, and he appeared to be struggling to control his emotions. He admitted afterward that he was trying hard not to cry. Joe had difficulty speaking at first because he was so emotional. It was obvious that the group had struck a chord with him. He stated that what Shina, Kim, and Mei had said affected him the most while they were portraying his parents and his supervisor. After the session, Joe reflected on his experiences in his journal.

I had an "aha" experience when the group addressed my trauma. I was able to take a vague and unspecific problem, such as anxiety, and turn it into something more concrete and deeper emotionally. What really hit home for me was listening to Shina portraying my father and Mei portraying my former supervisor. Somehow, when Shina (portraying my father) asked my forgiveness for failing to protect me from my mother's emotional excess and drama, it really got to me, I felt like I was going to lose it right then and there. Mei sensed it and asked me to close my eyes. I was then able to pull it together and continue listening to Shina.

When Mei took the role of my supervisor, I was amazed at how perceptive she was. She asked for forgiveness for shaming, blaming, and threatening me for my September 11 related reactions. When she further apologized for causing me so much anguish, fear, and pain, I realized it was exactly what I had wanted and needed all along. It truly amazes me how much an apology could mean to me. The fact that I was hurt and harmed and I deserved an apology was such a simple fact. However, it had somehow escaped me throughout my life.

Kim summed it up for me by portraying my mom with a simple, no-frills message, "I am sorry, and I love you even though I could not express it at times!" I had come further along in forgiving my mother than I realized.

Everybody surprised me that night! My sibling rivalry with Jim and Ron in the group ended that night. My transference with the leader melted away when she reached out to me in her enactment as my supervisor. I am so moved that even with their own struggles, all members stayed real, empathetic, caring, wise and perceptive.

The Impact of Psychodrama on Group Members Helping Joe

Anna's reflections:

When the leader invited the group to enact a role in Joe's life and say something to him, I struggled with it. I felt tears in my eyes, and I still am not sure of the reason. Maybe I feel as if I need an apology from people who hurt me in my past as well, but I am not brave enough to ask. In the session, I tried hard not to problem solve—something I tend to do. I felt close to Joe during and after the session. In the lobby, I hugged him. I realized my own needs for some sort of apology,

Ron's reflections:

As Joe shared the horror of not being able to find his sister and feeling so responsible and scared about how his parents would react if he didn't find her and watch out for her, I felt angry. When I heard of his mother's response when he did show up with his sister, I was even angrier. I could only imagine being that scared young Joe and getting a totally inappropriate response, not getting what he needed—to be held and cared for. I was very aware that my anger actually came from my own feelings about the lack of love, understanding, and being cared for in my own early life. I felt sad for Joe. I was deeply moved as each group member enacted a role in Joe's life and responded to him. I was especially moved as Shina took the role of Joe's father. As it turned out, that was one sharing that touched Joe deeply. I later realized that the "father" piece in my own life still remains unresolved but I learned so much about myself from Joe's story.

Jim's reflections:

When Joe said that he wished his mom could be made aware of her past transgressions, I remarked that she probably never will be cognizant of those past events. I was comparing my mom's similar reactions when I discussed my past with her. My mom has total amnesia about my childhood emotional distress. "That never happened!" she would say.

My mom never came to my rescue either. My stepfather was very authoritative and oppressive in his parenting style. He was also very distant with his feelings, and I cannot remember one nice thing he ever said to me. So, when Joe brought up this issue of abandonment, it really hit home!

This experience really shed a light on my own unresolved issues of abandonment. I wonder if this has any connection with how I am emotionally distant with my wife and kids?

I felt closer to Joe. I felt like I wanted to be his mentor. I wanted to educate him to be wise and selective about his disclosures at work. Joe naively thought that by boldly disclosing, in the work setting, about his unconventional life style practice and his addiction recovery, he would be rewarded with newfound freedom and it would be a cleansing catharsis for him. Instead, he only stumbled upon betrayal!

I saw a similar fellow at my agency do that and he experienced the same "fall from grace" that Joe did. I was thinking to myself, "My god, Joe, don't you realize how open you are to the wolves, sharks, and jerks out there?"

I wanted to teach Joe about human nature and office politics, but I realize that this insight must come from his own personal experience.

∞∞

In closing: There may come a time when a group member divulges unresolved pain, disenfranchised loss, trauma, and trapped emotions—a time when neither the empathy nor the here-and-now method proves inadequate for healing it. Facing this unique challenge, the leader needs an alternative method to optimize the group functioning, and simultaneously, expediting the healing for the person in pain.

Psychodrama foots the bill through its use of deep action to explore and work through issues identified by clients. Used properly, a small dosage of psychodrama techniques can set clients free from experiential avoidance and suppression, plunging them into a liberating kind of self-expression unimagined by the clients.

Two particular beginning levels of psychodrama techniques—reformed auxiliaries and the doubles—particularly fuel the group with its power to provide the members with *corrective emotional experiences,* as illustrated by the above four cases.

EXERCISES

Scenarios for Your Practice

1. Revisit Sami's psychodrama experience. In a double enactment, a group member says something that is perceived by Sami as culturally stereotypical. How do you navigate this situation as the group leader?

2. Revisit Jeff's psychodrama experience. After the experience, while still in session, Jeff was unable to share his appreciation with the group citing a "loss for words." In his reflection, he seemed to have a lot to say. In the next session, he did not offer to share this reflection. As the group leader, how might you assist Jeff?

3. In a reenactment exercise, Monica experiences panic-attack symptoms of perspiration, shortness of breath, tightening of the chest, and disorientation. As the group leader, how will you address this situation? How will you go about enactments in the future with this group?

4. During a reformed auxiliary re-enactment for Eric, Joseph takes the side of the oppressor and exerts his feelings that Eric was just weak for not being able to stand up to the bully. This irritates Joseph and other members of the group. Joseph replies, "I'm just sayin' . . . ." As the leader, what is your response?

5. In a group session, you attempt to introduce the double psychodrama exercise. After multiple explanations, the group finally seems to understand the exercise. After 3 minutes of allowing time and space for group members to volunteer as a double for Anna, no one has come forward, and there is an awkward silence. What action do you take?

6. During an auxiliary reenactment, Josefina seems to become very uncomfortable and finally shuts down after the fifth member speaks. Josefina's arms and legs cross, her eyes wander around the room, and she shifts constantly in her chair. What sort of response does this elicit from you as the leader of the group?

7. During a double reenactment, Ferdinand becomes enraged by Tony's response. He lashes out at the group member whom Ferdinand sincerely sees as the person Tony was reenacting (his brother). Tony freezes and finally sits down after Ferdinand's tirade. What action do you take as the group leader?

8. During a double reenactment, Jody says something that touches the heart of many in the group. Many members are in tears, nodding and shifting. Danny does not notice and quickly gets up to jump in for his turn as the double. What action do you take as the group leader?

9. During the previous five sessions, Shira has rarely spoken. When the group addresses her silence, group member Vera suggests a psychodrama exercise "since it really seemed to help Sandra." As the group

leader, what is your reasoning behind going through with or refraining from a psychodrama exercise?

10. In a particularly quiet group, one member of the group takes on the auxiliary roles by himself, repeatedly offering different perspectives in order to reduce the uncomfortable silence in the group. As the group leader, how do you address this issue?

Self-Reflection

1. What would be some of the indicators that prompt you to use psychodrama?

2. Have you ever experienced psychodrama? If so, what emotions and thoughts came up for you? If not, what emotions and thoughts do you anticipate from group members?

3. Consider the times when others have interpreted your thoughts or reactions to a situation. Did you readily accept their interpretation, or did you reject it? How did you react? Were there any insights as a result of the interpretation or your reaction?

4. Are you an abstract thinker, a concrete thinker, or both? How might each type of thinker react to a psychodrama situation?

5. Describe an experience where you were in both the here-and-now ("experience ego") and reflection mode ("observing ego"). What thoughts, feelings, or bodily sensations arose for you?

6. Brainstorm a psychodrama scenario. What sort of creative endeavors will you employ, and why? You may use the examples outlined in the chapter or incorporate your own unique style. Be specific in your examples.

CHAPTER 14

SKILLS OF TERMINATION

Completing the Cycle

The termination stage is to a group as the golden years are to a person. Although a theme of loss and grief (Beck, 1996; Lacoursiere, 1980) weaves through this stage, a beginning of a new journey also awaits ahead. To prepare for the new journey, leaders need to continue instilling a sense of hope, competency, direction, and self-identity.

This chapter presents the leadership skills needed to ensure a sense of closure for the group and a vision of continual growth after termination.

DEALING WITH UNCOMMON TERMINATION

While most groups commonly end in an expected timeframe, some will see one member leave at an earlier time, while in others, a member may drop out unannounced. This section will address these two uncommon types of termination. The normal termination will be covered in the section that follows.

Termination in Open-Ended Groups

Termination presents a special challenge for open-ended groups where new members will enter in conjunction with others leaving at any given time. The group does not end, but there will always be some members terminating their group experiences.

Although each session is built upon the previous one, for open-ended groups, each meeting should be treated as a stand-alone, with its own beginning, middle, and termination. This is to ensure that each member's entrance is given time to welcome, and each member's leaving is given time to terminate.

If terminated members struggle to succeed on their own outside the group, they are welcome to return to the same group, without judgment from others. This policy creates a safety net for members, encouraging them to venture out and try their lots.

Premature Termination in Closed Groups

Members in a closed group may terminate prematurely by dropping out or by indicating their desire to withdraw. Leaders must respect the freedom of a group member to withdraw, as mentioned in the ethical guidelines section in Chapter 3. If possible, however, it is wise to invite the person wanting to withdraw to return to the group for just a brief moment, to explain the reason for withdrawal. This helps the withdrawing member and the group obtain appropriate closure.

If a member simply drops out without explanation, it reinforces the person's poor habit of ditching a relationship when things get tough. It also leaves the remaining members feeling abandoned or blaming themselves for doing or saying something wrong to cause such a dropout.

Invite Explanation for Reasons of Premature Termination

When inviting the withdrawing member back to the group to discuss the reasons for dropping out, consider the following possibilities:

- *Withdrawal due to private reasons.* If the reason for withdrawal is rather private, the member should not be compelled to share with the group. Rather, he or she can say that an outside personal issue requires his or her complete attention for the time being. This is sufficient for closure, especially in the first few sessions of a new group.
- *Withdrawal due to unmet needs.* If withdrawal from the group is due to a conflict or neglect from the group, and the member is willing to return to the group for a short time to provide an explanation, chances are processing the misunderstanding or the unmet needs will mend the very feeling that drove the member to withdraw. There is a high likelihood the member will then stay in the group.
- *When an explanation is unavailable.* If the member withdrawing does not want to provide the group with an explanation, then the leader must

respect this right. However, *the remaining members will need to spend some time processing their feelings.* Some might feel guilty, believing the withdrawal is due to a conflict among them or negligence on their parts, and they may be right. Processing these feelings will help the group move forward without baggage.

Prevent Premature Termination in Closed Groups

First, before the group starts, prepare prospective members by letting them know that they may experience normal anxiety as they enter a new group. It can take several sessions for group members to begin building trust and alleviating some anxiety. For this reason, group leaders sometimes *ask members to commit to attending a minimum number of sessions (e.g., four sessions)* in order to give the group a chance to prove itself.

With a voluntary population, this is not meant to be a hard-and-fast rule. Rather, the four-session commitment primarily serves to notify potential group members that *building trust and a sense of comfort will take some time.*

Second, make a ground rule about leaving: Members who wish to withdraw midway shall inform the group of their departure at least one session ahead of time so that the group has the opportunity to process with the leaving member.

Third, encourage the regular expression of all emotions. Studies have found that clients who have difficulty in expressing their emotions, or who experience less positive affect in the first session, are more likely to terminate prematurely (McCallum, Piper, Ogrodniczuk, & Joyce, 2002; Oei & Kazmierczak, 1997). Given this, leaders should encourage group members to express both their doubts and questions about the group as well as their positive emotions. Exploration of doubts and questions can often diminish their intensity. Members also will realize that all feelings and experiences are good material to be expressed and examined in the group (Bernard, 1989).

THE TERMINATION STAGE OF A TYPICAL GROUP

How do members feel about ending when a typical group is ready to conclude? What's the nature of closing and termination in a typical group? This section tries to answer these questions.

Emotions Evoked by the Ending

As expected, the ending of therapeutic relationships can trigger various emotions. The entire group experience has been like a small life lived with others who have become significant in one's world; thus, the ending can feel like a big loss. In addition, some members may experience separation anxiety when sensing the ending approaching. For example, a member, Sara, who struggled with reclaiming her own voice, wrote in her reflective journal:

I feel a sense of panic that the group is almost at its end.

Ending as a Time for Celebration

The termination stage presents an opportunity to look back and to harvest the fruits of the season. It gives people a chance to reflect on and acknowledge the interpersonal learning that has occurred in the group; it allows members to explore ways that the learning may be put to use and continue in the future. Like a renewal of life, this ending enables members to approach old and new relationships with heightened levels of awareness. This sentiment was reflected by a member, Mary, in her journal:

> As the group nears the end, I feel that I will really miss the group, its process, and the feedback given from all members. This group has shown me so much about people and their core selves by just observing how we all interact with one another, at any given moment. I have become aware of things about me that have manifested themselves in the group. One thing I am becoming aware of is my defensiveness in interpersonal conflict. When Anna accused me of being in a clique, I reacted very defensively. I know that I often get this way whenever I am criticized. I have become aware that this defensiveness doesn't help solve any sort of conflict. I am now more cognizant of how I respond to situations where my buttons are pushed.

A Zen Story

A man is chased by a hungry tiger, as told in a Zen story (Tophoff, 2000). Running faster than he ever thought possible, the man is just managing to keep ahead of the tiger when he comes to a chasm in the earth. Without thinking, the man jumps. As he is going over the edge, he sees another hungry tiger waiting at the bottom of the cliff. Halfway down the cliff, the falling man manages to grasp a root sticking out from a tree. As he catches his breath, the man feels safe for a moment, just out of range of the tiger on the top of the cliff and well above the other tiger below.

Then he notices that a big rat has come along and is beginning to gnaw on the very root that is saving his life. The man, however, also notices a beautiful red, ripe strawberry on the side of the cliff. He takes the strawberry and puts it in his mouth—and it tastes so wonderful!

The termination of a group is akin to the Zen story. As a group ends, members must deal with hungry tigers (the loss of the group) and the gnawing rat (their *unknown* personal futures). Yet, amidst such grief is the delicious strawberry (the sense of accomplishments and hopes for the future).

The Cycle of Life, the Seeds of New Beginnings

Indigenous peoples are more in tune with the cyclic nature of things than those of us who live an urbanized life. Spring comes with fresh growth but is soon supplanted by the heat of summer, then the coolness of fall, and eventually the starkness of winter. The sequence of change can induce a terror of *impermanence* in us if we do not recognize, as the indigenous people do, that things continue to turn around—*life turns and cycles*. The same can be said of the life of groups.

The relationships in group blossom ever so slowly, then the petals are lost, and the flower is no more. *Yet, seeds know how to find their places under the soil* and, in due time, will grow into many new and colorful flowers. *The ending of a group contains many seeds of new beginnings.*

Given that charged feelings and precious insights are inherently present during the termination stage, these feelings and insights that members experience should be explored as the group moves toward a conclusion.

SEVEN PRINCIPLES OF TERMINATION

This section proposes seven principles of termination that leaders may want to keep in mind before venturing into the skill component.

1st Principle: Give Advance Warning

Leaders need to give advance warning about termination, getting members to tie up whatever loose ends remain (Macneil, Hasty, Conus, & Berk, 2010;

Rose, 1989). Pay special attention to difficult issues not yet worked through (Keyton, 1993). If left unaddressed, these issues may create emotional baggage for members that they will carry forward into their future relationships.

The briefer the group, the more important it is to forewarn members, throughout the life of the group, about time limitations (Spitz, 2013). The briefer the group, the more likely members will have unfinished business when closing, unlike long-term groups that usually can afford to deal with matters more completely. Leaders of brief group therapy, therefore, should take action to address unfinished business in the final sessions.

2nd Principle: Acknowledge the Polarity of Feelings

On the one hand, the ending of a relationship can bring about a sense of attainment and *relief* but on the other hand, a sense of *loss* a feeling that the window is closing on letting others know about us, to stretch ourselves in this intense way, to give, to connect, and to discover. This polarity of feelings must be acknowledged.

From a Mayan perspective, however, grief and celebration are intimately connected, rather than polarized. As stated in the recorded speech by Prechtel (2003), "When you are praising the thing you have lost, it is called grief; when you are grieving the thing you once had, it is called praise." In his view, praise cannot exist without grief, and grief cannot exist without praise. Despair often results from an inability to praise the things one has lost.

Prechtel reflects further in his speech, "the ability to laugh and the ability to cry often live in the same house." Learning to talk about and accept the polarity of feelings evoked by closure can help us embrace the rich meanings behind both the yin and the yang of a life lived.

3rd Principle: Overcome the Difficulty of Saying Goodbye

Saying goodbye can prove to be so difficult that some people elect to simply skip it. This is evident in individual counseling where some clients are a "no-show" when it comes to the termination session. The struggle with separation, in our society, can amount to the "farewell party syndrome" where a party meant for people to say goodbye ends up becoming an event where the partygoers seek food, light-hearted socialization, and talk of positive aspects of the relationships, and where deeply felt feelings are circumvented and little is said or done to acknowledge the rich meanings or unfinished business between people.

This kind of *avoidance* can create numerous unresolved feelings or issues and thus is labeled a *syndrome*.

The difficulty of saying goodbye may cause some members to detach themselves from the group, backing off from investing in their work in the last sessions (Lacoursiere, 1980). To overcome this difficulty, leaders need to think about ways to ease members into saying goodbye in ways that are meaningful to their interpersonal learning experiences in the group.

4th Principle: Set Goals for the Final Session

Since the difficulty of ending has specific impacts on the final few sessions, one way to ease members into saying goodbye is to set specific goals for these final sessions. Spitz (2013) identifies three goals for the final sessions:

- To assess the overall *therapeutic experience* on an individual and group level
- To examine to what degree members have *reached their goals*
- To complete the group experience in a *positive frame of mind*

To translate Spitz's concepts into actions, we can treat the ending of a group experience as a "graduation." The goal of the final few sessions, therefore, is to create an atmosphere of a graduation where members can take inventory of their *accomplishment, empowerment,* and *hope for the future.* A later section will present methods of conducting the termination session in line with the three goals identified by Spitz.

5th Principle: Transfer Interpersonal Learning From Inside to Life Outside the Group

Members transfer their in-group learning to their personal lives in two occurrences:

- *Transfer learning throughout the group life.* Members regularly transfer their interpersonal learning inside the group to life outside. The regular check-in at the beginning of the session often finds members reporting their efforts made beyond the confines of the group. The following snippet of a members' reflective journal exemplifies this kind of ongoing transmission of interpersonal learning:

> Each week as members do check-in, they share the growth and change they experienced outside the group, based on the work they did within the group. This was most evident in our last session. I noticed that members are learning to be true to themselves in their own lives. This is truly exciting for me to watch. Initially, I was doubtful as to whether our group sessions could bring about change to our outside lives in such a short time. Yet, as time passes, I can see that as long as a member is willing to try, change is possible!

- *Transfer learning after termination.* The end of the group represents a transition to a new stage of life—a "rite of passage." After termination, each person will take on the responsibility for his or her own growth for the road forward. The final session, therefore, marks a time for members to think about how to continue their progress once the group has ended. Following is a list of progress or interpersonal learning that members have made in the group, ready to be transferred to the life outside the group after termination:

  o The ability to emotionally connect with others
  o The ability to recognize and assert one's own needs in proper ways
  o The ability to manage and work through conflict
  o The ability to take reasonable interpersonal risks in telling one's own truth
  o The ability to communicate more clearly and truthfully
  o The ability to offer and invite meaningful input (feedback)
  o The ability to use journaling or other means to promote a healthy inner dialogue

Group leaders can offer a follow-up session within 6 months or 1 year after a group has been completed. Feedback from a follow-up session can provide valuable information as to how well former group members have been able to transfer and implement what they learned in the group.

6th Principle: Use Life-Review Therapy and Looking-Back Letters

A group leader can apply the principle of life-review therapy to the group at termination. In counseling elderly people, therapists often use life-review therapy to help them look back on their lives and remember their accomplishments via telling stories. This review of life experiences restores an elderly person's self-identity—identity too easily lost in retirement as well as in the loss of health, friends, and purpose in life.

In applying life-review therapy to group termination, the leader may ask members, before the end of the group, *to write themselves a "looking-back letter."*

In this letter, members may write about their original issues and goals, how their goals changed during the course of the group, what they learned about themselves, what they changed, the significant events in the group that propelled their self-discovery, the "aha" experience, or what the group has meant to them.

Letter writing may seem archaic or not in line with the click-click digital communication era. People don't slow down enough to engage in this most personal and candid way of expression. However, it takes the slow art of letter writing for our authentic voice to come through (Toepfer & Walker, 2009; Tubman, Montgomery, & Wagner, 2001).

When members come to the last session, they may share the feelings evoked when they were writing their looking-back letters or the major points in their letters. It is particularly meaningful for the group members to hear what they have meant to one another. This usually creates a warm and humorous atmosphere. Laughter, tears, and hugs may result from this sharing. Please find examples of members' looking-back letters at the end of this chapter.

7th Principle: Draw on Appreciative Inquiry

Appreciative inquiry (Hammond, 2013) emphasizes looking into the growth of members' experiences, similar to the technique of "positive reframing" often used in strategic therapy.

To use appreciative inquiry for termination, see whether you can wholeheartedly let in the following philosophical positions stated by Hammond (2013):

- There is always something there that has worked.
- What we focus on will become our reality.
- Reality is created in the moment, and there are multiple realities.
- The act of asking questions influences the outcomes.
- People will have more confidence and comfort to journey to the unknown when they carry forward parts of what they have learned.
- The language that we use creates our reality.

Carrying the spirit of appreciative inquiry into the termination session, you will fuel the group with positive energy, empowering members to continue to grow.

SKILLS FOR ENDING THE GROUP

This section presents a sequence of leadership skills and techniques a leader can use to help the group members say goodbye to each other. These skills are based on the seven principles addressed in the previous section.

Opt for an Opening Meditation

You may invite members to close their eyes for a 3-minute meditation. This inner focus can help them *get in touch with their feelings of the present moment.* You may guide the meditation by saying:

> This is a very special session—our last session. Before we start, let's relax in our chairs for a few minutes. Close your eyes. [pause] Pay attention to your breathing and any sensation in your body. [pause] Notice the thoughts and feelings that come to your mind. [pause] Allow those thoughts and feelings to come and go. [pause] If some of them are especially strong, stay with them for awhile. Listen to what they are trying to say. [pause] When the session starts, there will be time to voice these thoughts and feelings. So just stay in silence for 1 minute. [silence for one minute] Now that you are feeling centered, bring your attention back to the room. When you feel ready to join the group, you may open your eyes.

Acknowledge Present Feelings

After the opening, invite members to briefly share any feelings they have about termination—joy, pain, loss, separation anxiety, or relief. As a leader, you may provide modeling by sharing your here-and-now feelings and thoughts on the last session. Your self-disclosure will assist the group in the sharing of the polarity of feelings. About 10 minutes may be needed for this sharing. You may say something like,

[To the group] I hope the brief meditation has helped you become situated for today's session. We have anticipated this final session, and now it is here. Many of us probably have some mixed feelings brewing within us, so I would like to invite all of you to use the next 10 minutes to openly share those feelings. As you listen to other members sharing, please feel free to make comments if you feel moved to do so. Okay, let me start with my own reactions. As I sit here knowing that this is our last session, I am feeling. . . .

After members have shared their feelings, summarize the common feelings present in the moment. For example,

[To the group] There seems to be a common feeling of _____ [fill in the blank] tonight as we come here. . . .

Coach the Group to Say Goodbye in Meaningful Ways

If not coached, most members will feel at a loss as to what to say in bringing closure with one another. As a way of coaching, ask members to share one or two of the following experiences:

- The feelings they had when writing their looking-back letters
- Significant turning points—how they have made progress toward their personal goals
- What was learned—insight, growth, and change
- What other group members have meant to them

Ensure that every member has *equal airtime* in case the more verbal members expound on their thoughts and feelings, leaving little time for those who are less verbal. You may coach with the following guidance:

First,

[To the group] For the bulk of our last session, I would like to invite you to share what the group experiences have meant to you. This will help all of us to have a sense of closure to the experience. Maybe you can include one or two of the following: the feelings you had when you were writing your looking-back letter; [pause] any significant experiences within the group that have helped you reach a breakthrough in your progress toward your goal; [pause] the insight you have gained about yourself and how it has helped you change; [pause] or what this group has meant to you.

Second,

Each of you will have about 3 to 4 minutes to share. After each member has shared, we will have about 3 minutes for the group to make comments or provide the final feedback. Let's keep group discussions as open and free-flowing as possible. Okay, who would like to start?

Facilitate Group Interaction and Feedback

Allow the group interaction to be as open as possible, but intervene whenever the group members get sidetracked. Help members reframe their experiences in positive terms if negative or self-criticizing voices become evident:

[To the group] It seems like Mike feels he could have done better in improving his relationship with his mother. Do any of you see the progress that Mike has made that he might not have noticed himself?

Deal With Unfinished Business

Though the group has dedicated a portion of time in each session to work on unfinished business from its previous sessions, some unresolved issues may still exist in the final session. If unfinished business does surface, devote some group time for processing and hopefully bring a sense of closure to it.

Transfer In-Group Learning to the Life Outside the Group

To encourage members to look at the "road forward," you may have members reflect on how they will transfer their interpersonal learning to the life outside the group and how they will create a new beginning for themselves:

[To the group] I am so happy to hear that many of you have gained a major breakthrough in this brief period of time. To make sure that you continue your personal work and growth, I would like all of us to take a moment to think about the following questions: How will you carry what you learned in the group to your life outside? What outside support exists for you to help you implement the changes that you desire? What are some reasonable risks that you anticipate taking in the future?

Take Care of Referrals and Particular Needs

Most members grow in the span of the group life and can move on with their lives. For some members, however, life after the group may require additional counseling, depending on the clients' goals and whether they believe additional assistance is appropriate.

- *Referral to individual counseling.* Years of observation have taught us to appreciate one particular thing—the extent of difficulty some people have in opening up in front of a group. We, therapists and counselors, tend to take for granted the action of open sharing, not appreciating the fear that holds some people back from opening up in the group setting. These members can benefit from a referral to individual counseling—an easier setting where they can learn to open up and focus on themselves—before they can do so in the group.

For those who have had difficulty with separation issues, a referral to individual counseling is also advisable. The hope is that the private setting of individual counseling may help them resolve those issues from the past.

- *Referral to another group.* Just when some members reach the point of learning to open up and trust, the group has come to an end. For these people, referral to another group is much needed. Many members actually enjoy taking what they learn in one group on to the next and find themselves making progress by leaps and bounds there.

Complete the Group With a Symbolic Ceremony

The last gesture of saying goodbye may be a symbolic ceremony. Here are two examples of such ceremonies:

- Group hug
- Scheduling a follow-up

Whenever a follow-up session is decided, make it a real session. If arranged as a pot-luck dinner or a restaurant gathering, the session won't hold the same standard because food, small talk, and socialization distract and defeat the original purpose.

If the group members want to socialize with one another, they can schedule another time for a gathering where they can engage in lighter and freer mingling.

An Option to Close the Group for Youths: Create and Share Memory Books

For children and adolescent groups or groups in which members are less verbal, the leader may use a *structured exercise* called the "memory book" (devised by Dr. Chris Ryback and his colleague, Dr. Lori Russell-Chapin) to facilitate the group in saying goodbye.

In this exercise, each member is asked to put together a small memory book of their own that encompasses their group experiences. The book is made of pages of construction paper cut in half, with two holes punched along the left side for binding with colored ribbon or yarn.

On each page, members briefly symbolize their experiences in the group with a simple drawing or a few printed words or poetry. A memory book, for example, might contain the following:

- First page: What the member was like when entering the group
- Second page: A significant experience that changed him or her in some important way
- Third page: What the member is becoming like at the end of the group
- Fourth page: How others in the group contributed to the member's experience
- Fifth page: What the member will take with him or her from the group

The emphasis is not on artistic achievement but rather on highlighting the group experiences that the member wants to share with others.

Each page shall take no more than 5 minutes to complete. After completing the booklet, members can share what they will take forward with them from the group experience. As such, the entire session is spent on completing and processing the exercise, and the book itself will be a tangible reminder of what each member has gained.

In closing: Though a theme of loss and grief permeates the air, the termination stage marks the beginning of new journey waiting ahead. In helping members say goodbye in a meaningful manner, the leader continues instilling in group members a sense of hope, competency, direction, and self-identity.

EVALUATION OF THE GROUP EXPERIENCE

Program evaluation is an integral part of the program management circle (Lewis, Lewis, Daniels, & D'Andrea, 2011). Evaluation provides useful data that can create accountability and inform plans for future group programs. In evaluating group services, the focus is usually on *the quality* of the experiences and *the impact* the group has had on client change.

This section presents three types of evaluation surveys through which group leaders can gather evaluative data to assess group effectiveness.

Evaluation Immediately After Termination

While still in the meeting room with their experiences top of mind, most members are willing to respond to the leader's request to participate in an evaluation survey, immediately after termination.

The evaluation should be anonymous to allow group members the freedom to describe their experience and offer constructive feedback concerning how future groups may improve. A Likert 5-point scale can be used to facilitate statistical analysis (Allen & Seaman, 2007).

Following are examples of anonymous surveys that we have created. Example 1 can be used for postgroup evaluation, while Example 2 can be used for pregroup and postgroup evaluation. Comparing the pregroup and postgroup data may reveal the extent to which the group has been effective and the areas that warrant fine-tuning for the future.

Example 1: A Group Evaluation Survey

This is an anonymous survey. Your response will be kept private and confidential.

Please select the most appropriate rating for each statement.

1. This group helped me better understand myself.

   Strongly Agree   Disagree   Neutral   Agree   Strongly Disagree
   |_____|_____|_____|_____|_____|

2. With this group experience, I have a better understanding of my relationship styles with others.

   Strongly Agree   Disagree   Neutral   Agree   Strongly Disagree
   |_____|_____|_____|_____|_____|

3. With this group experience, I came to understand more about the ways I deal with difficult things and emotions in my life.

   Strongly Agree   Disagree   Neutral   Agree   Strongly Disagree
   |_____|_____|_____|_____|_____|

4. After this group experience, I now feel less alone in the world.

   Strongly Agree   Disagree   Neutral   Agree   Strongly Disagree
   |_____|_____|_____|_____|_____|

5. After this group experience, I now feel more open with those in my life with whom I want to be close.

   Strongly Agree   Disagree   Neutral   Agree   Strongly Disagree
   |_____|_____|_____|_____|_____|

6. The group experience has been useful for me in learning to take risks in new behaviors in order to better my life.

   Strongly Agree   Disagree   Neutral   Agree   Strongly Disagree
   |_____|_____|_____|_____|_____|

7. The group experience has been useful for me in learning to listen to others, verbally and nonverbally, with deeper sensitivity.

   Strongly Agree   Disagree   Neutral   Agree   Strongly Disagree
   |_____|_____|_____|_____|_____|

8. I will be able to apply what I've learned in this group to improve my relationships in my work setting.

Strongly Agree   Disagree   Neutral   Agree   Strongly Disagree

|_____|_____|_____|_____|_____|

9. I will be able to apply what I've learned in this group to improve my personal relationships.

Strongly Agree   Disagree   Neutral   Agree   Strongly Disagree

|_____|_____|_____|_____|_____|

10. I have felt that others in this group truly care about me.

Strongly Agree   Disagree   Neutral   Agree   Strongly Disagree

|_____|_____|_____|_____|_____|

11. I have been able to express to others in this group how I truly perceive them.

Strongly Agree   Disagree   Neutral   Agree   Strongly Disagree

|_____|_____|_____|_____|_____|

12. I have gained insights about myself through the input from group members regarding how they perceive me.

Strongly Agree   Disagree   Neutral   Agree   Strongly Disagree

|_____|_____|_____|_____|_____|

13. Based on my experience and the learning that I have had in this group, I have identified the following goal (or goals) that I plan to work toward achieving.

Goal #1:

Goal #2:

Goal #3:

14. Based on my experience and the learning that I've had in this group, I plan to achieve my goals by implementing the following change (or changes) in my life.

Change #1:

Change #2:

Change #3:

15. Other remarks:

Example 2: Pregroup Survey or Postgroup Survey

This is an anonymous survey. Your response will be kept private and confidential. Please circle the number that applies to your position on the following statements:

5: definitely true

4: somewhat true

3: neither true nor untrue

2: somewhat untrue

1: definitely untrue

Table 14.1 Anonymous Survey

1	I am aware of the way I interact with people and how I come across to others.	1	2	3	4	5
2	I am aware of some of my own blind spots in my relationships.	1	2	3	4	5
3	I am able to stay emotionally present in my interaction with people, instead of hiding behind my invisible shell or wall.	1	2	3	4	5
4	I am realistic about my own perceptions of myself. I am able to accurately perceive my own feelings in interaction with others.	1	2	3	4	5
5	When I talk about myself and give feedback to others, I am descriptive, with more shades of gray, regarding my perceptions about myself and others, rather than using general and abstract expressions.	1	2	3	4	5
6	I am able to own up to the suppressed or denied parts of myself and let these parts be integrated back to my wholesome self.	1	2	3	4	5
7	I am able to seek less external approval from others and more internal approval from myself.	1	2	3	4	5
8	I am able to engage in self-initiation and self-leadership in my relationships, instead of relying on others to make something happen for me.	1	2	3	4	5
9	I feel accepted and respected by people. My relationships with others feel safe and accepting, and I have contributed to the cohesion of my relationships.	1	2	3	4	5
10	I am able to decrease my habitual use of defensive walls and allow myself to be more trusting and more spontaneous in my self-expression.	1	2	3	4	5

Follow-Up and the Evaluation

A follow-up survey allows you to see whether former members have been able to transfer their learning forward. It also helps gather information regarding any roadblocks or setbacks that group members might have experienced after termination. Such data give you the opportunity to determine what adjustments you can make regarding group treatment services for future members.

If you are sending the survey by mail, accompany it with *a cover letter* explaining that this is a follow-up survey on the group experience, results will be kept confidential, and that respondents' feedback will assist you in improving the group services to be offered in the future. Following is an example of a group follow-up survey we have created.

Example 3: A Group Follow-Up Survey

This is an anonymous survey. Your response will be kept private and confidential. Please select the most appropriate rating for each statement.

1. As I look back on the period of time since the group finished, I can say that this group has helped me to better understand myself.

    Strongly Agree   Disagree   Neutral   Agree   Strongly Disagree

    |_____|_____|_____|_____|

2. Since completing this group experience, I have improved my relationships with others.

    Strongly Agree   Disagree   Neutral   Agree   Strongly Disagree

    |_____|_____|_____|_____|

3. Since this group experience, I have felt less alone in the world.

    Strongly Agree   Disagree   Neutral   Agree   Strongly Disagree

    |_____|_____|_____|_____|

4. Since completing this group experience, I have been able to take more risks with new behaviors in order to better my life.

    Strongly Agree   Disagree   Neutral   Agree   Strongly Disagree

    |_____|_____|_____|_____|

5. I have been able to apply what I've learned in this group to improve my work relationships.

   Strongly Agree   Disagree   Neutral   Agree   Strongly Disagree
   |_____|_____|_____|_____|_____|

6. I have been able to apply what I've learned in this group to improve my social relationships.

   Strongly Agree   Disagree   Neutral   Agree   Strongly Disagree
   |_____|_____|_____|_____|_____|

7. As I look back to the group experience, I feel that others in this group truly cared for me.

   Strongly Agree   Disagree   Neutral   Agree   Strongly Disagree
   |_____|_____|_____|_____|_____|

8. As I reflect back on the group experience, I believe that I was able to express to others in the group how I perceived them.

   Strongly Agree   Disagree   Neutral   Agree   Strongly Disagree
   |_____|_____|_____|_____|_____|

9. As I recall my group experience, I can remember that others in this group expressed how they perceived me.

   Strongly Agree   Disagree   Neutral   Agree   Strongly Disagree
   |_____|_____|_____|_____|_____|

10. After completing the group experience, I have made substantial progress in achieving the following goal (or goals) that I set at the conclusion of the group.

    Goal #1:

    Goal #2:

    Goal #3:

11. After completing the group experience, I have been able to make the following change (or changes) in my life, based on my experience and the learning that I had in this group.

    Change #1:

    Change #2:

    Change #3:

12. Other remarks:

EXAMPLES OF LOOKING-BACK LETTERS

1. Keith's Letter

Looking back and reflecting on this group gives me a bittersweet feeling. It's sweet because I've learned so much about myself but bitter because I'm going to miss the group and wish we could continue.

I Didn't Expect the Group to Be This Way. The group gave me an opportunity to openly and honestly talk about "real stuff" that was affecting me. In fact, it was the first time in my life that I was able to go beneath the surface and deal with issues that were having an impact on my life. I was able to do this because of the environment the group provided for me. It is important to note, however, that I didn't come into this group expecting it to be this way. The group experience exceeded my expectations. A nurturing yet challenging environment was critical for me to uncover many of the issues that I face in my life.

Moving Beyond the Mental. Most of the learning in my life has been mental; this group allowed me to move beyond the mental and into the emotional. I am grateful for this group and will regard this experience as the most critical step in my life. There were several experiences in this group that stood out for me. They were nurturing, challenging, conflicting, or enlightening.

My Walls of Defense Against the Authority Figure Tumbling Down. I have to admit that I came into this group with baggage. I wasn't sure how I would interact with the leader. The reason behind this is because I had a previous bad experience with an authority figure. I was not sure why; I didn't know whether it was a personality thing or a cultural thing. The previous authority figure was Asian, and the leader of this group is also Asian. As a result, I immediately became defensive because I didn't want to relive the past experience.

However, the biggest moment for me came when the leader disclosed something about herself. Her disclosure allowed me to see things from a different and more accurate perspective. At that moment, I felt the walls of defense start tumbling down. It was such a relief for me, and it allowed me to truly experience the impact of the group process.

From Shame to Clarity. The nurturing experience for me happened in the beginning when I told the group how I usually take on too much and make things difficult for myself. I shared that I would like to live more in the moment. I let the group know that the reason I work so hard is because of some shameful things I did in the past that hurt my credit and still today drag on me financially. The group validated me. They did not necessarily agree with my lifestyle, but they validated that my emotions made sense.

The validation gave me the clarity I needed to realize that my lifestyle didn't make sense and was unnecessary. I could still accomplish what I wanted to financially without killing myself in the process. This experience was so relieving and nurturing that I have changed my schedule and feel so much better.

Being Challenged. The challenging time came when Rosy told me that I was probably "emotionally no good" for anyone because of the way I worked myself. She said it in a way that made me look within myself and really investigate what was going on with me. I appreciated her candor and her ability to be frank with me. I was also able to receive it well because the trust factor was already built into the group.

Another challenging time came when Jane said that she thought I intellectualized too much. This stimulated me to be more reflective about myself. I remember my immediate reaction was to defend the way I was. However, the more I thought about it, the more I realized that I do overintellectualize. This allowed me to come to terms with the idea that being too intellectual can prevent me from reaching the heart of the matter. It can prevent me from letting go and relaxing. I am appreciative of Jane's honest comment.

Grateful for the Transformation Made Possible Through "Stirring the Pot." The enlightening point of the group came when we started to "stir the pot" and engage in confrontation. It is so easy to run from confrontation because of the discomfort attached to it. However, it may be the very experience that is needed to help us overcome our own issues. As a result of this experience, I have coined the phrase that "confrontation has its up sides."

Overall, I was able to accomplish two things during the group. First, I am no longer overloading myself and have reduced my schedule significantly. I am not where I started 12 weeks ago at the beginning of the group. As a result of my experience in the group, I will be more conscious about my actions.

Secondly, I was able to work on and improve the skill of saying exactly what's on my mind, without editing or thinking too deeply all the time. These have been very significant accomplishments for me, and I am immensely grateful.

I feel a little inadequate because I can't find the words to express the level of gratitude I have for the leader and to all the group members who invested their hearts, time, and minds. All I can say is thank you . . . straight from my heart. From Keith.

2. Mike's Letter

As I look back at my group experiences, several sessions stood out.

Bursting Into Tears at Session 7. Session 7 was my turning point. It was one of the most surprising sessions for other members because they were seeing a different side of me for the first time. I cried during the closing comment because I really wanted the group's attention that night but was not strong enough to ask for it. Instead, I chose to withdraw and remained silent. This strategy had served me well over the years, but I was no longer able to run away from my feelings. At the moment when I burst into tears, I felt extremely exposed, but the reaction of the group gave me comfort. It was at that point that I knew I could trust this group to help me with my issues. It was very comforting to see other members shed tears for me and show concern for my feelings. I was very touched by their tears.

My Alcoholic Father and His Impact on Me. Session 8 was very powerful. The group empowered me to share my innermost thoughts and feelings about my father and his impact on my life. I have always struggled with the fear of becoming my father. His failure as a father was primarily due to the fact that he was an alcoholic. He was unable to change his way of life. As a result, he died at an early age and never acknowledged his disease to my sister and me.

This was my struggle. I wanted an explanation, but I was never strong enough to ask for it. Thankfully, the group was able to help me in a way that I could not have imagined.

Having Closure With My Father Through the Psychodrama Experience in Session 10. Unexpectedly, Session 10 was also extremely powerful. As I was trying to elicit a response from Terry, I found myself reliving my experience. I was soon overwhelmed with emotion to the point where I could not stop crying. Taking on the role of my father, Cindy and Jean were able to give me the words that I so desperately wanted to hear from my father. Their words were exactly what I needed to hear because, for the first time, they were coming from someone who was not trying to protect me.

I was finally able to have some closure on this issue. However, I am cognizant of the fact that I will need to continue to work on self-growth. I am very thankful that I was a part of this group. It served as an agent of change in my life. I will cherish this experience for the rest of my life.

∞∞

In closing: The termination stage is to a group as the golden years are to a person. Although a theme of loss and grief weaves through this stage, a beginning of a new journey also awaits ahead.

Ending is part of the cyclic nature of things. Life turns and cycles. Spring comes with fresh growth but is soon supplanted by the heat of summer, then the coolness of fall, and eventually the starkness of winter.

The relationships in group blossom ever so slowly, then the petals are lost, and the flower is no more. Yet, seeds know how to find their places under the soil and, in due time, will grow into many new and colorful flowers. Just the same, the ending of a group contains many seeds; and seeds, in due time, will find their ways to germinate and sprout into many hopes and vibrant journeys.

EXERCISES

Scenarios for Your Practice

1. At the final session of a group, Chow states, "I don't want the group to end. I'm not ready for that!" What factors would you consider in making your response? Are there issues that you would explore with Chow?

2. Jake and Woodrow fail to show up for the final group session. They have seemed less connected to the group over the last several weeks. You have reason to believe that they have resumed abusing alcohol even though they had supposedly maintained sobriety for several years prior to the group sessions. How would you deal with their absence in the final meeting?

3. A group member, Helmut, says "I deeply appreciate the support and friendships that grew in here. I'm inviting everyone here, members and leaders alike, to a backyard cookout at my house next Saturday." As the group leader, how would you respond to this statement?

4. Karen has recently been diagnosed with a life-threatening sexually transmitted disease. She feels unprepared to tell the group members that she needs to terminate group therapy in order to receive treatment. She is ashamed and worried about their reaction. As the group leader, how do you address this situation with Karen and with the group?

5. Dimitri has announced his plan to leave the group due to the final stages of his mother's illness. He has been very quiet for the last six sessions, and members have tried to encourage him to speak. How might group members respond, and how can you strive to make the most effective termination?

6. What appreciative inquiry can you use in the following situation: Emilio has stated that he has become even more guarded and angry as a result of group counseling. He wishes to terminate and blames a few specific members of the group.

7. Jennifer has rarely spoken in the group. In the final session, she begins to open up and states that she felt comfortable in doing so because she would never see the group members again. As the group leader, how will you keep the group on track with closure while still addressing Jennifer's thoughts, feelings, and unfinished business?

8. Jack's answers between the pregroup and the postgroup evaluations fluctuated very minimally even though he seemed to make significant progress in the group. How do you interpret this information? What may be a factor in Jack's perceived minimal change and growth?

9. After a very successful group, your group members decide to continue meeting on their own. They invite you to come to their sessions and group social outings. What advice do you have for them? Do you continue to work and/or socialize with them? What will your response be? Are there any ethical issues influencing your choice?

10. In a closing ceremony, you decide to incorporate a rock ceremony where each member writes a word on a rock for a selected member of the group. One of your group members thinks this ceremony is "infantile" and refuses to participate. A few of the group members are disappointed by this. How do you address this situation?

Self-Reflection

1. What are some of the ways in which your family handled significant losses? Do you still use the same approaches?

2. As a group leader, how will it be for you to let go of group members with whom you have shared emotional closeness? What will be an appropriate way for you to handle this loss?

3. What kind of continuing obligation do you feel you have toward members of a completed group?

4. If you were a member, what would you like to take away from the termination session of a group? What will best prepare you for terminating a group experience?

5. What experiences have you had with closure (or lack thereof)? Reflect on the times when you were satisfied or unsatisfied with the closure of a relationship. What feelings were roused? What behaviors ensued?

6. Have you ever experienced abandonment? If so, how did it affect your relationships with others? Were there unresolved issues? How did they manifest in other areas of your life? Did you feel responsible or guilty in any way?

7. Have you ever felt compelled to leave a situation (job, relationship, etc.) with or without explanation? What was your reasoning for terminating the relationship? What manner of explanation did you provide or refrain from providing? What reasons did you have for the method you chose?

CHAPTER 15

WRITING AS A REFLECTIVE PRACTICE IN GROUP COUNSELING

Slightly touched upon in Chapter 2, the topic of reflective practice will now gain traction in this chapter, especially the following two types of reflective writing:

- Member reflective journals
- Leader narrative session notes

Both types of reflective practice bolster the therapeutic effect of groups, carrying it to a peak without needing extra sessions. This has a great appeal in a time when cost containment has become a major thrust in the health care industry, and we have to conduct groups in briefer time periods.

LEADERS' REFLECTIVE PRACTICE

In cultivating our inner leader, we have to consistently engage in reflective practice. This section elaborates how you, as a leader, can use reflective practice to advance your personal and professional development.

Reflective Practice: A Self-Examination Central for Leaders' Development

Reflective practice is deemed the most important tool in the development of any professional (Atieno Okech, 2008; Bolton, 2010). As emphasized by Bolton (2010), all professionals in training should regularly engage in reflective practice to critically examine their values, concepts, and assumptions. Spending time in self-examination serves to widen your perspective, develop the authority of your personal voice, and give clarity to your own roles, responsibilities, and principles.

The importance of this kind of reflective self-examination looms even larger for group leaders.

Two Essential Forms of Reflective Practice

Valli (1997) proposes five types of reflection: technical reflection; reflection in- and on-action; deliberative reflection; personalistic reflection; and critical reflection. Among these five, the following two seem to deeply affect leaders' cultivation of their inner leaders:

- Personalistic reflection: Reflecting on one's *inner voice* (feelings, emotions, and cognition) and the *voices of others*
- Critical reflection: Reflecting on interpersonal dimensions of group practice with open-mindedness, discernment, moral principles, and creativity

There is no better way to engage in these two forms of reflective practice than by writing.

Writing as an Essential Component of a Leader's Reflective Practice

In line with Bolton's (2010) suggestion to let writing be the most essential component of our reflective practice, we encourage group leaders to put their personal reflections into writing. The writing process creates meanings for you and helps you communicate at a more substantial level with others.

I (Mei) left home at an early age to study in a city far away. Being separated from friends and families added up to a towering challenge for me as a youngster. Fortunately, upon departure, a friend gave me a beautiful notebook for jotting down all my inner thoughts and feelings. Ever since then, the practice of reflective journaling has become a major vehicle for me to tap into my inner resources and personal strength, creating the kind of richness for my life that benefits me still today. When rereading those early journal entries, I never cease to be awed by the transcendent power that writing has.

Bolton (2010) states once more, reflecting on our experiences through writing, that we create meaning for ourselves and produce a version of us that can be communicated to others. I can personally attest to the trueness of this statement. Growing up in a reserved family, I had never learned how to communicate my internal experiences; they seemed foreign. Thankfully, through reflective journaling, I learned to give a voice to my inner life, which deepens my communication with people who I come to know and trust.

MEMBER'S REFLECTIVE PRACTICE

Research Findings on Benefits of Reflective Writing

Writing offers members a way to open up to their inner experiences. As evidenced by various research studies, the benefits are rather striking.

Decreased need for health care services. Pennebaker (1997) conducted a study investigating the effect of therapeutic writing. In the study composed of college students, the control group wrote about mundane topics, while the experimental group wrote about their traumatic experiences. Participants were asked to write about these topics for 15 minutes per day, for 4 days.

Of those in the experimental group (writing about their traumas), one subgroup was asked to just express their emotions; a second subgroup was to write about fact-oriented descriptions of their traumas; while a third subgroup wrote about both their emotional experiences and the facts of the situations.

The researcher then used the frequency of participants' use of health care services during the following few months as data for comparison.

In the two subgroups who wrote about their emotions concerning trauma, results showed that participants decreased their use of health care services by 50%. Those in the control group increased their use of health care services by 50% on the same measure.

Improved immune system functioning. Pennebaker (1997) and colleagues further examined the effect of writing with regard to the functioning of the immune system. For this study, blood was drawn from participants at three different periods of time: the day prior to writing, the day after completing the writing, and 6 weeks after the writing occurred.

Once again, participants were divided into groups and subgroups, similar to that of the previous study. The participants were asked to write about their assigned topics for 20 minutes per day, for 4 days.

Results showed parallel findings to the previous study: Only those who wrote about both their thoughts and feelings concerning a trauma demonstrated a strengthened immune system functioning. Though the benefits reached their peak immediately following the writing, the effect of a strengthened immune system remained 6 weeks after the writing was finished.

Keeping Things to Ourselves Can Take a Toll on Our Health

We might ask, why not just mull things over in the recesses of our mind? Pennebaker (1997) answered: The acts of concealing and inhibiting their emotional expression can actually take a toll on people's psychological and physical health.

For example, in a study of individuals with eating disorders, he found that *it was the covering up of the disorder that contributed most to the emotional difficulties of those with the disorder.* In other words, people who cover up their problems pay a price for the covering. Not only is so much energy and time spent in covering, but the very act of covering causes the individual to feel isolated and alienated from others who might have otherwise provided support.

On the other hand, research has continuously demonstrated that writing can contribute to one's well-being. Pennebaker (1997) echoes this sentiment: Writing can clear the mind and pave the way to complete complex tasks; writing can help the writer work through traumas that otherwise might block that person's ability to focus on important tasks. Writing can help the writer acquire and integrate new information and promote problem-solving.

Scriptotherapy and the Reason It Works

There exists a tradition of using writing to enhance therapeutic effect— scriptotherapy (Riordan, 1996). Widely used in individual and group therapy, scriptotherapy requires the client to slow down, thus leaving him or her in a more reflective state.

During an individual or group therapy session, clients who have difficulty with their information processing speed are often preoccupied and unable to fully absorb what has transpired in the session. It is only when in the privacy of their home that clients are able to think through and digest the complicated and charged interpersonal processes of the session through the reflective pace of writing.

In addition, reflective writing allows clients to express themselves without the fear of being judged. Through uncensored self-expression, they come to a sense of authorship of their thinking, feelings, and actions.

To Write a Reflective Journal With Ease

To write a reflective journal with ease, follow the principles suggested by several authors (Adams, 1990; DeSalvo, 2000; Stone, 1998):

- Spend as little as 20 minutes for the writing; it is enough to capture the highlights and the essence of your experience.
- Set your own pace. Write as fast or as slow as you want. Set no deadlines!
- Choose *when* you want to write.
- Keep your journal private, or only share a piece of your writing with a selected reader, like a close friend or a mentor.
- Write anywhere. With a small notebook and pen, opportunities abound for jotting down thoughts and feelings that flash through your mind— while waiting for others in the car, in the airport, at the mall, or at home. Pull out your notebook, laptop, or smartphone, and type away.
- Write even if you are not in top physical condition; even if you are ill, writing can actually contribute to your healing since it helps boost immune function, as demonstrated by Pennebaker's (1997) study.
- Write from your current level of understanding, growth, and healing. Don't wait until you get that special talent of writing. As you continue to put your experiences into words, you will gain a greater degree of eloquence in writing.
- Write without censoring yourself. Accept all feelings that arise. Write in your own natural voice. No need to mimic those of others.
- Settle on a way of writing that works for you. You can express yourself with just words, with drawings, photos, poems, or with collages.

APPLYING REFLECTIVE JOURNALING IN GROUP COUNSELING

Group members can benefit tremendously from weekly reflective journaling.

This section suggests ways leaders should encourage members to journal, using it as a tool to bolster the power of interpersonal learning.

Assign Weekly Reflective Journal for Reflection on Group Experiences

Within a single session of a group, a great deal of exchange happens verbally, nonverbally, intrapersonally, and interpersonally. Without the opportunity to digest and process the sensory, cognitive, and emotional experiences in the session, members may struggle to independently handle unexamined issues and unarticulated reactions that surface at home.

To prevent sensory overload, leaders may assign members to write a weekly journal in which they reflect on the experiences and issues that surfaced. Journaling after each group session will help members make sense of their entire group experience.

Using the time between group sessions to do reflective journaling empowers members to build upon the growing awareness when they return to the group. Some members even volunteer during check-in to share whatever has come up in their reflections from the previous session.

Use Writing to Deepen Members' Self-Discovery

Journaling deepens members' self-discovery. What members write does not matter as much as the fact that writing provides a means for them to become more aware of their unsuspecting processes.

Self-exploration through journaling deepens a member's self-discovery. Going beyond conscious thoughts, feelings, and future plans, members' reflective journals usually tap into the interpersonal patterns that manifest in their lives, even into what lies in the subliminal (Adams, 1990). This kind of practice has an even greater bearing for short-term groups, for which this book is designed.

Minority clients—especially those from a cultural background where their modes of communication are not as vocal as those of the majority culture—can benefit from using reflective journaling to deepen their self-discovery. Journal writing gives them the opportunity to tap into their unarticulated reactions to the session, where verbal expression seems inaccessible (White & Murray, 2002).

Members' Reflections on Writing About Group Experiences

The following snippets of members' journal entries exemplify the ways in which they appreciate the value of journal writing:

After the group session, I felt very emotional. When I left the room, I was wondering what to do with my emotions. I soon found that reflecting in my mind as well as in the journal allowed the therapy to continue even in the absence of the group environment. I see this reflective journal writing as being an integral part of my progress between sessions. It helps me chart my progress as well as provide me with an outlet for expressing the emotions that the therapy sessions have brought to the surface.

Another member wrote the following:

Throughout the group, I have found writing the reflective journal to be most beneficial. Writing allows me to take more risks and to write down patterns that I see happening in members and in the group as a whole. Like some people, I am not able to verbalize my thoughts on the spot or in any succinct manner in the group. Writing allows me time to process and compose my reactions. The combination of writing and verbal expression in a group empowers me to speed up my personal transformation.

Have Members Share Parts of Their Journals: A Possibility for Small Group

Riordan (1996) observed that members can benefit greatly from sharing parts of their journal entries, especially if the group is rather small. When shared, these written insights, responses, and questions can make the group meetings even more dynamic and beneficial.

In an ideal world, a leader might even read members' journals and provide feedback. Of course, tight schedules are a reality in a therapist's life; we can only do so much in a certain period of time. Actually, we do not necessarily need to read members' journals: The writing alone is still highly beneficial to the group members.

LEADERS' NARRATIVE SESSION NOTES

Though traditionally not a part of leaders' reflective practice, a leader's progress notes—narrative session notes—can become a powerful tool in speeding up the group process. This section introduces the benefits of narrative session notes and how to use them as a therapeutic tool in group work.

How Leaders Benefit From Writing Narrative Session Notes

As a part of clinical practice, leaders must keep progress notes for each group session. As routine as they are, progress notes can be used as a therapeutic tool—narrative session notes that benefit not only the members but also the leaders.

First, as they engage in the act of writing narrative session notes (sometimes called session summaries), group leaders are given an opportunity to ponder the group processes outside the rapidly evolving here-and-now group inter actions. The fact is, after the session has ended, leaders often come up with their best ideas. Writing narrative session notes gives leaders the opportunity to reflect on these afterthoughts and ideas.

Second, leaders may elect to distribute the narrative session notes electronically through a confidential and safe medium. This way, their afterthoughts and ideas can be conveyed to members efficiently, without having to wait until the next session to do so (Parry & Doan, 1994).

Third, the narrative session notes can act as a leader's "narrative letter" to group members. The literature demonstrates that therapists who write narrative letters to their clients are able to decrease the length of treatment (Nylund & Thomas, 1994; White, 1995). In the group setting, when the progress notes are written in the form of a "narrative letter," the group may reach its potential within a shorter period of time. Group therapists are able to meet the expectations of cost-conscious managed care by decreasing the number of group sessions.

Use Narrative Session Notes to Increase Leader Transparency

Above all, narrative session notes increase the leaders' transparency. Because they are distributed to the group, narrative session notes help to convey group therapists' afterthoughts and perceptions to group members. The increased transparency of the group leader can help members experience the therapist as a human being, rather than an expert who merely dispenses professional exper tise (White, 1991).

Through this practice, not only can therapists share their ideas about the group process with members, but it also helps to solidify a relationship of trust. Additionally, it can temper the hierarchical imbalance between therapists and clients.

How Members Benefit From Reading Narrative Session Notes

The ones who benefit the most from the narrative session notes are, indeed, the group members. First, reading narrative notes prior to attending group sessions gives members the time and space needed to see the immediacy and intensity of a group session's here-and-now exchanges, from the perspective of the leader.

Second, written session notes give life and credibility to what has happened in the session. Words in written form, as Epston (1994) states, "don't fade and disappear the way conversation does; they endure through time and space, bearing witness to the work of therapy and immortalizing it" (p. 31). What a magnificent description!

By reading the written session notes, members get a chance to absorb and retain what has transpired in a session. The notes become something tangible to refer to on a regular basis (Parry & Doan, 1994).

Third, as members accumulate narrative session notes each session, they benefit from the cross-session reminders that reignite the insight gained during critical instances and point them toward the path of growth. When made visually available, these narrative notes are accessible for group members to revisit, especially in times of self-doubt or crisis.

Client Rights to Have Access to Their Treatment Records

Legally and ethically, therapists are obligated to keep progress notes—as a type of *treatment records*—in order to keep track of significant elements of individual or group sessions (Spitz, 2013). However, record keeping, or client documentation, often consumes a great amount of the therapist's time. Few therapists enjoy this specific aspect of service delivery (Mitchell, 2001). After much time and effort have been put into writing case notes, these records are then put to rest in charts. It is no surprise then that few clinicians look forward to the work of record keeping.

Does record keeping have to be such a chore? If handled with intelligence, client documentation can actually serve to create a more effective treatment.

Research has shown that if clients are allowed *access to certain types of recorded* information, their treatment can be improved (Roth, Wolford, & Meisel, 1980). However, the therapeutic community has not implemented a system that would promote greater client accessibility to charts.

Most clients are unaware that the information contained in their records *belongs to them*. This may be because these records reside with the mental health providers and are released only to third-party payers (Anderson & Hopkins, 1996). Nevertheless, any notes concerning a client are part of the record and belong to the client.

Distributed "Process Summary" Makes "Progress Notes" a Treatment Vehicle

To promote greater client access to such information, Yalom has devised a way of writing session notes that he calls "process summary" (Yalom & Leszcz, 2005). This is a special type of client documentation or treatment record in which the here-and-now of the group process is highlighted.

Breaking from traditional record-keeping methods, Yalom combines case notes and process notes into the process summary. Most uniquely and powerfully, Yalom shares these notes with his clients. He *sends this process summary for his clients to read before the next session.*

This sharing of documentation has the power to reinforce client change (Yalom & Leszcz, 2005). It represents a major step toward transforming the treatment record into an effective intervention strategy.

Our idea of narrative session notes resembles Yalom's process summary but adds an emphasis on narrative language. This aspect will be elaborated below.

To Write or Not to Write: Time Constraints and Confidentiality

The practice of narrative session notes is vastly different from the documentation style preferred by many insurance companies. However, the potency of writing and sharing these notes leads us to believe that the time and effort spent on it will pay off. The potency of this practice is not an issue, but time is.

In deciding whether to write and share narrative session notes, the leader must evaluate his or her own resources. If time is an issue, the leader can choose to write narrative session notes only in the most critical, conflict-filled, transition stage of group development.

The narrative session notes can be distributed and shared immediately prior to the group session, or they may be electronically delivered to the members through a confidential medium. Since the session notes involve clients' intimate life experiences, their safekeeping must be enforced as strictly as with individual case notes. To maintain confidentiality, therapists can ask group members to plan for the safekeeping of these written documents (White, 1995).

Steps of Writing Narrative Session Notes

The following three steps may serve as useful guidelines for writing narrative session notes:

Retrace Key Episodes and Striking Events—After each group session, the leader may want to first jot down key phrases describing his or her immediate reactions to the session. The purpose of this immediacy is to capture the leader's unfiltered thoughts. The narrative can be refined later. This first step helps keep the leader's initial impressions fresh.

Next, the leader mentally retraces key episodes in the session. While doing so, he or she tries to recall any striking feelings, utterances, and interactions attached to vital episodes. In a sense, group leaders are like "the historians of the therapeutic process" and the ones who keep a "chronicle of events" (Yalom, 2009, p. 161).

Refine the Narratives—In this step, the leader conceptualizes and adds meaning to the pivotal episodes. At this phase, *the use of language is especially critical*. Try to avoid analytical or diagnostic language in the narrative session notes. The use of therapeutic language will be discussed in the next section. To model transparency, the group therapist is encouraged to share any observations, thoughts, and reactions in the notes.

Obtain Feedback in the Following Sessions—After the session notes have been distributed to the members, the leader should spend some time in the following session processing members' responses to the notes. This does not take away from dealing with the here-and-now or new agendas because the therapist can phrase questions in such a way that will bridge responses to current issues. For example, the leader may say to the group,

I wonder, how do you react to the session notes? Does anything strike you?

Remember, neither the notes nor the leader defines the client experience; the client has the final say. This collaboration makes the narrative notes a product of co-authorship.

USING THERAPEUTIC LANGUAGE IN NARRATIVE SESSION NOTES

The language used by the therapist to describe clients' experiences can have an enormous influence on clients' self-concept. It is imperative that group therapists use only restorative and therapeutic language when writing the narrative notes for the group. Chen, Noosbond, and Bruce (1998) have developed principles for using therapeutic language in writing session notes. This section briefly recaps these principles.

Externalize the Problem

Many members suffer from a negative self-concept because they see their problems as a kind of pathology residing within themselves. Viewing themselves this way, they inevitably subjugate themselves, blocking their ability to act on their own resources. In writing the narrative notes, therapists can use depathologizing language, reshaping the relationship that members have with their problems.

The easiest way to depathologize a client's negative self-view is by externalizing the client's problems. Here, the therapist separates a client's identity from the problem by describing the maladaptive patterns as an external force that the client has to confront. By externalizing the problems or maladaptive patterns, the therapist first gives the problem, or pattern, a *name* and then personifies it.

In doing so, the member becomes a protagonist, and the problem becomes an antagonist. The member's self-identity is kept separate from the problem, and the member is forced to confront and reshape the oppressive relationship he or she has with the problem.

For example, rather than write that Sue was defensive (as a maladaptive pattern) to members' feedback, the therapist names the defensiveness as "the old fear" and animates the fear by describing its action on Sue:

> *The old fear* once again *persuaded* Sue to shut out the feedback that other members were trying to give her. It succeeded in blocking Sue from hearing the truth about herself that might cause the old fear to lose its power and status in Sue's life.

Search for Exceptions to the Problems

The second principle in writing narrative session notes is to search for the exceptions to a member's problems. Exceptions to problems are the counterplots of clients' stories that are often missed when the story is told. Members often forget to mention their personal triumphs, strengths, and resources.

Because members think these are irrelevant to their problems, they often neglect to report these to the group. However, these exceptions to problems are extremely important in therapy.

If used with wisdom, these exceptions can actually restore a client's self-esteem, which is a valuable asset in therapy. For example, rather than simply write that Sue reported a relapse last week, the therapist who wrote the following notes searched for an exception to the problem and then highlighted that exception:

> Although there was a point last week that Sue was seduced by the pull of alcohol, there were also 6 days that week when she stood firm against the power of that pull, despite her feelings of sadness and grief over the loss of her significant relationship.

Maintain a Not-Knowing Position

A "not-knowing" position is one where therapists convey something to group members, from a one-down position—a position of curiosity and wonderment—instead of from the position of an expert. As the therapist extends her curiosity, members' curiosity about themselves also peaks. This puts members in a position to gain more self-knowledge than they might otherwise.

For example, instead of writing that Dale was being aloof and distant to Sue's pain in the session, a mirror to the deficient relationship Dale has with his mother, the therapist might write about the issue from a "not-knowing" position:

> I wonder what might happen if Dale would allow himself to stay emotionally present with Sue's pain, amidst her loss of a significant relationship.
>
> How would his understanding of the pain experienced by people in his life potentially increase as a result?

Internalize Client Personal Agency

Typically, therapists would externalize members' problems in the session notes, but when it comes to personal agency, therapists are to do the opposite: They need to be relentless in helping group members internalize a sense of personal efficacy.

To do this, the group therapist describes positive traits such as courage, positive intentionality, and competence. The traits are described as being within the members—something possessed by members as part of their character traits that will not be taken away, under any circumstances.

For example, instead of simply describing her observation of a member's self-deferring behavior, the group therapist might highlight something within the member that denotes personal agency:

> Jean demonstrates a lot of sensitivity and awareness of Sue's needs, consistently deferring her opportunity to speak in an effort to allow Sue to go first. This behavior can be easily misunderstood as a lack of self-assertion, but this sensitivity and responsiveness that the group has witnessed in Jean is indeed a gift.

To summarize, the language used in the narrative session notes should be therapeutic and restorative for the members. Week after week, as the members read the narrative session notes that display them in the changing light, they may start to adopt this language for future self-narration. Thus, the narrative session notes can elicit the use of transformative descriptions by members when they talk and think about themselves and others.

Examples of Narrative Session Notes

- **Session 2 Narrative Notes (Names are all masked)**

The group began the second session with a check-in on each member's current feelings. After that, a structured activity was conducted where all members wrote *inside the circle* on papers, the names of the significant people in their life with whom they are able to express themselves and their emotions genuinely. On the *outside of the circle*, they wrote the names of the significant people in their life with whom they *wish* they could be able to express themselves and their emotions genuinely.

Finally, the group shared their feelings and their learned experiences from the activity. <u>I was amazed to see how this exercise made the group interact with each other so emotionally and openly.</u>

<u>I was also amazed to see how the group members had more difficulty putting names inside the circle than outside the circle.</u>

Ginger: Ginger was the first one to share her experience after the exercise and explained how her relationship with her niece was disturbing for her. Sabrina asked if this niece was the daughter of Ginger's recently deceased sister, whom Ginger had talked about in the previous session. Getting emotional, Ginger nodded and expressed how she tries to be there for her niece, but that the niece definitely doesn't like her.

Though Ginger shared her inability to get close to her niece, her sense of responsibility and love for her niece show that she is very courageous and has positive intentions.

Joseph: When Joseph expressed his feelings about the exercise, he mentioned how he has always needed validation from his father. The group then observed a connection between his goal presented in the first session and his relationship toward his father. Members gave Joseph a lot of positive feedback, including *his insecurity and need for acceptance.*

Despite being oppressed by a sense of insecurity, Joseph responds to group members proactively, and the feedback he provides is usually insightful and taken with gratitude.

As the session moved on, there was a theme observed in Tim's, Sabrina's, and Eleshia's stories about the people on the outside of their circles, and so we tried to work on the theme with these three members simultaneously.

Tim: As Tim was sharing his story, there was an emotional connection observed within the group. *Tim's tears moved the group,* and almost every member provided him with feedback. When he mentioned that he couldn't really name any significant person in his life with whom he is able to express himself and his emotions genuinely, Eleshia responded that she couldn't either. They were able to connect with each other at a deeper level, even though their stories were undoubtedly different from each other.

I see Tim as a confident, strong individual with important opinions. I wonder if Tim sees this in himself yet, and I wonder whether or not he has displayed this strength of character with his boyfriend. Since he has lost all his significant others in his life, he is unable to be expressive with his boyfriend the way he is with the group. As he puts it, *he can be very open and expressive with strangers where the stakes are low, and there's no fear of losing them. What a great level of self-awareness!*

Sabrina: Sabrina was able to provide her responses to both Tim and Eleshia. She got emotional and cried, and the group was able to participate in Sabrina's experience and provided feedback. Sabrina, however, felt overwhelmed by the fact that she was taking most of the group's time and didn't want to burden anyone with her problems. Eleshia responded by telling her that she is learning from Sabrina as she sees that their stories and situations are very similar.

The old feeling once again persuaded Sabrina to feel that she was burdening the group by sharing her problems. I wonder what might happen if Sabrina would allow herself to overcome this feeling of burdening others? How would this new ability change Sabrina's ways of expressing herself with her family and friends?

Eleshia: Eleshia responded to Tim and Sabrina openly, while mentioning that she was not yet comfortable enough to talk about her own family issues on a deeper level. She also got emotional; *a connection could be seen between her and Emma.*

Emma: Emma also had to deal with a situation somewhat similar to Eleshia's. However, Emma was also not yet ready to go into detail and had tears in her eyes.

Mike: While Eleshia was sharing her part, Mike was able to connect with her, too, and gave his feedback. However, Mike's feedback to all the members was usually surrounded by his own feelings and experiences. *I wonder what might happen if Mike would allow himself to be emotionally present with the member he is addressing and come out of his own experience for the time being. How would this learning help him connect to and understand his family's feelings and reactions?*

Sabrina again: At this point, Sabrina was overwhelmed with emotion. The responses that she was receiving helped her open up more and gave her courage and strength to speak and not judge herself. The group was quite supportive of her. *Sabrina tends to be the strong one in her family, which is why she became emotional when she felt vulnerable and exposed.*

Although the session was becoming highly emotional, *I was pleased to see how all the members of the group were interacting at a deeper level.*

Terri: I was also glad to hear Terri's comments about her past experience and *how she would not want to rush through her turn* just to get it over with. While checking out, Terri expressed that even though she wasn't able to share her part, she still learned a lot from other members' experiences and sharing.

I wonder if Terri will go first in the next session, just like she did in the first session or will she wait again? Will she be able to express herself openly in the group?

Ted: Ted was quite assertive, on the other hand, and gave feedback to almost all the members and tried to encourage them.

Although Mike, Emma, Ted, and Terri didn't get a chance to share their experience with the activity, every single member took some steps toward reaching his or her interpersonal session goal during this session. In interacting with other members of the group, they practiced the interpersonal skill that they committed to working on during check-in.

Having a shared structured activity for members to get in touch with their feelings, themselves, and their significant others was a powerful technique to use in the second session, and it allowed members to open up significantly.

- **Session 6 Narrative Notes (Names are all masked)**

Members present for Session 6 were Lori, Nita, Kelly, Maria, Jane, Helen, Marcy, Peter, and Nelson.

Here-and-now session goals: The group began with a presentation of each member's *here-and-now session goals.* I was surprised at the similarities between all group members' here-and-now goals. All members expressed their difficulty in communication, which is a powerful commonality for the group. It is very interesting to me that so many group members express an interest in improving their ability to communicate "unpleasant" or assertive emotions.

Helen: After each member presented his or her here-and-now session goals, Helen presented her concerns. Helen tends to be reluctant about taking "center stage" in the group; we, therefore, made an effort to have her be the focus. Because we tried to work on multiple presenting issues simultaneously, no feedback was given to Helen until the other issues were presented.

Kelly: Next, we proceeded to Kelly's issue. As Kelly's story continued, group members began to physically pull back and had confused looks on their faces. Several group members asked clarifying questions. Kelly's answers to these questions, however, caused more confusion. I could sense Kelly's frustration as the group was unable to understand her story.

Lori: While others were confused by Kelly's stories, Lori seemed to be able to provide powerful feedback to Kelly when she just opened up honestly and told Kelly that she "overexplains" things.

Watching Lori's interaction with Kelly made me proud of the progress she has made within the group. I see her as a confident, strong individual with important opinions. I wonder if Lori sees this in herself yet, and I wonder if she might already display this strength of character with her family and friends.

The group: Following Lori's model, the rest of the group showed tremendous bravery by opening up honestly to Kelly. Many of them felt they were not being heard by Kelly.

Maria: Maria reiterated what Lori had said in a more compassionate way. She expressed that she would like to know Kelly better, but sometimes she simply could not understand her messages. Maria later expressed to Kelly that she often feels that Kelly cannot hear what is being said to her.

Maria said this with pain in her face. Throughout this part of the session, I was trying to say something to Kelly that would give her the message and at the same time show her compassion. Maria was able to do that in a way that I could not. I have also noticed that recently, Maria seems more comfortable taking time from the group to express her thoughts.

Helen again: Helen was trying to tell Kelly that she was simply confused and wanted to get a better understanding of Kelly's story. *I was amazed at how easily Helen shifted from her own presenting issue to being completely involved in Kelly's. She was able to put her own needs on hold for another person.*

It became clear that *a parallel* exists between Helen's behavior in the group and her behavior with her sister. *Helen is so good at making other people feel important and putting their needs before hers. The question is, how much is she sacrificing to do this?*

Kelly again: At this point, Kelly was overwhelmed with emotion. The reactions she was receiving disturbed her, because she perceived them as being negative. It seemed to me that Kelly has been unable to let herself and her own emotions receive attention. She tends to focus on others.

Because she was so uncomfortable with the focus being on her, she felt attacked. Although the session was becoming highly emotional, I was pleased to hear both Nita and Peter speak up about the issue.

Nita: Nita's reaction to Kelly was clear, concise, and direct. *This is the first time I have seen Nita be assertive.* She really reached a new level in moving toward her goal by *refusing to back down,* even when *Kelly seemed to be blocked by a wall of fear surrounding her.*

Peter: Peter was able to self-disclose when providing reactions to Kelly. I have seen him doing this more and more often as the group progresses. *Each time he speaks, he lets the group in on a different part of himself.*

The group: Kelly's pain was immense. The group assured Kelly that the reactions were coming from a place of caring and not with any intention to hurt her.

The Parallel in Helen's Role Inside and Outside the Group. Helen, in particular, seemed to be overcome by guilt saying that expressing herself may not be worth it if it causes someone a great deal of pain. I can see the parallel between Helen's role in the group and her role in her everyday life, especially with her sister. The fact that the group spent so little time on Helen's presenting issue, and was instead stuck on Kelly's stories, illustrated Helen's role in our social microcosm.

Every single group member made strides in reaching his or her goal during this session. I saw a side of everyone that I hadn't seen in previous sessions. Asking members to present their here-and-now session goals is a powerful technique.

- **Session 9 Narrative Notes (Names are all masked)**

I (Ed) and Tonja began Session 9 with a check-in, asking the group members how they would like to spend the time that we had together in this session.

Due to the intensity of the previous (eighth) session, there seemed to be <u>a little bit of apprehension</u> in how the group wanted to move forward.

Eventually, members, one-by-one, <u>took a leap</u> to express what direction they would like to see the group move. From this, there were two themes that would come to <u>play a central role</u> in the life of this session. Krisandra reported that there were several lingering feelings and thoughts she wanted to share with specific group members, and Allison wanted to know how group members deal with disappointment. <u>These two themes</u> would end up being <u>the catalyst for the group's growth</u> in this session.

Krisandra: <u>Krisandra kicked off the sharing</u> by revealing <u>her profound respect for Dante</u>. She revealed that during a previous session, when Dante had wondered if people at his work dismissed him because he is an African American man, she had been <u>very moved</u>—so much so that she has felt a <u>strong, persistent desire</u> to let Dante know that she <u>stands in awe at the struggles that he and other people of color must go through</u> on a daily basis. She said that African Americans endure the microaggressions daily, and the accumulation of such microaggression is like the accumulation of "a thousand little paper cuts."

Krisandra seemed <u>overcome with tears</u>—tears of gratitude for being able to comprehend the magnitude of these thousand little paper cuts; <u>tears of sadness</u> at the injustice of it; and <u>tears of humility</u> at the <u>strength, courage, and tenacity</u> it takes to live in the midst of such injustice.

Dante: <u>Krisandra's heartfelt sharing</u> clearly had a <u>strong impact on Dante</u>, and he was <u>quite moved</u>. The group then shifted its attention to Dante, and the group remarked on <u>a noticeable change</u> in his demeanor: He seemed much more <u>relaxed</u>. As if to thank Krisandra's validation, Dante let us in on a new change that he took. <u>For the first time at work, he had found his voice</u>: In a recent staff meeting he had let his coworkers know that they must ask him before they schedule anything on his calendar, and if they don't, he let them know that he would cancel the appointment.

Wow! Let's hear that again: For the first time at work, Dante had found his voice: In a recent staff meeting he had let his coworkers know that they must ask him before they schedule anything on his calendar, and if they don't, he let them know that he would cancel the appointment.

In this one story, it was clear that Dante had taken momentous strides in the direction of his goal—to kick his passivity to the curb. Dante seemed lighter, calmer, and more at peace, and the group immediately perked up: We were curious as to what this experience was like for Dante? How did he get to the point where he was able to do this? And what could we learn from him?

Sharing in <u>Dante's joy</u>—we told Dante that we love him, and we love that he was able to do this. This really felt like <u>a victory for the whole group</u>.

I wonder how Dante would feel about being <u>the group's resident "Finding Your Voice" consultant</u>? If he is willing, we will need to remember to <u>confer with him whenever we need help with speaking up, setting boundaries, and getting our needs met</u>.

And if Dante struggles with finding his voice in future situations, perhaps <u>he, too, can confer with himself by remembering this story</u> about his staff meeting. And, if <u>his passivity ever tries to get him to forget</u>, perhaps <u>we, as witnesses</u> to this story, <u>can remind him of it</u>?

<u>Dante's success</u> led to <u>a group discussion on the themes</u> of <u>not being seen, of being invisible</u>, as well as <u>speaking up to get our needs met</u> and being able to <u>say "no."</u>

Amber: Amber, for instance, recently was able to say "no" to a family member, as well as to ask for help—she even <u>asked for hugs</u> from her husband. <u>To ask for help is actually a strength</u>, and this paradox was apparent in Amber as she told us about this development.

Allison: Allison was commenting on this theme when we asked for <u>clarification</u> about her check-in: Did she have a disappointment she wanted to share, or did she want to ask the group members how they manage disappointments? Still struggling with the mission of being more assertive, Allison indicated the latter. Since Allison often speaks to people in an indirect way, we encouraged her to ask the group directly, "Would you please share with me about your life disappointments?"

Ella: Somehow, though, the conversation changed directions, and it wasn't until <u>Ella astutely brought it to our attention</u> did we realize that we had <u>left Allison out in the cold</u>.

The group immediately worked to <u>rectify</u> this. We especially wanted to know if this feeling of Allison being left out had happened before.

Allison again: Indeed it had; with bravery, Allison let us know. She had felt ignored and forgotten by the group <u>several times</u> in the group's history. <u>The bravery and courage</u> that it takes for Allison to be this <u>honest</u> really perked up the group.

Mei, our adjunct co-leader, wanted to <u>stretch Allison's courage</u> a bit. So, she asked Allison if she would be willing to <u>tell the group directly that she was disappointed *in the group*</u> for skipping over her. This seemed a bit daunting, but <u>Allison was up for this</u> leap forward, and <u>she told the group directly and unequivocally, "Yes, I am disappointed in you for leaving me in the cold."</u>

Wow! What was this like for you, Allison, to so directly tell the group "I am disappointed in you"? You <u>took a risk</u> in communicating your feelings, and you seemed a bit <u>more peaceful</u> afterward, <u>kind of like Dante</u>. Did anyone else notice this too?

I wonder, <u>how can Allison build upon this</u>? And how can we <u>support her if this is something she wants to continue doing</u>?

The group responded to Allison's statement, immediately offering her with their various takes on how they manage the disappointment in their lives. It turned out, as Mei pointed out, no matter how members' offerings were almost contradictory to her question, Allison seemed <u>lighter, almost giddy upon hearing each member's direct address to her</u>. In a way, Mei noted, <u>it almost didn't matter what people said, as long as they said something to her</u>.

Allison confirmed that she really <u>just wanted some care and nurturance from the group</u>. I wonder, how can we make sure that <u>we continue to give Allison care and nurturance</u>? And <u>who else</u> would like some care and nurturance from the group?

The group as a whole: The group then focused its concentration on <u>decoding the mystery</u> of *why* <u>the group forgot about Allison</u>.

Tanzy: Tanzy shared how he personally experienced Allison: During the check-in and then later when Allison repeated her question, <u>Tanzy wasn't exactly sure what Allison was asking for</u>. He could have shared how he, himself, deals with disappointment, but he hesitated, thinking it might not actually be helpful for Allison.

<u>Allison, what do you make of this? What do you take away from Tanzy's implication that you will be more likely to get what you want when you directly ask for it, rather than going around about it?</u>

Other members: Others echoed this sense of confusion and their reasons for holding back. The group members came to the same voice: They wish Allison would give a hand gesture, and even, as Dante suggested, <u>proclaim loudly "WHOA"</u> if Allison is not being heard in future sessions.

I (Ed) am humbled at <u>the group's ability to be honest with one another</u>. It seems <u>we made good on our group goal</u> of speaking our feelings honestly and of giving and receiving honest feedback—<u>no small feat</u>!

∞∞

In conclusion on this text: Beneath any ordinary interaction among a group of people lies a fascinating world of interpersonal process—a world we often let pass as we go about our lives. However, upon a closer look, stretches of interpersonal terrain often lay themselves bare in front of our eyes. The journey—to marvel this spectacular interpersonal terrain—has been like a trek to the peak of Mt. Everest. It starts with a humble step and ends with a courageous last push.

This last push—the reflective practice—lands us at two types of reflective writing: member reflective journals and leader narrative session notes. Both bolster the therapeutic effect of groups, carrying the group to a peak without needing extra sessions.

It has been rejuvenating staying in this reflective mood throughout the journey of acquiring group leadership skills, particularly aiming for the holy grail of the group—the elusive and ever electrifying group dynamics and their interpersonal processes. We hope your leadership muscles are getting beefier through this expedition. And we hope, at the end of the rainbow, your groups all delight at their pots of gold.

APPENDICES

APPENDIX A

A SAMPLE OF THE GROUP PROPOSAL

Rationale

Gender dysphoria refers to the distress that accompanies "the incongruence between one's experienced/expressed gender and one's assigned gender" (DSM-5, 2013, p. 451). The incongruence itself is not a dysfunction; the distress surrounding the incongruence, however, is worthy of attention and care. Despite a growing trans* population in Chicago, no experiential groups exist in the city to support such a vulnerable population. As I take interest in working with this population and feel a great deal of compassion and empathy for trans* individuals, I would like to propose a hybrid of support and experiential group at our center for trans*.

The proposed group will provide understanding to trans* individuals who deserve to live within society whilst having their true, authentic selves honored. The hybrid group can provide a mechanism of support, psychoeducation, and growth while lessening the distress that trans* members may feel. The group can also serve as a place of empowerment and advocacy.

Terminology

It is essential for all counselors working with trans* individuals to understand and stay up to date with relevant transgender terminology and policy.

Permission for use by Kimberly Buikema

The following terminology is current and relevant in regard to the trans* population, which I will continue to use throughout this proposal and in future work with trans* clients (Killermann, 2013).

- Transgender—an umbrella term for those who do not follow the gender norms that have been assigned by society.
- Trans*—a broader (than transgender) umbrella term for those who do not identify themselves within the binary gender spectrum. This includes those who identify as transgender, transsexual, genderqueer, genderfluid, transvestite, genderless, and so on. Our group will welcome all trans* individuals, not just those who identify as transgender. Therefore, trans* will be used throughout the remainder of my proposal.
- Transition—the process a trans* individual goes through when changing gender expression.
- Transman, Female to Male, FTM, F2M—An individual who was assigned as a female at birth but identifies herself as male.
- Transwoman, Male to Female, MTF, M2F—An individual who was assigned as a male at birth but identifies himself as female.

Type and Purpose of Group

Group counseling can especially help trans* individuals by providing a supportive network of acceptance and a kind of understanding from those who share similar experiences and by allowing individuals to work through and process their distress to their fellow members who not only support them but also understand and have lived through and learned from similar experiences.

Group also provides a great opportunity for members to discuss barriers and practical issues. Members can receive both emotional support and practical feedback. Aware of the power of the group, I am confident that the hybrid of a support and experiential group can be especially beneficial for trans* individuals.

While many types of the group can be helpful for trans* individuals, pscyho-educational, mindfulness, topic-based, or process to name a few, the proposed group will be a hybrid support and experiential group.

The support aspect will be naturally built into the group since members will be able to bring in their own topics or issues to work through in a supportive and understanding environment.

The experiential aspect of the group, however, will make the best use of the power and growth inherent in the group process that focuses on examining the "here-and-now" materials that organically occur within the group.

I was able to consult with a trans* therapist who works at an LGBTQ specific practice in Andersonville. She has found this type of hybrid group to be incredibly successful. In fact, the group was so successful that her practice started a second group of the same nature, and she encouraged me to run this type of group here in our center, given how powerful and effective the group can be. She said that many group members have claimed that "it feels like home" (R. McDaniel, personal communication, March 28, 2016). Given the large trans* population that frequents our center, I am confident this type of group will be of great need for them.

Membership

Group members will commit to the group on a voluntary basis. In regard to emotional safety and comfort level, all members will be trans*. That means they could be all over the stages of questioning, working through finding identity, transitioning, or living and expressing as trans*.

Closed or Open Group

The group will be a closed, longer-term, ongoing group. However, if a spot opens up within the group, a new member may join. Admission is pending on both permission by the group and an individual screening procedure with my co-leader or myself.

Group Size

As it is a hybrid support/experiential group, the group size will be kept slightly smaller. Eight members would be an ideal number (Chen & Ryback, 2004), but the group could be run with members numbering between six and 10. A group with fewer than four members will not be conducive, and if more than 10 members are willing and eligible, creating two groups will be the proposed choice.

Session Length and Frequency

Sessions will run 90 minutes, once a week, from 7 p.m. to 8:30 p.m. on a weeknight. This would allow group members to arrive after work but still have time to get home safely via walking, cycling, or public transport.

Location

The group's meeting place needs to be accessible, private, and sensitive, whilst creating a feeling of safety. It may be upsetting, offensive, or triggering for group members to attend a meeting in a religious institution or place of worship, considering the discrimination or rejection some members have faced from such places (Dickey & Loewy, 2010). Fortunately, in the center, we have space in our facility to hold group sessions every week; neither privacy nor security is an issue.

Leaders' Qualifications

According to WPATH's (World Professional Association for Transgender Health) *Standards of Care*, group leaders must have, at a minimum, an MA in mental health counseling, counseling psychology, or social work. They must also be licensed as an LPC, LCPC, or LCSW (World Professional Association for Transgender Health, 2012, p. 22).

However, as I only just completed my MA, I am still waiting for my LPC credentials to come through. I also don't have a lot of experience working with trans* individuals. Therefore, I will seek out consultation and supervision from a therapist experienced in working with trans* individuals, as outlined in ACA's (American Counseling Association) *Competencies for Counseling With Transgender Clients* (American Counseling Association, 2010).

Fortunately, Joe, the LCPC in our center, has agreed to act as my supervisor and consultant in this instance, as he has received specific trans* counseling training and has the required experience. He has also agreed to co-lead the group with me, as he also realizes that this type of group could be very beneficial for our trans* population. In this case, he could fill the roles of mentor/consultant, co-leader, and supervisor. This could benefit both myself (getting the supervision and mentoring I would need) and the group, as they would have two therapists facilitating the group.

Once I have received my LPC licensure, attended a trans* specific training at Live Oak or Center on Halsted, and received substantial supervision from Joe, I will be able to run a trans* hybrid group independently, as I'll have the necessary degree, credentials, training, and experience.

Joe and I will ensure that we are compliant with both ACA's *Competencies for Counseling With Transgender Clients* (ACA, 2010) and WPATH's *Standards of Care* (2012). This includes having a strong understanding of the transition process, state and federal policy in regard to discrimination, documentation and medical intervention, and appropriate knowledge of terminology, including correct pronouns.

Screening Procedure

Group members will go through a screening intake interview with both Joe and myself. From there, we will make a decision in regard to whether members are appropriate for the group setting. Individuals with more serious diagnoses such as bipolar disorder, borderline personality disorder, schizophrenia, or other psychoses will not be appropriate in this group setting, as they could affect the safety of other group members (Chen & Rybak, 2004, p. 63).

Since many trans* individuals are susceptible to distress, depression, anxiety, and PTSD due to discrimination, lack of acceptance, and microaggressions (Riley, Wong, & Sitharthan, 2011), those who may have these separate diagnoses will be appropriate candidates for admission.

However, if individuals are suicidal or suffering from extreme depression, anxiety, or PTSD, they may not be suitable for the group setting at this time. In this case, we may refer them to individual counseling or a diagnosis-based trans* group, of which there is a limited number in Chicago. This is for the safety of the individual wanting to attend and the safety of group members.

Joe and I will also carefully consider other factors such as identifying or expressing gender of group members. Transmen (female to male) may feel less supported in a group setting, as transwomen (male to female) are more predominant (Dickey & Loewy, 2010). This is a worthy consideration in regard to group make-up. We will also take into consideration those who identify as genderqueer, gender fluid, or gender expansive and how that may impact the group.

Ground Rules

As with all other groups, confidentiality and safety are of the highest priority, as is maintaining a respectful and nonjudgmental atmosphere. Hateful language will not be allowed or tolerated. In order to feel safe, all members of the group must identify as trans*. Members have the power to choose which pronouns they would like to be referred to and have permission to change that pronoun at any time.

Joe and I will also be very cognizant of the unspoken pressure that group members may feel within the group setting. We will regularly remind members that it is very important to remember that each trans* individual's journey is different. In no way should a group member feel pressured by other members to identify or express gender in a way that they are not ready for or that does not feel authentic to them, including medical interventions. According to Bockting, Knudson, and Goldberg (2006), this kind of pressure can be a very real issue.

Judgment about others' gender identity and expression will not be tolerated. This rule will be clearly laid out and repeated if and when it is necessary.

We will also keep an atmosphere of respect throughout and remind group members to do so. This extends to the topics that are brought in by group members. We will ask all members to maintain a willingness to discuss the topics others bring in. We will also establish a rule to encourage members to work in the "here and now" processing moments. With the use of both methods (process and topic-based support), the group can work within both spheres simultaneously.

Structure

We will run the group structured for the first three to four sessions, then move into an unstructured format. However, a regular check-in every week will be maintained. This will allow members to share topics they'd like to discuss in the bulk of the session. If processing needs to continue from the previous session, that will also be encouraged. If we run out of time before presenting issues can get discussed, we will put something on hold until the following week. We will also manage crises as and when they arise.

Special Needs and Characteristics of the Trans* Population

Many trans* individuals are at a greater risk of depression, anxiety, suicide, and PTSD due to both gender identity incongruency and regular discrimination and microaggressions. Discrimination also places trans* individuals at a greater risk of unemployment and homelessness (ACA, 2010; Bockting et al., 2006).

Many trans* individuals also suffer from lack of self and lack of self-acceptance, again making them more susceptible to mental health issues and distress. This lack of self, identity, and distress whilst navigating regular discrimination can make trans* individuals particularly vulnerable.

Minority trans* and trans* individuals who live in poverty are in a double bind in regard to discrimination and oppression, which also merits particular attention and care (ACA, 2010).

Understanding, honoring, and acknowledging these vulnerabilities will inform our approach and work within the group, alongside the theories and techniques outlined in the section below.

Concepts and Techniques

Aaron Devor created a 14-step model of transgender identity formation (Devor, 2004), which we plan to use as a tool to help gain a general idea of where group members may be in regard to their identity.

Queer theory also provides a helpful perspective from which to draw understanding about gender identity and expression. The following quote by Dilley (1999) helps clarify:

> Queer theory is not easily understood partly because it challenges basic tropes used to organize our society and our language: even words are gendered, and through that gendering, an elliptical view of the hierarchy of society, and presumption of what is male and what is female, shines through. Queer theory rejects such binary distinctions as arbitrarily determined and defined by those with social power. (p. 460)

This tenet of queer theory provides a lens through which to examine, understand, and deconstruct the binary, gender-normative, and heteronormative bias of most Western cultures.

Gaining this perspective can help the group leader cultivate compassion and empathy in regard to the bias in which trans* individuals live. This perspective and theory will also inform our group work with trans* individuals.

Dickey and Loewy (2010) have pointed out that multicultural, feminist, and social justice frameworks can prove helpful to both empower and advocate for trans* individuals. I've also been advised that relational, trauma-informed, systemic, strength-based, and internal family systems could prove helpful (R. McDaniel, personal communication, March 25, 2016).

Joe and I have decided that a holistic, collaborative, respectful, trauma-informed approach that encourages empowerment could be very powerful in the group setting. We may draw on the aforementioned frameworks as and when the need arises.

We will also draw guidance from Jack Annon's PLISSIT model of intervention as outlined by Riley et al. (2011) and Henkin (2007).

The following are ways we plan to incorporate the PLISSIT model of intervention into the group setting:

- Permission—Give permission for members to define their own gender identity and expression, both of which can be fluid and exist on a spectrum.
- Limited Information—Members share how much they are comfortable sharing in the moment.

- Specific Suggestions—Help members brainstorm ways of expression that are safe.
- Intensive Therapy—Members can choose how intensely they want to participate in the group each week.

Using this model and application reflects the emphasis on mutual respect toward each member's pace of identity and acceptance whilst encouraging discussion, which could be particularly empowering for trans* individuals.

Possible Issues or Topics

In 2004 or 2005, a cognitive behavior therapy (CBT) research group was run in a VA Hospital in Boston. Six transgender women (MtF) participated. The group met for 60 minutes for 12 weeks. Topics in the study included identity, development, personal safety, family issues, parenting, medical issues, body issues, and intimate relationships (Maguen, Shipherd, & Harris, 2005). Joe and I found that these topics could be useful in our group, too. These topics may arise naturally, or we may bring them up if it seems appropriate and relevant.

Other topics could include self-acceptance, transition, authenticity, friendships, disclosure, discrimination and microaggressions, housing, employment, gender expression, legal issues, dating, sexuality, and any other topics that members choose to discuss.

We may repeat topics as necessary, as there are many layers involved in a lot of these topics. Of course, members' topics and processing will get priority.

Conclusion

Trans* individuals constantly search for identity, authenticity, self-acceptance, and self-validation. This does not differ greatly from many other individuals seeking out group or individual counseling. What is unique when working with the trans* population is helping them figure out how to identify, navigate, and operate within society, families, and workplaces that insist upon the either/or, gender binary identification and expectation. Joe and I look forward to exploring all of this within our group.

References

American Counseling Association. (2010). Competencies for counseling with transgender clients. *Journal of LGBT Issues in Counseling, 4*(3–4), 135–159. doi:10.1080/15538605.2010.524839

American Psychiatric Association. (2013). *Diagnostic and statistical manual of mental disorders* (5th ed.). Washington, DC: Author.

Bockting, W. O., Knudson, G., & Goldberg, J. M. (2006). Counseling and mental health care for transgender adults and loved ones. *International Journal of Transgenderism, 9*(3–4), 35–82. doi:10.1300/J485v09n03_03

Chen, M., & Rybak, C. J. (2004). *Group leadership skills: Interpersonal process in group counseling and therapy.* Belmont, CA: Brooks/Cole.

Devor, A. H. (2004). Witnessing and mirroring: A fourteen stage model of transsexual identity formation. *Journal of Gay & Lesbian Psychotherapy, 8*(1–2), 41–67. doi:10.1300/J236v08n01_05

Dickey, L. M., & Loewy, M. I. (2010). Group work with transgender clients. *The Journal for Specialists in Group Work, 35*(3), 236–245. doi:10.1080/01933922.2010.492904

Dilley, P. (1999). Queer theory: Under construction. *International Journal of Qualitative Studies in Education, 12*(5), 457–472. doi:10.1080/095183999235890

Henkin, W. A. (2007). Coming out trans: Questions of identity for therapists working with transgendered individuals. *Electronic Journal of Human Sexuality, 11.* Retrieved from http://mail.ejhs.org/volume11/Coming_out_trans.htm

Killermann, S. (2013). *The social advocate's handbook: A guide to gender.* Austin, TX: Impetus Books.

Maguen, S., Shipherd, J. C., & Harris, H. N. (2005). Providing culturally sensitive care for transgender patients. *Cognitive and Behavioral Practice, 12*(4), 479–490. doi:10.1016/S1077-7229(05)80075-6

Riley, E. A., Wong, W. T., & Sitharthan, G. (2011). Counseling support for the forgotten transgender community. *Journal of Gay & Lesbian Social Services, 23*(3), 395–410. doi:10.1080/10538720.2011.590779

World Professional Association for Transgender Health. (2012). Standards of care for the health of transsexual, transgender, and gender-nonconforming people, version 7. *International Journal of Transgenderism, 13,* 165–232. doi:10.1080/15532739.2011.700873

APPENDIX B
Pregroup Orientation Handouts

ORIENTATION TO BEING IN A THERAPY GROUP

Student Counseling Services, Iowa State University. Reprinted with Permission

If this is your first experience in a therapy group, along with some excitement and anticipation, you probably have some apprehensions as most people do. People have common concerns such as, "What will the other members be like?" and "Will the experience be helpful and meaningful to me?" In this orientation, we will outline some of the benefits of being in a group as well as guidelines to assist you in taking advantage of the experience.

WHAT CAN YOU EXPECT FROM BEING IN GROUP THERAPY

Group therapy affords opportunities to address the issues that concern you, identify with others, and examine life patterns that are interfering with your personal growth. In a group, you have the opportunity to gain immediate feedback from other group members and the leaders. By receiving feedback from others (that is, how they perceive you), you increase your awareness of yourself and aspects of your life you wish to change.

Group therapy also gives you an opportunity to try out new behaviors, to express feelings you have been hesitant to express, to assert yourself in new ways, or to experiment with new ideas. You will also be able to learn from other members as you identify and connect with their struggles and successes.

With the assistance of the group leaders and your fellow group members, you will have the task of determining how you take advantage of these opportunities. You determine the amount of energy—mental and emotional—you wish to invest in the group process. Needless to say, the more you invest, the more you benefit.

WHAT TO DO TO GET THE MOST OUT OF A THERAPY GROUP

1. *Be yourself.* Start from where you are, not how you think others want you to be. This might mean asking questions, expressing anger, or communicating confusion and hopelessness. Growth begins by taking the first step of sharing in the group.

2. *Define goals.* Take time before each session to define your goals for that session. Nevertheless, being flexible about your goals is also important. You may be surprised to find that your goals continue to change throughout the group process.

3. *Recognize and respect your pace for getting involved in the group.* Some group members will easily be ready to disclose their thoughts and feelings; others need more time to gain feelings of trust and security. By respecting your needs you are learning self-acceptance. If you are having a difficult time with how to discuss your problems with the group, then ask the group to help you.

4. *Take time for yourself.* You have the right to take group time to talk about yourself. Many people may feel that other's issues are more important than their own, may have a difficult time facing feelings, or may have fears of appearing "weak." By recognizing what the reluctance means, you begin the growth process.

5. *Recognize and express thoughts and feelings.* The use of either thoughts or feelings alone is insufficient in working through problems. If you are having difficulties recognizing and expressing your thoughts or feelings, ask the group to help. Learning to express yourself fully, without censorship, enables exploration and resolution of interpersonal conflicts and self-affirmation.

6. *Take risks.* Experiment with different ways of behaving and expressing yourself. By taking risks, you can discover what works for you and

what doesn't. This may mean expressing difficult feelings, sharing information you usually keep secret, or confronting someone about something upsetting to you.

7. *Give and receive feedback.* Giving and receiving feedback is a major aspect of group therapy. The best way to get feedback is to request it from specific individuals, those whose impression means the most to you. You have the right to ask for either negative or positive comment (or both), depending on what you are ready to hear.

   Feedback should be concrete and specific, brief but to the point, and representative of both your feelings and thoughts. It is provided in the spirit of helpfulness and respect. The purpose is to help others identify patterns, personal presentations, unrecognized attitudes, and inconsistencies.

   Most group members learn that **giving advice**, suggestions, and solutions is seldom helpful. For advice-givers, it takes time to learn how to express *personal reactions*, communicate understanding, give support, and listen attentively.

8. *Become aware of distancing behaviors.* All of us have ways of behaving that prevent others from getting close to us such as remaining silent and uninvolved, telling long involved stories, responding to others with intellectual statements, and talking only about external events. As you become involved in the group, you will have the opportunity to identify what you do to distance yourself from others. Keep in mind that distancing behaviors have had a purpose in the past. The question you will face is whether the behavior is preventing you from getting what you want such as close relationships with people.

9. *Be patient with yourself.* Growth takes time, effort, and patience. Changing what has become such an integral part of ourselves is very difficult and slow. By having patience with ourselves and accepting and understanding these blocks to growth, we set the foundation for growth and change.

10. *Work outside the group.* In order to get the most from the group experience, you will need to spend time between sessions thinking about yourself, trying out new behaviors, reflecting on what you are learning, reassessing your goals, and paying attention to your feelings and reactions.

THE GROUP LEADERS

Usually, groups have two leaders whose function is to use their knowledge and experience to facilitate individual and group growth. Leaders will promote an atmosphere of safety and encourage open communication between members. Group leaders will also help to identify group patterns, feelings, and underlying meanings.

The activity level of the group leaders will vary, depending on what is happening in the group. When the members are relating freely with each other and the energy level and involvement is high, the leaders tend to be less active. You are also encouraged to communicate your reactions and thoughts to them concerning their role and activities.

ADDITIONAL QUESTIONS?

We hope this orientation guide will help you to prepare for the group experience. If you have questions about being in a group that are not addressed in this orientation, ask your group leader.

GROUP THERAPY AGREEMENT

Student Counseling Services, Iowa State University. Reprinted with Permission

Group therapy is often the treatment of choice for people who experience troubled relationships, loneliness, depression, anxiety, grief/loss, and low self-esteem. People who participate in groups have the opportunity to benefit from sharing personal experiences, giving and receiving support/constructive feedback, and experimenting with new interpersonal behaviors. In order for the group to work, a safe environment must be created and expectations for members and co-leaders must be understood by the participants. The best way to create a safe environment for personal growth is for you to understand and to agree to these guidelines.

> *Confidentiality*—Feeling safe in the group is very important to a successful group experience. Confidentiality is the shared responsibility of all group members and leaders. Please keep discussions that occur in group confidential and keep names and identities of other group members confidential. You are free to disclose to people that you are a member of a group

and that you attend group, but to protect confidentiality, please do not discuss person-specific details of other group members to persons outside the group.

Attendance—Group members are expected to make a commitment to attend group the entire term. Members also agree to come on time every week. If you are running late or have an emergency/illness that prohibits you from coming to the group, we ask that you call or email one of the co-leaders or let the front desk staff know. If you know ahead of time that you will miss a later group session, we ask that you share the date of your absence with the group beforehand. Individual and group sessions are provided at no charge but failure to attend group without canceling will result in a $25 charge. If you are unable to attend group consistently, you may be asked to discontinue group.

Members often feel anxious about participating in groups and seeing the results can take time. If you do decide to discontinue attending the group and have explored your concerns with the leaders and other members, we ask that you come back to the group to say good-bye. Members will begin to care about one another and though this may feel hard to imagine now, members may experience unresolved feelings if you leave without any explanation.

Relationships With Other Members—Outside relationships between members can disrupt group cohesion and the therapeutic process. As long as group members are in a group, relationships outside of group should be avoided. This includes texting and social media. If you do have contact with someone outside of group (e.g. see someone on campus), we ask that you share that contact with the group at the next meeting.

Safety—If you experience thoughts of self-harm, suicide, or harm to others, it is expected that you will bring this up in the group and/or make separate contact with an SCS counselor to discuss your thoughts. If you are in crisis, you are expected to seek out the help that is required to keep you and others safe. Possible actions include coming to SCS for a walk-in crisis appointment (M–F 8:00–5:00), calling the National Crisis Line at 800-273-8255, contacting the Crisis Text Line by texting "ISU" to 741741, calling 911, or going to the hospital emergency room.

Questions—If you have questions or concerns, please discuss these with the group leaders. In addition, you may contact the group coordinator (name, phone, email) or the associate director (name, phone, email).

Your signature below indicates that you have read and understood this Group Therapy Agreement and you agree to adhere to the boundaries specified for group therapy.

_____

_____

_____

Name:(Please Print)   Signature   Date
_____

Therapy Goals for the Semester:

_____

_____

_____

_____

APPENDIX C

EXAMPLES OF INTERPERSONAL SKILLS FOR MEMBER TO PRACTICE IN THE SESSION

1. *Maintaining one's center and identity in interpersonal relationships*

   In this session, I want to try to articulate my feelings, whether they are positive or negative, to the person I am interacting with.

   In today's session, I want to try to take good care of myself and be truthful about my feelings, even if that requires me to bring up difficult subjects.

   I want to resist my tendency toward withdrawal and try to stay engaged with people, even if I feel nervous or rejected.

   I want to lower the wall I build in my relationships with people. I want to be able to show others who I really am, without being controlled by fear of rejection.

   I want to respond nondefensively when I face criticism.

   I want to be my true self without always wearing a smiling persona or constantly trying to change my behaviors to please or control others.

   I want to stand comfortably for myself, without second-guessing or worrying about what others think of me.

   I want to say no to what I don't want, without feeling guilty.

   I want to express my feelings, positive or negative, diplomatically without worrying about others' approval and without making others feel defensive.

2. *Comforting and soothing oneself when faced with stress or difficulties*

In today's session, I want to try to use my inner resources to calm myself and step back from interactions when others are in the midst of anger and hostility, or step back from situations that can cause trauma.

I want to slow down, instead of leaping into an argument or losing my temper.

I want to stay present with my own feelings when under stressful interactions, instead of engaging in compulsive or addictive behaviors.

3. *Having one's self-esteem and mood remain constant in the presence of others' anxieties and worries*

In this session, I want to try to remain empathic and supportive without feeling compelled to rescue others or worry about them when they are anxious, depressed, or going through a hard time.

I want to remain a loving witness to others' struggle and growth, without absorbing their painful feelings or feeling responsible for fixing problems for them.

4. *Knowing that one's values are constant*

In today's session, I want to try to let my sense of self-worth remain stable whether I am praised, criticized, making progress, failing, in pain, or in a cheerful mood.

I want to hold the ground that my value is inherent in being who I am and being alive, without needing to please others.

I want to foster my self-worth through internal validation. I won't let my self-worth rely on what kind of praise, grades, status, looks, or weight I get.

5. *Being able to self-assert and self-confront*

In this session, I want to try to routinely reflect on my behaviors and confront myself. I want to be able to stop and ask myself, "How did I contribute to the problem in this interaction?" I want to keep the focus inward, own up to my own mistakes, apologize when appropriate, and stop other people when they are hurtful to me.

I want to set boundaries for myself. When an interaction is intruding into one of my boundaries, I want to be able to say no and leave that interaction without fear of feeling alone.

6. *Asking for and receiving support without feeling weak or compromised*

Today I want to learn to accept help from others without feeling indebted.

I want to reach out for help when I am in need.

I want to connect with others through receiving. I want to experience that my ability to receive allows someone else to experience the gift of giving.

I want to ask for what I desire, without feeling embarrassed.

7. *Developing a set of values through reflection, awareness, learning, and experimentation*

Here in this session, I want to practice trusting my own inner wisdom that comes through my experiences and my own personal reflections, instead of relying on my family, school, or religious institutions to determine what is important for me.

8. *Feeling comfortable with different belief systems and perspectives*

Today I want to try to feel comfortable, whether or not anyone agrees with me. I want to learn to appreciate differences as unthreatening, enriching, and interesting.

I want to allow myself to be curious, rather than jumping into self-defensiveness immediately when differences surface in my interactions with people.

9. *Seeing others clearly*

In this session, I want to practice dropping my preconceived beliefs and expectations about people. I want to get to know the persons in front of me as who they truly are, allowing myself to feel close to their unique idiosyncrasies.

APPENDIX D

EXAMPLES OF BRIEF RELAXATION EXERCISES FOR OPENING THE GROUP

The key to guiding a relaxation exercise is personalized pacing, as explained below:

- First, do what you instruct others to do.

If you say, "Breathe in for four counts," you yourself need to also breathe in for four counts. If you say, "Breathe out for six counts," you must do the same. This way, you won't hasten in your instructions that are out of pace with the actual actions.

- Second, use a slow, soothing, and calm voice to guide this exercise.

EXAMPLE 1:

Before we dive into the session, let's spend 3 to 4 minutes on a relaxation exercise. Please find a comfortable sitting position. [pause] Take a quiet and slow breath. Notice how your stomach rises when you inhale. Notice your stomach slowly descend as you exhale.

Continue to take quiet and slow breaths. [pause] When you feel comfortable, slowly close your eyes.

Concentrate on your body sensations as you breathe. If your mind begins to wander, just allow the competing thoughts to dissipate and bring your focus back to your breathing sensations. [pause]

Allow yourself to remain in this total state of relaxation for 2 minutes. [pause]

As your eyes remain closed, allow yourself to gather thoughts about whatever you would like to share or to accomplish today in the group meeting. [pause]

When you are ready, you may open your eyes.

EXAMPLE 2:

This example involves reprogramming the mind in order to override the stress caused by daily life:

Before we start today's session, let's do a simple relaxation exercise. Please sit comfortably on your chair. Close your eyes, and breathe slowly. Let your arms and legs go limp. [pause]

As you continue to breathe in and out slowly, notice your arms and hands begin to feel heavier and heavier. [pause]

Next, notice your legs and feet begin to feel heavier and heavier. [pause] At the same time, notice your arms and legs begin to feel warmer and warmer. [pause]

Your heart is calm and relaxed. Your heartbeat is slow and relaxed. [pause] Your breathing is slow and comfortable. Your stomach is calm and relaxed. Your forehead is cool and calm. Your entire body is calm and relaxed. [pause]

Allow yourself to be in this total relaxation for awhile. [pause] While you are relaxed, let your attention go to the thoughts, feelings, or issues that you want to share with the group today. [pause]

When you are ready, please open your eyes.

EXAMPLE 3:

The most relaxing exercise is one that *uses less wording* so as to allow members to completely tune in and connect with their inner self. It goes like this:

Before we start today's session, let's do a simple relaxation exercise. Sit comfortably on your chair. Close your eyes and breathe slowly. Take a deep breath in (four *silent* counts) and out (six *silent* counts).

Continue this slow and deep breathing for the next 2 minutes. We will sit in silence while we do this.

[3 minutes later] Now we are all rested, let's open our eyes.

REFERENCES

Adams, K. (2009). *Journal to the self*. New York, NY: Warner Books.

Agazarian, Y., & Simon, A. (1967). *Sequential analysis of verbal interaction*. Philadelphia, PA: Research for Better Schools.

Alexander, F., & French, T. (1946). The principle of corrective emotional experience. *Psychoanalytic therapy: Principles and application, 66–70*.

Alexander, F., & French, T. (1980). *Psychoanalytic therapy: Principles and applications*. Lincoln, NE: University of Nebraska Press.

Allen, I. E., & Seaman, C. A. (2007). Likert scales and data analyses. *Quality progress, 40*(7), 64.

American Counseling Association. (2014). *ACA code of ethics*. Alexandria, VA: Author.

Anderson, B. S., & Hopkins, B. R. (1996). *The counselor and the law* (4th ed.). Alexandria, VA: American Counseling Association.

Aponte, H. J. (1994). How personal can training get? *Journal of Marital and Family Therapy, 20*(1), 3–15.

Association for Specialists in Group Work. (2000). Professional standards for the training of group workers. *Journal for Specialists in Group Work, 25*(4), 327–342.

Atieno Okech, J. E. (2008). Reflective practice in group co-leadership. *The Journal for Specialists in Group Work, 33*(3), 236–252.

Bach, G., & Deutsch, R. M. (1971). *Pairing: How to achieve genuine intimacy*. New York, NY: Avon Books.

Baldwin, M. (2013). *The use of self in therapy*. New York, NY: Routledge.

Bales, R. F. (1953). The equilibrium problems in small groups. In T. Parsons, R. F. Bales, & E. A. Shils (Eds.), *Working papers in the theory of action* (pp. 111–161). New York, NY: Free Press.

Bannister, A. (2003). *Creative therapies with traumatized children*. London, UK: Jessica Kingsley.

Barker, P. (2013). *Using metaphors in psychotherapy*. New York, NY: Brunner/Mazel.

Barkowski, S., Schwartze, D., Strauss, B., Burlingame, G. M., Barth, J., & Rosendahl, J. (2016). Efficacy of group psychotherapy for social anxiety disorder: A meta-analysis of randomized-controlled trials. *Journal of Anxiety Disorders, 39*, 44–64.

Beck, A. P. (1996). Group processes: A developmental perspective. *International Journal of Group Psychotherapy, 46*(3), 443–446.

Becvar, D. S., & Becvar, R. J. (2013). *Family therapy: A systemic integration*. Boston, MA: Pearson Education.

Behroozi, C. S. (1992). Groupwork with involuntary clients: Remotivating strategies. *Groupwork, 5*, 31–41.

Bemak, F. (2005). Reflections on multiculturalism, social justice, and empowerment groups for academic success: A critical discourse for contemporary schools. *Professional School Counseling, 8*(5), 401–406.

Bemak, F., Chung, R. C. Y., & Siroskey-Sabdo, L. A. (2005). Empowerment groups for academic success: An innovative approach to prevent high school failure for at-risk, urban African. *Professional School Counseling*, 377–388.

Bemak, F., & Epp, L. R. (1996). 12th curative factor: Love as an agent of healing in group psychotherapy. *Journal for Specialists in Group Work, 21*(2), 118–127.

Berg, R. C., Landreth, G. L., & Fall, K. A. (2013). *Group counseling: Concepts and procedures* (4th ed.). New York, NY: Routledge.

Berg, R., & Wages, L. (1982). Group counseling with the adolescent learning disabled. *Journal of Learning Disabilities, 15*(5), 276–277.

Bernard, H. S. (1989). Guidelines to minimize premature terminations. *International Journal of Group Psychotherapy*, 39, 523–529.

Bernard, H., Burlingame, G., Flores, P., Greene, L., Joyce, A., Kobos, J., Leszcz, M., Macnair Semands, R. R., Piper, W. E., Slocum Mceneaney, A. M., & Fierman, D. (2008). Clinical practice guidelines for group psychotherapy. *International Journal of Group Psychotherapy, 58*, 455–542.

Bernstein, B. (2010). A public language: Some sociological implications of a linguistic form. *The British Journal of Sociology, 61*(s1), 53–69.

Bhaskar, R. (2008). *Dialectic: The pulse of freedom*. New York, NY: Routledge.

Blaney, P. H. (1986). Affect and memory: A review. *Psychological Bulletin, 99*(2), 229–246.

Bohart, A. C. (1993). Experiencing: The basis of psychotherapy. *Journal of Psychotherapy Integration, 3*(1), 51–67.

Bohart, A. C. (1999). Intuition and creativity in psychotherapy. *Journal of Constructivist Psychology, 12*(4), 287–311.

Bolton, G. (2010). *Reflective practice: Writing and professional development*. Thousand Oaks, CA: Sage.

Borg, J. (2009). *Body language: 7 easy lessons to master the silent language*. Upper Saddle River, NJ: FT Press.

Borg, J. (2012). *Body Language: How to know what's REALLY being said*. London, UK: Pearson.

Braaten, L. J. (1989). The effects of person-centered group therapy. *Person-Centered Review, 4*(2), 183–209.

Brown, B. (2015). *Daring greatly: How the courage to be vulnerable transforms the way we live, love, parent and lead*. New York, NY: Avery.

Brown, N. W. (2011). *Psychoeducational groups: Process and practice* (3rd ed.). New York, NY: Routledge.

Brown, N. W., & Brown, N. W. (2011). *Psychoeducational groups: Process and practice* (3rd ed.). New York, NY: Routledge.

Buber, M. (1937/2003). *I and Thou* (R. G. Smith, Trans.). London, UK: T & T Clark.

Buber, M. (1952). *Eclipse of God: Studies in the relation between religion and philosophy*. Atlantic Highlands, NJ: Humanities Press.

Budman, S. H. (1994). *Treating time effectively: The first session in brief therapy*. New York, NY: Guilford.

Budman, S. H., & Gurman, A. S. (2002). *Theory and practice of brief therapy*. New York, NY: Guilford.

Budman, S. H., & Gurman, A. S. (2016). *Theory and practice of brief therapy*. New York, NY: Guilford.

Burgoon, J. K., Beutler, L. E., LePoire, B. A., Engle, D., Bergan, J., Salvio, M., & Mohr, D. C. (1993). Nonverbal indices of arousal in group psychotherapy. *Psychotherapy: Theory, Research, Practice, Training, 30*(4), 635–645.

Calvin, W. (1996). *How brains think: Evolving intelligence, then and now.* Washington, DC: Basic Books.

Cantora, A., Mellow, J., & Schlager, M. D. (2016). Social relationships and group dynamics inside a community correction facility for women. *International Journal of Offender Therapy and Comparative Criminology, 60*(9), 1016–1035.

Carlson, J., Watts, R. E., & Maniacci, M. (2006). *Adlerian therapy: Theory and practice.* Washington, DC: American Psychological Association.

Carter, E. F., Mitchell, S. L., & Krautheim, M. D. (2001). Understanding and addressing clients' resistance to group counseling. *Journal for Specialists in Group Work, 26*(1), 66–80.

Casement, P. J. (2014). *On learning from the patient.* London, UK: Routledge, Taylor & Francis Group.

Cashdan, S. (1989). *Object relations therapy: Using the relationship.* New York, NY: W. W. Norton.

Casson, J. (2004). *Drama, psychotherapy and psychosis: Dramatherapy and psychodrama with people who hear voices.* Hove, UK: Brunner-Routledge.

Center for Substance Abuse Treatment. (2005). Group leadership, concepts, and techniques. In *Substance abuse treatment: group therapy* (Treatment Improvement Protocol [TIP] Series, No. 41). Rockville, MD: Substance Abuse and Mental Health Services Administration. Retrieved from http://www.ncbi.nlm.nih.gov/books/NBK64211

Champe, J., & Rubel, D. J. (2012). Application of focal conflict theory to psychoeducational groups: Implications for process, content, and leadership. *Journal for Specialists in Group Work, 37*(1), 71–90.

Chen, M., & Giblin, N. J. (2018). *Individual counseling and therapy: Skills and techniques.* New York, NY: Routledge.

Chen, M., Noosbond, J. P., & Bruce, M. A. (1998). Therapeutic document in group counseling: An active change agent. *Journal of Counseling and Development, 76*(4), 404–411.

Choate, L. (2010). Interpersonal group therapy for women experiencing bulimia. *The Journal for Specialists in Group Work, 35*, 349–364.

Christiansen, T. M., & Kline, W. B. (2000). A qualitative investigation of the process of group supervision with group counselors. *Journal for Specialists in Group Work, 25*(4), 376–393.

Christiansen, T. M., & Kline, W. B. (2001). The qualitative exploration of process sensitive peer group supervision. *Journal for Specialists in Group Work, 26*(1), 81–99.

Clarkson, P., & Nuttall, J. (2000). Working with countertransference. *Psychodynamic Counseling, 6*(3), 359–79.

Clemans, S. E. (2011). The purpose, benefits, and challenges of "check-in" in a group-work class. *Social Work with Groups, 34*(2), 121–140.

Comacho, S. F. (2001). Addressing conflict rooted in diversity: The role of the facilitator. *Social Work With Groups, 24*(3/4), 135–152.

Comstock, D. L., Duffey, T., & St. George, H. (2002). The relational-cultural model: A framework for group process. *Journal for Specialists in Group Work, 27*(3), 254–272.

Conyne, R. K. (1998). What to look for in groups: Helping trainees become more sensitive to multicultural issues. *Journal for Specialists in Group Work, 23*(1), 22–32.

Conyne, R. K. (1999). *Failures in group work: How we can learn from our mistakes.* Thousand Oaks, CA: Sage.

Conyne, R. K., Rapin, L. S., & Rand, J. M. (2008). A model for leading task groups. In H. Forester-Miller & J. Kottler (Eds.), *Issues and challenges for group practitioners.* Denver, CO: Love.

Corey, G. (2017). *Theory and practice of counseling and psychotherapy* (10th ed.). Boston, MA: Cengage Learning.

Corey, G., Corey, M., Callahan, P., & Russell, M. (1992). *Group techniques.* Pacific Grave, CA: Braaks.

Corey, M. S., & Corey, G. (2014). *Groups: Process and practice* (9th ed.). Belmont, CA: Brooks/Cole.

Cowger, C. D. (1992). Assessment of client strengths: Clinical assessment for empowerment. *Social Work, 39,* 262–268.

Cozolino, L. (2010). *The Neuroscience of psychotherapy: Healing the social brain* (2nd ed.). New York, NY: W. W. Norton.

Cozolino, L. (2016). *Why therapy works: Using our minds to change our brains.* New York, NY: W. W. Norton.

Csikszentmihalyi, M. (2008). *Flow: The psychology of optimal experience.* New York, NY: Harper Perennial.

Cummings, A. L. (2001). Teaching group process to counseling students through the exchange of journal letters. *Journal for Specialists in Group Work, 26*(1), 7–14.

Damasio, A. (2006). *Descartes' error: Emotion, reason, and the human brain.* London, UK: Vintage.

Daniel, R. J., & Gordon, R. M. (1996). Interpersonal conflict in group therapy: An object relations perspective. *Group, 20*(4), 303–311.

Davidson, T. (2014). STRENGTH: A system of integration of solution-oriented and strength-based principles. *Journal of Mental Health Counseling, 36,* 1–17.

Dayton, T. (1994). The drama within: Psychodrama and experiential therapy. Deerfield Beach, FL: Health Communications.

Dayton, T. (2005). The use of psychodrama in dealing with grief and addiction-related loss and trauma. *Journal of Group Psychotherapy, Psychodrama & Sociometry, 58*(1), 15–34.

Delucia-Waack, J. (2009). Helping group leaders sculpt the group process to the unique needs of college students. *International Journal of Group Psychotherapy, 59,* 553–562.

DeSalvo, L. (2000). *Writing as a way of healing: How telling stories transforms our lives.* Boston, MA: Beacon Press.

Desetta, A., & Wolin, S. (2000). *The struggle to be strong: True stories by teens about overcoming tough times.* Minneapolis, MN: Free Spirit Press.

Deutsch, M., & Krauss, R. (1962). Studies in interpersonal bargaining. *Journal of Conflict Resolution, 6*(1), 52–76.

Dewane, C. J. (2006). Use of self: A primer revisited. *Clinical Social Work Journal, 34*(4), 543–558.

Dierick, P., & Lietaer, G. (2008). Client perception of therapeutic factors in group psychotherapy and growth groups: An empirically-based hierarchical model. *International Journal of Group Psychotherapy, 58*(2), 203–230.

Dinerstein, R. D. (1990). Client-centered counseling: Reappraisal and refinement. *Arizona Law Review, 32,* 501.

Doidge, N. (2014). *The brain that changes itself.* New York, NY: Viking.

Doyle, T. (2004). *Communication unbound.* Boston, MA: Pearson Education.

Drumm, K. (2006). The essential power of group work. *Social Work With Groups, 29*(2–3), 17–31.

Edwards, K. J., & Davis, E. B. (2013). Evidence-based principles from psychodynamic and process-experiential psychotherapies. *Evidence-Based Practices for Christian Counseling and Psychotherapy,* 122.

Elliott, R., & Greenberg, L. (2007). The essence of process-experiential: Emotion-focused therapy. *American Journal of Psychotherapy, 61*(3), 241–254. TP Enos, G. A. (2006). Mandated clients finding their way. *Addiction Professional.* Retrieved from http://www.addictionpro.com/article/mandated-clients-finding-their-way

Epstein, M. J. (1998). Assessing the emotional and behavioral strengths of children. *Reclaiming Children and Youth, 6,* 250–252.

Epston, D. (1994). Extending the conversation. *Family Therapy Networker, 18*(6), 30–37, 62–63.

Fall, K. A. (2013). *Group counseling: Process and technique.* New York, NY: Routledge.

Fehr, S. S. (2014). *Introduction to group therapy: A practical guide.* New York, NY: Routledge.

Ferencik, B. M. (1991). A typology of the here-and-now: Issues in group therapy. *International Journal of Group Psychotherapy, 41*(2), 169–183.

Ferguson, A. J., & Peterson, R. S. (2015). Sinking slowly: Diversity in propensity to trust predicts downward trust spirals in small groups. *Journal of Applied Psychology, 100*(4), 1012–1024.

Fishbane, M. D. (2014). "News from neuroscience": Applications to couple therapy. In *Critical topics in family therapy* (pp. 83–92). New York, NY: Springer International.

Fosha, D., Siegel, D. J., & Solomon, M. (2011). Introduction. In D. Fosha, D. J. Siegel, & M. Solomon (Eds.), *The healing power of emotion: Affective neuroscience, development & clinical practice* (pp. vii–xiii). New York, NY: W. W. Norton.

Fox, M. (2000). *Original blessing: A primer in creation spirituality.* New York, NY: Jeremy P. Tarcher/Putnam.

Friedman, W. (1989). *Practicing group therapy.* San Francisco, CA: Jossey-Bass.

Furman, R., Bender, K., & Rowan, D. (2014). *An experiential approach to group work.* Chicago, IL: Lyceum Books.

Gaylin, W. (2000). *Talk is not enough: How psychotherapy really works.* Boston, MA: Little, Brown.

Gazda, G. M. (1989). *Group counseling: A developmental approach.* Needham Heights, MA: Allyn & Bacon.

Gelso, C. J., Hill, C. E., & Kivlighan, D. M. (1991). Transference, insight, and the counselor's intentions during a counseling hour. *Journal of Counseling and Development, 69*(5), 428–433.

Getz, H. G. (2002). Family therapy in a women's group: Integrating marriage and family therapy and group therapy. *The Family Journal: Counseling and Therapy for Couples and Families, 10,* 220–223.

Gillem, A. R. (1999). Teaching counselor trainees to identify and manage countertransference through a counseling analogue. *Teaching of Psychology, 26*(4), 274–276.

Gitterman, A. (2005). Building mutual support in groups. *Social Work with Groups, 28,* 91–106. doi:10.1300/J009v28n03_07

Gladding, S. T. (2015). *Group work: A counseling specialty* (7th ed.). New York, NY: Pearson.

Goldenberg, I., & Goldenberg, H. (2013). *Family therapy: An overview (8th ed.).* Belmont, CA: Brooks/Cole.

Gonzalez, J. M., & Prihoda, T. J. (2007). A case study of psychodynamic group psychotherapy for bipolar disorder. *American Journal of Psychotherapy, 61,* 405–422.

Graybar, S. R., & Leonard, L. M. (2005). In defense of listening. *American Journal of Psychotherapy, 59,* 1–18.

Greenberg, J., & Mitchell, S. (1983). *Object relations in psychoanalytic theory.* Cambridge, MA: Harvard University Press.

Greenberg, L. (2008). Emotion and cognition in psychotherapy: The transforming power of affect. *Canadian Psychology, 49,* 49–59.

Greenberg, L. S., Korman, L. M., & Paivio, S. C. (2002). Emotion in humanistic psychotherapy. In D. J. Cain & J. Seeman (Eds.,), *Humanistic psychotherapies: Handbook of research and practice* (pp. 499–530). Washington, DC: American Psychological Association.

Greenberg, L. S., & Pascual-Leone, A. (2006). Emotion in psychotherapy: A practice-friendly research review. *Journal of Clinical Psychology, 62,* 611–630.

Greenberg, L. S., Rice, L. N., & Elliott, R. (1996). *Facilitating emotional change: The moment-by-moment process.* New York, NY: Guilford.

Gutheil, T. G. (2010). Ethical aspects of self-disclosure in psychotherapy. *The Psychiatric Times, 27*(5), 39–41.

Gutheil, T. G., & Gabbard, G. O. (2008). The concept of boundaries in clinical practice: Theoretical and risk-management dimensions. *Personality Disorder: The Definitive Reader, 150,* 245.

Hagedorn, W. B. (2011). Using therapeutic letters to navigate resistance and ambivalence: Experiential implications for group counseling. *Journal of Addictions & Offender Counseling, 31*(2), 108–126.

Hagedorn, W. B., & Hirshhorn, M. A. (2009). When talking won't work: Implementing experiential group activities with addicted clients. *Journal for Specialists in Group Work, 34,* 43–67.

Haley, J. (1991). *Problem-solving therapy.* San Francisco, CA: Jossey-Bass.

Haley-Banez, L., Brown, S., Molina, B., D'Andrea, M., Arrendondo, P., Merchant, N., & Wathen, S. (1999). Association for Specialists in Group Work: Principles for diversity-competent group workers. *Journal for Specialists in Group Work, 24*(1), 7–14.

Hall, E. T. (1989). *The dance of life: The other dimension of time.* New York, NY: Anchor Books.

Halverson, C. B., & Cuellar, G. (1999). Diversity and T group development: Reaping the benefits. In A. L. Cook, M. Brazzel, A. S. Craig, & B. Greig (Eds.), *Reading book for human relations training* (8th ed., 111–116). Alexandria, VA: NTL Institute for Applied Behavioral Science.

Hammond, E. S., & Marmarosh, C. L. (2011). The influence of individual attachment styles on group members' experience of therapist transitions. *International Journal of Group Psychotherapy, 61,* 597–620.

Hammond, S. A. (2013). *The thin book of appreciative inquiry* (3rd ed.). Bend, OR: Thin Book.

Hammond, W. R., & Wyatt, J. M. (2005). Anger management therapy with adolescents. In A. Freeman, S. H. Felgoise, A. M. Nezu, C. M. Nezu, & M. A. Reinecke (Eds.), *Encyclopedia of cognitive behavior therapy* (pp. 26–29). New York, NY: Springer.

Han, A. L., & Vasquez, M. J. T. (2000). Group intervention and treatment of ethnic minorities. In J. F. Aponte & J. Wohl (Eds.), *Psychological intervention and cultural diversity* (2nd ed., pp. 110–130). Needham Heights, MA: Allyn & Bacon.

Hannah, P. J. (2000). Preparing members for the expectations of social work with groups: An approach to the preparatory interview. *Social Work with Groups, 22*(4), 51–66.

Heider, J. (2015). *The Tao of leadership: Lao Tzu's Tao Te Ching adapted for a new age.* New York, NY: Bantam.

Heitler, S. M. (1993). *From conflict to resolution: Skills and strategies for individual, couple, and family therapy.* New York, NY: W. W. Norton.

Hensley, L. G. (2002). Teaching group process and leadership: The two-way fishbowl model. *Journal for Specialists in Group Work, 27,* 273–286.

Hetzel, R. D., Barton, D. A., & Davenport, D. S. (1994). Helping men change: A group counseling model for male clients. *Journal for Specialists in Group Work, 19*(2), 52–64.

Hill, W. F. (1965). *Hill interaction matrix: A method of studying interaction in psychotherapy groups.* Los Angeles, CA: University of Southern California.

Hofstede, G., Hofstede, G. J., & Minkov, M (2010). *Cultures and organizations: Software of the mind* (3rd ed.). London, UK: McGraw-Hill.

Horvath, A. O. (1995). The therapeutic relationship: From transference to alliance. *In Session: Psychotherapy in Practice, 1*(1), 7–17.

Horvath, A. O., & Symonds, B. D. (1991). Relation between working alliance and outcome in psychotherapy: A meta-analysis. *Journal of Consulting and Clinical Psychology, 38*(2), 139–149.

Howe, E. (2011). Should psychiatrists self-disclose? *Innovations in Clinical Neuroscience, 8*(12), 14.

Hoyt, M. F. (1995). *Brief therapy and managed care: Readings for contemporary practice.* San Francisco, CA: Jossey-Bass.

Jacobs, E. E., Masson, R. L., & Harvill, R. L. (2016). *Group counseling: Strategies and skills* (8th ed.). Boston, MA: Cengage Learning.

Jacobs, E., & Schimmel, C. (2013). *Impact therapy: The courage to counsel.* Star City, WV: Impact Therapy Associates.

Johannessen, L. R. (2003). Achieving success for the "resistant" student. *The Clearing House, 77*(1), 6–13.

Johnson, D. (2012). *Reaching out: Interpersonal effectiveness and self-actualization* (11th ed.). New York, NY: Pearson.

Johnson, S. M. (2004). *The practice of emotionally focused couple therapy: Creating connection.* New York, NY: Routledge.

Jones, K. D., & Robinson, E. H. M., III (2000). Psychoeducational groups: A model for choosing topics and exercises appropriate to group stage. *The Journal for Specialists in Group Work, 25,* 356–365.

Jong, P. D., & Berg, I. K. (2013). *Interviewing for solutions* (4th ed.). Belmont, CA: Cengage Learning.

Juhnke, G. A., & Hagedorn, W. B. (2013). *Counseling addicted families: An integrated assessment and treatment model*. New York, NY: Routledge.

Kane, C. M. (1995). Fishbowl training in group process. *The Journal for Specialists in Group Work, 20*, 183–188.

Karp, M., Holmes, P., & Tauvon, K. B. (Eds.). (2005). *The handbook of psychodrama*. New York, NY: Routledge.

Kauff, P. F. (2009). Transference in combined individual and group psychotherapy. *International Journal of Group Psychotherapy, 59*, 29–46.

Keats, P., & Sabharwal, V. (2008). Time-limited service alternatives: Using therapeutic enactment in open group therapy. *Journal for Specialists in Group Work, 33*(4), 297–316.

Kees, N. L., & Leech, N. L. (2002). Using group counseling techniques to clarify and deepen the focus of supervision groups. *Journal for Specialists in Group Work, 27*(1), 7–15.

Kellermann, P. F. (1979). Transference, countertransference, and tele. *Group Psychotherapy, Psychodrama & Sociometry, 32*, 38–55.

Kernberg, O. F. (1995). *Object relations theory and clinical psychoanalysis*. New York, NY: Jason Aronson.

Keyton, J. (1993). Group termination: Completing the study of group development. *Small Group Research, 24*(1), 84–100.

Khantzian, E. J. (2001). Reflections on group treatments as corrective experiences for addictive vulnerability. *International Journal of Group Psychotherapy, 51*(1), 11–20.

Kiesler, D. J. (1982a). Interpersonal theory for personality and psychotherapy. In J. C. Anchin & D. J. Kiesler (Eds.), *Handbook of interpersonal psychotherapy* (101, 3–24). New York, NY: Pergamon Press.

Kiesler, D. J. (1982b). Confronting the client-therapist relationship in psychotherapy. In J. C. Anchin & D. J. Kiesler (Eds.), *Handbook of interpersonal psychotherapy* (pp. 274–295). New York, NY: Pergamon Press.

Kiesler, D. J. (1988). *Therapeutic metacommunication: Therapist impact disclosure as feedback in psychotherapy*. Palo Alto, CA: Consulting Psychologists Press.

Kiesler, D. J., & Van Denburg, T. F. (1993). Therapeutic impact disclosure: A last taboo in psychoanalytic theory and practice. *Clinical Psychology and Psychotherapy, 1*(1), 3–13.

Kivlighan D. M., III & Kivlighan D. M., Jr. (2016). Examining between-leader and within-leader processes in group therapy. *Group Dynamics: Theory, Research, and Practice, 20*(3), 144.

Kivlighan, D. M. (1985). Feedback in group psychotherapy review and implications. *Small Group Research, 16*(3), 373–385.

Kivlighan, D. M., & Jauquet, C. A. (1990). Quality of group member agendas and group session climate. *Small Group Research, 21*(2), 205–219.

Kivlighan, D. M., Jauquet, C. A., Hardie, A. W., Francis, A. M., & Hershberger, B. (1993). Training group members to set session agendas: Effects on in-session behavior and member outcome. *Journal of Counseling Psychology, 40*(2), 182–187.

Kleinberg, J. L. (2000). Beyond emotional intelligence at work: Adding insight to injury through group psychotherapy. *Group, 24*(4), 261–278.

Kline, W., Falbaum, D., Pope, V., Hargraves, G., & Hundley, S. (1997). The significance of the group experience for students in counselor education: A preliminary naturalistic inquiry. *Journal for Specialists in Group Work, 22*(3), 157–166.

Kluckhohn, F. R., & Strodtbeck, F. L. (1976). *Variations in values orientations*. Westport, CT: Greenwood Press.

Knox, R., Wiggins, S., Murphy, D., & Cooper, M. (2012). Introduction: The in-depth therapeutic encounter. In R. Knox, D. Murphy, S. Wiggins, & M. Cooper (Eds.), *Relational depth: New perspectives and developments* (pp. 1–11). Basingstoke, UK: Palgrave Macmillan.

Kohut, H. (2014). *The restoration of the self*. Chicago, IL: University of Chicago Press.

Kormanski, C. (1982). Leadership strategies for managing conflict. *Journal for Specialists in Group Work, 7*(2),112–118.

Kormanski, C. (1999). *The team: Explorations in group process*. Denver, CO: Love.

Kottler, J. (1996). *Beyond blame: A new way of resolving conflicts in relationships*. San Francisco, CA: Jossey-Bass.

Kottler, J. A., & Englar-Carlson, M. (2015). *Learning group leadership: An experiential approach*. Thousand Oaks, CA: Sage.

Kraus, K. L., DeEsch, J. B., & Geroski, A. M. (2001). Stop avoiding challenging situations in group counseling. *Journal for Specialists in Group Work, 26*(1), 31–47.

Kreilkamp, T. (2015). *Time-limited, intermittent therapy with children and families*. New York, NY: Routledge.

Kupers, T. A. (2005). Toxic masculinity as a barrier to mental health treatment in prison. *Journal of Clinical Psychology, 61*(6), 713–724. doi:10.1002/jclp.20105

Lacoursiere, R. B. (1980). *The life cycle of groups: Group developmental stage theory*. New York, NY: Human Sciences.

Lanza, M. L. (2007). Modeling conflict resolution in group psychotherapy. *Journal of Group Psychotherapy, Psychodrama & Sociometry, 59*(4), 147–158.

Lasky, G. B., & Riva, M. T. (2006). Confidentiality and privileged communication in group psychotherapy. *International Journal of Group Psychotherapy, 56*, 455–476.

Lazarus, R. S. (2003). Does the positive psychology movement have legs? *Psychological Inquiry, 14*(2), 93–109.

LeDoux, J. (2015). *The emotional brain: The mysterious underpinnings of emotional life*. New York, NY: Simon & Schuster Audio.

Leichtentritt, J., & Shechtman, Z. (2010). Children with and without learning disabilities: A comparison of processes and outcomes following group counseling. *Journal of Learning Disabilities, 43*(2), 169–179.

Leszcz, M. (1992). The interpersonal approach to group psychotherapy. *International Journal of Group Psychotherapy, 42*(1), 37–62.

Levant, R. F., & Shlien, J. M. (1984). *Client-centered therapy and the person-centered approach: New directions in theory, research, and practice*. Westport, CT: Praeger Publishers/Greenwood.

Levenson, H. (1995). *Time-limited dynamic psychotherapy: A guide to clinical practice*. New York, NY: Basic Books.

Levesque, D. A., Velicer, W. F., Castle, P. H., & Greene, R. N. (2008). Resistance among domestic violence offenders: Measurement development and initial validation. *Violence Against Women, 14*(2), 158–184.

Levine, R. (2011). Progressing while regressing in relationships. *International Journal of Group Psychotherapy, 61*, 621–643.

Lewin, K. (2008). *Resolving social conflicts and field theory in social science*. Washington, DC: American Psychological Association.

Lewis, J. A., Lewis, M. D., Daniels, J., & D'Andrea, M. J. (2011). *Community counseling: A multicultural-social justice perspective.* Pacific Grove, CA: Brooks/Cole.

Li, X., Kivlighan D. M., Jr. & Gold, P. B. (2015). Errors of commission and omission in novice group counseling trainees' knowledge structures of group counseling situations. *Journal of Counseling Psychology, 62*(2), 159.

Lieberman, M., Yalom, I., & Miles, M. (1974). *Encounter groups: First facts.* New York, NY: Basic Books.

Lietaer, G., Rombauts, J., & Balen, R. (1990). *Client-centered and experiential psychotherapy in the nineties.* Leuven, Belgium: Leuven University Press.

LoFrisco, B. (2012). *The skill of self-disclosure: What you need to know.* MastersInCounseling.org. Retrieved from https://www.mastersincounseling.org/self-disclosure-what-you-need-to-know.html

Longo, R. E. (2004). An integrated experiential approach to treating young people who sexually abuse. *Journal of Child Sexual Abuse, 13*(3–4), 193–213.

Lothstein, L. M. (2014). The science and art of brief inpatient group therapy in the 21st century: Commentary of Cook et al. and Ellis et al. *International Journal of Group Psychotherapy, 64*, 229–244.

Lowenstein, L. (2011). *Favorite therapeutic activities for children, adolescents, and families: Practitioners share their most effective interventions.* Retrieved from http://www.lianalowenstein.com/e-booklet.pdf

Luft, J. (2000). *Group processes: An introduction to group dynamics* (3rd ed.). Palo Alto, CA: Mayfield.

Lundahl, B., & Burke, B. L. (2009). The effectiveness and applicability of motivational interviewing: A practice-friendly review of four meta-analyses. *Journal of Clinical Psychology, 65*, 1232–1245.

Macneil, C. A., Hasty, M. K., Conus, P., & Berk, M. (2010). Termination of therapy: What can clinicians do to maximise gains? *Acta Neuropsychiatrica, 22*(01), 43–45.

Mahon, L., & Flores, P. (1993). Group psychotherapy as the treatment of choice for individuals who grew up with alcoholic parents: A theoretical view. *Alcoholism Treatment Quarterly, 9*(3–4), 113–125.

Makinson, R. A., & Young, J. S. (2012). Cognitive behavioral therapy and the treatment of posttraumatic stress disorder: Where counseling and neuroscience meet. *Journal of Counseling & Development, 90*(2), 131–140.

Malan, D. H. (2012). *Frontier of brief psychotherapy: An example of the convergence of research and clinical practice.* New York, NY: Springer.

Marmarosh, C., Holtz, A., & Schottenbauer, M. (2005). Group cohesiveness, group-derived collective self-esteem, group-derived hope, and the well-being of group therapy members. *Group Dynamics: Theory, Research, and Practice, 9*(1), 32.

Marmarosh, C. L., & Tasca, G. A. (2013). Adult attachment anxiety: Using group therapy to promote change. *Journal of Clinical Psychology, 69*(11), 1172–1182.

Marshak, R. J., & Katz, J. H. (1999). Covert processes: A look at the hidden dimensions of group dynamics. In A. L. Cook, M. Brazzel, A. S. Craig, & B. Greig (Eds.), *Reading book for human relations training* (8th ed., 251–257). Alexandria, VA: NTL Institute for Applied Behavioral Science.

Maslow, A. H. (1943). A theory of human motivation. *Psychological Review, 50*, 370–396.

Mason, C. P. (2016). Using reality therapy trained group counselors in comprehensive school counseling programs to decrease the academic achievement gap. *International Journal of Choice Theory and Reality Therapy, 35*, 14–24.

May, R. (1983). *The discovery of being: Writing in existential psychology.* New York, NY: Norton.

McCallum, M., Piper, W. E., Ogrodniczuk, J. S., & Joyce, A. S. (2002). Early process and dropping out from short-term group therapy for complicated grief. *Group Dynamics: Theory, Research, and Practice, 6*(3), 243.

McCarthy, P. R., & Betz, N. E. (1978). Differential effects of self-disclosing versus self-involving counselor statements. *Journal of Counseling Psychology, 25*(4), 251–256.

McClure, B. A., Miller, G. A., & Russo, Y. J. (1992). Conflict within a children's group: Suggestions for facilitating its expression and resolution strategies. *The School Counselor, 39*(4), 268–272.

McGoldrick, M., & Giordano, J. (2005). *Ethnicity and family therapy* (3rd ed.). New York, NY: Guilford.

Meyer, C. L., Tangney, J. P., Stuewig, J., & Moore, K. E. (2014). Why do some jail inmates not engage in treatment and services? *International Journal of Offender Therapy and Comparative Criminology, 58*(8), 914–930.

Miller, W. R., & Rollnick, S. (2012). *Motivational interviewing.* New York, NY: Guilford.

Miltenberger, R. G. (2012). *Behavior modification: Principles and procedures* (5th ed.). Belmont, CA: Wadsworth.

Mitchell, R. W. (2001). *Documentation in counseling records* (2nd ed.). Alexandria, VA: American Counseling Association.

Molina, B., Monteiro-Leitner, J., Garrett, M. T., & Gladding, S. T. (2005). Making the connection: Interweaving multicultural creative arts through the power of group counseling interventions. *Journal of Creativity in Mental Health, 1*(2), 5–15.

Moreno, J. (1978). *Who shall survive: Foundations of sociometry, group psychotherapy and* sociodrama (3rd ed.). New York, NY: Beacon House.

Moreno, J. L. (1946). *Psychodrama: Volume 1.* Beacon, NY: Beacon House.

Moreno, J. L. (2005). Brief report: The magical music shop. *Journal of Group Psychotherapy, Psychodrama & Sociometry, 58*(1), 35–42.

Moro, R. R., Scherer, R., Ng, K., & Berwick, A. C. (2016). Addressing personalization issues with trainees using solution-focused supervision. *International Journal of Solution-Focused Practice, 4*, 10–19.

Morran, D. K., Stockton, R., Cline, R. J., & Teed, C. (1998). Facilitating feedback exchange in groups: Leader interventions. *Journal for Specialists in Group Work, 23*(3), 257–268.

Munn-Giddings, C., & McVicar, A. (2007). Self-help groups as mutual support: What do careers value? *Health & Social Care in the Community, 15*(1), 26–34.

Needham-Didsbury, I. (2012). The use of figurative language in psychotherapy. *UCL A Working Papers in Linguistics, 24*, 75–93.

Nicholas, M. W. (2013). The compulsion to repeat relationships with abusive partners and how group therapy can help. *International Journal of Group Psychotherapy, 63*, 347–365.

Nichols, M. P. (2016). *Family therapy: Concepts and methods* (11th ed.). Boston, MA: Pearson.

Nylund, D., & Thomas, J. (1994). The economics of narrative. *Family Therapy Networker, 18*(6), 38–39.

Oei, T. P., & Kazmierczak, T. (1997). Factors associated with dropout in a group cognitive behaviour therapy for mood disorders. *Behaviour Research and Therapy, 35*(11), 1025–1030.

Ogden, T. (1979). On projective identification. *International Journal of Psychoanalysis, 60*(3), 357–373.

Ohrt, J. H., Ener, E., Porter, J., & Young, T. L. (2014). Group leader reflections on their training and experience: Implications for group counselor educators and supervisors. *Journal for Specialists in Group Work, 39*(2), 95–124.

Osbeck, L. M. (2001). Direct apprehension and social construction: Revisiting the concept of intuition. *Journal of Theoretical and Philosophical Psychology, 21*(2), 118–131.

Osborn, C. J. (1999). Solution-focused strategies with "involuntary" clients: Practical applications for the school and clinical setting. *The Journal of Humanistic Education and Development, 37*(3), 169–181.

Ottens, A. J., & Klein, J. F. (2005). Common factors: Where the soul of counseling and psychotherapy resides. *Journal of Humanistic Counseling, Education and Development, 44*, 32–45.

Overholser, J. C. (2005). Group psychotherapy and existential concerns: An interview with Irvin Yalom. *Journal of Contemporary Psychotherapy, 35*, 185–197.

Page, R. C., & Berkow, D. N. (2005). *Unstructured group therapy: Creating contact, choosing relationship.* Bath, UK: Bath Press.

Page, R. C., Weiss, J. F., & Lietaer, G. (2002). Humanistic group psychotherapy. In D.J. Cain & J. Seeman (Eds.,), *Humanistic psychotherapies: Handbook of research and practice* (pp. 339–368). Washington, DC: American Psychological Association.

Pan, P. J. D., & Lin, C. W. (2004). Members' perceptions of leader behaviors, group experiences, and therapeutic factors in group counseling. *Small Group Research, 35,* 2, 174–194.

Paré, D., Bondy, J., & Malhotra, C. (2006). Performing respect: Using enactments in group work with men who have abused. *Journal of Systemic Therapies, 25*(2), 64–79.

Parry, A., & Doan, R. E. (1994). *Story re-visions: Narrative therapy in the postmodern world.* New York, NY: Guilford.

Pascual-Leone, A., & Greenberg, L. S. (2007). Emotional processing in experiential therapy: Why "the only way out is through." *Journal of Consulting and Clinical Psychology, 75*(6), 875.

Pease, A., & Pease, B. (2006). *The definitive book of body language.* New York, NY: Bantam Books.

Pender, R. L. (2012). ASGW best practice guidelines: An evaluation of the Duluth model. *The Journal for Specialists in Group Work, 37*(3), 218–231.

Pennebaker, J. W. (1997). *Opening up: The healing power of expressing emotions.* New York, NY: Guilford.

Perlmutter, M. S., & Hatfield, E. (1980). Intimacy, intentional metacommunication and second order change. *American Journal of Family Therapy, 8*(1), 17–23.

Perls, F. (1992). *Gestalt therapy verbatim* (2nd ed.). Gouldsboro, ME: Gestalt Journal Press.

Perrin-Boyle, H. (2012). \'Ber\ing' it all. *International Journal of Group Psychotherapy, 62,* 343–349.

Petrocelli, J. V. (2002). Effectiveness of group cognitive–behavioral therapy for general symptomatology: A meta-analysis. *Journal for Specialists in Group Work, 27*, 95–115.

Pierce, K. A., & Baldwin, C. (1990). Participation versus privacy in the training of group counselors. *Journal for Specialists in Group Work, 15*(3), 149–158.

Pines, M. (1986). Psychoanalysis, psychodrama and group psychotherapy: Step-children of Vienna. *Group Analysis, 19*(2), 101–112.

Pinsoff, W. M. (1994). An integrative systems perspective on the therapeutic alliance: Theoretical, clinical, and research implications. In A. O. Horvath & L. Greenberg (Eds.), *The working alliance: Theory, research, and practice* (pp. 173–199). New York, NY: John Wiley.

Pistrang, N., Barker, C., & Humphreys, K. (2008). Mutual help groups for mental health problems: A review of effectiveness studies. *American Journal of Community Psychology, 42*(1–2), 110–21. doi:http://dx.doi.org/10.1007/s10464-008-9181-0

Potter-Efron, R. T. (2005). *Handbook of anger management: Individual, couple, family, and group approaches.* New York, NY: Routledge.

Prechtel, M. (Speaker). (2003). *Grief and praise: An evening with Martin Prechtel* (CD). Ojo Caliente, NM: Flowering Mountain.

Prochaska, J. O., DiClemente, C. C., & Norcross, J. C. (1992). In search of how people change: Applications to addictive behaviors. *American Psychologist, 47*(9), 1102.

Rains, S. A., Brunner, S. R., & Oman, K. (2016). Self-disclosure and new communication technologies: The implications of receiving superficial self-disclosures from friends. *Journal of Social and Personal Relationships, 33*(1), 42–61.

Reilly, P. M., & Shopshire, M. S. (2014). Anger management for substance abuse and mental health clients: A cognitive-behavioral therapy manual. *Journal of Drug Addiction, Education, and Eradication, 10*, 199–238.

Remocker, A. J., & Storch, E. T. (1999). *Action speaks louder: A handbook of structured group techniques* (6th ed.). New York, NY: Churchill Livingstone.

Richards, B. M. (2000). Impact upon therapy and the therapist when working with suicidal patients: Some transference and countertransference aspects. *British Journal of Guidance & Counseling, 28*(3), 325–337.

Riegel, K. F. (1976). The dialectics of human development. *American Psychologist, 31*(10), 689–700.

Riester, A. E. (1994). Group psychotherapy for youth: Experiencing in the here-and-now. *Journal of Child and Adolescent Group Therapy, 4*(3), 177–185.

Riordan, R. J. (1996). Scriptotherapy: Therapeutic writing as a counseling adjunct. *Journal of Counseling and Development: JCD, 74*(3), 263–269.

Riva, M. T., Lippert, L., & Tackett, M. J. (2000). Selection practices of group leaders: A national survey. *Journal for Specialists in Group Work, 25*(2), 157–169.

Rizvi, S. L., Steffel, L. M., & Carson-Wong, A. (2013). An overview of dialectical behavior therapy for professional psychologists. *Professional Psychology: Research and Practice, 44*, 73–80.

Rogers, C. R. (1965). The therapeutic relationship: Recent theory and research. *Australian Journal of Psychology, 17*(2), 95–108.

Rogers, C. R. (2003). *Client-centered therapy.* London, UK: Constable & Robinson.

Rogers, C. R. (2007). The necessary and sufficient conditions of therapeutic personality change. *Psychotherapy: Research, Practice, Training, 44*(3), 240–248. doi: 10.1037/0033-3204.44.3.240

Roisman, G. I., Madsen, S. D., Hennighausen, K. H., Sroufe, L., & Collins, W. (2001). The coherence of dyadic behavior across parent–child and romantic relationships as mediated by the internalized representation of experience. *Attachment & Human Development, 3*(2), 156–172.

Roney, T., & Cannon, J. (2014). Dialectical behavior group therapy for borderline personality disorder. *International Journal of Group Psychotherapy, 64*, 400–408.

Ronnestad, T. M., & Skovholt, M. H. (1993). Supervision of beginning and advanced graduate students of counseling and psychotherapy. *Journal of Counseling & Development, 71*(4), 396–405.

Rose, J., & Steen, S. (2014). The achieving success everyday group counseling model: Fostering resiliency in middle school students. *Professional School Counseling, 18*(1), 28–37.

Rose, S. (2016). The emotional growth of teens: How group counseling intervention works for schools by Fibkins, W. L. *Social Work With Groups, 39*(1), 84–85.

Rose, S. D. (1989). *Working with adults in groups: Integrating cognitive-behavioral and small group strategies.* San Francisco, CA: Jossey-Bass.

Rose, S. R. (1989). Members leaving groups: Theoretical and practical considerations. *Small Group Behaviors, 20*(4), 524–535.

Roth, L. H., Wolford, J., & Meisel, A. (1980). Patient access to records: Tonic or toxin? *American Journal of Psychiatry, 137*(5), 592–596.

Rubel, D., & Atieno Okech, J. E. (2006). The supervision of group work model: Adapting the discrimination model for supervision of group workers. *The Journal for Specialists in Group Work, 31*(2), 113–134.

Rutan, J. S., Sonte, W. N., & Shay, J. J. (2014). *Psychodynamic group psychotherapy* (5th ed.). New York, NY: The Guilford Press.

Salmon, C. (2003). Birth order and relationships. *Human Nature, 14*(1), 73–88.

Salzberg, K., & Kabat-Zinn, J. (2003). Mindfulness as medicine. In D. Goleman (Ed.), *Healing emotions: Conversations with the Dalai Lama on mindfulness, emotions, and health* (pp. 107–144). Boston, MA: Shambhala.

Sandler, J. (1981). Unconscious wishes and human relationships. *Contemporary Psychoanalysis, 7*(2), 180–196.

Schimmel, C., & Jacobs, E. (2014). The toughest kinds of groups. *Counseling Today.* Retrieved from http://ct.counseling.org/2014/02/the-toughest-kinds-of-groups

Schlapobersky, J. R. (2015). On making a home amongst strangers: The paradox of group psychotherapy. *Group Analysis, 48*, 406–432.

Schutz, W. C. (1958). *FIRO: A three-dimensional theory of interpersonal behavior.* New York, NY: Rinehart & Co.

Schwartz, D., Nickow, M. S., Arseneau, R., & Glissow, M. T. (2015). A substance called food: Long-term psychodynamic group treatment for compulsive overeating. *International Journal of Group Psychotherapy, 65*, 387–409.

Seaward, B. L. (2015). *Managing stress: Principles and strategies for health and well-being* (8th ed.). Burlington, MA: Jones and Bartlett.

Secemsky, V. O., Ahlman, C., & Robbins, J. (1999). Managing group conflict: The development of comfort among social group workers. *Social Work With Groups, 21*(4), 35–49.

Selekman, M. D. (1997). *Solution-focused therapy with children: Harnessing family strengths for systemic change.* New York, NY: Guilford.

Seligman, M. E., & Csikszentmihalyi, M. (2000). Positive psychology: An introduction. *American Psychologist, 55*(1), 5–14.

Seppala, E., Rossomando, T., & Doty, J. R. (June 1, 2013). Social connection and compassion: Important predictors of health and well-being. *Social Research, 80*(2), 411–430.

Shaffer, J. B. P., & Galinsky, M. D. (1989). *Models of group therapy.* Englewood Cliffs, NJ: Prentice Hall.

Shapiro, J. S. (1978). *Methods of group psychotherapy and encounter: A tradition of innovation.* Itaskca, IL: Peacock.

Shechtman, Z. (2014). Group counseling in the school. *Hellenic Journal of Psychology, 11,* 169–183.

Shechtman, Z., & Pastor, R. (2005). Cognitive–behavioral and humanistic group treatment for children with learning disabilities: A comparison of outcomes and process. *Journal of Counseling Psychology, 52,* 322–336.

Shechtman, Z., & Toren, Z. (2009). The effect of leader behavior on processes and outcomes in group counseling. *Group Dynamics: Theory, Research, and Practice, 13*(3), 218.

Shen, W. W., Sanchez, A. M., & Huang, T. (1984). Verbal participation in group therapy: A comparative study of New Mexico ethnic groups. *Hispanic Journal of Behavioral Sciences, 6*(3), 277–284.

Shields, W. (1999). Aliveness in the work of the group: A subjective guide to creative character change. *International Journal of Group Psychotherapy, 49*(3), 387–398.

Siegel, D. (2015). *The developing mind: How relationships and the brain interact to shape who we are.* New York, NY: Guilford.

Sklare, G., Keener, R., & Mas, C. (1990). Preparing members for "here-and-now" group counseling. *Journal for Specialists in Group Work, 15*(3), 141–148.

Sklare, G., Thomas, D. V., Williams, E. C., & Powers, K. A. (1996). Ethics and an experiential "here-and-now" group: A blend that works. *Journal for Specialists in Group Work, 21*(4), 263–273.

Skudrzyk, B., Zera, D. A., McMahon, G., Schmidt, R., Boyne, J., & Spannaus, R. L. (2009). Learning to relate: Interweaving creative approaches in group counseling with adolescents. *Journal of Creativity in Mental Health, 4*(3), 249–261.

Slavin, R. L. (1993). The significance of here-and-now disclosure in promoting cohesion in group psychotherapy. *Group, 17*(3), 143–150.

Slife, B. D., & Lanyon, J. (1991). Accounting for the power of the here-and-now: A theoretical revolution. *International Journal of Group Psychotherapy, 41*(2), 145–167.

Smith, E. (2006). The strength-based counseling model. *The Counseling Psychologist, 34,* 13–79.

Snyder, C. M. J., & Anderson, S. A. (2009). An examination of mandated versus voluntary referral as a determinant of clinical outcome. *Journal of Marital and Family Therapy, 35*(3), 278–292.

Söchting, I., O'Neal, E., Third, B., Rogers, J., & Ogrodniczuk, J. S. (2013). An integrative group therapy model for depression and anxiety in later life. *International Journal of Group Psychotherapy, 63,* 503–523.

Sommers-Flanagan, J., & Sommers-Flanagan, R. (2015). *Counseling and psychotherapy theories in context and practice: Skills, strategies, and techniques* (2nd ed.). Hoboken, NJ: John Wiley & Sons.

Spitz, H. I. (2013). *Group psychotherapy and managed mental health care: A clinical guide for providers*. New York, NY: Brunner/Mazel.

Stockton, R., & Toth, P. (1996). Teaching group counselors: Recommendations for maximizing preservice instruction. *Journal for Specialists in Group Work, 21*(4), 274–282.

Stone, M. (1998). Journaling with clients. *Journal of Individual Psychology, 54*(4), 535–545.

Strupp, H. H., & Binder, J. L. (1984). *Psychotherapy in a new key: A guide to time-limited dynamic psychotherapy*. New York, NY: Basic Books.

Sullivan, H. S. (2013). *The interpersonal theory of psychiatry*. New York, NY: Routledge.

Sullivan, H. S., & Perry, H. S. (1971). *The fusion of psychiatry and social science*. New York, NY: Norton.

Swogger, G. (1981). Human communication and group experience. In J. E. Durkin (Ed.), *Living groups: Group psychotherapy and general system theory* (pp. 63–78). New York, NY: Brunner/Mazel.

Taft, C. T., & Murphy, C. M. (2007). The working alliance in intervention for partner violence perpetrators: Recent research and theory. *Journal of Family Violence, 22*(1), 11–18.

Taylor, R. E., & Gazda, G. M. (1991). Concurrent individual and group therapy: The ethical issues. *Journal of Group Psychotherapy, Psychodrama & Sociometry, 44*(2), 51.

Teachman, B. A., Goldfried, M. R., & Clerkin, E. M. (2013). Panic disorder and phobias. In L. G. Castonguay & T. F. Oltmanns (Eds.,), *Psychopathology: From science to clinical practice* (pp. 88–142). New York, NY: The Guilford Press.

Teyber, E. (2000). *Interpersonal process in psychotherapy: A relational approach* (4th ed.). Pacific Grove, CA: Brooks/Cole.

Thomas, G., Martin, R., & Riggio, R. E. (2013). Leading groups: Leadership as a group process. *Group Processes & Intergroup Relations, 16*(1), 3–16.

Thomas, R. V., & Pender, D. A. (2008). Association for Specialists in Group Work: Best practice guidelines 2007 revisions. *The Journal for Specialists in Group Work, 33*(2), 111–117.

Thylstrup, B., & Hesse, M. (2011). The impulsive lifestyle counseling program for anti-social behavior in outpatient substance abuse treatment. *International Journal of Offender Therapy and Comparative Criminology, 60*(8), 919–935.

Ting-Toomey, S. (1999). *Communicating across cultures*. New York, NY: Guilford.

Ting-Toomey, S., & Oetzel, J. G. (2001). *Managing intercultural conflict effectively*. Thousand Oaks, CA: Sage.

Toepfer, S. M., & Walker, K. (2009). Letters of gratitude: Improving well-being through expressive writing. *Journal of Writing Research, 1*(3), 181–198.

Tootle, A. E. (2003). Neuroscience applications in marital and family therapy. *The Family Journal, 11*(2), 185–190.

Tophoff, M. (2000). Zen Buddhism and the way of sensory awareness. In K. T. Kaku (Ed.), *Meditation as health promotion: A lifestyle modification approach*. Delft, the Netherlands: Eburon.

Toth, P. L., & Erwin, W. J. (1998). Applying skill-based curriculum to teach feedback in groups: An evaluation study. *Journal of Counseling and Development, 76*(3), 294–301.

Trotzer, J. P. (2006). *The counselor and the group.* New York, NY: Routledge.

Trotzer, J. P. (2013). *The counselor and the group: Integrating theory, training, and practice.* New York, NY: Routledge.

Tubman, J. G., Montgomery, M. J., & Wagner, E. E. (2001). Letter writing as a tool to increase client motivation to change: Application to an inpatient crisis unit. *Journal of Mental Health Counseling, 23*(4), 295–312.

Tuckman, B. W. (1965). Developmental sequence in small groups. *Psychological Bulletin, 63,* 384–399.

Tuckman, B. W., & Jensen, M. A. C. (1977). Stages of small-group development revisited. *Group & Organization Management, 2*(4), 419–427.

Valli, L. (1997). Listening to other voices: A description of teacher reflection in the United States. *Peabody Journal of Education, 72*(1), 67–88.

Vannicelli, M. (2001). Leader dilemmas and countertransference considerations in group psychotherapy with substance abusers. *International Journal of Group Psychotherapy, 51*(1), 43–62.

Vannicelli, M. (2014). Supervising the beginning group leader in inpatient and partial hospital settings. *International Journal of Group Psychotherapy, 64,* 145–163.

Velasquez, M. M., Stephens, N. S., & Ingersoll, K. (2006). Motivational interviewing in groups. *Journal of Groups in Addiction & Recovery, 1*(1), 27–50.

Vriend, J. (1985). We've come a long way, group. *Journal for Specialists in Group Specialists in Group Work, 10*(2), 63–67.

Waldo, M. (1985). A curative factor framework for conceptualizing group counseling. *Journal of Counseling and Development, 64*(1), 52–58.

Waldrop, M. (1992). *Complexity: The emerging order at the edge of order and chaos.* New York, NY: Simon & Schuster.

Walsh, W. B. (2014). *Counseling psychology and optimal human functioning.* New York, NY: Routledge.

Washton, A. M., & Zweben, J. E. (2006). *Treating alcohol and drug problems in psychotherapy practice: Doing what works.* New York, NY: The Guilford Press.

Watson, N.J. (2006). Martin Buber's *I and Thou*: Implications for Christian Psychotherapy. *Journal of Psychology and Christianity, 25,* 35–44.

Weber, R. C. (1999). The group: Opportunity and reality. In A. L. Cooke, M. Brazzel, A. S. Craig, & B. Greig (Eds.), *Reading book for human relations training* (8th ed., pp. 283–287). Alexandria, VA: NTL Institute for Applied Behavioral Science.

Werner, E. E. (1995). Resilience in development: Current directions. *Psychological Science, 4,* 81–82.

Werner, E. E., & Smith, R. S. (1992). *Overcoming the odds: High risk children from birth to adulthood.* Ithaca, NY: Cornell University Press.

Westwood, M., Keats, P., & Wilensky, P. (2003). Therapeutic enactment: Integrating individual and group counseling models for change. *The Journal for Specialists in Group Work, 28*(2), 122–138.

White, J., & Freeman, A. S. (2000). *Cognitive-behavioral group therapy for specific problems and populations.* Washington, DC: American Psychological Association.

White, M. (1991). Deconstruction and therapy. *Dulwich Centre Newsletter, 3,* 21–40.

White, M. (1995). *Re-authoring lives: Interviews and essays.* Adelaide, South Australia: Dulwich Centre.

White, M., & Epston, D. (1990). *Narrative means to therapeutic ends*. New York, NY: Norton.

White, V. E., & Murray, M. A. (2002). Passing notes: The use of therapeutic letter writing in counseling adolescents. *Journal of Mental Health Counseling, 24*(2), 166–176.

Wolin, S. J., & Wolin, S. (2010). *The resilient self: How survivors of troubled families rise above adversity*. New York, NY: Villard.

Woodward, G. (2004). Acting for change: The evolution of a psychodrama group. In B. Reading (Ed.), *Group psychotherapy and addiction* (pp. 133–144). Philadelphia, PA: Whurr.

Yalom, I. D. (1980). *Existential psychotherapy*. New York, NY: Basic Books.

Yalom, I. D. (1983). *Inpatient group psychotherapy*. New York, NY: Basic Books.

Yalom, I. D. (2009). *The gift of therapy: An open letter to a new generation of therapists and their patients*. New York, NY: Harper Perennial.

Yalom, I. D., & Leszcz, M. (2005). *Theory and practice of group psychotherapy* (5th ed.). New York, NY: Basic Books.

Young, T. L., Reysen, R., Eskridge, T., & Ohrt, J. H. (2013). Personal growth groups: Measuring outcome and evaluating impact. *The Journal for Specialists in Group Work, 38*(1), 52–67.

Zarrett, N., & Eccles, J. (2006). The passage to adulthood: Challenges of late adolescence. *New directions for youth development, 111*, 13–28.

Zaslav, M. R. (1988). A model of group therapist development. *International Journal of Group Psychotherapy, 38*(4), 511–519.

Zastrow, C. (1990). Starting and leading therapy groups. *Journal of Independent Social Work, 4*(4), 7–26.

Ziv-Beiman, S. (2013). Therapist self-disclosure as an integrative intervention. *Journal of Psychotherapy Integration, 23*(1), 59–74.

INDEX